THE CHOSEN

Also by Dwight K. Nelson:
Creation and Evolution
Outrageous Grace
Pursuing the Passion of Jesus

To order, **call 1-800-765-6955.**
Visit us at **www.reviewandherald.com** for information
on other Review and Herald® products.

GOD'S
DREAM
FOR YOU

THE CHOSEN

Dwight K. Nelson

REVIEW AND HERALD® PUBLISHING ASSOCIATION
Since 1861 | www.reviewandherald.com

Published by Review and Herald® Publishing Association, Hagerstown, MD 21741-1119.

Review and Herald® titles may be purchased in bulk for educational, business, fund-raising, or sales promotional use. For information, e-mail SpecialMarkets@reviewandherald.com.

The Review and Herald® Publishing Association publishes biblically based materials for spiritual, physical, and mental growth and Christian discipleship.

The author assumes full responsibility for the accuracy of all facts and quotations as cited in this book.

This book was
Edited by Penny Estes Wheeler
Copyedited by Delma Miller and Judy Blodgett
Cover designed by Bryan Gray and Ron J. Pride
Cover art by thinkstock.com
Typeset: Bembo 10/12

PRINTED IN U.S.A.

15   14   13   12   11   5   4   3   2   1

Library of Congress Cataloging-in-Publication Data
Nelson, Dwight K.
  The chosen : a daily devotional / Dwight K. Nelson.
    p. cm.
  Includes bibliographical references and index.
  1. Devotional calendars. I. Title. II. Title: Daily devotional.
  BV4811.N45 2011
  242'.2—dc22

                                            2010035709

ISBN 978-0-8280-2541-6

Dedicated to

Pioneer Memorial Church of Seventh-day Adventists

"The chosen lady and her children, whom I love in the truth—and not I only,
but also all who know the truth—because of the truth, which lives in us
and will be with us, forever."
—2 John 1, 2, NIV

Acknowledgments

"Of making many books there is no end" (Eccl. 12:12). I'm not certain if the wise king was describing the never-ending task of publishers, or was opining the unending joy of the writer. But either way, I'd like to say thank you.

Thank you, Mario Martinelli and Jeannette Johnson on the Review and Herald Publishing Association team. When the two of you, along with Gerald Wheeler, dropped by my office at the Pioneer Memorial church that wintery afternoon, I had no idea that this book would be the result. And when you explained the magnitude of the task in writing a devotional book like this, I was certain you had found the wrong author. Nevertheless, now that, at last, the task is completed, I am grateful for your invitation, and especially thankful, Jeannette, for your cheerful verve and encouragement along the way. I'm also grateful to Penny Estes Wheeler for the gift of her editing skills. And thank you, JoAlyce Waugh, for bringing this project to completion. It is an honor to have partnered with all of you.

And thank you to my publishers over the years who have enabled me to translate sermonic broodings into published books. You will recognize what I wrote for you in some of the daily readings of this book. Thank you, Hart Books (*The Godforsaken God, A New Way to Pray, Countdown to the Showdown,* and *The Jesus Generation*). Thank you, Review and Herald Publishing Association and Hart Books (*What "Left Behind" Left Behind*). And thank you, Pacific Press Publishing Association (*Outrageous Grace, Built to Last* [now *Creation and Evolution*], *The Claim, The Eleventh Commandment,* and *Pursuing the Passion of Jesus*).

Finally, I would like to express my thanksgiving to God for the members of the Pioneer Memorial church—a university congregation of students, faculty, and community alike—who since 1983 have been my and our spiritual family and home. They, more than anyone, have shared the God-journey of "the chosen." And because they have, my life and ministry have been profoundly shaped and indelibly enriched. To all of them I gratefully dedicate this book.

A Word Before . . .

Robert Raines, in his book *Creative Brooding*, describes his reticence to read devotional books, likening the experience to being "stoned to death with popcorn"—with pious, airy, weightless fluff. And to be honest with you, I, too, have kept my distance from most devotional collections. After all, what can you possibly gain from a daily two-minute reading?

And if you too have shared the same hesitation, allow me, please, this brief appeal.

This isn't your grandfather's devotional book—366 (because the new year is a leap year) disconnected daily readings offering a two-minute spiritual send-off into your busy day. Rather *The Chosen* is the narrative of a divine calling that is connected and continued from New Year's Day in the beginning all the way through to New Year's Eve at the ending. Day by day, week by week, month by month, the story of *The Chosen* will grow, and I am praying that the conviction will deepen that you really are "the chosen one" God has been waiting for all these years.

But *The Chosen* can simply be read as a book, meaning you may wish to brood over the opening pages and then skip to the March readings, where a new way to pray and worship at the beginning of your day is carefully, methodically laid out. No more two-minute specials for you. Then, once you've begun this new spiritual discipline, you can return either to read the book a page and day at a time or to read it thematically instead. For every month's theme builds a biblical case for your high calling as "the chosen one":

January	The God of the Chosen
February	The Call of the Chosen
March	The Heart of the Chosen
April	The Day of the Chosen
May	The Love of the Chosen
June	The Hope of the Chosen
July	The Community of the Chosen
August	The Truth of the Chosen
September	The Mission of the Chosen
October	The Mobilization of the Chosen
November	The Character of the Chosen
December	The Crossing Over of the Chosen

The point is that this new book isn't an invitation to a hurried early-morning pause for worship, but rather an appeal to enter deeply into a growing friendship with the God who is calling you. If you daily put into practice what the March chapter is teaching, I believe you will never be the same again. That conviction has nothing to do with me and everything to do with the Christ who is calling us.

And given this increasingly urgent hour of history (read June's chapter, if you have any doubts), isn't this new year the right year to plumb the depths of God's character and pursue the uncharted adventure of His claim and calling upon your life? Why put off your destiny as "the chosen one" any longer?

One morning a schoolboy raced out the door of his home to catch his bus. Panting and gasping for air, he arrived at the bus stop just in time to see the red taillights vanish around the corner. Late again! A bystander called out, "Too bad, sonny. Looks like you didn't run fast enough." To which the honest boy gulped back, "Oh no, sir—I ran fast enough. I just didn't start soon enough."

The chosen can run fast enough—of that I am certain. But will they—will you and I—start soon enough? Jesus' promise—"My grace is sufficient for you"—surely means that if we will start right now . . . with Him . . . it will be soon enough.

—Dwight K. Nelson
Pioneer Memorial Church of Seventh-day Adventists
Andrews University

THE NIGHT YOU WERE CHOSEN

Before I formed you in the womb I knew you, before you were born I set you apart.
Jer. 1:5, NIV.

Have you ever wondered what it was like the night you were conceived? I hadn't either, until I came across a stunning description that biologists on this campus assure me is true for all of us. Your parents came together—whether they stayed together, ever really got together, or were strangers doesn't change this incredible scenario for any of us—and father deposited half a billion tiny male reproductive cells, or sperm, inside mother. That's right—500,000,000 sperm, each with the solitary mission to find the single ovum, mother's egg, and penetrate it. And only one of those sperm could make you you—which meant that it had to "outswim" the 499,999,999 other sperm in that race for life!

In the words of Anthony DeStefano: "*Half a billion* potential human beings, each one completely different from you, could have been born in place of you had not that one, unique sperm cell fertilized that one, unique ovum. In a very real sense, half a billion other potential human beings had to forgo life to make way for you." And then comes his stunning conclusion: "From a strictly statistical point of view, your presence on this planet is a miracle. At the very dawn of your life you had to overcome overwhelming odds—odds higher than any you will ever have to face in any other situation. No matter what you may think of yourself now, . . . no matter what ills may befall you in life, no matter what suffering you may be forced to endure, no matter what family or money problems you may eventually have to face, it is imperative that you understand this: You came into this world as a champion" (*Ten Prayers God Always Says Yes To,* pp. 167, 168).

Do you know why? Because you were chosen! It is the shining truth of this new year—*God chose you.* Any other reproductive cell combination, and we'd have gotten your sister instead! God chose you the night you were conceived.

And He has chosen you now to make this uncharted journey with Him. "'For I know the plans I have for you,' declares the Lord, 'plans to prosper you and not to harm you, plans to give you hope and a future'" (Jer. 29:11, NIV). And when the One who chose us before we were born promises to journey with us all the days we live, can you imagine our destination!

YOU'RE STILL GOD'S CHOSEN ONE

But even before I was born, God chose me and called me by his marvelous grace.
Gal. 1:15, NLT.

Did you catch that? God called and chose Paul and you and me *before* we were even born. Great news for those dark and mournful episodes when you and I, in self-pitying tears, whimper to God (or anyone else we can get to listen) about how meaningless and pointless "my life really is!"

But you don't know about me, you protest. My parents didn't plan me, didn't want me—I'm one big "oops!" And you may be right. But our text is compellingly clear—there is Someone in the universe who *did* want you and plan you. Just like the unplanned, unwanted twins, Perez and Zerah, who ended up in the Messiah's family tree! (See Genesis 38 and Matthew 1.) Because no matter your parents, you're still God's chosen.

But I was born with a terrible disability, you point out, which makes me a mistake of nature. Then meet my blind friend, Ray McAllister, a doctoral student at this university. He e-mailed me this beautiful prayer: "O God—let me be one blind in body but who can see You in spirit most clearly and who can show You to others and lead others to You, to Your love, to Your providence, and in so doing I may help others who are blind in spirit but sighted in body receive sight." Because no matter Mother Nature, you're still your heavenly Father's chosen.

But, you respond, the reality is that I'm too old now to be chosen for anything. Are you serious? Tell that to Anna, the widowed elderly prophet, whose entire life was a countdown to five minutes of recognizing the infant Messiah in His mother's arms and proclaiming Him to everyone in the Temple who would listen! Tell that to Moses, whose entire first 80 years were but a prelude to a surprise extra 40 years of unexpected leadership. Because no matter your age, you're still God's chosen one.

And if you're God's chosen, then that can only mean He has a destiny for you, a very unique mission for a very unique creation. That's why the object of this new year isn't to discover our dreams, but rather to follow His destiny. And that makes David's prayer the right prayer to the One who has chosen us: "Therefore, for Your name's sake, lead me and guide me" (Ps. 31:3). Who better to lead us this new year than the One who chose us?

CHOSEN @ THE BEGINNING

All praise to God, the Father of our Lord Jesus Christ, who has blessed us with every spiritual blessing in the heavenly realms because we are united with Christ. Even before he made the world, God loved us and chose us in Christ. Eph. 1:3, 4, NLT.

Thanks to the Internet, the whole world knows the meaning of the "at," or @, symbol. Without it we'd never find our way in cyberspace. So perhaps it wasn't surprising that a young Chinese couple, wanting to be both original and thoughtful, asked the government to register their newborn's name as "@." In Chinese the letters "a" and "t" can be pronounced to sound like the phrase "love him." And love their baby they did, throwing the officials into consternation.

Our text proclaims that as a sign of His love for His earth children, God *chose* us—you and me—long before we were born, long before the world was even created. Why? "God decided in advance to adopt us into his own family by bringing us to himself through Jesus Christ. . . . And it gave him great pleasure" (Eph. 1:5, NLT).

Can you believe it! Choosing the likes of you and me has given God "great pleasure." But then, that's the heart of any adoption, isn't it? The joyful pleasure of *choosing* your child—no "oops" or accidents with an adoption—you *choose* your child very carefully and intentionally. Just as God did when He chose us to be His children. But sadly, how easy it is for us to forget our chosenness. The King of the universe has adopted us into His family; and yet we drag through life, eking out an existence, moping as paupers, when we've been adopted as princes and princesses! What an affront to God must be my worries, my whining, my forgetting the glorious truth of that old gospel song "My Father is rich in houses and lands, He holdeth the wealth of the world in His hands!" Isn't it a crime to be pouting and complaining when "I'm a child of the King"?

Our adoption papers were registered and signed in crimson at Calvary—good news! "He made us accepted in the Beloved" (verse 6). Chosen, adopted, accepted! What more could you ask for?

"Such love is without a parallel. Children of the heavenly King! Precious promise! Theme for the most profound meditation! The matchless love of God for a world that did not love Him!" (*Steps to Christ,* p. 15).

DESTINY'S OUTSTRETCHED HAND

You made all the delicate, inner parts of my body and knit me together in my mother's womb. . . . You saw me before I was born. Every day of my life was recorded in your book. Every moment was laid out before a single day had passed. Ps. 139:13-16, NLT.

God is like a master artist, isn't He? A few weeks ago I was craning my neck in the Sistine Chapel at Saint Peter's Cathedral in Rome, trying to grasp the magnitude of Michelangelo's genius in painting that ceiling. The finger of God still reaches to touch the outstretched hand of newly created Adam. But do you suppose Michelangelo shaped that masterpiece on the spot, without forethought and sketches? Hardly!

Then do you suppose you arrived in this life, a blank slate, with no sketches or advance planning in the mind of the God who chose you? No, David exclaims in this psalm. The divine Artist who shaped us in our mother's womb is the divine Historian who recorded our lives before they were even lived—a provocative thought worth pondering, is it not?

To this divine handiwork we may respond in two ways. We may rue the notion that our Creator's forethought means our lack of independence or individuality. After all, how can I be me and free, if my Maker has already planned out my life?

Or we can celebrate the suggestion that this fallen creation notwithstanding, the Master Artist who has shaped both our existence and our destiny has intricately fitted us (i.e., outfitted us, at times even retrofitting us) for the unique mission He willed us into life to accomplish. In this prayer David celebrates an individuality so unique that God's life and mission for you can be lived and accomplished by no other individual in history—but you.

Are we bound by God's destiny? Hardly. The tragic life of King Saul is proof enough that all of us are free to choose our own way. But why reject the destiny of the One whose love from the beginning has shaped us to soar with Him to our highest potentials in life?

"Each has his place in the eternal plan of heaven. Each is to work in cooperation with Christ for the salvation of souls. Not more surely is the place prepared for us in the heavenly mansions than is the special place designated on earth where we are to work for God" (*Christ's Object Lessons*, pp. 326, 327).

Then shall we not take the outstretched hand of God and live His destiny today?

THE GREAT LIE

So [Adam] said, "I heard Your voice in the garden, and I was afraid because I was naked; and I hid myself." Gen. 3:10.

So who is this God who has chosen us? Don't expect the truth from the devil—who was cocked, loaded, and waiting on that glorious primeval morning when shafts of golden sunlight streamed through the emerald patchwork ceiling of that sprawling orchard garden, and dew shimmered like diamond drops on the fruit-laden boughs. She stepped gently through the sunlight, innocently into the trap.

"Psst. Up here." For the first time (and not the last) their eyes met, the first woman and the first serpent. And in a ploy as old as Eden he snared her soul by engaging a conversation. You see, when you argue with the devil, you lose every time. She did, and she lost. Took the bait, jumped to the defense of her Creator, got blindsided with the deception, disobeyed God, ate the fruit, persuaded her husband, and together they brought down an entire race.

What's a heartbroken Creator to do? What every parent with a runaway child instinctively does—race out into the night to find him or her. "Then [in the cool of the evening] the Lord God called to Adam and said to him, 'Where are you?'" (Gen. 3:9). And in the trembling response of Adam (and Eve) hiding behind the bush—"I was afraid"—we hear the tragic refrain of the serpent's primordial lie: God is somebody to be afraid of.

Buddhist temples, Shinto shrines, Hindu courtyards, Muslim mosques, Jewish synagogues, Christian churches—it matters not the sacred site—the lie is always the same. God is someone to be afraid of. So by the millions, the faithful of earth perform their rituals, read their holy books, plead their prayers, all with the hope of appeasing an angry, fearful God.

Why? "[Because] the enemy of good blinded the minds of men, so that they looked upon God with fear; they thought of Him as severe and unforgiving . . . as a being whose chief attribute is stern justice, . . . watching with jealous eye to discern the errors and mistakes of men, that He may visit judgments upon them" (*Steps to Christ*, pp. 10, 11). Is there then no hope for us either?

"It was to remove this dark shadow, by revealing to the world the infinite love of God, that Jesus came to live among men" (*ibid.*). Good news for the greatest lie! We don't have to believe it any longer. Someone has come to tell the truth.

15

THE GREATER TRUTH

Blessed is the Lord God of Israel . . . to grant us that we, being delivered from the hand of our enemies, might serve Him without fear. Luke 1:68-74.

Remember the story about the elderly, childless couple that Heaven stunned with the too-good-to-be-true announcement they were going to have a baby boy, leaving the old man literally speechless for nine months? The miraculous birth of the baby who became John the Baptist loosed father Zacharias' tongue, you remember, with a paean of praise to God for the coming Savior. And did you catch the prophesied outcome? People would once again be able to worship and serve God "without fear." But did the song come true?

Remember that early morning when that ravaged woman taken in adultery was tossed in a heap at Jesus' feet? They were ready to stone her! And the prophesied young Messiah that Zacharias sang of? Reading a trap by the haughty elders, He stooped to the Temple floor and etched the private sins of the woman's accusers in the dust. He'll not embarrass them, either. Tails tucked between their legs, they disappeared as quickly as did the record of their sins in the dust. Alone with the woman, Jesus revealed a side of God she hadn't expected: "Neither do I condemn you; go and sin no more" (John 8:11). That early-morning pronouncement only confirmed His earlier late-night declaration: "For God did not send His Son into the world to condemn the world, but that the world through Him might be saved" (John 3:17). No condemnation. What kind of a God is this who chose us *before* we were ever born and chooses us *after* we've fallen into sin a thousand times ten thousand times over? And with no condemnation?

He is the same God who looks into the face of His betrayer, who was also the company embezzler, and calls him a name. Look, if you've ever been betrayed by someone you love, someone close to you, then you know well the dictionary of invectives available to you to call that wretch every name in the book! But not Jesus. Instead, by the light of Gethsemane's angry torches, He gazes deeply into Judas' orange-cast eyes and calls him "friend" (Matt. 26:50). He called His betrayer "friend."

Thus Jesus shredded the devil's lie, proving instead that God is *not* somebody to be afraid of—he is someone to be a friend of. After all, "perfect love casts out fear" (1 John 4:18).

THE DEATH OF DAG HAMMARSKJOLD AND THE CHOICE

Choose this day whom you will serve, whether the gods your ancestors served . . . or the gods of the [people] in whose land you are living; but as for me and my household, we will serve the Lord. Joshua 24:15, NRSV.

Dag Hammarskjold was secretary-general of the United Nations from 1953 until his tragic death in 1961. A Swedish Christian, he authored a collection of meditations, and was regarded by many as the greatest diplomat of the twentieth century.

Sometime in the night between September 17 and 18, while on a United Nations peace mission to the Congo, Hammarskjold's plane went down in Zambia in a fiery explosion. The circumstances surrounding the plane crash remained a mystery, until investigators discovered a fresh clue in the evidence. In the cockpit of the wreckage someone noticed an open map to Ndolo, the airport in Leopoldville (now Kinshasa), Congo. However, the intended destination that night was the city of Ndola in Zambia. The pilot had mistakenly grabbed the wrong map, and in the pitch-black of that night the plane slammed into the ground when the pilot thought he still had a thousand more feet to descend. All because he'd grabbed the wrong map.

Ndolo. Ndola. The only difference in those names is a single letter. But it was the difference between life and death.

Afraid or *a friend*. Just the difference of a few letters. But when it comes to the map of God, it too is the difference between life and death.

So which map shall we follow? The appeal of the aged leader Joshua is still as relevant today: "Choose this day the God you will serve." Because the new year isn't only about God choosing us—it's also about our choosing Him.

And we don't have forever. The litany of global headlines of late is proof enough that time is running out for this planet and *all* its inhabitants. Just because God is someone to be a friend of, not afraid of, doesn't mean we can put off till tomorrow the decision urgently needed today. "Choose *this day* the God you will follow." The gathering night is dark. We *must* have the right map; we *must* choose the right God; we *must* land at the right destination!

Then won't you bow right now and invite the God who has already chosen you to be the God of your choice, too, by declaring, "As for me and my household, we will serve the Lord."

17

GOD'S FIRE RESCUE METHOD

Long ago God spoke to our ancestors in many and various ways by the prophets, but in these last days he has spoken to us by a Son. Heb. 1:1, 2, NRSV.

What if you woke up one night to discover your next-door neighbor's house enveloped in flames? And when you raced outside, you spotted their little girl screaming from the second-floor bedroom window. With her parents nowhere in sight, you race through the front door and up the stairs to her bedroom. Paralyzed by panic and still screaming, the child refuses to leave the illusive security of her room. You try coaxing, cajoling, but all to no avail. She's too afraid.

But the flames are roaring down the hallway—it's now or never. So what do you do? What every firefighter would do in the same circumstance. You grab the girl, your arm over her flailing limbs, your hand over her mouth, and you run for dear life. Why? Because when the house is burning down, there's no time for polite niceties. The firefighter's rule is simple—extricate now, explain later.

Could that be what God was doing in the Old Testament? How many times did it appear His house of faith was going up in flames? His children sound asleep or distracted or even panicked—and all the divine coaxing and pleading through prophets and patriarchs alike didn't seem to rouse them or change them. What's a rescuer to do? If your goal is to save those entrapped, you'll have to extricate now, and explain later. Not because you don't have a heart for dialogue and reasoned conversation—but because the danger is too imminent for protracted visitations!

And so God did just that, practically dragging His children out of one crisis after another. The fuller explanations would simply have to wait, for their survival depended on the rough-and-tumble of immediate divine rescue.

Our text declares: "Long ago God spoke to our ancestors in many and various ways by the prophets, but in these last days he has spoken to us by a Son" (NRSV). Because "in these last days" Jesus is still God's clearest explanation of all. And when at Calvary His own house went up in flames and no one was there to rescue *Him,* then at last we saw the depths of the love divine that sacrificed itself in a final rescue, that we might be saved from the flames forever and ever. Amen.

A SIGN OF LOVE

And have you forgotten the encouraging words God spoke to you as his children?
He said, "My child, don't make light of the Lord's discipline, and don't give up
when he corrects you. For the Lord disciplines those he loves, and he punishes
each one he accepts as his child." Heb. 12:5, 6, NLT.

I know of some who've announced they've gone through the Bible and counted more than 60 stories in which God has punished people. No wonder Satan's lie gets traction—God is someone to be afraid of. After all, who wants to get chosen by a God like that! Perhaps we need to brood a bit longer over today's text: "The Lord disciplines those he loves."

Karen and I have been blessed with two wonderful children, Kirk and Kristin. When they were young, I remember kneeling down, looking straight into their wide eyes, and explaining to them the dangers of playing on the neighborhood road in front of our house. "Car come along—go *boom!*" So the law in our little kingdom was—the road is off-limits.

But let's say a few minutes after those instructions, Kirk is playing in the middle of the forbidden street. What's a father to do? I hurry out, take my boy firmly by the hand, escort him to the house, and, being a dad of grace and mercy, reexplain the law of the off-limits road. "Do you understand?" He nods his head in full agreement.

But a few minutes later there he is again, playing in the street. Though I am still a father of grace and mercy, I can assure you that this time the story has a slightly different ending. To show him my love, I will warm one part of his anatomy so that the truth will be red-hot in another portion of his anatomy! Why? Parents know that if you really love your child, discipline is an integral part of demonstrating that saving love.

Is it any different with our divine Parent? Count all the stories you wish. The biblical paradigm shifts when we remember that God is our Father and that we are His children. And chosen by Him as we all are, is it so counterintuitive to realize that in order to teach us and shape us for our intended destinies He allows us to experience some of life's painful realities? Not all the time, not even most of the time—but still there *are* those times when with His arm around us He leads us "through the valley of the shadow" (Ps. 23). If we would only trust His love, would there be any discipline we could not endure, as long as He was *with* us?

ON PLAYING MARBLES WITH GOD — 1

*Then the father said to him, "Son, you are always with me, and all that is mine is yours.
But we had to celebrate and rejoice, because this brother of yours was dead and has come to
life; he was lost and has been found." Luke 15:31, 32, NRSV.*

Jean Piaget, the Swiss developmental psychologist, once studied children playing marbles in order to understand how a child deals with right and wrong. In
the process he discovered three stages children go through with marbles.

The first stage is the **rules stage**, when young children accept the rules of the
game as having been handed down to them by an unquestionable higher authority, their father. Rules are to be obeyed, not challenged. If you want to win the
game, keep the rules.

Not surprisingly, the second stage is the **rebel stage**, when the older children
begin challenging the traditional rules and experiment by inventing new rules of
their own.

The third stage can be called the **relationship stage**, when finally the grown
children realize how silly their own made-up rules really were, and now out of mu-
tual respect they return to the rules—not because of authority, but rather for the
sake of relationship.

Once upon a time Jesus told a story about all three stages. For when the
farmer's younger son nearly slammed the kitchen screen door off its hinges, the father knew his boy was as good as gone. And so dividing up the farm, he gave both
sons their share of the inheritance. Whereupon the younger boy (stage two) rode
off into the sunset, plunged into city life, dissipated his fortune with fury and passion, ending up broke and broken in a pigsty. But coming to his senses, he turned
his rags toward home, where the father (stage three) had been waiting night and
day. Spotting his boy's familiar gait in the distance, he flew off the porch and down
the road with open arms. The party they threw that night was off the charts! And
out-of-bounds for the older brother (stage one), who in jealous anger refused to
share his father's joy. The End.

So which stage are you in? Stage one (the rules boy who stays home and gets
lost), stage two (the rebel boy who leaves home and gets lost), or stage three (the
relational father who loved them both)? Jesus' good news for today is that the
Father values relationships most of all—even more than the rules we break and the
rules we keep—which is why He hurries out of the house for *both* His boys. What's
not to love about that?

ON PLAYING MARBLES WITH GOD—2

But he answered his father, "Look! All these years I've been slaving for you and never disobeyed your orders. Yet you never gave me even a young goat so I could celebrate with my friends. But when this son of yours who has squandered your property with prostitutes comes home, you kill the fattened calf for him!" Luke 15:29, 30, NIV.

Hear what the elder brother is saying? "I've *slaved* for you all these years"—those are Jesus' words—"I've kept every single one of your rules, I've never sinned grossly, I've denied myself pleasures, all because I figured that's what you demanded of me. And what do I get for living such a drab and joyless life? *Nothing!*"

Sound familiar? Could there be an elder brother or sister in the corner of our hearts, too? Have we been following God all these years out of a sense of sullen obligation—a fearful obedience that keeps thinking, *If I don't obey Him, He's going to cut me out of His will?*

Don't misunderstand me, please. I'm not opposed to the rules and commandments of God. Our loving Father, like any good parent, carefully provides protective rules for His children. But sullen submission to those rules for the sake of earning His inheritance—where is the joy, the peace, and the freedom in that? Could this be the reason for the stern faces in church these days? Elder brothers and sisters (who may not be older) who have never physically run away but who've run away spiritually from the grace and love and joy and peace of the Father's house. We hear the "music and dancing" (Luke 15:25) spilling out of the Father's home, but we refuse to go in, sweating in His fields but so far away from His heart.

You can almost hear the catch in the father's voice as he leaves the party behind and steps into the gathering dusk to love his elder boy. "Son, all that I have is yours"; i.e., didn't you know my inheritance was already yours? I never expected you to slave for it or for me. You're my child. You have both my heart and my land. If only you wanted my friendship.

Because that's the stage-three truth about God, isn't it? He is a being questing for friends. "All that I have is yours," which really means, "All that I want is *you*."

And with all that the Father has to offer you and with all that you have to give Him, isn't it the right time to cease slaving for Him and to start celebrating with Him? After all, haven't you chosen each other?

21

ON PLAYING MARBLES WITH GOD—3

*In the same way, there is more joy in heaven over one lost sinner who repents and returns
to God than over ninety-nine others who are righteous and haven't strayed away!*
Luke 15:7, NLT.

What's the mind-set of a stage-two rebel? Look at the prodigal son. More
often than not it's a reaction, a bold, flagrant reaction to the stage-one mentality of an elder brother. And it can sound like this: "I've had it with the conservatives—all their authority, their restraints, their rules. I don't need anybody telling
me how to live—not my family, not my church, not my school, not my government, not anybody! Because I'm me—freethinking, independent, grown-up me.
And I'll live as I please—thank you!"

I've known more than a few of these stage-two younger brothers and sisters
(who aren't necessarily younger chronologically). Many are bright and perceptive,
who consider the church, and God, as too authoritarian, too preoccupied with
rules and behaviors. And so they choose to live on the edge, just beyond the pe-
riphery of the community of faith, noisily proclaiming their newfound freedom,
bedecked with their trinkets of rebellion, hoping to be noticed, but not wanting
to be found. You may know them, too. You may be one.

It would be funny were it not so sad. For you see, the two brothers are very
much alike down deep inside. Oh, it's true—stage-two prodigals call the stage-one
elders conservatives, and the elders call the rebels liberals. But beyond the name-
calling, both boys really want the same thing: they want to be free. Both boys see
the father as an authoritarian rule giver. Because of his rules, one boy leaves home
and gets lost. Because of his rules, the other son stays home and gets lost. Both of
them are wrong, both are lost, because both have missed the stage-three truth
about the father.

And that is that when it's all said and done, *the father values relationships more
than rules.* In Jesus' story the father leaves his house looking for *both* boys. Same father, same wide-open embrace, same eager and loving heart. It's the same truth it's
always been throughout eternity—what matters most to God in the beginning and
in the end is *relationship.* He doesn't hurry from His home to restore broken rules—
His heart races toward His children in order to restore a broken relationship. For
the truth is, the Father isn't somebody to be afraid of. He is someone to be a friend
of, a truth so simple that even children with marbles can teach us.

A BLACK-AND-WHITE EMBRACE

But when he was still a great way off, his father saw him and had compassion, and ran and fell on his neck and kissed him. Luke 15:20.

Ever wonder why Jesus died with His arms outstretched? Perhaps the award-winning photograph from *Life* magazine tells it best.

It was a news photograph from that day in 1973 when the prisoners of war came home from Vietnam. The giant gray C-140 Hercules transport had landed and taxied up the runway at a West Coast air base. Down the lowered stairway they stepped, the first returning POWs, to the boisterous welcome of their cordoned-off loved ones. But our eyes are drawn to one soldier in particular, dressed in crisp military khaki, his pleated cap perched atop a face gaunt but proud.

Something has caught his attention. Somebody has broken out of the roped-off crowd and is racing toward him, a look of joyful ecstasy on her face, her long hair streaming in the airport wind. He must have heard her call to him. Because in spotting her, he has instinctively dropped his duffel bag and is bending at his knees, his arms thrown wide open to catch his little girl. And when the camera shutter clicks, her feet are off the ground, her arms suspended in midair reaching out to her returning father. Freeze frame. A black-and-white moment of timelessness, the portrait of a father-and-child reunion.

And that is why Jesus died with His arms outstretched. So that we would never forget they are the arms of "our Father which art in heaven." Arms wide open with the glad and glorious truth that what has always mattered most to God are His children, younger brothers and older sisters, stepping into His wide-open embrace.

Then shall we not freeze that frame in our minds, too? Because if what matters most to the God of the universe are relationships, then shouldn't they matter most to His church, to His friends, to you and me, as well? Isn't that black-and-white moment the very reason the chosen exist? Chosen by God not only to step into that wide-open embrace ourselves, but chosen to take this glorious snapshot of Him to the farthest corners of our lives and our world?

With a picture like this, for the life of me and the life of you, I can't think of a reason *not* to step into those outstretched arms. Can you?

THE TRUTH ABOUT THE TRUCKER AND GOD

"For I know the plans I have for you," declares the Lord, "plans to prosper you and not to harm you, plans to give you hope and a future." Jer. 29:11, NIV.

For two weeks now we've been examining the portrait of this God who has chosen us. Maybe we've known Him all our lives, or perhaps we're discovering Him all over again (like the old cornflakes commercial—"Taste them again for the first time"). But it's more than clear that the truth about Him has gotten terribly distorted out there, and sometimes even in here.

The papers back east carried the story of a woman driving alone late one night on an abandoned stretch of interstate, when from out of nowhere materialized a rumbling 18-wheeler. The driver was passing her when suddenly his air brakes whooshed and he slowed back in behind her, his blinding halogen lights blazing into her car. Nervous, the woman sped up. So did the trucker. She slowed down. So did he. No matter what she did, he was on her tail. Panicking now, she desperately searched the black stretches ahead for some sign of life and help. Finally she spotted a gas station that was still open. Again she attempted to lose the trucker, but he veered off the same exit ramp right behind. Screeching into the station, the woman fled from her car screaming for help. The trucker leaped from his cab and raced toward the car. When he got there, he stopped, threw open her back door, reached inside, and pulled out a man who had been crouched behind her seat.

Sometime in the night an unknown assailant had hidden in her car, waiting for the opportune moment to attack her. But in that same dark night a trucker passed by and from his high vantage point saw the hiding assailant. The woman had been running from the wrong one. For the one who was chasing her was the only one who could save her.

How many in this twilight of earth's history have mistaken the evidence and are running from the wrong one, running from the only One who can save them? "For I know the plans I have for you," declares the Lord, "plans to prosper you and not to harm you, plans to give you hope and a future."

With an offer like that, who wouldn't want to be chosen by God? Why, even if this were the only promise He made, wouldn't we have every reason to hope for the future? So is there any reason then for you to keep this offer to yourself?

A TALE OF THREE MOUNTAINS—1

How you are fallen from heaven, O Lucifer, son of the morning! . . . For you have said in your heart: "I will ascend into heaven, I will exalt my throne above the stars of God; I will also sit on the mount of the congregation . . . ; I will ascend above the heights of the clouds, I will be like the Most High." Isa. 14:12-14.

One afternoon I made a pastoral visit to an elderly couple in my parish, great-grandparents several times over. On their fireplace mantel family snapshots crowded into high school portraits, all telling the colorful stories of their seven children and their offspring. As we relived the memories, the aged parents came to the last portrait on the shelf, their youngest. A note of sadness crept into the mother's voice as she told of her boy who had grown up in the same home with the same family values as the rest had, but, for reasons nobody knew, had turned his back on it all. Rejected them. Rebelled.

Imagine this family gathered at a Thanksgiving dinner reunion. Six of the children and their broods have come home to be with Mother and Father. Laughter and smiles and joy all crowd around the family table. But wait a minute. As Father stands to pray, what is that that trickles from the corner of Mother's praying eyes? A tear? But dear Mother, six of your seven children have come home—isn't that reason enough to be happy? But we all know the universal truth, don't we? How can a mother's heart be happy when one of her children is missing?

Once upon a very long time ago there was a perfect Parent and a perfect home. But one of the children rebelled against everything the family stood for and valued, leaving a broken heart and a broken home in a heaven now broken, too.

You can't tell the story of the Father without reliving the tale of Lucifer. Same home, same Father—but such tragically opposite results with the family favorite, who secretly coveted to "sit on the mount of the congregation" (read "throne of God"). "Ah, if only I were God," he insidiously whispered. And the rest is history—the heartbreaking history of a divided universe and a planet in rebellion.

He was the highest of the chosen ones, but he chose to become unchosen. And he broke the maternal heart of our Father in heaven, a heart that still weeps for a boy not coming home.

A TALE OF THREE MOUNTAINS—2

Then the Lord saw that the wickedness of man was great in the earth, and that every intent of the thoughts of his heart was only evil continually. And the Lord was sorry that He had made man on the earth, and He was grieved in His heart. Gen. 6:5, 6.

You have to hand it to God, don't you? Failure after failure, and He keeps on going. A rebellion in His own home, and a third of the children are gone. A rebellion in His new garden planet, and all of the children are gone. How much failure can a parent take? And at what point do you start getting mad? Instead, sacred history describes the pain of divine failure with the simple words, "He was grieved in His heart." Grieved, because He must now make the terrible decision every surgeon faces in order to save His patient.

And it is this decision that Satan has fanned into a roaring diatribe against the notion of a loving Creator and God. Why, just look at the Flood! What kind of God would in rage destroy an entire civilization? Let's face it—the divine destruction stories of the Bible have played havoc with God's reputation on earth. What shall we do with the Flood (and Sodom and Gomorrah, the slaughter of the Canaanites, Uzzah, an entire Assyrian army, et al.)?

My lung is diseased with cancer. I visit the surgeon. He has two choices—(1) let the cancerous lung metastasize throughout my body or (2) take radical, invasive action and remove the diseased organ. Save the organ or save the life? Is it really a choice if you're in the lifesaving business?

Our text today describes an earth in the advanced stage of sin's cancer. Not all God's children have abandoned Him. But if the cancer is allowed to metastasize, He loses the entire race. Shall He save the cancer, or take radical invasive action to remove the hopelessly diseased portion in order to save the race? You make the call. You be the divine doctor.

"Turn to me and be saved, all you ends of the earth; for I am God, and there is no other" (Isa. 45:22, NIV), God pleaded with the antediluvians. Eight of them—count them—did turn to Him. But when the waterlogged doors of the ark swung open atop Mount Ararat, Noah and his family were the sole survivors of that radical surgery.

"Turn to me." These are not the words of a raging, consuming God. They are the plea of a compassionate Savior, a plea this diseased world needs desperately to hear again.

A TALE OF THREE MOUNTAINS—3

So Abraham called that place "The Lord Will Provide." And to this day it is said, "On the mountain of the Lord it will be provided." Gen. 22:14, NIV.

Long, long ago a pile of wooden planks in the form of an ark atop a mountain was the revelation of divine love. Not as long ago a pair of wooden boards in the form of a cross became the expression of His love. Today nothing has changed.

The same God, the same love, the same urgent plea, the same final decision—to excise the cancer before the race is lost, the same clock counting down to eternity, the same arms outstretched, the same merciful invitation. "As it was in the days of Noah, so it will be at the coming of the Son of Man" (Matt. 24:37, NIV). Nothing has changed: come home, come back to the Father before it's too late. Come now. The divine appeal turns out to be the same.

What is there about the human heart that is so susceptible to an appeal?

I was deeply moved by a picture I saw in a newspaper some years ago. A picture of a mysterious sign that had appeared nailed to a tree in Nappanee, Indiana. It isn't one of those slick Madison Avenue billboards with smiling faces and a catchy logo. Just a simple sign, with a few hand-painted words on it. And nobody knew from whence it came, not even the farmer on whose land the tree grows and the sign was affixed. Three times he had removed it, and three times it reappeared.

Makes you wonder who put it up. A heartbroken mother? A lonely father at midnight? No one knows. But no one who reads the sign can forget it. Four simple words: "Son, please come back."

They are the same four words that God painted in crimson and nailed to a tree long ago, the four words of His nailed-open embrace: "Child, please come back."

It's more than obvious that Lucifer won't be coming back. Nor will the antediluvians. But of the almost 6.9 billion other sons and daughters of the Father alive today, how many of them are still susceptible to His appeal? Could it be that's why you've been chosen? Oh sure, God could write the words across the heavens for all to see. But who would be moved? Truth is, there's nothing that moves the heart more than a personal invitation from someone you know who cares.

WHY GOD CAN'T SLEEP AT NIGHT

In all their affliction He was afflicted. Isa. 63:9.

I live in a small rural community, half of which consists of the university campus where I pastor. So whenever I hear sirens in the distance, I catch myself instinctively tensing and wondering if they wail for someone I know. They often do.

Have you noticed that no matter where you live, sirens wail in the same gut-twisting language? Emergency rooms the world over specialize in knotted stomachs and crumpled tissues, while we wait for word from behind the curtain. Suffering is our way of life.

Is it God's way of life, too? Does He suffer the way we do?

I remember those times when my children would come into the house sobbing, knee torn and bleeding from a bicycle tumble. Why was it that as I scooped them into my arms—I tell you the truth—I could feel the pain in my own knee? Why do *their* tears still well up in *my* eyes?

Could it be this is the way of parents because it is the way of the Father? *Our* tears well up in *His* eyes—isn't that what "in all [our] affliction He [is] afflicted" means? "Not a sigh is breathed, not a pain felt, not a grief pierces the soul, but the throb vibrates to the Father's heart" (*The Desire of Ages,* p. 356). It doesn't take away the suffering, to be sure, anymore than holding your child removes her pain. But when you know there is someone who is sharing your pain, in some mysterious way the pain is tempered.

"In all [our] affliction He [is] afflicted." Because He has already been there. He has already been *here.* The naked scream from the center cross is evidence enough. Suffering is God's way of life, too. And that is why the ultimate word regarding human suffering is that ultimately, intimately, God is with us in the midst of it . . . until it ends.

Three young men from campus died tragically in a winter's plane crash. At one of the funerals I conducted, a colleague and I stepped to the casket for the family's last goodbye. As they wept over the stilled form of their son and grandson, we felt their tears in our own eyes and hearts. After several minutes of muffled quiet, my pastor friend leaned over to me and whispered, "It's no wonder God can't sleep at night."

Because in all our affliction, He not only is afflicted; He is also with us. And for now that's the best news there is. God really truly is with us.

THE BONES OF JEHOHANAN BEN HAGQOL

And when they had come to the place called Calvary, there they crucified Him, and the criminals, one on the right hand and the other on the left. Luke 23:33.

They don't have his death certificate, but they have found his bones, bleached and dusty in an abandoned crypt. And from the disintegrating skeleton, his tragic story emerges: his name, Jehohanan ben Hagqol (Aramaic for John, son of Hagqol); nationality, Jew; age, somewhere between 24 and 28 years old; height, five feet six inches; economic status, member of a wealthy family; occupation, no apparent form of hard labor; health, no indication of any serious illness (although the asymmetrical formation of his cranium indicates that in the first weeks of his mother's pregnancy and again later—shortly before or during his birth—his life was threatened by unknown traumatic events); residence, Jerusalem; date of death, sometime during the A.D. 30s and 40s.

Manner of death? Violent. The shin of his left leg had been broken, probably by the blow of a club. And presumably as a consequence of that blow, both bones of the right lower thigh had also been broken. Moreover, after expiration, his feet had to be amputated by a hatchet blow in order to extricate his body. Why? Simple. Jehohanan was the victim of Roman crucifixion. The five- to six-inch nail that spiked his heels to the cross has been found. (Apparently the bent tip of the nail had stuck in a knot in the wood, which explains the amputation of the young man's feet.) Traces of nail were also found between the radius and cubitus of the left forearm, indicating that his arms as well as his feet had been nailed to the cross. Traces of the cross indicate it was made from olive wood.

Nobody knows his story. His dusty pile of bones was discovered by the Israeli Ministry of Housing in June 1968 at a burial site in north Jerusalem. What makes this archaeological find so significant is that it marks the first time the remains of a crucified man, dating from the Roman Era, have been found.

But then the world never needed the tale of Jehohanan to remember the tragedy of crucifixion, did it? The story of another young Man from that same city in that same time has told the tale all too well. We know what killed Jehohanan. But what killed Jesus? It is imperative we find the answer. For in it there must surely be the truth about the God who has chosen us.

WHAT KILLED JESUS?

But when they came to Jesus and saw that He was already dead,
they did not break His legs. But one of the soldiers pierced His side with a spear,
and immediately blood and water came out. John 19:33, 34.

I own a piece of paper given to me by a friendly parishioner who owns a funeral home. I'm grateful he didn't fill it out for me in advance, since it's a death certificate. And while the fact remains that if time should last long enough, your name one day will appear on a similar piece of paper, I have a hard time bringing myself to admit that one of these days, if Jesus doesn't come soon, there will be a certificate with my name on it, too.

On that fated Friday afternoon before the sinking sun turned the sky over the Holy City bloodred, what did the somber coroner annotate on the death certificate of Jesus? On line 27, "cause of death," what did he scribble down? Three Roman nails? One centurion's lance? Forty less one flagellations on the back by that legionnaire? That twisted crown of thorns plaited and pressed on His bloody brow? Or was it the gasping, spasmodic breathing that eventually suffocated the victim of the cross? What killed Jesus?

A physician friend of mine once sent me a cover story from the *Journal of the American Medical Association (JAMA)*, in which a physician, a minister, and an anatomical artist collaborated to research how Jesus died. Their conclusion? "A fatal cardiac arrhythmia may have accounted for the apparent catastrophic terminal event" (vol. 255, no. 11, p. 1463). Is that what killed Jesus?

But most of us have been taught from childhood a quick and simple answer—our sins. What sins? Well, you know, our pride and self-centeredness, our evil tempers and vile tongues, our lustful hearts and addicted minds, our hate and anger and murder and rebellion, our perverted appetites, our utter faithlessness and dishonesty. In short, all our sins—they're what killed Jesus.

But are they really? Or could it be we're so right that in fact we're wrong? With our Western sensibilities, we analyze, theorize, philosophize, scrutinize, and even theologize the cross. And then with a unanimous vote, we declare our sins to have killed Him.

But in hurrying away from Calvary, we are 12 hours too late. The answer we seek glistens in the bloody sweat of a midnight garden.

THE GARDEN OF HELL — 1

He took Peter, James, and John with him, and he became deeply troubled and distressed. He told them, "My soul is crushed with grief to the point of death. Stay here and keep watch with me." Mark 14:33, 34, NLT.

S ay what you will about Mel Gibson's *The Passion of the Christ*, he certainly got this part right. The road to Golgotha always leads *through* Gethsemane. Once upon a time the human race fell in a garden. Once upon another time the human race got saved in a garden.

Beneath the full Passover moon a band of 12 young men hurries through the patches of silver and black out the eastern gate of the sleeping city, down into the valley notch, and back up a wending path to a hillside orchard garden called in their tongue "olive press" or Gethsemane. When at the gate they stop, we catch a glimpse of the face of Jesus, darkly and strangely twisted. Was it this night He soothed, "My peace I leave with you"? No, for there is no peace etched in the shadows of His face now.

Something is happening to the Master, and the Gospel writers are silent. The only cryptic clue is a long Greek word found in Mark alone: "horror-struck." As He now staggers to the garden's inner sanctum, "He groaned aloud, as if suffering under the pressure of a terrible burden. Twice his companions supported Him, or He would have fallen to the earth" (*The Desire of Ages*, p. 686). He turns to His three closest friends, "My soul is crushed with grief to the point of death." It is as if He were dying. Could it be that He is?

Choking sobs rend the heavy night mist: "Abba, Father, all things are possible for You. Take this cup away from Me" (Mark 14:36). Not even Christ can name what rends His soul with terror and tears. "This cup" is all He can moan. What is that mysterious cup He trembles to even touch? Is it a fear of physical suffering, pain, and death? Why, even Socrates hardly flinched when drinking his hemlock, leading John Stott to wonder, "So was Socrates braver than Jesus? Or were their cups filled with different poisons?" (*The Cross of Christ*, p. 74).

The Scriptures Jesus was steeped in repeatedly describe drinking from the cup of God's holy "wrath" against unholy sin (Job 21:20; Ps. 75:8; Isa. 51:17; also Rev. 14:10). Could that be the reason the soul of Jesus shudders? Could there really be a Love so strong it was willing to drink the cup of my own poison?

31

THE GARDEN OF HELL—2

Surely He has borne our griefs and carried our sorrows; yet we esteemed Him stricken, smitten by God, and afflicted. . . . All we like sheep have gone astray; we have turned, every one, to his own way; and the Lord has laid on Him the iniquity of us all. Isa. 53:4, 6.

Sometimes I come home late at night, and by the sliver of light from the half-ajar closet door I look on the sleeping face of my wife. And I wonder how I could ever survive being separated from Karen. It's bad enough for a weekend, or a week, but to be cut off from her love for eternity? My heart shudders at the very thought.

Three times in that midnight garden, fingernails clinging to the moist earth, Jesus pleads for another way. "If it is Your will, Abba, Father, I beg of you take this cup away." Already "the Lord [was laying] on Him the iniquity of us all." Already the awful struggle of sin's eternal-separation-from-the-Father reality was choking out the life of the Son. If He drinks the cup, the poison is eternal death, forever separation from the One who has been the love of His life.

"The fate of humanity trembled in the balance. Christ might even now refuse to drink the cup apportioned to guilty man. It was not yet too late. He might wipe the bloody sweat from His brow, and leave man to perish in his iniquity" (*The Desire of Ages*, p. 690).

Was it a temptation? You don't think Jesus was alone in that garden, do you? If the fallen angel rebel had personally assaulted Christ in the wilderness at the beginning of His ministry, would not the dark leader with all his demonic legions be present in the garden, too? Only now the stakes are exponentially higher for Satan and his kingdom. For if Jesus exits this garden tonight and goes to Calvary tomorrow as the divine sacrifice for sin and sinners, then it is the death knell for the serpent— who surely tonight shrieks with all his diabolical rage: "Go home to Your abba, Daddy's boy—they sleep, for whom You would die—this sorry wretch of race is mine—for I am their prince. Go home, Daddy's boy. Why should You die forever!"

It is the physician Luke who alone records the rare condition called hematidrosis, the hemorrhaging of surface vessels into the sweat glands under extreme mental anguish (Luke 22:44). The sweaty, bloody ground beneath the bowed form of the Man in the garden is evidence enough that the cup of our salvation trembled in His hand.

And again we wonder, is there a Love so strong it would choose to die forever . . . for us?

THE GARDEN OF HELL—3

*And He was withdrawn from them about a stone's throw, and He knelt down and prayed,
saying, "Father, if it is Your will, take this cup away from Me; nevertheless not My will,
but Yours, be done." Then an angel appeared to Him from heaven, strengthening Him.
Luke 22:41-43.*

Let's be honest. We really don't take sin that seriously, do we? After all, when was the last time we sweat blood over a temptation? Unfair analogy, you protest. Is it really? "In your struggle against sin, you have not yet resisted to the point of shedding your blood" (Heb. 12:4, NIV). The point is that far too lightly and too quickly you and I dismiss our nagging, naughty little sins. Shame on me—tsk, tsk, tsk—I shouldn't do that again, should I—hee-hee-hee. Apart from Gethsemane we have no consciousness of the magnitude of evil that grips our careless souls.

Beneath the Passover moon Jesus shed blood in His struggle over sin (not His, mind you, but yours and mine), and whether or not He should drink the cup and bear the sins of a race that at best was sleeping and at worst couldn't care less. Gethsemane's bloody battleground is proof enough of the high cost of our own sins.

"Three times has He uttered that prayer. Three times has humanity shrunk from the last, crowning sacrifice. . . . [Then] His decision is made. He will save man *at any cost to Himself.* He accepts His baptism of blood, that through Him perishing millions may gain everlasting life. . . . Having made the decision, He fell dying to the ground from which He had partially risen" (*The Desire of Ages*, p. 690-693; italics supplied).

Did you catch that? "He fell dying." Had not the angel who was His guardian resuscitated Him, Jesus would have died in the garden, a sacrifice for the sins of the human race. But Love's supreme sacrifice, at last embraced by Christ, must not be made hidden in a garden cloister. Rather, in the full light of day suspended between heaven and earth for heaven and earth to witness, God will die for this rebel race.

Therein lies the passion of the Christ and the Father. For from both the heart of Gethsemane and the summit of Calvary shines the same resplendent truth: lost people matter most to God.

EXCRUCIATUS

And when they had come to a place called Golgotha, that is to say, Place of a Skull, they gave Him sour wine mingled with gall to drink. But when He had tasted it, He would not drink. Then they crucified Him. Matt. 27:33-35.

Who is this God who has chosen us? Twelve hours later at noon on Friday Jesus hangs from a Roman cross. His lacerated back rubs the splintery wood—a back shredded into a messy, bloody gouge, ripped open by tiny pieces of bone and metal embedded in the leather straps of the scourging whip that flailed His skin.

The nerves, the tendons, the vessels of His wrists and feet have been crushed by the six inch iron nails hammered into the wooden stake. Nailed in a position cruelly intended to bring on spastic strangulation of the breathing process, Jesus must raise His chest simply to breathe. But in order to expand His diaphragm long enough to suck in more air, He must drag His shredded back against the wood, while jamming His weight against His nailed wrists and ankles, producing a searing hot pain.

It is no wonder the Latins coined the word *excruciatus,* which means "from out of the cross," and from whence comes our word "excruciating." Calvary was no anesthetized picnic. And as a consequence we have come to envision the cross as the ultimate in physical suffering, haven't we? Mel Gibson's bloody rendition would certainly lead one to that conclusion.

But is the cross about ultimate human pain? Once I watched a friend die from cancer, connected to his morphine drip night and day. Surely the six hours of Calvary are not equivalent to six weeks of advanced cancer, are they? There must be more to the cross than the graphic depiction of human suffering and physical pain.

"All His life Christ had been publishing to a fallen world the good news of the Father's mercy and pardoning love. Salvation for the chief of sinners was His theme. But now with the terrible weight of guilt He bears, He cannot see the Father's reconciling face. The withdrawal of the divine countenance from the Savior in this hour of supreme anguish pierced His heart with a sorrow that can never be fully understood by man. So great was this agony that His physical pain was hardly felt" (*The Desire of Ages,* p. 753).

Hardly felt? Then what was it that drew such a cry of anguish before He died?

SCREAM IN THE DARK

When it was noon, darkness came over the whole land until three in the afternoon. At three o'clock Jesus cried out with a loud voice, "Eloi, Eloi, lema sabachthani?" which means, "My God, my God, why have you forsaken me?" Mark 15:33, 34, NRSV.

I have heard few human screams. As a father I've heard my children scream out their hurt or fear. As a pastor I've walked hospital corridors and have listened to the muffled cries of pain from behind closed doors. But I have never heard the sheer and naked terror in Golgotha's scream: "My God, my God, why have you forsaken me?" It was no whimper this "loud voice" cry (the Greek reading *megale phone*, from whence comes our "megaphone"). It was no doubt like His final cry, a "shriek, shrill and agonizing" (*Signs of the Times*, Apr.14,1898).

What is this God-forsaken terror from the middle cross? Could it be the noise-less, slithering approach of the second death that Jesus senses in the darkness—that death that is eternal, that death that heretofore has never been witnessed anywhere in the universe? Called the "second" death in Revelation 20:6, and the "eternal" death in Romans 6:23 (as the antithesis of "eternal life"), was it the nameless terror of this nameless foe that triggered Christ's naked scream?

The supernatural, funereal darkness enveloping His cross was cryptic evidence that the separation Jesus had pleaded against in the garden was in fact now coming to pass. "My God, my God!" No "Abba, Father" now. Just the horror of the re-alization that the One with whom He had shared eternity past is gone. "Why have You abandoned me?" But to that scream comes no reply, save the silence of the tomb in the darkness of the cross. He has been cut off forever. The jeering prelates and rabble were right. "He saved others; Himself He cannot save" (Matt. 27:42). And that is the gospel truth. For had He saved Himself that Friday afternoon, that would have been all that was saved. Just Himself. It is the incomprehensible truth of divine love, God's love in Christ, that kept Him from saving Himself, leading Him instead to sacrifice Himself forever and ever, just to save sinners the likes of you and me. Not even His scream in the dark could change His mind or reverse His choice. The God who chose us in the beginning chose us in the ending, when for Him it all ended that afternoon.

THE FOREVER PRICE

Who will separate us from the love of Christ? Will hardship, or distress, or persecution, or famine, or nakedness, or peril, or sword? . . . No, in all these things we are more than conquerors through him who loved us. Rom. 8:35-37, NRSV.

How can it be that Jesus died an eternal death for our sins? Consider this quotation and a story in response.

"Satan with his fierce temptations wrung the heart of Jesus. The Savior could not see through the portals of the tomb. Hope did not present to Him His coming forth from the grave a conqueror, or tell Him of the Father's acceptance of the sacrifice. He feared that sin was so offensive to God that Their separation was to be eternal. . . . It was the sense of sin, bringing the Father's wrath upon Him as man's substitute, that made the cup He drank so bitter, and broke the heart of the Son of God" (*The Desire of Ages*, p. 753).

I remember the story from childhood, the story of a young boy who was terribly sick, so sick in fact that the doctors said he was going to die. Unless (and here his fate hung) they could find someone with his rare match of blood. And the whole family was tested, but it was his little sister who offered the perfect match. The doctors and her parents explained to her the nature of the emergency, and asked whether she would be willing to give some of her blood to save her very sick brother. Turning away, she pondered their proposition. Finally she looked back and nodded her curls. Yes, she would give her blood for her sick brother.

Soon she was connected to that little plastic bag that began to drip full with her lifesaving blood. The minutes ticked by; the procedure finally ended. And as they led the little girl back out of the laboratory, with a quivering lip and tear-brimmed eyes she looked up into her father's face and quietly asked, "Daddy, when will I die now?" For a split second the father looked puzzled. And then like a flash of lightning it hit him—his little girl had just gone through the entire ordeal of donating her blood, believing that when it was over, she would die!

Did she die for her brother? The shining truth is that *in her mind* she truly did give up her life for someone she loved dearly. Just like Jesus, who *in His mind* that Friday afternoon gave up His life forever, so that you and I might live forever and ever.

No wonder nothing will ever be able to separate us from the love of God in Christ Jesus!

"O LOVE THAT WILT NOT LET ME GO"

For I am convinced that neither death, nor life, nor angels, nor rulers, nor things present, nor things to come, nor powers, nor height, nor depth, nor anything else in all creation, will be able to separate us from the love of God in Christ Jesus our Lord.
Rom. 8:38, 39, NRSV.

So how shall we answer our question from a week ago: What killed Jesus? Standing between Gethsemane and Golgotha, our hearts are confronted with two undeniable and ultimate realities: How utterly terrible is our sin; but how utterly wonderful is His love! He was willing to be separated from God forever so that we might be saved by God forever. Forsaken so that we might be found, rejected so that we might be redeemed, He died the second death so that we would have a second chance. In all our feeble human language there is no word for such a sacrifice save the word "love."

George Matheson was in love. He and the girl of his dreams were soon to be married. Then tragedy struck. George was smitten with a mysterious blindness. But though his eyes could no longer see, his heart could go on loving the woman who was to become his wife.

Until a second tragedy struck. One morning Matheson heard her footsteps approaching. But when his fiancé spoke, she announced that she could not find it in her heart to marry a blind man. And as her steps echoed out of his life forever, eyes that could not see cried tears that could only be felt. She had loved him, but she chose not to keep him.

In his own private agony Matheson one day groped for a pen and wrote of another love:

> O Love that wilt not let me go,
> I rest my weary soul in Thee;
> I give Thee back the life I owe,
> That in Thine ocean depths its flow
> May richer, fuller be.

What killed Jesus? A garden and a cross declare that greater than our sin against Him was His love toward us. And that is what took His life on Calvary—the nailed-open embrace of a love that will never let you go.

Forever and ever.

Amen.

ANOTHER FRIEND

I will talk to the Father, and he'll provide you another Friend so that you will always have someone with you. . . . This Friend is the Spirit of Truth. John 14:16, 17, Message.

Is there a friendlier word than "friend"? Can you imagine someone not wanting to have one? The whole world loves a friend!

That's why I like Eugene Peterson's translation of Jesus' upper room promise. As we've pondered the God of the Chosen these past few weeks, we've thought about God the Father and about God the Son. But what about "another Friend," God the Spirit?

The Greek word is *parakletos*, "one called to the side of." Multiple translations reveal the richness of this name Jesus gave the Spirit that night: "Comforter" (KJV), "Counselor" (NIV), "Helper" (NASB), "Advocate" (NRSV), and "Friend" (Message). But then isn't that just like a friend—to comfort you when you're down, to counsel you when you're perplexed, to help you when you're exhausted, to stick up for you when you're defeated? Talking about a forever friend, what a wonderful person to know! Makes you wonder why we don't talk about Him more, doesn't it?

Look how the Scriptures describe Him: the very embodiment of the Father, the very embodiment of Jesus (but without a body); walks through walls, walks through life; lives in the light, sees in the dark; lives in you, talks in you; reads your mind, speaks your language; taps your conscience, touches your heart; warns you of evil, woos you to righteousness; knows your future, knows your past; loves you anyway, loves you always; the Best Friend you ever had, the Best Friend you'll ever have!

I had a best friend in elementary school. And I must confess, I wanted to be his exclusive best friend, too. Because having to share such a good friend with everyone else meant having less time with him myself. Not so our Spirit Friend! Even with nearly 7 billion children on His list, he abides with us 24/7 as if we were His only friend in the universe. I repeat, what a Friend!

In fact, with just as much passion and joy we can resing the old gospel hymn "What a friend we have in [*the Spirit*], all our sins and griefs to bear; what a privilege to carry everything to [Him] in prayer!" "Can we find a friend so faithful, who will all our sorrows share? [*The Spirit*] knows our every weakness; take it to the Lord in prayer!"

NO GOD HUMBLER — 1

But when the Helper comes, whom I shall send to you from the Father, the Spirit of truth who proceeds from the Father, He will testify of Me. John 15:26. He will glorify Me, for He will take of what is Mine and declare it to you. John 16:14.

Have you ever heard of the psychiatric diagnosis "acquired situational narcissism"? "Narcissism" you recognize as excessive fascination or interest in one's self, or self-love. "Acquired" and "situational" describe how individuals, for example, can acquire this intense self-focus when they assume a position of great power or influence, leading some to conclude that presidents are particularly susceptible to acquired situational narcissism. Perhaps we can all think of people infected with an overinflated sense of power and prominence.

Is God one of them? I was intrigued with some study a classmate of mine, Fred Bischoff, did regarding the leadership paradigm of the Trinity and how humble these three Supreme Leaders are—the Father, who leads the universe through humbly serving all His creatures and His entire creation; the Son, who leads by humbly submitting to the leadership of the Father; and the Spirit, who humbly leads by quietly remaining unseen as He assists in carrying out the agenda of both the Father and the Son.

And when you ponder the Spirit, is it not profound that all that He is and all that He does takes place without the universe ever witnessing His person? In the media–dominated world we occupy, where vanity of appearance and physical attraction have been insanely elevated to supreme value, isn't it refreshing to have a Friend who is perfectly content to remain utterly unseen and usually unnoticed? Can you name a humbler God than He?

In fact, Jesus declared on the eve of His death (our text today) that when the Holy Spirit comes to us, He comes with a solitary preoccupation: "He will glorify and testify of Me." Without a doubt the Holy Spirit is the most Christ-centered being in the universe, completely sublimating Himself for the sake of revealing and glorifying Jesus to all! No God humbler.

And that, by the way, means that whenever you pray to be filled with the Spirit, you are in fact requesting that you might be filled to the full with Jesus. For wherever the Spirit goes and whomever the Spirit fills, the dominant public impression is *always* of Jesus. "And they took note that these men [and women] had been with Jesus" (Acts 4:13, NIV).

NO GOD HUMBLER—2

Let the same mind be in you that was in Christ Jesus, who, though he was in the form of God, did not regard equality with God as something to be exploited, but emptied himself, taking the form of a slave, being born in human likeness. And being found in human form, he humbled himself and became obedient to the point of death—even death on a cross
Phil. 2:5-8, NRSV.

In our show-biz, media-saturated, hero-starved age perhaps it's understandable that when a religious personage such as the pope travels, there is such a frenzy of paparazzi-type news coverage. The entourage of black limousines, the flag-draped poles and banisters, the crush of the faithful and the curious lining the motorcade route, the military guard snapped to attention upon arrival, the band's loud fanfare, the welcoming line of dignitaries . . . and on and on and on.

And yet when the God of the universe descends to our planet to become Emmanuel, "God with us," what a stunning contrast! Born in a box of cow feed, raised as a carpenter's boy, traversing the land as an itinerant Messiah, arrested for disturbing the peace, executed for speaking truth to power—Jesus would never have survived our star-crossed hunger for hype, would He? He who "made Himself of no reputation" (Phil. 2:7, NKJV) would have been so compellingly at odds with our thirst for stardom and fame.

"Whom shall I release to you?" Makes you wonder, doesn't it, if Pilate were to raise that query today, whom we would ask for? The "no God humbler" One or the celebrity pick of the day?

"Looking upon the crucified Redeemer, we more fully comprehend the magnitude and meaning of the sacrifice made by the Majesty of heaven. The plan of salvation is glorified before us, and the thought of Calvary awakens living and sacred emotions in our hearts. Praise to God and the Lamb will be in our hearts and on our lips; for *pride and self-worship cannot flourish in the soul that keeps fresh in memory the scenes of Calvary*" (*The Desire of Ages*, p. 661; italics supplied).

Maybe we need to keep our no humbler God more actively in our consciousness. Could it be that the scenes of Calvary need revisiting day after day, if ever we would reflect the humility of this God who has saved us and who in saving us asks to let His mind be in us too?

THE GREAT WHITE THRONE

*Therefore God also highly exalted him and gave him the name that is above every name,
so that at the name of Jesus every knee should bend, in heaven and on earth and under
the earth, and every tongue should confess that Jesus Christ is Lord, to the glory of God
the Father. Phil. 2:9-11, NRSV.*

Will there be no comeuppance for this no humbler God? Do not the Father,
Son, and Holy Spirit rightfully deserve the accolades and honor, the worship
of all the galaxies They have so humbly served all these millennia? But of course!

In one of the most breathtaking scenes in all the Apocalypse, there comes the
moment when the great white throne of the Most High God is raised—and all the
Spielberg and Lucas special effects animation could not possibly capture the daz-
zling majesty and grandeur of this cosmic scene—high above the assembled universe. "Then I saw a great white throne and Him who sat on it, from whose face
the earth and the heaven fled away" (Rev. 20:11).

And we will all stare, for we will all be there, be assured. Is this the Man who
stripped Himself naked to the waist, and with towel and basin in hand washed the 12
pairs of dirty feet that belonged to the 12 men (one of whom is just like you and me)
who should have been lined up, each to have his turn to wash their Master's feet?

Is this the same God—how can it be!—who with hands tied behind Him endured the slaps, the fists, the spit in the face, who with face now black-and-blue
was stripped naked to be flogged one lash short of death, who with battered face
and bloody back and legs is finally nailed to that splintery cross and hoisted to co-
agulate between heaven and earth until He expired?

"Far above the city, upon a foundation of burnished gold, is a [white] throne,
high and lifted up. Upon this throne sits the Son of God, and around Him are the
subjects of His kingdom. The power and majesty of Christ no language can describe, no pen portray. The glory of the Eternal Father is enshrouding His Son. The
brightness of His presence fills the City of God, and flows out beyond the gates,
flooding the whole earth with its radiance" (*The Great Controversy*, p. 665).

It is any wonder, then, we shall all one day bow before this humble God? And
is there any question we should begin that bowing right now?

MEMORIES OF RECESS

For you are a holy people to the Lord your God; the Lord your God has chosen you to be a people for Himself, a special treasure above all the peoples on the face of the earth. Deut. 7:6.

When you think of being chosen, does your mind go back to recess days on that schoolyard playground long ago, when Teacher asked the two biggest boys in the class to choose up teams for some sport in which winning mattered? Remember how the rest of you lined up, dutifully waiting for your name to be called? And remember how you stood there, nervously holding your breath, shifting your weight from one sneaker to the other, hoping against hope that this time you'd be chosen? But as the captains picked their choosy way through that line that was getting shorter and shorter with every name called out, a line that still had you in it, did the dreadful thought occur to you, *I may not get chosen at all. Guess I'll have to stand on the sidelines again and watch the kids who were "chosen" play their game?*

Some of us painfully know that it's no fun *not* to be chosen. Whether it's an election for president or an invitation to a party, nobody likes to be left out.

So what shall we do with these words of God dutifully relayed to the children of Israel by their aged leader Moses? Forty years of wilderness wandering are nearly over. Except for Joshua and Caleb, an entire generation older than 60 is now dead. These words are a part of the longest farewell in sacred literature, as one last time Moses reviews with the grown-up children God's leadership throughout the past four decades. Their mothers, fathers, and grandparents are all dusty burial mounds in the wilderness behind them. Unbelief has robbed an entire generation of the Promised Land. And even their beloved senior leader will in a few days climb a lonely mountain and die alone this side of Canaan, the very high price for the moral accountability of spiritual leaders.

"The Lord your God has chosen you to be a people for Himself." There really isn't a politically correct way to put this. Moses simply pronounces the truth. Over all the peoples of the human race, you—this liberated band of slaves from Egypt—have been chosen by God to be His own "special treasure." Period. But in our age of egalitarian fairness, this hardly seems polite or proper, does it? Unless, of course, being chosen is more about God than us.

THE SELECTION PROCESS

You have been set apart as holy to the Lord your God, and he has chosen you from all the nations of the earth to be his own special treasure. Deut. 14:2, NLT.

Let's be honest. There is an obvious selection process throughout the Scriptures. Adam and Eve have two sons—one gets chosen by God and the other rejected. The antediluvian world includes a man named Noah and his family—these eight get chosen and the rest of the world rejected.

A pagan family in Ur of the Chaldees has a boy named Abram—he gets chosen by God and the rest of the family left out. Abraham has two sons—both are chosen by God, but only one gets the highest destiny. That one, Isaac, has two sons—one gets chosen by God and the other gets left on the sidelines of a lesser destiny. The chosen son Jacob has 12 sons—the second-youngest one gets chosen by God to be the deliverer and the others end up bowing down to him. The land of Egypt is filled with children of Israel—and after a couple centuries God chooses the slaves and rejects the taskmasters.

Israel crosses over into the Promised Land and clamors for a king—God chooses Saul, but then "unchooses" him for a young shepherd named David. The kingdom of Israel prospers and grows and then apostatizes and falls—king succeeds king, some chosen by God and others rejected, until finally all that's left is a "remnant."

After the long and painful Exile, the scattered remnant returns home, and centuries later God shows up in the person of Emmanuel, Jesus of Nazareth, loved by the masses but rejected by the leadership and executed. And when He is resurrected, a new "chosen" emerges unfettered by DNA or geographical boundaries or even Jerusalem's Temple. And thus the story of "the chosen" goes on and on and on.

The point? Throughout sacred history God has had a community of faith that He has identified as "the chosen." There on the borders of the Promised Land, Moses drives home that incontrovertible point: "You have been set apart as holy to the Lord your God, and he has chosen you from all the nations of the earth to be his own special treasure."

Because, you see, when you're on the very borders of the Promised Land, it is high time you understood the divine mission to which you're being called.

"THE TWO GREATEST RELIGIOUS MOVEMENTS OF ALL HISTORY"

Now then, if you will indeed obey My voice and keep My covenant, then you shall be My own possession among all the peoples, for all the earth is Mine. Ex. 19:5, NASB.

Years ago Taylor G. Bunch asserted: "The Bible is a book of parallel events and movements; of types and their antitypes. This makes the Bible an up-to-date Book from Genesis to Revelation to the very close of human history. . . . One of the greatest parallels . . . is found in what we call the Exodus and Advent movements of ancient and modern Israel. . . . *These are the two greatest religious movements of all history*" (*The Exodus in Type and Antitype*, pp. 2, 3; italics supplied). Would you agree?

Consider these parallels. **1.** Both movements were called to "cross over" into the Promised Land (Ex. 3:8; Rev. 21:1). **2.** Both were raised up in fulfillment of definite time prophecies (Gen. 15:13; Dan. 8:14). **3.** Both were called to champion God as Redeemer and Deliverer from human bondage (Ex. 14:13, 14; Rev. 1:5, 6). **4.** Both were to journey "under" the blood of the Lamb as a symbol of salvation by faith alone in the divine sacrifice (Ex. 12:13; Rev. 12:11). **5.** Both were called out of sun worship (Ex. 12:12; Rev. 14:7). **6.** Both were raised up to champion the Law of God (Deut. 4:13, 14; Rev. 14:12). **7.** Both were called to restore worship of the Creator God through the preservation of His seventh-day Sabbath (Ex. 20:8-11; Rev. 14:7). **8.** Both would passionately look forward to the coming Messiah (Num. 24:17; Rev. 22:20). **9.** Both were called to reject the fallen culture and debased religions of the nations around them (Deut. 7:3, 4; Rev. 18:4). **10.** Both were led by a divinely called prophet (Deut. 18:15; Rev. 12:17; 19:10). **11.** Both were called to adopt a lifestyle and diet that would reveal the stunning health differences between them and society at large (Ex. 15:26; Rom. 12:1, 2). **12.** Both would discover in the sanctuary system a defining revelation of God's salvation history on earth and in heaven (Ex. 25:8, 9; Heb. 8:1, 2; Rev. 11:19). **13.** Both were to champion the Word of God as the authoritative revelation of divine truth (Deut. 6:4-9; Rev. 12:17). **14.** Both were called the chosen (Deut. 7:6; Rev. 14:12). **15.** Both were capable of failing their mission and being replaced by a community of faith more faithful and obedient than they (Deut. 30:15-17; Rev. 3:15, 16).

Two "crossing over" movements—are we surprised? But then, couldn't the God who chose you and me before we were born choose entire communities for His divine mission, too?

44

MOTHER'S MORALITY PLAYS

Now all these things happened to them as examples, and they were written for our admonition, upon whom the ends of the ages have come. 1 Cor. 10:11.

What is there about parents that makes them such great moralizers? We lived in a small community and my mother, God bless her, was forever drawing morals and on-the-spot lessons from the lives of the adults, teens, and children around us. "Now, see what happened to him when he did that? You don't ever want to do that, now do you?" And of course, my siblings and I all dutifully shook our heads with appropriate vigor and obvious conviction.

Like a spiritual parent, Paul drives home the same point. The wandering of "the chosen" across the hot sands of those 40 long wilderness years is one continuous morality play from which the rest of us are to carefully learn our lessons. All those stories of the children of Israel in Exodus, Leviticus, Numbers, and Deuteronomy "were written for our admonition."

And did you catch it? All those narratives were written as spiritual and moral lessons for the generation *"upon whom the ends of the ages have come,"* i.e., for the generation living at the end of time, or as the *New Living Translation* renders it: "They were written down to warn us, who live at the time when this age is drawing to a close."

Taylor Bunch was right. Those chronicles about the movement God raised up to cross over into the *earthly* Canaan are to be a primer for the spiritual movement God has raised up to cross over into the *heavenly* Canaan. All that happened to Israel of old, Paul admonishes us, now serves as Exhibit A for the generation living at the end of time. After all, the God who had His "chosen ones" in the beginning is the same God who has His "chosen ones" at the ending. Surely then, the lessons He sought to teach them He seeks to teach us, too, "upon whom the ends of the ages have come."

Shall we not then teach *our* children, too? "[We] should make [our children] acquainted with the great pillars of our faith, the reasons why . . . we are called, as were the children of Israel, to be a peculiar people, a holy nation, separate and distinct from all other people on the face of the earth" (*Testimonies for the Church*, vol. 5, p. 330). That was precisely Paul's point—we must prayerfully learn the lessons of ancient history, lest we forget the high calling God has always had for "the chosen."

THE QUANDARY OF AGING BOOMERS

But you are a chosen people, a royal priesthood, a holy nation, a people belonging to God, that you may declare the praises of him who called you out of darkness into his wonderful light. Once you were not a people, but now you are the people of God; once you had not received mercy, but now you have received mercy. 1 Peter 2:9, 10, NIV.

But does this generation in our community of faith know that it's chosen? Do they even know they are a part of a movement that has been raised up by God as surely as He raised up the children of Israel long ago? I look at the 3,500 students at the university where I serve and I wonder if they realize their generation has the stunning potential of being the movement that will "cross over" into the Promised Land , , , without seeing death

I have baby boomer friends who are hesitant whenever this notion of being chosen is entertained. And I'm sympathetic. After all, some of us grew up in Sabbath schools and churches where this notion of "the chosen" was trumpeted as a "we're better than everybody else" sort of calling. And sadly the emphasis on "exclusive" truth pedigree alienated those congregations from their communities and certainly didn't win many friends for Jesus.

But the counteracting response is just as mistaken. Not wanting to offend anyone and seeking to be accepted by the wider culture and surrounding world may be well intentioned, but when it jettisons the biblical recognition of a "chosen people," as Peter so clearly reinforces in our text, and when it rejects the divine and apocalyptic raising up of a movement, then that boomer response ends up throwing out the baby with the bathwater!

Perhaps we fear what Richard John Neuhaus insightfully observes: "God's chosen ones live out the drama and destiny of God himself. It is a fearful thing to be chosen. It is as though God enters history through his chosen ones" (*Death on a Friday Afternoon*, p. 138).

To deny that corporate divine chosenness is to deny the very biblical undergirding that stretches from Genesis through Revelation. Yes, "it is a fearful thing to be chosen." For it is a high calling no movement on earth has ever been up to or worthy of. Nevertheless it is a *divine* calling. And whom God calls, surely He enables.

So rather than apologizing for the divine calling, the appropriate response may be to humbly bow before the One who chose us before we were born and follow wherever He leads.

THE CHOICE

I no longer call you servants, because a servant does not know his master's business. Instead, I have called you friends, for everything that I learned from my Father I have made known to you. You did not choose me, but I chose you. John 15:15, 16, NIV.

Let's go back to that recess playground for another moment. I never was one of the jocks in school. I couldn't hit the ball the farthest, couldn't run the field the fastest, couldn't raise the score the highest. Why, if I'd ever been asked by Teacher to be the captain of a team for recess, I for sure wouldn't have chosen me!

But I wasn't entirely without hope. For I had a friend who had way more athletic prowess than I. And whenever Teacher chose him to be captain, I secretly knew that sooner or later I'd get chosen on his team. (I must confess I never really sat down and worked out all the psychological angles to determine whether he chose me out of sympathy or friendship. It didn't matter—because I got chosen!)

On the eve of His execution Jesus looked into the faces of those who had stuck with Him all through the months and even years. Tomorrow He would die for them. Tonight He must tell them how much they meant to Him. And so, did you catch what He called them in our text? "I have called you *friends*." And the wonderful reality about having a friend as Captain is the assurance that you're going to get chosen. And sure enough, no sooner does Jesus call us His friends than He declares, "I have chosen you."

And He's clear, isn't He? "You didn't choose Me—but I chose you." Which, of course, is the truth about the chosen: You choose the One who chooses you. Just as at recess. When your name at last is called and you go racing over to join the friend who just delivered you from that lonely line, you gladly choose to be on the captain's team. Hallelujah! Why? Because he chose you first, you chose him back. "You did not choose me, but I chose you."

And that's the truth about the two "crossing over" movements God has raised up. Neither chose Him first—He chose them. And out of humble gratitude both chose Him right back, at least in the beginning.

"Today the Lord has proclaimed you to be His special people, just as He promised you" (Deut. 26:18). So, when you've been chosen, out of gratitude quickly choose Him back!

47

JUVENILE DETENTION CENTER

The Lord did not set his affection on you and choose you because you were more numerous than other peoples, for you were the fewest of all peoples. Deut. 7:7, NIV.

Let's say you're the head of a juvenile detention center, as a friend of mine is. What will you do with that locked-down building filled with rebellious kids that have been turned over by the courts to the state for discipline and correction? Because it's your mission to turn those incorrigible kids around, how are you going to win their young hearts?

Every leader knows that in order to win over a large group—be they peaceful or rebellious—the strategic key is to get close to one. That means that in your detention center you must first win the trust of one of those teenagers, a boy or girl, it doesn't matter. Obviously you would like to connect with a youth who would have the influence to reach the others.

Why? Because the effective way to win all their hearts is to first win one of their hearts. Isn't that true? So you must pick out one of those young rebels who seems to have a heart that is open to you as a leader. Maybe you see it in his eyes, or you sense it in the thoughtful way she listens to you when it seems everybody else is ignoring you. And so you drop by his room, or the table where she's eating lunch, and you engage in a bit of conversation. You want to win his trust, her loyalty, right? So you show some extra attention to this one you're hoping will be the key to reaching all the rest.

Question: By this are you playing favorites? Answer: No, you are not—your simple strategy is to *win the heart of one in order to reach the lives of the many.*

Once upon a time there was a rebellious planet, just like the juvenile detention center—and the only way for the Leader to reach *all* of them was to choose *one* of them. And so God did. And he called them "the chosen." As Moses declared, "The Lord your God has chosen you to be a people for Himself" (Deut. 7:6). But were they chosen because there was something special about them—physically, financially, socially, spiritually, or morally? No. Moses is clear that the chosen were among the least. In fact, he goes on, "God is not giving you this good land to possess because of your righteousness, for you are a stiff-necked people" (Deut. 9:6). Ever wake up with a stiff neck? It's a pain. But God puts up with the pain of the chosen for the sake of His passion to save the whole detention center!

NOT SUPERSTARS!

The Lord did not set his affection on you and choose you because you were more numerous than other peoples, for you were the fewest of all peoples. But it was because the Lord loved you and kept the oath he swore to your forefathers that he brought you out with a mighty hand and redeemed you from the land of slavery. Deut. 7:7, 8, NIV.

God's chosen are not superstars—they are super-loved! Twenty-five times in this single book (in the dusty heart of the Old Testament, at that), Moses speaks of "love." Here the Hebrew word *ahabah* is the identical word Moses used to tell one of the great love stories of all time.

Remember the story of the runaway boy who, after deceiving both his dad and his older brother out of the birthright, flees to a faraway land to find his uncle? Physically exhausted after days and nights on the lam, Jacob arrives in the country of his mother's kin and collapses beside a shepherd's well. Sheep bleating in every direction, Jacob looks up to spot a young woman leading her flock to the watering trough. "Rachel was beautiful of form and appearance" (Gen. 29:17). And it was, for the vagabond, love at first sight. So smitten was he that after meeting her father, his uncle Laban, Jacob blurted out his proposal: "I'll work for you seven years if you'll let me marry your daughter." Deal! And as Moses tells the story: "So Jacob served seven years for Rachel, and they seemed only a few days to him because of the love [*ahabah*] he had for her" (verse 20).

It is that same "love" that Moses uses to describe the reason the chosen got chosen in the first place. God loved that movement of liberated slaves, just like Jacob loved Rachel. Love at first sight, love for life. "For forty years," Moses declares, "your God has been trying to win your hand in marriage." There's only one word to describe a God who would spend 40 long years trying to win the love of any us—and that word is *g-r-a-c-e*.

How else shall we explain the God of the universe, so passionate about winning the entire juvenile detention center back to Him, that He picks out one of the occupants, the one who showed Him a semblance of interest, a modicum of openness, and sets out to win that collective heart for the sake of His global mission? That God would choose a movement at all to help Him reach and save this world is truly amazing.

Amazing grace, amazing love. Obviously the only superstar in our story is He!

THE SHOWCASE

He will love you and bless you and increase your numbers. He will bless the fruit of your womb, the crops of your land—your grain, new wine and oil—the calves of your herds and the lambs of your flocks in the land that he swore to your forefathers to give you. You will be blessed more than any other people. Deut. 7.13, 14, NIV.

I knew a man once who was a champion race car driver, and had the scars to prove it! Not that he needed the scars to tell his story. Step into his eighth-floor suite overlooking the city, and you'll see a wall of bright-colored photographs capturing the glory and beauty of his fast cars. Then you'll see, displayed out on the shelves, shiny replicas and models of his racing machines. Look behind the glass, and you'll gaze upon his collection of ribbons and cups and trophies. It is the showcase of a winner (most of the time).

When you put a showcase together, you've got something you want to share with the world. That's why showcases are more than simple collections—they often tell the story about the one who put them together.

And that's Moses' point in his farewell address of Deuteronomy. Again and again he not only reminds the grown-up children of Israel that they've been chosen by God—he repeatedly tells them why. As our text today reveals, the chosen are especially blessed by the Chooser so that the world around, when admiring the blessings of the chosen, will ask about their Chooser. It's that simple.

If you obey God's laws carefully, "you will display your wisdom and intelligence among the surrounding nations. When they hear all these decrees, they will exclaim, 'How wise and prudent are the people of this great nation!' For what great nation has a god as near to them as the Lord our God is near to us whenever we call on him?" (Deut. 4:6, 7, NLT). What kind of a movement is this that has a God like that!

And that is why God calls the chosen and raises them up, with the promise to bless them, if they'll follow Him. It's the law of the showcase. When you put a showcase together, you've got something you want to share with the world. After all, showcases aren't supposed to be dusty old collections. They're the visual demonstration that somebody rather special is behind it all. As it turns out, Somebody very special, if you're talking about the divine movement of the chosen.

THE WISEST MAN ON EARTH

Now it shall come to pass, if you diligently obey the voice of the Lord your God, to observe carefully all His commandments which I command you today, that the Lord your God will set you high above all nations of the earth. Deut. 28:1.

Who is the wisest man who ever lived (besides your dad, of course)? Wise King Solomon, we're all agreed. And was he an old man or a young man when he became wise? He was a very young man when God came to the newly crowned monarch in the middle of the night and asked him what he wanted from God.

Quick was Solomon's reply: "Now, O Lord my God, You have made Your servant king instead of my father David, but I am a little child; I do not know how to go out or come in. . . . Therefore give to Your servant an understanding heart to judge Your people, that I may discern between good and evil. For who is able to judge this great people of Yours?" (1 Kings 3:7-9). And God was so pleased with the mature request of this young king that he promised Solomon not only wisdom but riches and honor as well! (Which only goes to show that whether you're 18 or 80, if you'll be humbly dependent upon God, He will make Himself dependent upon you. God needs those who need Him.)

Just look what happened to Solomon!

"And God gave Solomon wisdom and exceedingly great understanding, and largeness of heart like the sand on the seashore. Thus Solomon's wisdom excelled the wisdom of all the men of the East and all the wisdom of Egypt" (1 Kings 4:29, 30). And what was the point of this incredible divine largesse? To increase the hat size of the young king by making him a superstar? Hardly! The record is clear: "And men of all nations, from all the kings of the earth who had heard of his wisdom, came to hear the wisdom of Solomon" (verse 34).

And when the queen of Sheba with her glittering entourage departed Jerusalem after testing the famed wisdom of Israel's young king, her testimony is proof enough that when God chooses the chosen, they aren't chosen for *their worth*—they are chosen for *His work*: "Your wisdom and prosperity exceed the fame of which I heard. . . . Blessed be the Lord your God, who delighted in you, setting you on the throne of Israel!" (1 Kings 10:7-9). A pagan queen sings the praises of Israel's God—the very reason that God chooses the chosen in the first place!

A BEACHHEAD, NOT A BOUNDARY

[Darius wrote,] I make a decree that in every dominion of my kingdom men must tremble and fear before the God of Daniel. For He is the living God, and steadfast forever; His kingdom is the one which shall not be destroyed, and His dominion shall endure to the end. Dan. 6:26.

He is a young exile enrolled in a pagan university, far, far from home. And he is no sooner enrolled in this boarding school than he has to choose—shall I follow the majority on this campus or shall I follow God? It's not always an easy choice, as I've observed during my years on a university campus. But Daniel makes the right choice: I will honor the God of my fathers and mothers and obey the commands of Deuteronomy for the chosen, and I will not defile my body by eating what they eat or drinking what they drink in this university. I am chosen, and I choose to live like the chosen are to live (see Dan. 1).

And the rest is history—the story of how, out of a seemingly inconsequential choice to be true to what some would consider a minor detail of God's will, Daniel's life was catapulted into political and national prominence, until finally he becomes the most trusted adviser to three pagan monarchs, spanning two global empires.

Beyond the obvious recognition that God blesses those who honor Him, what's going on with this meteoric rise to influence and position for the young exile? As it was with Solomon, so with Daniel—God isn't interested in puffing the pride of a young man, but He is passionately committed to signally blessing that young adult who is available for heaven's strategic mission—reaching an entire world with the proffer of divine salvation. And unlike Solomon, Daniel never falters his entire life, thus winning the humble confessions of two of the three pagan kings that Daniel's God, the God of Israel (the chosen), is truly the supreme ruler of the cosmos. Read again the amazing faith confession of pagan king Darius in our text today!

I like the way Derek Kidner in his commentary on the Psalms once described the mission of Israel as God's chosen: "His little nation was His beachhead, not His boundary." Israel was never raised up to box up the supernatural blessings of God within their own borders. Rather the chosen have always been called to become a divine beachhead in a world still living behind enemy lines. They are to be a beachhead for God, winning first the attention and then the hearts of the high and low, all for the sake of Love's passionate mission.

NOT A BIG HEAD, BUT A BIG HEART

I will make you a great nation; I will bless you and make your name great; and you shall be a blessing. I will bless those who bless you, and I will curse him who curses you; and in you all the families of the earth shall be blessed. Gen. 12:2, 3.

This unsigned article is one of the most cogent descriptions I've read of God's mission for Israel *and what might have been* had the chosen chosen to remain faithful to Him.

"As the nations of antiquity should behold Israel's unprecedented progress, their attention and interest would be aroused. . . . Desiring the same blessings for themselves, they would make inquiry as to how they too might acquire these obvious material advantages. Israel would reply, 'Accept our God as your God, love and serve Him as we do, and He will do the same for you.'"

Now, note the reason for God's tangible blessings upon the chosen: "The material advantages that Israel enjoyed were designed to arrest the attention and catch the interest of the heathen, *for whom the less obvious spiritual advantages had no natural attraction.* They would 'gather themselves together' and 'come from far' (Isa. 49:6, 8, 9, 12, 18, 22; Ps. 102:22), 'from the ends of the earth' (Jer. 16:19), to the light of truth shining forth from the 'mountain of the Lord' (Isa. 2:3; 56:7; 60:3; cf. ch. 11:9, 10). Nations that had known nothing of the true God would 'run' to Jerusalem because of the manifest evidence of divine blessing that attended Israel (ch. 55:5). Ambassadors from one foreign country after another would come to discover, if they might, the great secret of Israel's success as a nation, and its leaders would have the opportunity of directing the minds of their visitors to the Source of all good things. *From the visible their minds were to be directed to the invisible, from the seen to the unseen, from the material to the spiritual, from the temporal to the eternal.* . . . The house of God in Jerusalem would eventually 'be called an house of prayer for all people' (Isa. 56:7)" (*The SDA Bible Commentary*, vol. 4 pp. 28, 29; italics supplied).

Such was the passionate dream of God for "the chosen" once upon a time. Do you suppose it still is? In the locked-down juvenile detention center of this world, could it be that God focuses His heart on one in order to win the hearts of all? If that's true, then clearly the raison d'être of the chosen today has nothing to do with a big head, but everything to do with the very big heart that *still* longs to save this lost world, if He possibly can.

TALE OF A FORGETFUL KING

For many are called, but few are chosen. Matt. 22:14.

Once upon a time there was a very sick king. So deathly ill was he that his friend, the prophet, made a bedside visit with the dire pronouncement that it was time for the king to draw up his personal will and put his house in order since death would be the next visitor knocking at the royal door. No sooner had the prophet left than the good-hearted king turned his face to the wall and burst into tears in a sobbing plea to God. And God, who can be more tenderhearted than the one who delivers the medical prognosis, stopped the prophet before he was out of the palace. "Go back and tell My friend that I'm going to extend his life by 15 more years." And as confirmation (because some medical reversals need empirical evidence), the shadow on the sun dial went backwards 10 degrees!

As happy as a death row inmate with a presidential pardon, King Hezekiah set out to live his extra 15 years with joyous gusto. And also, unfortunately, with a very short memory. For when a delegation of Babylonian emissaries showed up at the same palace door excited by the news of the king's miraculous healing, Hezekiah was so flattered by their attention that he blew the golden opportunity to testify of the God who had supernaturally (even fiddling with a sundial) healed him. Instead, the king took them on a guided tour of his royal treasury. And so the pagan ambassadors, who had come to learn of Israel's God, went home instead with a map to Israel's gold (a map that came in handy a few decades later when they sacked Jerusalem and stole the gold).

Makes you wonder, doesn't it? How quick are you and I to point to God as the source of our successes? When over a sandwich in the lunch room or a book in the library or the backyard fence at home, we're asked for the reason for our success, how easy it is to demur with an "aw shucks" humility about our ability, when in fact we've just been handed on a platter a golden opportunity to point to our God. Maybe we shouldn't be so hard on good king Hezekiah!

On His way to the cross Jesus was right. "Many are called, but few are chosen." Do you suppose the reason so few are chosen is that the many who are called have forgotten that *the whole point of the blessings is to point to the Blesser?* That was why God had His chosen in the beginning, and that is why He will have his chosen at the end—to point the world to Him.

WILL YOU BE MINE?

For God so loved the world that He gave His only begotten Son, that whoever believes in Him should not perish but have everlasting life. John 3:16.

I know it isn't a church holiday, but when we were kids, giving each other those little red-and-pink cards on Valentine's Day was a favorite pastime. I don't suppose we ever really figured out the meaning of that innocuously short query that we scribbled in third-grade penmanship on those floppy heart-shaped cutouts. Nevertheless we handed it out to all our friends at school: "Will you be mine?"

It's the call of the chosen, isn't it? "Will you be Mine?" asks the God of the universe, who for millennia now has been desperately trying to win back the hearts of a runaway and rebel race. "Will you be Mine?" Why, it's as if all the children God already has around His dinner table in heaven aren't enough—as if He'll never be really, truly happy and content until we say "Yes" and come and join Him too. "Will you be Mine?"

When I fell in love with Karen, before I'd even gotten to know her it was the utter preoccupation of my teenage heart to get her attention. Each day I knew that as I headed for the cafeteria at SMC (Southern "Matrimonial" College), she'd be coming out of one of her nursing classes and I could pass her on the sidewalk. And so every day, in one of those foolish (but effective) teenage rituals, I'd drop my head when I spotted her and pretend to be deep in thought while staring at the sidewalk in front of me, but all the while maneuvering my steps so that I would practically run straight into her. Then there'd be the burst of laughter, the quick apology about "not" seeing her there, and with her face fresh in my mind I'd be on my way. Who can know "the way of a man with a maiden" (Prov. 30:19, NIV)?

But then, the ways of Love divine are as inexplicable at times, aren't they? Explain to the rest of us, please, the compelling passion that drives a God from His great white throne to our dark, fallen earth, all for what? That we might be granted the chance to cry at the top of our lungs, "We have no king but Caesar"? And with that ugly refrain repeating inside of Him, this rejected God stumbles on to the place of His execution. And as they stretch out His naked frame and pin Him to that stake, with every thud of the mallet upon those nails the question He came to earth to ask is hammered out: "Will you be Mine?"

CAN A PAGAN BE SAVED?

Indeed, when Gentiles, who do not have the law, do by nature things required by the law, they are a law for themselves, even though they do not have the law, since they show that the requirements of the law are written on their hearts, their consciences also bearing witness, and their thoughts now accusing, now even defending them. Rom. 2:14, 15, NIV.

Can a pagan remain a pagan and still be saved? Does God choose pagans, too? Before you scramble for an answer, consider a story or two. Once upon a time a close friend of God's lied about his wife to a nomadic pagan warlord—telling him that she was his sister. Whereupon the man promptly commandeered the other man's wife and added her to his harem. That night in a dream God declared to the warlord, "You are dead meat if you touch that man's wife." The man cried, "In the integrity of my heart and innocence of my hands I have done this" (Gen. 20:5). And of course, God knew that, and said, "I also withheld you from sinning against Me; therefore I did not let you touch her" (verse 6). Thus, Abimelech the pagan was spared. Why? There were no Ten Commandments to tell him the difference between right and wrong. He simply lived up to the light that he had. And God honored him, his worship of pagan gods notwithstanding.

Once upon another time a good king went out against a pagan king. But the God of the good king actually sent a message to him through the pagan king: "Refrain from meddling with God, who is with me, lest He destroy you" (2 Chron. 35:21). But Josiah refused to listen to Pharaoh Necho, and the next day he was slain in battle. He should have listened to God's message to him through the pagan Pharaoh! God must not be totally down on pagans, don't you suppose?

After all, he's the God who inspired Psalm 87. "I will record Rahab and Babylon among those who acknowledge me—Philistia too, and Tyre, along with Cush—and will say, 'This one was born in Zion'" (verse 4, NIV). "The Lord will write in the register of the peoples: 'This one was born in Zion'" (verse 6, NIV). Amazing! When the register of the saved and chosen is read one day, God declares that among the names will be the people of the great pagan neighbors of Israel!

Then how could He be down on pagans? Through the centuries God has communed with them, sent messages through them, and even promised to include them in His book of life. It certainly appears that God is looking for every reason in the book to save pagans, doesn't it?

PAGAN FAITH

When Jesus heard it, He marveled, and said to those who followed, "Assuredly, I say to you, I have not found such great faith, not even in Israel!" Matt. 8:10.

There are three little words stamped on my back: "Made in Japan." I was born in Tokyo and spent the first 14 years of my life a missionary's kid in the Land of the Rising Sun—boasting today 130 million inhabitants and the world's largest city. Will God destroy them all because they are pagans? And what about the 1.5 billion Muslims in the world? What about the millions in the pagan, secular West? Will God save pagans?

As Jesus was entering Capernaum one day, a pagan Roman centurion approached the Savior. His beloved servant lay dying. Would the Master please heal him? And when Jesus offered to go to the centurion's home, the Roman warrior quickly protested that he wasn't worthy to have Jesus come under his roof. "But only speak a word," the commander suggested, "and my servant will be healed" (Matt. 8:8). And as our text today describes, Jesus was dumbfounded! For months He had been traversing the land of "the chosen," wildly acclaimed at times by the masses, but more often than not rejected by a faithless ecclesiastical hierarchy. Shaking His own head in wonder, Jesus turned to the entourage around Him and declared, "I haven't found such great faith, not even among 'the chosen'!"

But then His punch line becomes even punchier. "And I say to you that many will come from east and west, and sit down with Abraham, Isaac, and Jacob in the kingdom of heaven. But the sons of the kingdom will be cast out into outer darkness. There will be weeping and gnashing of teeth" (verses 11, 12). Ouch! Was Jesus declaring that pagans from the east (read Japan or Islam) and west (read secular atheists and humanists) will sit down one day at God's banqueting table, while those who'd originally been "the chosen" would be lost in their own unbelief? Mercy!

Which is precisely what we all need, isn't it? Mercy for the pagans, mercy for "the chosen," mercy for the lost in all of us. Apparently the kingdom of heaven and divine mercy operate with a paradigm that is *inclusive* rather than *exclusive*. And just as apparently the ones that get chosen in the end are the ones who have lived up to the light (whether much or little) that divine love and mercy have shined upon their pathway.

FUZZY WUZZY PAGANS, FUZZY CHRISTIANS

But someone who does not know, and then does something wrong, will be punished only lightly. When someone has been given much, much will be required in return; and when someone has been entrusted with much, even more will be required. Luke 12:48, NLT.

Once upon a time a master embarked on a very long trip. And so he summoned his wise and trusted servant and told him, "I am placing my entire family and household under your supervision and administration. Take good care of them for me, until I return." The servant gratefully bowed, accepting the commission and pledging his obedience. And with that the master was off and gone.

Time went by, and the lead servant soon tired of the responsibilities his master had placed upon him. Why did he have to live under such stringent expectations and regulations? After all, he hadn't seen the master in a long, long time.

And so the unthinkable happened. The wise and trusted servant cast aside his obligations like a heavy old coat. "My master is delayed—and I'm tired of waiting. Let's eat, drink, and be merry!" And he did, becoming so inebriated that he began to beat the members of the master's household. It was an ugly scene.

But it got even uglier when the master unexpectedly and suddenly returned. After describing the brutal fate of the trusted servant in this parable, Jesus drives home His punch line in our text. "Much is required from those to whom much is given" carries with it the corollary "Little is required of those to whom little is given." It's the law of commensurate returns, the law that calibrates outcome commensurate to income. The more you have, the more will be expected of you—the less you have, the less will be expected. It is both obvious and fair.

Does that mean, for example, that the animist who worships the spirits of trees will be held to a different standard than the Christian who values her clothes and her car more than her God? Actually, not at all. It means rather that they *both* will be held to the identical standard. *What did you do with what you had?* It's a standard as fair as the God who maintains it.

So how much do you and I and the chosen have? And what about our pagan neighbors on this planet? The very fact that God hasn't made our lives a standard by which they will be judged is proof enough that He is eager to save as many of us as He can, isn't He?

WHALE OF A TRUTH

I knew that you are a gracious and compassionate God, slow to anger and abounding in love, a God who relents from sending calamity. Jonah 4:2, NIV.

What's not to love about the Jonah story? There's the perfect "bad boy," the recalcitrant, runaway prophet, and a boatload of cussing pagan sailors. Throw in a Level 5 hurricane at sea, and you've got a humdinger of a storm—and story. You've also got divine roulette that picks the rebel out of the crowd, and, of course, that dark, mysterious sea creature that swallows Jonah the moment he sinks beneath the heaving, foaming surface. What could be better!

But there's more. The whale vomits up the runaway prophet, his skin bile-yellowed from three days and nights in that marine belly. No wonder the entire city listened as this messenger pronounced a divine nuking in 40 days! And surprise of surprises, the populace, from the king on down, fall to their faces in one of the classic citywide revivals of all time.

And Jonah? The largest altar call response in history, and this preacher is furious that his prophecy didn't come true. You can't win them all. But don't tell that to God, who actually did win the entire city this time. God saves a cityful of pagans, and He does it without asking them to join "the chosen." There is no record of the saved of Nineveh ever proselytizing to Israel's faith. They repented of their wicked ways before the God of Jonah, and the God of Jonah forgave them and saved them, every last one of them. The End.

And by the way, not only did God save that entire Assyrian city—He also saved the entire boatload of pagan sailors plus one prophet. It's one saving story! Proof enough that Peter's words about pagan Cornelius are indeed true: "I truly understand that God shows no partiality, but in every nation anyone who fears him and does what is right is acceptable to him" (Acts 10:34, 35, NRSV).

"Among the heathen are those who worship God ignorantly, those to whom the light is never brought by human instrumentality, yet they will not perish. Though ignorant of the written law of God, they have heard His voice speaking to them in nature, and have done the things that the law required. Their works are evidence that the Holy Spirit has touched their hearts, and they are recognized as the children of God" (*The Desire of Ages*, p. 638).

It's a whale of a truth, isn't it? God has His chosen everywhere!

THIS LITTLE LIGHT OF HIS

That was the true Light which gives light to every man coming into the world. John 1:9.

For decades we've sung the chorus "This little light of mine, I'm going to let it shine." But in actuality the light doesn't belong to any of us, does it? It's the light of Christ, "the Light of the world." And as our text declares, He is the Light that shines upon all who enter this life.

"As through Christ every human being has life, so also through Him every soul receives some ray of divine light. Not only intellectual but spiritual power, a perception of right, a desire for goodness, exists in every heart" (*Education,* p. 29). The wicked, cruel Assyrians of Nineveh, pagan centurions, postmodern seculars, spirit-worshippers—it doesn't matter. Jesus is the Light of the world that flickers inside of us all.

For that reason God's final call to "the chosen" will include vast swaths of Sunni and Shiite Muslims, Hindus, Buddhists, Jews, Christians, and even atheists. What will be the standard in the end that will determine their chosesnness? It will be that measure of light that shone into their souls. None of us will be judged for the light we didn't have. All of us will be accountable for the light we did have.

"Our standing before God depends, not upon the amount of light we have received, but upon the use we make of what we have. Thus even the heathen who choose the right as far as they can distinguish it are in *a more favorable condition* than are those who have had great light, and profess to serve God, but who disregard the light, and by their daily life contradict their profession" (*The Desire or Ages,* p. 239; italics supplied).

A few days ago we asked, Can a pagan remain a pagan and still be saved? The evidence of Scripture leads to the conclusion, Yes. Then what's the point of being missionaries, evangelists, and witnesses for Jesus anymore? Simple. The vast majority of God's pagan children aren't living up to the light they have. The prisons, brothels, casinos, universities, governments, and neighborhoods of the world are filled with pagans who have blatantly rejected God's light. They are the second thief on the cross, cursing and defiant. But given another chance, were you or I to walk into their lives right now, they could become the first thief on the cross and be saved in the end! It is *that hope* that compels us to join with God in seeking to reach every man, woman, and child on this planet. For this little light of His shines inside them, too.

THE PLEA OF TWO MOTHERS

As it is written: "There is none righteous, no, not one; there is none who understands; there is none who seeks after God. They have all turned aside; they have together become unprofitable; there is none who does good, no, not one." Rom. 3:10-12.

It was surreal and bizarre at the same time. There he was on trial for his life, Scott Peterson, convicted of murdering both his wife and their unborn child. In the penalty phase of the trial (while the nation gaped on live cable TV), both mothers were brought before the court to address the jury. First it was Laci Peterson's mother, who in that hushed courtroom wept and screamed invectives at Scott for taking the life of her daughter and unborn baby boy. Then Scott Peterson's mother addressed the jury. She, too, wept as she pleaded for her son's life. Two mothers begging for two diametrically opposed judgments.

Is that the way it will be in the final judgment when God ratifies His choice of the chosen? A furious voice screaming for our execution? Another voice of tears pleading that we might be spared? *Does the final judgment come down to the final verdict?* Am I guilty or not guilty, lost or saved? And which mother will the jury believe?

Let's face it. If it's a matter of guilt or innocence, we all lose, don't we? Just like Scott Peterson. For how could Scripture be clearer than our text for today? You can search the world over, it declares, and you will find not one, no one, none who is innocent or righteous. There are zero innocent, not-guilty human beings living on this planet at the present time! Which means that if you went door to door in this country, and then door to door in every other nation on earth, your methodical survey would reveal that not a single individual in any domicile on earth is morally guiltless. "There is none who does good, no, not one." You can't get more categorical than that, can you?

Sorry, God—looks like Your search for the chosen begins with one big zero! And yet—and this is a huge "and yet"—the shining declaration of Holy Scripture, as we've been reading this month, is just as categorical in announcing that God is gathering a community of men, women, and children (a movement, if you please) from across the face of this earth and is declaring them to be His "chosen ones"! All of them as guilty as sin, and yet somehow they end up being handpicked by God. If that isn't grace in the courtroom, what is?

MISCARRIAGE OF JUSTICE

For all have sinned and fall short of the glory of God. Rom. 3:23.

The furor over capital punishment is hardly quieting down. Because of advances in DNA testing, the murder convictions of more than a few death-row inmates have been overturned by new DNA evidence. The wrong man had been sentenced to death. An innocent man was about to be executed. I watched an interview with just such an exonerated former inmate. He'd spent decades of his life behind bars as the result of the state's rush to judgment. As the camera zoomed in on his face, the emotions of relief and anger mixed were nearly palpable.

Even more tragic, of course, have been those posthumous discoveries that the state, thinking it had the guilty one behind bars, had proceeded to execute the wrong man, who turned out to be innocent. Only the resurrection can rectify so terrible a wrong.

Paul's declaration here in Romans, however, cannot be overturned by new DNA evidence. "All have sinned." Period. "All fall short of God's glory." Period. No need for an appeal to the Supreme Court, for the highest Court in the universe has already declared with perfect prescience that the prisoner, the sinner, stands guilty as charged. From Mother Teresa to Adolf Hitler to you and me, *all have sinned*. The verdict is guilty, and the sentence is death. "For the wages of sin is death" (Rom. 6:23). Period. The End.

Then how shall we, who long to be chosen, be freed from the terrible sentence? Are our offenses, our transgressions, our iniquities, our sins unpardonable?

Our only hope, as it turns out, is the greatest miscarriage of justice in all of history. On that day that now has forever divided the past from the future, an innocent Man was rushed by the state to His execution. The DNA evidence from that fateful Friday is now more than clear—they executed the wrong Man; an innocent Man went to His death. Only a resurrection could possibly rectify so grievous a wrong.

And that, of course, is the everlasting gospel! "For He [God] made Him [Christ] who knew no sin [innocent] to be sin for us [guilty], that we [sinners longing to be chosen] might become the righteousness [rightness of innocence] of God in Him" (2 Cor. 5:21).

The greatest miscarriage of justice in the history of the universe has thrown wide the gates of heaven to all the guilty that God has called to be chosen. Amazing grace!

THE JUDGMENT OF ADOLF HITLER

There is no difference between Jew and Gentile, for all have sinned and fall short of the glory of God, and all are justified freely by his grace through the redemption that came by Christ Jesus. Rom. 3:22-24, TNIV.

What does that mean, "all are justified"?

It would be as if Adolf Hitler had survived and was brought to judgment, where on the morning of the final sentencing the judge addressed the court: "Ladies and gentlemen of the jury, for the past few days I have been pondering your verdict of the accused long and hard. I know you have found Adolf Hitler guilty of heinous crimes against humanity. And I concur—he is indeed guilty. But now in the penalty phase of this trial, I have made a judicial decision. I am going to acquit Mr. Hitler of his terrible crime. I am going to waive the death sentence against him."

No sooner does the judge pronounce those words than the courtroom turns electric with furious buzz. The judge pounds his gavel to quiet the chamber. "I know what you are thinking and saying. I, too, am committed to upholding the law and maintaining justice. And so I have decided that in pardoning Adolf Hitler and declaring him 'Not guilty' I myself will pay the penalty. I will forfeit my life on his behalf." And after a long pause: "This court is adjourned."

Can you imagine the furor, the headlines, the global outcry were that to have happened? "Judge Acquits Hitler and Offers Own Life for Execution," the headline would have shouted.

And yet as bizarre as it sounds for our contemporary jurisprudence, "to justify" in the New Testament context means to do just that. "All are justified [pardoned, acquitted, declared no longer guilty] freely by his grace through the redemption that came by Christ Jesus." Through the death of Christ, *all*—that's correct, *the entire human race*—have had the divine charges dropped against them.

It is the stunning pronouncement of the everlasting gospel. All sinners are deservedly accused, but all sinners have been undeservedly acquitted. All have been accused, and all have been acquitted "by his grace." At Calvary the Judge bore the death sentence for an entire human race. He can justify all, because He paid the penalty for all. Amazing grace indeed!

WILL ALL BE SAVED?

This is right and is acceptable in the sight of God our Savior, who desires everyone to be saved and to come to the knowledge of the truth. 1 Tim. 2:3, 4, NRSV.

Does "all are justified" mean "all are saved"? I wish it did. There is a teaching called "universalism" that declares that in the end God will save every human being who has ever lived, including Adolf Hitler, Joseph Stalin, Idi Amin, Osama bin Laden, and you and me. Everyone gets saved in the end.

And in my heart of hearts I have to believe that God Himself wishes it could be true, don't you think? If you were the Father, wouldn't you long for every child of yours to be saved in the end? How many times have I listened as heartbroken parents anguished over choices their children were making. Is there a parent in the world who wouldn't do almost anything to make sure their child was saved in the end? God surely knows that longing.

That's why the Scriptures are replete with verses just like our text today. "We have our hope set on the living God, who is the Savior of all people" (1 Tim. 4:10, NRSV). "For the grace of God has appeared, bringing salvation to all" (Titus 2:11, NRSV). "Look to Me, and be saved, all you ends of the earth!" (Isa. 45:22). "For Christ's love compels us, because we are convinced that one died for all" (2 Cor. 5:14, NIV). All, all, all—notice the repetition. "The Lord is . . . not willing that any should perish but that all should come to repentance" (2 Peter 3:9). It is clear that God universally desires that *all* of His earth children might come to Him, that *all* might take their place among His chosen ones.

But while the Bible teaches salvation's universal provision, it does not suggest salvation's universal acceptance. God acquits all, but not all accept Him. And that's why God won't save the entire human race. He values *our freedom to choose* too much to force all to choose Him and thus be saved. Love, in order to be love, must not only grant us the right to say YES to it—it must also grant us the right to say NO. Hence divorce courts and broken hearts, because *love cannot be forced.* And God will not people heaven with people who don't want to be there.

But you want to be there, and I want to be there. And the everlasting gospel declares that God has done everything divinely and humanly possible to make certain we're all there.

THE GOSPEL ACCORDING TO ABRAHAM LINCOLN

Therefore if the Son makes you free, you shall be free indeed. John 8:36.

On January 1, 1863, President Abraham Lincoln signed the Emancipation Proclamation, declaring free all slaves residing in territory in rebellion against the federal government. And by that proclamation the Civil War was declared to be a war for the freeing of the slaves. On December 18, 1865, eight months after the end of the war, the ratification of the Thirteenth Amendment to the Constitution was verified, finally assuring the end of slavery. But the president who signed the Emancipation Proclamation was dead, gunned down by a political fanatic.

The moment President Lincoln signed the document and it was enacted, every slave was set free *legally*. But not every slave was free *experientially*. My friend Jerry Finneman has observed that in order to be freed *experientially*, slaves needed to: (1) hear the good news; (2) believe the good news; (3) determine that the good news was true in their case; (4) refuse to remain in subjection as slaves any longer; (5) assert their freedom from their former taskmasters; and (6) count on the authority and power of the government that declared them free to now help them remain free (*1888 Glad Tidings*, vol. 20, no. 5, pp. 3, 4).

And so it was and is at Calvary. "With His own blood [Jesus] has signed the emancipation papers of the race" (*The Ministry of Healing*, p. 90). There at the cross the God of the universe in crimson proclaimed that the entire human race was forthwith declared emancipated and liberated from the tyrannical dominion of their cruel taskmaster—every man, woman, and child who had ever, or would ever, live was declared set free.

But as U.S. history has shown us, there were some slaves who never went free—either because they never heard the good news, or they didn't believe the good news, or they simply didn't want to be set free. Universal emancipation must still be personally embraced if it would ever be individually experienced.

For that reason the call of the everlasting gospel is *good news twice over*: first, it announces to us God's universal acquittal of all sinners by grace ("The Son has set you free"); and second, it invites our personal acceptance of His saving grace through faith ("Come to Me, and I will give you rest"). Good news universally through grace, good news personally through faith—how could God's news get any better than that!

TC-3

DIVINE ALZHEIMER'S

I, even I, am he who blots out your transgressions, for my own sake, and remembers your sins no more. Isa. 43:25, NIV.

Is it a sin to walk on your roof? Not if you're careful. Then is it sin to look down from your roof? Not really. But what if your neighbor's wife is in her backyard taking a bath?

Therein lies the tragic downfall of King David, who got far too close and fell off the edge, not of his roof but of his soul. There's nothing wrong with a spring-time stroll on top of your palace. After all, you are king. But when all that power goes to your head instead of your humility, and you insist on having your neighbor's wife, impregnating her, deceiving her guileless husband, having him killed, and covering up the whole sordid affair from heaven and earth—you'll end up breaking all 10 of the commandments in a matter of hours! Guilty as sin.

It is to the king's credit, in this tale of such terrible moral deficits, that when the prophet Nathan blindsided him with a self-incriminating parable and David realized the jig was up and that God knew all, he collapsed in remorseful tears before the prophet and God.

"Have mercy upon me, O God, according to Your loving kindness; according to the multitude of Your tender mercies, blot out my transgressions. . . . Against You, You only, have I sinned, and done this evil in Your sight—that You may be found just when You speak, and blameless when You judge" (Ps. 51:1-4).

And how does God respond to the prayer of the penitent? Decades later God rebuked another king with these startling words: "You have not been as My servant David, who kept My commandments and who followed Me with all his heart, to do only *what was* right in My eyes" (1 Kings 14:8). Wait a minute, God—time out! Do You have Alzheimer's? What do You mean that David kept Your commandments, followed You with *all* his heart, and did *only what was right*? You must have the wrong David!

Ah, it is the truth of the everlasting gospel. "If you give yourself to [Christ], and accept Him as your Savior, then, sinful as your life may have been, for His sake you are accounted righteous. Christ's character stands in place of your character, and you are accepted before God *just as if you had not sinned*" (*Steps to Christ,* p. 62; italics supplied). Good news for the chosen who fall, as did David, but who find, as did David, the God who remembers their sins no more.

WHEN MERCY GREW ON TREES

You shall call His name Jesus, for He will save His people from their sins. Matt. 1:21.

Going through someone else's family tree is about as intriguing as reading the phone book. When was the last time you thrilled with "the begats" in Matthew 1's dusty opening? And yet tucked inside Jesus' family tree are seven surprise entries that tell the truth about the chosen.

Surprise entry 1: "Judah begot Perez and Zerah by Tamar" (verse 3). Tamar was a woman, and finding any woman in the branches of Jewish family trees was a shocker! Playing a prostitute, she became pregnant by her father-in-law. She gave birth to twins that should've been Judah's grandsons, but were his sons instead. And all four end up in the Messiah's family tree!

Surprise entry 2: A real live prostitute, the madam of Jericho's brothel— "Salmon begot Boaz by Rahab" (verse 5). But the prostitute was saved and married into Jesus' family line.

Surprise entry 3: "Boaz begot Obed by Ruth" (verse 5). She was a descendant of incest: Lot's daughter sleeping with him. And God was adamant that no Moabite would ever be allowed to worship with Israel "forever" (Deut. 23:3). Yet Ruth the Moabite became a grand matriarch of the Messiah. Clearly divine mercy overruled divine justice.

Surprise entries 4 and 5: "David the king begot Solomon by her *who had been the wife* of Uriah" (Matt. 1:6). Instead of calling her Bathsheba, Matthew intentionally describes her as another man's wife, underscoring that she didn't belong to David and that she was the wife of a pagan convert—all three of whom will be in heaven one day. Will mercy ever top that one!

Surprise entry 6: "And Jacob begot Joseph the husband of Mary, of whom was born Jesus who is called Christ" (verse 16). The young Mary is proof enough that you don't have to be sexually fallen to end up in Jesus' family tree—good news for all those who quietly, obediently follow after God, just as Mary did.

Surprise entry 7: The greatest surprise of all. For there are two family trees in Matthew—one at the beginning and one at the end, one woven with "begats" and the other stained with blood. The first tree is closed to further entries, but not the second. For at the family tree of Calvary the door to God's chosen has been thrown wide to all, making you and me the seventh surprise entry, which, thanks to His undying mercy, need be no surprise at all!

THE RESTORED MASTERPIECE

So if anyone is in Christ, there is a new creation: everything old has passed away; see, everything has become new! 2 Cor. 5:17, NRSV.

But with all this good news about God accepting the chosen as they are (we even sing it: "Just as I Am"), encircling us with His grace, emancipating, acquitting, and pardoning us, and entering us into His family tree—shall we conclude that when He calls us to come as we are, we remain as we are?

Alister McGrath, the English scientist turned theologian, tells how during his two years of study at Cambridge University he often made his way to the nearby chapel of King's College. There in the quiet magnificence of the sanctuary he would rest his mind and refresh his soul. Hanging in the chapel was an old painting, the work of a master, that McGrath often stopped to contemplate. One day a protester, attempting to make some sort of political point, stepped up to that painting, drew a knife, and slashed the canvas. Several days later when Alister returned to the chapel he discovered a notice had been placed beside the ruined painting: "It is believed that this masterpiece can be restored" (*Justification by Faith*, p. 18).

Once upon a long ago time the whole human race was lost, slashed by a crazed and demented fallen angel. But a few days later, outside the barred and shuttered Eden garden, Someone posted a notice: "It is believed that this masterpiece can be restored."

It is the truth of the everlasting gospel. For when God chooses a man or a woman, or even a community, and calls them to Him and His salvation, it is not only for the sake of redemption—it is also for the sake of restoration.

"If anyone is in Christ, there is a new creation" promises our text today. Yes, the divine acquittal and emancipation are instantaneous, but the divine work of restoring the original human creation and masterpiece is truly the work of a lifetime, day after day, night by night.

Yes, we come as we are. But no, we do not remain as we are. For in Christ there is a new creation in progress. And that is why the rogues' gallery of the chosen has reason to hope, "being confident of this, that he who began a good work in you will carry it on to completion until the day of Christ Jesus!" (Phil. 1:6, NIV).

THE VERDICT IS IN

There is no fear in love; but perfect love casts out fear. 1 John 4:18.

Remember the question we raised a few days ago: Does the final judgment come down to the final verdict? A stomach-twisting, nerve-racking nail-biter to the very end? Am I guilty or am I not? Am I lost or am I saved? After reflecting on the call of the chosen in the everlasting gospel as we have, how shall we now answer?

Let's revisit for a moment that handful of verses in Romans that Martin Luther called "the chief point, in the very central place of the Epistle, and of the whole Bible," and what Leon Morris describes as "possibly the most important single paragraph ever written." In the heart of Romans 3:21-26 are these familiar words: "There is no difference between Jew and Gentile, for all have sinned and fall short of the glory of God, and all are justified freely by his grace through the redemption that came by Christ Jesus" (verses 22-24, TNIV).

It is the heart of the everlasting gospel, the hinge of all truth: we fallen humans—hopelessly lost, all of us—have been gloriously redeemed by the God of the universe who in Christ sacrificed Himself for the salvation of the human race, so "that whoever believes in Him should not perish but have everlasting life" (John 3:16). Amen.

When was that divine verdict *against* sin and *in favor* of sinners pronounced? According to the calendar on the wall, that supreme sacrifice was made 2,000 years ago. That is, two millennia ago the divine judgment on both sin and sinners was rendered at the cross, when God brought down His gavel and declared sinful human beings acquitted, pardoned, and emancipated. "It is finished!" (John 19:30). And it was. "[Christ] took in His grasp the world over which Satan claimed to preside as his lawful territory, and by His wonderful work in giving His life, He restored the whole race of [men and women] to favor with God" (*Selected Messages,* book 1, p. 343).

And because of this everlasting, always-lasting good news, the final judgment doesn't come down to the verdict at the end, but rather the verdict in the beginning. We need not live in uncertainty over its outcome. Whether the judgment be concluded tonight, tomorrow, in a hundred years or a thousand years—it matters not. For the verdict that counts in the end is in the beginning. "This grace was given us in Christ Jesus before the beginning of time" (2 Tim. 1:9, NIV). No wonder they call the gospel good news!

AN EXTRA DAY WITH GOD

Then Jesus said, "Come to me, all of you who are weary and carry heavy burdens, and I will give you rest." Matt. 11:28, NLT.

If your birthday is today, you've had one fourth as many as the rest of us. No wonder you look so young! But then, that's your reward for the fact that earth orbits the sun every 365.242 days. It's not your fault. They say the odds of being born on leap day is 1 in 1,461, which means there are more than 4.5 million leap-day babies just like you on this planet. Like the Canadian quadruplets who today are turning age 6, or the three Norwegian siblings whose mother made sure each of them was born on consecutive February 29s. Happy birthday!

But speaking of adding a day now and then, how would you like to have been a Roman in 46 B.C.? That's the year that their astronomers figured out their calendar was *way* off. So to correct decades of drift they made that year keep lasting and lasting and lasting for 445 days. Try calculating your birthday on that calendar!

Ever wonder if God would like to add a day to His calendar? Come to think of it, He has, hasn't He? An extra day every week, "extra" simply because He could have made the earth week six days long. After all, Genesis 1 declares that His physical creation was completed in six days. But because the Creator and His creation are not only physical, but are truly social and spiritual, God added an "extra" day to the six days and called it the birthday of the world. We still remember it as His Sabbath, from the Hebrew *Shabbat,* which means "to cease, to rest."

And can you think of a more perfect day in which to rest in the friendship of our Forever Friend than the Sabbath? "Come to Me," Jesus still invites us, "and I will give you rest." The rest of His friendship is the heart and soul of the Sabbath, isn't it?

"'Come unto Me' is His invitation. Whatever your anxieties and trials, spread out your case before the Lord. Your spirit will be braced for endurance. The way will be opened for you to disentangle yourself from embarrassment and difficulty. The weaker and more helpless you know yourself to be, the stronger will you become in His strength. The heavier your burdens, the more blessed the rest in casting them upon the Burden Bearer" (*The Desire of Ages,* p. 329).

With a promise like that why wait for God's "extra" day? Celebrate His rest right now!

"PLEASE DIAL 9-9-9"

Then he said to me, "Do not fear, Daniel, for from the first day that you set your heart to understand, and to humble yourself before your God, your words were heard; and I have come because of your words. But the prince of the kingdom of Persia withstood me twenty-one days." Dan. 10:12, 13.

Just how jittery our world has become became clear from our bus ride outside London. Karen and I had hardly been seated when a recording in a very proper male English accent announced over the PA system: "This bus is under attack. Please dial 9-9-9 [our 9-1-1]." We looked around—everyone seemed fairly normal. The recording repeated itself. I looked up at the driver—he seemed normal, too, except for the fact he was pounding the dashboard. Turns out that the prerecorded terrorist alert (that British buses now carry ever since the London attacks several years ago) had accidentally come on, and the driver couldn't turn it off! What's more, the alarm was blaring outside as well. We drove for miles with people staring, some even dialing their cell phones for help.

We live in a world on the jittery edge of uncertainty, don't we? And the stunning headlines keep mounting. We are in a war of terror in many more ways than one.

The words of Gabriel to Daniel draw back the veil between the seen and the unseen as nowhere else in Scripture. For three weeks Daniel had fasted and prayed. "I'm sorry," Gabriel said. "I couldn't get here sooner, for the dark and evil prince of Persia has been fighting me!"

We are in a war today, not only visible, but in actuality even more real in the realm of the *invisible*. For decades we've called it "the great controversy"—the forces of light and darkness in desperate "hand-to-hand" spiritual conflict over vast swathes of the human race. For 21 days the mighty Gabriel has been locked in a supernatural struggle with fallen Lucifer.

And all the while, though he is not a witness to the galactic conflict in the unseen, Daniel fasts and prays. Do you suppose therein lies a compelling invitation to the likes of you and me? "The great controversy between good and evil will increase in intensity to the very close of time" (*The Great Controversy*, p. ix). Which simply means we are now living in the most explosive hour of human history. Then shall we not, like Daniel, pray and pray and pray? Over the next few days you and I must ponder how it is we must pray our way through this cosmic war.

CALLING FOR MICHAEL

But for twenty-one days the spirit prince of the kingdom of Persia blocked my way. Then Michael . . . came to help me, and I left him there with the spirit prince of the kingdom of Persia. Dan. 10:13, NLT.

Who is Michael? Philipp Melanchthon, the brilliant associate of Martin Luther in the opening salvo of the Reformation, concluded that Michael is the apocalyptic name for none other than Christ Himself (see Jude 9; 1 Thess. 4:16; John 5:28). And I agree. For Christ has ever been the divine go-between for the Godhead and creation—for humans, He is Emmanuel ("God with us"), and for the angels He is the archangel Michael ("Who is like God"). His name appears only in apocalyptic literature (Daniel, Jude, Revelation) when there is a battle between the forces of light and darkness. *And whenever He shows up, He wins!*

Which being interpreted means that given the hour of history and the intensity of the war we are now surviving, can you think of a more critical time for us to be calling upon the Lord Jesus? And not for just two minutes a day! How could we possibly be fooled into thinking that this spiritual conflict can be survived with a two-minute devotional-quickie on the run? Please don't misunderstand me. Obviously, I'm in favor of devotional books such as this one. But the inescapable point is that we live in unprecedented times. Earth is literally tearing at its seams (as June's readings will remind us). If ever we needed to set aside greater blocks of time for personal worship, study, and prayer, wouldn't now be the time? I'm not suggesting we all embark on a 21-day fast from delicacies and bathing as Daniel did (see Dan. 10:3)—we no doubt could live without the sweets, but not the showers—but shouldn't we seriously be carving out more and more time to be alone with God and His Word?

Can you imagine rushing into battle with *no communication* from or with our commander? Then we cannot, we must not, race out of our homes, our rooms without being alone with Jesus. "We are living in the most solemn period of this world's history. The destiny of earth's teeming multitudes is about to be decided. . . . We need to humble ourselves before the Lord, with fasting and prayer, and to meditate much upon His word. . . . We should now seek a deep and living experience in the things of God. We have not a moment to lose" (*The Great Controversy*, p. 601). Given that, how will you daily call on Michael?

PRAYER CLOSET

Leaving the crowd behind, they took him along, just as he was, in the boat.
Mark 4:36, NIV.

"In contemporary society our Adversary majors in three things: noise, hurry, and crowds" (*Celebration of Discipline*, p. 13). Richard Foster is right, isn't he? And that is why it is essential that we do just as the disciples did in this gospel story: "Leaving the crowd behind, they took [Jesus] along." We must leave the noise and crowds behind.

That's why we still need what the ancients called a prayer closet—a room in your house, or a corner in your room or apartment or mobile home—someplace where you and Jesus can be alone together each day. We are creatures of habit. We eat breakfast in the same spot, we surf the Web or read the newspaper in the same chair. Even so we need to find a "sacred corner" that can become our prayer closet. It doesn't have to be fancy—but it must be consistent. Changing your prayer closet location from day to day will only distract you—whether it be in your house or in a room. Being the curious creature that you are, you'll spend the first precious moments noticing all that's "new" within your field of vision. So go back day after day, or night after night, to the same familiar and comfortable setting—no distractions there to divert you from why you have the prayer closet in the first place—to be alone with your Savior.

But you need quiet as well as consistency. That means you are away from the thoroughfare of life and noise where you live. Turn off all the background noise you can. No iPod, no stereo, no TV, no cell phone, no sleeping spouse in the bed next to you (in fact, forget turning your bed into a prayer closet—you'll never keep awake!), no children in the family room, no roommate in your field of vision (though perhaps still in the room, since you do share the space). For all of us who share our domiciles, there needs to be some sort of "devotional agreement" whereby we pledge to honor each other's quest for this daily quiet corner with God.

In the words of Ralph Carmichael's great hymn: "There is a quiet place, far from the rapid pace where God can soothe my troubled mind. . . . There in my quiet hour with Him my cares are left behind" (*The SDA Hymnal*, no. 503).

In the exponentially heightened noise and commotion of this hour of history, how vital that we, too, "leave the crowds behind" each day and hurry to that "quiet place" with the only One who can keep us both sane and secure in these uncertain times.

HOW MUCH TIME?

And in the morning, a long time before daylight, he got up and went out to a quiet place, and there he gave himself up to prayer. Mark 1:35, BBE.

Can you believe it? Even the God of the universe made flesh needed a quiet place to pray. Consider this from *Thoughts From the Mount of Blessing*: "Jesus had select places for communion with God, and so should we. We need often to retire to some spot, however humble, where we can be alone with God" (p. 84).

But how much time should we spend each day in prayer? Given the pell-mell rat race we're all trying to survive, how many minutes a day should we spend alone with God?

As someone once quipped—when it comes to prayer, it's not mind over matter, but rather *mind over mattress!* Which simply means we all face the perennial morning struggle of getting out of bed and getting to our prayer closet. And so it really becomes a matter of programming our schedules around our renewed quest to intensify our faith and prayer lives.

When both our children were born, I had in place some deeply entrenched habits that included sleeping peacefully through the night. But then along came the babies, and guess what? My life was turned upside down, or at least my nights were—or (truth in advertising) Karen's nights were! And we loved it—almost. Why? Because we had a brand-new priority in our lives. And our schedules went through radical reorganization to accommodate our new priority.

It's the same way with Jesus and prayer. Unless we radically reorganize our daily schedule to accommodate Him, what's the point? When a university student comes in to my office trying to carve out this new priority, I suggest 20 minutes a day, seven days a week, in his or her prayer closet. Yes, Jesus sorrowfully asked Peter in Gethsemane, "Could you not watch [with me] one hour?" (Mark 14:37). But for some an hour is too formidable, and I'd rather have you succeed than plunge in over your head and quit. So start small and grow. A half hour, an hour—you'll soon discover with this new way of praying (which we'll share here over the next few days) that time will no longer be an obstacle.

But if *Late Night With David Letterman* is your habit, you'll find *Early Morning With Jesus* a whole lot more difficult. Go to bed earlier so you can set your alarm earlier. When there's Somebody new in your life, it's essential to radically reorganize your schedule.

HIGH-CONCENTRATE SOUL FOOD

Let us fix our eyes on Jesus, the author and perfecter of our faith. Heb. 12:2, NIV.

Have you ever read the entire book of Hezekiah? Most people haven't. It doesn't exist. But that's how the Bible feels to a lot of us—a dusty old collection of no-name ancients who had no clue how complicated our survival would be today.

The prayer method that I'm going to suggest here will keep you away from Hezekiah and Lamentations for a while. Like an athlete—spiritually, Paul describes all of us competing in the race of our lives (see 1 Cor. 9:24)—we need high-concentrate "soul food." And the highest concentration of nutritional spiritual power in all the Bible is embedded in the life of Jesus as recorded in Matthew, Mark, Luke, and John. For that reason *The Desire of Ages* invites us: "It would be well for us to spend a thoughtful hour each day in contemplation of the life of Christ. We should take it point by point, and let the imagination grasp each scene, especially the closing ones" (p. 83). And that's what this new way of praying will do.

You see, your time with Jesus in the Gospels will prove true the ancient law, "What we behold, we become." We can't break that law, but it can break us. Because whatever we intently, intensely focus our minds upon becomes embedded in our very selves. I read of an experiment in which a young man, placed under hypnosis, was given a piece of chalk to "smoke." The researchers assured him it was a cigarette, and so the young man "smoked" the chalk. Suddenly they feigned alarm that the "cigarette" had burned the young man, bandaged his fingers, brought him out of hypnosis, explained the "accident," and told him to return the next day. Sure enough, when the bandages were removed, the man had developed blisters where his fingers had held the chalk. His body literally became what his mind thought. By beholding, we become changed.

Given this critical hour in earth's history, how essential then that the chosen intently, intensely focus their minds and hearts upon Jesus! For who else but Michael can deliver us?

So here in your prayer closet, as you're ready to begin, invite the Spirit of Jesus to take these next few minutes and infuse the portrait of your Savior deep into your heart and mind. As our text today teaches, ask the Spirit to "fix your eyes on Jesus."

As that old chorus sings: "Turn your eyes upon Jesus, look full in His wonderful face; and the things of earth will grow strangely dim in the light of His glory and grace."

FROM SMORGASBORD TO SINGLE DISH

But grow in the grace and knowledge of our Lord and Savior Jesus Christ. 2 Peter 3:18.

Now what? Open to the Gospel of your choice. (Mark is the most dramatic, Luke the most pagan-friendly, Matthew the most majestic, and John the most profound.) And now do something a bit counterintuitive. We usually feel compelled to read as much of God's Word as we can in a sitting—the more spiritual food, the better, right? Wrong, actually. Like any smorgasbord, you can get too much of a good thing, which is true of the Bible, too. This method isn't about that old "three chapters a day and five on Sabbath" strategy to read your Bible through in a year. This is a "go as slow as you want and take all the time you need" method. Why? Because the object of our worship is to focus on Jesus. But if we've crammed three chapters of Gospel stories into our mind first thing in the morning, what will we possibly retain?

So this "new way to pray" takes just one story a day—one miracle, one parable, one teaching, one incident. You want to be saturated with what the Holy Spirit will bring to you out of that single story. Two or three stories, and you'll wonder which lesson He wants you to focus on. So stick to one (usually three to ten verses long). The modern translations are conveniently divided into paragraphs, which highlight the logical breaks in the narrative for you.

Obviously, one story won't take much time at all to read, especially when you're already familiar with it. (Avoid the temptation, by the way, to skip those familiar ones—sometimes God has His deepest lessons tucked away in the "old, old story.") So here's the strategy: *reread to relive.* Make it a full-sensory experience— turn the story into a DVD in your mind. See it the first time, add the sounds the second, the smells the third, the taste and the touch, as well. Remember, what we behold, we become. So make sure that the eyes of your soul are drinking in the incredibly rich detail of Jesus that the Spirit will bring to mind. *The Desire of Ages* noted yesterday: "Let the imagination grasp each scene." Reread it to relive it.

And all the while ask yourself, What does this story tell me about my Savior and Friend? The Spirit inspired the Gospel writer with every story. Something divine is tucked away inside it, something deeply significant for your spiritual survival and growth. What does God want you to learn from this single story? Ask Him. Search for it. And I promise you, the God of the universe will draw near to your mind and reveal a picture of Jesus you'll never forget!

A BOWL OF WHEATIES AND
THE TRUTH ABOUT PRAYER

Give all your worries and cares to God, for he cares about you. 1 Peter 5:7, NLT.

A picture of Jesus you'll never forget? While the last line of yesterday's reflection is true, please don't conclude that every breakfast is a five-course buffet. There are some mornings, let's be honest, when your bowl of Wheaties turns soggy pretty quick! Nothing to write home about, nothing to report to the rest at the office or at class about—just a bowl of flakes that didn't crunch or munch much at all. Then shall we swear off breakfasts? Hardly. Everybody knows that you're not always served Belgian waffles and Spanish omelets when you sit down for breakfast.

And it's that way with prayer and worship, too. There will be days when the Spirit of Jesus thunders loudly in your heart or whispers profoundly in your mind, and you'll leave your prayer closet revived, energized, and ready to conquer the world—or at least that day for God. But worship can be a soggy bowl of Wheaties as well. Not because God has failed you and me, or the Gospel story let us down. But simply because we're human—we kept falling asleep during our worship or kept getting distracted by the agenda of a day already begging for attention, or we were too bothered (read: troubled, agitated, upset, angry, guilty, worried, et al.) by what happened yesterday or last night. There are a thousand reasons for our frail humanity. And a soggy bowl of Wheaties may be all you dish up today.

But that's OK, because the One we've come to meet and have grown to love knows all about us children, doesn't He? Does a loving mother scold her child who falls asleep in midsentence? Does a kind father berate his little tyke who keeps interrupting their conversation? Then do you suppose God gets a bit huffy and puffy with us for our frailties?

Here's a way to turn those soggy Wheaties into prayer advances. Talk to God about whatever it is that has "sogged up" your worship, your life lately. Tell Him you're tired, bothered, worried about the day. Tell Him you're feeling guilty over yesterday. Tell Him everything. He already knows, so why pretend you're enjoying Belgian waffles with Him when it's soggy Wheaties all the way through. Talk to Him. What could bring more joy to a parent's heart? Cast all your cares upon Him—He really does care for you. And who knows? Maybe the soggy Wheaties are a part of His strategy to get you really hungry for what He has already planned for tomorrow's breakfast!

WRITING TO GOD

That which we have seen and heard we declare to you, that you also may have fellowship with us; and truly our fellowship is with the Father and with His Son Jesus Christ.
1 John 1:3.

Would you like to write a letter to God, and receive one back from Him? You can. All you need is a journal and a pen (or a laptop). I realize that this isn't going to be for everybody, but then again it may be the very corner your prayer life has been waiting to turn. It was for mine.

Let's say your Gospel story for the morning is Peter walking on water. Now, there's something to write home about. Which, of course, was what nearly sank Peter to Davy Jones's locker—pride, the nemesis of us all. So here you are reading and rereading that familiar but stormy midnight encounter on the high seas with Jesus. You feel the stinging drench of the gale-driven spray on your face as you peer into darkness to track Peter. Sure enough, he really truly is walking on the waves! But in another split second you hear an awful cry from the darkness— "Lord, save me!" And the next thing you know, you see Peter, soaked and subdued, grasping Jesus' hand and heaving himself back into the skiff. The End.

What does this story tell me about my Forever Friend? Once your brooding settles on an answer to that guiding question (i.e., the lesson you sense Jesus would draw for you were He sitting in a chair beside you), grab your journal and pen (or your laptop) and scribble out a letter to Him. "O Jesus, how very much like Peter I really am! So bold and courageous at the outset, but 10 paces into the project, I'm so cocky over myself that I take my eyes off You. Every time! And down I go. My prayer this morning is Peter's—Lord, save me! Keep my eyes on You all through the day. Amen." You're not writing for a Pulitzer; you're having a two-way conversation with your Master. His Spirit talked to you through the story, and now you're talking back through the letter. "Prayer is the opening of the heart to God as to a friend" (*Steps to Christ,* p. 93). It really is that simple.

Keep your heart and eyes on Jesus. Sure, take a good long glance at Peter (or whoever else is coming to the Savior in the story) to see how the Spirit positions you in the narrative. But keep focused on the Master. Do you have to write anything? Not at all. This prayer method works through quiet pondering and/or through simple writing. What matters most for the chosen is that they "follow the Lamb wherever He goes" (Rev. 14:4).

FORWARD ON OUR KNEES

Oh come, let us worship and bow down; let us kneel before the Lord our Maker. Ps. 95:6.

Before you hurry out of your prayer closet to face the new day, there is one more posture that is vital. Yes, you and Jesus through the Spirit have been in "conversation" together for the past few minutes. As you've opened His Word, He has spoken to you through sacred history (His story). And as you've meditated upon His story, your own heart has spoken back to Him. Every one of these minutes together is praying, is it not? Of course. And at the conclusion of them you could walk away from your "inner sanctum," knowing you have been in dialogue with God.

But may I suggest that you conclude this time with God on your knees? It is the familiar posture of worship. And it is to that posture that the psalmist in our text calls us, "Let us kneel before the Lord our Maker." After all, it's what people often did when they approached Jesus. As He descended from the Mount of Transfiguration, you remember the desperate father who ran to the Savior and knelt before Him (Matt. 17:14). It's the posture the mother of James and John assumed when she came to Jesus with a petition on behalf of her two boys (Matt. 20:20). Why, even a leper desperate for healing fell on his knees before Jesus (Mark 1:40).

Why kneel? Because it is a physical reinforcement in my own mind and heart that I have been worshipping the God of the universe. Yes, He is my forever friend. And yes, Jesus is still the same approachable companion He was 2,000 years ago. But I remind you that were you and I able to see Christ as He is today, our response would be no different than that of the closest earthly friend Jesus ever had. "And when I saw Him, I fell at His feet as dead" (Rev. 1:17). When Jesus came down to His elderly friend's prayer closet there on that rocky outcropping of Patmos in the Aegean Sea—while John was having his private worship before God—not even their intimate friendship could temper the instantaneous response of John before the glorified Christ! He fell down on his face before Him.

He is the same Jesus you meet in your own prayer closet. So, end your prayer time—even though it will not be granted you to physically see the glorified Savior . . . yet—on your knees before Him. In that posture your mind and spirit will be unleashed to worship the Lord your God "with all your heart, with all your soul, with all your mind, and with all your strength" (Mark 12:30).

What better way to walk with God than forward on our knees?

PETITIONS FOR YOUR AUDIENCE WITH THE KING

I urge that supplications, prayers, intercessions, and thanksgivings be made for everyone, for kings and all who are in high positions, so that we may lead a quiet and peaceable life in all godliness and dignity. This is right and is acceptable in the sight of God our Savior, who desires everyone to be saved and to come to the knowledge of the truth. 1 Tim. 2:1-4, NRSV.

If with their petitions they came to Jesus on their knees, then you and I may certainly do the same. Include those on your prayer list in the moments you spend on your knees at the end of your worship. Oswald Chambers describes intercessory prayer as "a work which has no snare. Preaching the gospel has a snare; intercessory prayer has none" (*My Utmost for His Highest*, Mar. 30). His point? Our public service, be it preaching or serving of any kind, carries the latent risk of becoming self-centered, self-promotional. But praying for others before God in private brings no accolades or applause—for it is all done in *private*.

In today's text the apostle Paul reminds us that such private interceding "is right and is acceptable in the sight of God our Savior." Why? Because God "desires everyone to be saved," that's why! Which is a strong hint that our prayer lists ought to be weighted by the names of family, friends, neighbors, colleagues, and even strangers whom we've met who need to meet the Savior. But more on that tomorrow.

You can start building a prayer list of your own right now, if you wish. My current list (which I keep in my prayer journal) began with an e-mailed prayer request someone sent long ago, and I've been scribbling in names ever since. (Not a very neat or attractive list, but who cares—it's only for private consumption—and it works.) Who should go on *your* list? Pray for "everyone," Paul enjoins us, which surely is divine permission to pray for whomever the Spirit places upon your heart. And given the conditions on this planet these days, his suggestion that we include our political leaders is a good one. Yes, let's pray for those who need physical healing (more on them later). Yes, let's intercede for those in need of financial deliverance or marital intervention or academic or career success, et al. But as your list grows longer, treasure this incredible promise: "The more earnestly and steadfastly we ask, *the closer will be our spiritual union with Christ*" (*Christ's Object Lessons*, p. 146; italics supplied). What a promise for our prayer lists!

TURNING A CURSE INTO A PRAYER!

So when Pilate saw that he could do nothing, but rather that a riot was beginning, he took some water and washed his hands before the crowd, saying, "I am innocent of this man's blood; see to it yourselves." Then the people as a whole answered, "His blood be on us and on our children!" Matt. 27:24, 25, NRSV.

My own prayer journey is a rather eclectic one. I have borrowed the methods of others and am the richer for it. For example, years ago I read one of the letters Dietrich Bonhoeffer wrote while incarcerated, and he mentioned to a dear friend that he found strong comfort in reading a psalm a day. And so ever since I've done the same and have been immensely blessed. As soon as I finish Psalm 150, the next morning I'm back to Psalm 1. They are the richest prayers in all of literature, and I know they will stir your own soul, too.

One Christmas my mother-in-law gave me Oswald Chambers' *My Utmost for His Highest*, a collection of daily Christ-centered devotional readings from a century ago. And for 20-plus years now, my soul has been enriched every new morning.

I learned a third prayer practice from my late friend Roger Morneau, who suggested that every day we read the story of Jesus' crucifixion and thus go to the summit of all divine power. If it's good for him, I concluded, it will be good for me. And so every morning I read Matthew 27:23-54. "Kneeling in faith at the cross, [the sinner] has reached the highest place to which [we] can attain" (*The Acts of the Apostles*, p. 210). What better place to daily kneel than at the summit of Calvary!

In reading Matthew 27 one day I suddenly realized that the cry of the rabble that Friday morning outside Pilate's judgment hall could become a powerful prayer. "His blood be on us and on our children!" Isn't that what I and every believing parent longs for on behalf of our children? That the blood of the Lamb, even as it was painted on the doorposts of the chosen the night they were delivered from Egypt, might be splashed upon the lintels of our homes and the hearts of our children. "His blood be on us [we mustn't leave ourselves out from the protective covering of Jesus' sacrifice] and on our children!" And when your children grow up and leave home, why stop the prayer? In your mind's eye you can still tiptoe to wherever it is they are sleeping and symbolically place your child under God's protective and saving love.

Come to think of it, is there a name on your prayer list that *doesn't* need this prayer?

81

THE BLOOD

But they have conquered him by the blood of the Lamb and by the word of their testimony, for they did not cling to life even in the face of death. Rev. 12:11, NRSV.

I was preaching in Sacramento, California. The Friday evening meeting was soon to begin, when I spotted a young man walking down the center aisle of the church. He wore a black T-shirt, and across his shirt in giant bright-red letters was the name SATAN. I did a quick double take. No question about it. I hadn't read wrong—and suddenly I began to wonder about the crowd and convocation I'd come to. But as he moved closer and extended his hand for a handshake, I could read the small print in white letters under Satan's name: "is defeated." Whew—I was still among friends!

"Satan is defeated." That was the triumphant pealing of every bell in the universe on that Friday afternoon when Jesus cried out the victorious "It is finished!" The ugly earth battles would yet continue, but the outcome of the war was forever decided. "Satan is defeated!"

No wonder the Apocalypse describes God's chosen through the centuries conquering the great red dragon (Satan) "by the blood of the Lamb." Why such a bloody metaphor? Simply because the very blood that the archenemy of heaven and earth shed that Friday in his slaughter of the Son of God has become the crimson symbol of the divine counteroffensive that crushed the deadly grip of Satan upon earth and the human race. Love substituted itself for the rebel race, and in its sacrificial death triumphed over the dark kingdom, emancipating humanity forever and ever. Amen.

And it is that Amen that bids us appeal to the crimson symbol of "the blood of the Lamb" in our worship and in our prayer. Thus "His blood be upon us and our children" becomes a mighty petition to Calvary's Conqueror to conquer now in our own lives and the lives of those we love. The enemy knows well the crippling power of such an appeal. "Tell [Satan] of the blood of Jesus, that cleanses from all sin. You cannot save yourself from the tempter's power, but *he trembles and flees when the merits of that precious blood are urged.* Then will you not gratefully accept the blessings Jesus bestows?" (*Testimonies for the Church,* vol. 5, p. 317; italics supplied). Blessings unleashed and unlocked because of Jesus' triumph on the cross.

No wonder we, too, may overcome through "merits of that precious blood."

MORE THAN 1,200 STUDIES

Bless the Lord, O my soul, and forget not all His benefits: Who forgives all your iniquities, who heals all your diseases, who redeems your life from destruction, who crowns you with lovingkindness and tender mercies. Ps. 103:2-4.

On Faith for Today's *The Evidence* telecast, I had the opportunity to interview Larry Dossey, recognized for his writings and research on the power of prayer. Though he grew up an evangelical Christian yet later became a New Age enthusiast, nevertheless he strongly advocates prayer intervention for the sick, going so far as to suggest that research shows even plants that are prayed for are physically affected.

At this time more than 1,200 empirical studies have examined the relationship between prayer and physical healing. From San Francisco General Hospital to Duke University Medical Center, you can examine the research for yourself by simply "googling" the key words.

The inescapable point is that we would do very well to include those in need of physical healing on our personal prayer lists. But what believer needed that assurance! After all, Jesus was the Master Healer. His disciples moved among the populace "and anointed with oil many who were sick, and healed them" (Mark 6:13). And the Bible declares: "And the prayer of faith will save [Greek, *sōzō*—"heal" or "save"] the sick, and the Lord will raise him up" (James 5:15).

Over the years, part of my life as a pastor has been praying for the sick. By the hospital bed or the bedside at home, no part of my ministry is more sacred than this intercessory privilege. Are all healed? Of course not. Why? God didn't answer the same query from Job, or from Elisha, the greatest miracle worker outside of Jesus in all of Scripture. Job was eventually healed; Elisha was not. Then because we don't know why some are healed and some not, shall we cease praying for the sick? Never. "You do not have because you do not ask" (James 4:2).

I interviewed John Polkinghorne, the famed English physicist and Anglican churchman, and asked him about prayer. He said that while we cannot know the mechanics of intercessory praying, perhaps it is as a laser beam, in which bundled strands of light are able to penetrate the greatest of obstacles. Could it be that in united prayer, the accumulated bundles of our focused petitions release God to do the unpredictable and sometimes unbelievable? We may never know until eternity, but until eternity we must never stop asking our wise and loving God to intervene.

GOD'S THREE "ALWAYS" PRAYERS

In this manner, therefore, pray: Our Father in heaven, hallowed be Your name. Your kingdom come. Your will be done on earth as it is in heaven. Matt. 6:9, 10.

Would you like to pray a prayer in which you are "guaranteed" that your petition is God's will? How about three prayers? Wesley Duewel, in his book *Mighty Prevailing Prayer*, describes what he calls God's "always" prayers, prayers that are *always* God's will (pp. 96, 97).

Prayer 1—It is *always* God's will to save the sinner. "The Lord is not slack concerning His promise, as some count slackness, but is longsuffering toward us, not willing that any should perish but that all should come to repentance" (2 Peter 3:9). Then let's crowd our prayer lists with the names of those who need the salvation of Jesus. Lost children, lost neighbors, lost colleagues, lost friends, lost cities and villages, and even nations—we must add them to our prayer lists. And never need we add the condition "If it is Your will," for we already know it *is* God's will to save the lost—all of them, if only they were as willing as He.

Prayer 2—It is *always* God's will to bless and revive the church. "Will You not revive us again, that Your people may rejoice in You?" (Ps. 85:6). Why would God *not* want to revive His church on earth? Why would He *not* long for our home congregations to become the explosive headquarters for the ministry of the Holy Spirit in our neighborhoods, our towns, our cities? We never have to pray, "If it is Your will, please revive our church." It *is* God's will.

Prayer 3—It is *always* God's will to glorify His name. On the eve of His death during His final visit to Jerusalem's temple, Jesus lifted His eyes to heaven and there before the multitude prayed, " 'Father, glorify Your name.' Then a voice came from heaven, saying, 'I have both glorified it and will glorify it again' " (John 12:28). Not like us—God doesn't glory in Himself when He glorifies His name. Rather, the name of God captures the full-orbed glory of the divine character of love. And when God glorifies His name in our midst, it is just as it was in the Temple—the attention is fully on Jesus. What better prayer to pray then than this petition that seeks for the glory of God to be revealed in our midst, personally and corporately?

While we cannot know the *mind* of God for every need we've scribbled onto our prayer lists, this much is clear—we can know His *heart*. And knowing His heart, can we not pour out our hearts to Him on behalf of all that He and we hold so dear?

THE PRAYER OF THE CHOSEN

Remember me, O Lord, with the favor You have toward Your people. Oh, visit me with Your salvation, that I may see the benefit of Your chosen ones. Ps. 106:4, 5.

Isn't that an amazing prayer? "O God, even as You have blessed the chosen down through the centuries of time, would You please grant me the same favor, visit me with the same salvation, and let me experience the very same benefit ["prosperity," NIV] You have given Your chosen ones." Don't you suppose God passionately longs for us to petition Him for that life of benefits He has promised the chosen?

What could make a parent happier (or more flabbergasted) than to have the resident teenager announce at the supper table that he or she would love to spend the evening with you—just the two of you—so that he or she might learn from your wisdom, benefit from your counsel, come to know your heart more deeply, and in the process hopefully be drawn closer to you? After picking yourself up from the floor, wouldn't you be glad to give your teen all of that, plus more!

Then why would it be an iota different with our heavenly Father who chose us from the very beginning? Brood over this heartful promise: "You need not go to the ends of the earth for wisdom, for God is near. It is not the capabilities you now possess or ever will have that will give you success. It is that which the Lord can do for you. We need to have far less confidence in what man can do and far more confidence in what God can do for every believing soul. He longs to have you reach after Him by faith. He longs to have you expect great things from Him. He longs to give you understanding in temporal as well as in spiritual matters. He can sharpen the intellect. He can give tact and skill. Put your talents into the work, ask God for wisdom, and it will be given you" (*Christ's Object Lessons*, p. 146).

All of that plus more for the chosen? Why not! Then why shouldn't we petition our heavenly Father daily for the abundance that He alone can provide? But aren't petitions a form of immaturity and self-centeredness? Shouldn't we outgrow petitionary prayer?

I suppose we'll outgrow that the day we outgrow the Lord's Prayer. It comes as a surprise to some to learn that in fact Jesus' model prayer consists of a string of seven petitions (count them for yourself) between the "Our Father in heaven" and the "for Yours is the kingdom. . . ." Seven petitions, evidence enough that God longs for us, too, to pray the prayer of the chosen.

THE GIFT THAT KEEPS ON GIVING

So I say to you, ask, and it will be given to you; seek, and you will find; knock, and it will be opened to you. For everyone who asks receives, and he who seeks finds, and to him who knocks it will be opened. Luke 11:9, 10.

Ever get the impression God wants you to ask? Ask, seek, knock—take the first letter of each of Jesus' imperatives, and what you have? A-s-k. Then why don't we do it more?

Once upon a time there was a man who had an out-of-town friend show up at midnight. After all the boisterous welcoming and hugging were through, the host suddenly realized he had nothing to feed his famished friend (grocery shopping wasn't until Friday). Thank God for our neighbors. But as he rang and rang the doorbell next door, he couldn't seem to rouse the family. Finally an upstairs window scraped open. After his neighbor's necessary apologies and explanation, the man upstairs grumbled that it was too late to look for food in his pantry, the kids were asleep, all the fuss might wake them up. But the needy host refused to budge. "I've got to have some bread for my visitor, *please!*" How long that kept up nobody knows. What Jesus' parable makes clear is that the man upstairs *finally* yielded to his persistent neighbor and gave him all the food he needed. The End.

The parable's punch line? Ask. Ask for what? Jesus is ready with the answer: "If you sinful people know how to give good gifts to your children, how much more will your heavenly Father give the Holy Spirit to those who ask him" (Luke 11:13, NLT). Ask for the Holy Spirit!

Asking for the Holy Spirit would be like asking your parents for a major credit card in their name with unlimited purchasing privileges. Get the card, and you've access to unimaginable blessings. (Of course, no wise, thinking parent is going to give an unlimited credit card to their children!) But ask your heavenly Father for the Holy Spirit, and it's even better than a credit card with unlimited credit. For God will bring every other gift you've ever needed (or deeply wanted) in tow. "With the reception of this gift [the Holy Spirit], *all other gifts* would be ours" (*My Life Today*, p. 57; italics supplied).

What kind of a parent would do that? Our heavenly Father, says Jesus. Apparently the gift of the Spirit is so monumentally significant in the eyes of heaven that when we have Him we have the one Being in the universe who can access for us the very treasury of God's kingdom!

THE JIGSAW PUZZLE — 1

After these things I saw another angel coming down from heaven, having great authority, and the earth was illuminated with his glory. Rev. 18:1.

Do you like jigsaw puzzles? For me, putting a nature scene together is a wonderfully relaxing pastime. But to be honest, my patience maxes out at 750 pieces. Put 1,000 randomly mixed pieces in a box, and it's goodbye relaxation!

So let's put a simple seven-piece jigsaw puzzle together right here. Why? Because from these seven pieces emerges a compelling prayer agenda that the chosen must embrace.

Jigsaw piece 1 is our text for today. Angels abound in Revelation; have you noticed? Most of us recall the three angels of Revelation 14. But here is a fourth angel that, like a shaft of exploding light, descends from heaven to earth near the end of time. (We know it's near the end, because three verses later there is a Voice from heaven that cries out, "Come out of her, my people, . . . lest you receive of her plagues" [Rev. 18:4].) So just before the end, a fourth angel, with great authority, sets the earth ablaze with glory. Whose glory? His own? Hardly.

Scholars are agreed that nearly every phrase of Revelation is borrowed from the Old Testament. The unlocking key for this jigsaw piece is Ezekiel 43:2: "And behold, the glory of the God of Israel came from the way of the east. His voice was like the sound of many waters; and the earth shone with His glory." Clearly John is citing this text. Put the two together and we know whose glory fills the earth at the end of time, don't we? It is the glory of *God* rising from the *east* like the sun. "But to you who fear My name the Sun of Righteousness shall arise with healing in His wings" (Mal. 4:2). Who do you suppose that Sun is? Who declared "I am the light of the world" (John 8:12; 9:5)? Whom did John describe as One whose "countenance was like the sun shining in its strength" (Rev. 1:16)?

Letting the Bible interpret itself, **jigsaw piece 1** dramatically describes the outpouring of the glory of Jesus upon earth's final generation, one last global revival. But with Jesus now bound to humanity with a body like ours, how could He pour Himself out? "He will glorify Me" (John 16:14). Who? The mighty Holy Spirit, the most Christ-centered Being in the universe. When He is poured out, it is the glory of Jesus that explodes all around. No wonder we are to "plead for the Holy Spirit" (*Christ's Object Lessons*, p. 147). No wonder this prayer request should head our list!

THE JIGSAW PUZZLE—2

Then I looked, and behold, a white cloud, and on the cloud sat One like the Son of Man, having on His head a golden crown, and in His hand a sharp sickle. And another angel came out of the temple, crying with a loud voice to Him who sat on the cloud, "Thrust in Your sickle and reap, for the time has come for You to reap, for the harvest of the earth is ripe."
Rev. 14:14, 15.

God is a farmer. Where do you think we learned it from? It is amazing how often the agricultural metaphor is woven throughout Scripture, from parables to prophecies. Here King Jesus sits upon the glorious Second Advent cloud, and what is in His hand? A sickle. Why? Because "the harvest of the earth is ripe." Remember the point of Jesus' parable about the wheat and the tares? Earth ends with a mighty harvest—John's point, too, here in **jigsaw piece 2.**

And it's also Joel's point in **jigsaw piece 3** when he describes God's last judgment with these words: "Let the nations be wakened, . . . for there I will sit to judge all the surrounding nations. Put in the sickle, for the harvest is ripe" (Joel 3:12, 13). The world of Judean agriculture is the language of Scripture, and it is clear the harvest metaphor describes the end of the world.

Now take **jigsaw piece 4:** "Be glad then, you children of Zion, and rejoice in the Lord your God; for He has given you the former rain faithfully, and He will cause the rain to come down for you—the former rain, and the latter rain in the first month. The threshing floors shall be full of wheat" (Joel 2:23, 24). How is the final harvest brought to ripe readiness? Through an abundant rainfall, Joel responds. Hebrew farmers knew only two seasons, wet and dry. And so they planted their seed at the beginning of the wet season of the early rains (autumn) in order to ensure their crops would take root and grow. And then they eagerly anticipated the season of the latter rain (spring) when that final burst of rainfall would accelerate the grain to full maturity for the harvest before the dry season set in.

But Joel clearly has much more than the weather patterns of Palestine on his mind. **Jigsaw piece 5:** "And it shall come to pass afterward that I will pour out My Spirit on all flesh; your sons and your daughters shall prophesy, your old men shall dream dreams, your young men shall see visions. . . . I will pour out My Spirit in those days" (verses 28, 29). The rain God promises is the outpouring of His Spirit. Only two more jigsaw pieces to go. But already we have enough of the picture to realize *this is one rainfall we must be asking for now.*

THE JIGSAW PUZZLE—3

Peter, standing up with the eleven, raised his voice and said to them, "Men of Judea and all who dwell in Jerusalem, let this be known to you, and heed my words. . . . This is what was spoken by the prophet Joel: 'And it shall come to pass in the last days, says God, that I will pour out of My Spirit on all flesh.'" Acts 2:14-17.

An unforgettable memory tucked away in my heart is of standing in the sacred quiet of that Jerusalem upper room that archaeologists are certain was the setting for the Holy Spirit's outpouring at Pentecost. A group of us Adventist pastors and religion professors from around the world gathered in that stillness to worship and pray together, remembering that "in this very place" a roaring wind and flaming tongues of fire swirled around 120 men and women in prayer.

From that outpouring, Peter hurried out to the balcony beneath which, it seemed, all of Jerusalem was abuzz over the strange manifestations emanating from that upper story. And I'm so grateful that in our text for today, **jigsaw piece 6**, Peter intentionally inserted words that never appeared in Joel's prophecy, for the phrase "in the last days" is unique to Luke's history of Acts. Peter knew Joel's words to be more than the ancient past—they were intended by God to portray the explosive future of the chosen. "In the last days . . . I will pour out My Spirit on all!"

And because of that insertion, it is clear that the Bible applies the prophetic words of Joel to *both* the outpouring of God's Spirit upon His chosen ones at the beginning of the history of the church (early rain) *and again* at the end of the history of the church (latter rain). Remember, the early rains soften the soil for the planting of new seed (Acts 2), and the latter rains ripen the grain for the final harvest (Rev. 14 and 18). And it is that final, supernatural, apocalyptic outpouring of God's Spirit that Revelation 18:1 (**jigsaw piece 1**) predicts and promises.

We may call it "the second coming of the Holy Spirit," as my friend Norman Gulley does. For if Pentecost was His mighty "first" coming, then indeed the latter rain of the Spirit will be His even mightier "second" coming! "The outpouring of the Holy Spirit on the day of Pentecost was the former rain, but the latter rain will be more abundant. The Spirit awaits our demand and reception. Christ is again to be revealed in His fullness by the Holy Spirit's power" (*Christ's Object Lessons*, p. 121). Did you catch that? A "more abundant" outpouring of Jesus' Spirit "awaits our demand and reception"? Shall we not then pray and pray and pray, and ask and ask and ask?

THE JIGSAW PUZZLE—4

For I will pour water on him who is thirsty, and floods on the dry ground; I will pour My Spirit on your descendants, and My blessing on your offspring. Isa. 44:3.

Here is **jigsaw piece 7.** "On the one who is *thirsty,* I will pour out My Spirit," God promises. There's only one condition. You must be thirsty—as thirsty as the dry cracked brown of Sudan's barren landscape, as thirsty as the baked brittle yellow of your dying front lawn. "For I will pour fresh water upon those who are thirsty and floods of water upon the dry ground."

All this talk of rain is simply the biblical call for spiritual revival and reformation. These seven jigsaw pieces now assembled together are but the impassioned appeal of God to His chosen ones to awaken to both the world's and the church's desperate thirst. "Let anyone who is thirsty come to me, and let the one who believes in me drink. As the scripture has said, 'Out of the believer's heart shall flow rivers of living water.' Now [Jesus] said this about the Spirit, which believers in him were to receive" (John 7:37-39, NRSV). Is anybody thirsty for the Spirit of Jesus?

May I be a bit more blunt? The urgent reality is that unless you and I are seeking the second coming of the *Holy Spirit,* we will never be ready for the second coming of *Jesus.* The former must precede the latter, or the latter will never come. "Let anyone who is thirsty come to me," Jesus still cries. Is anyone praying for His latter rain anymore?

You can imagine that somebody in this cosmic war is desperately praying we never will! "There is nothing that Satan fears so much as that the people of God shall clear the way by removing every hindrance, so that the Lord can pour out His Spirit upon a languishing church and an impenitent congregation. If Satan had his way, there would never be another awakening, great or small, to the end of time. . . . [But] Satan can no more hinder a shower of blessing from descending upon God's people than he can close the windows of heaven that rain cannot come upon the earth" (*Selected Messages,* book 1, p. 124).

Hallelujah! The enemy of our souls cannot stop the rain. He cannot indefinitely prevent Revelation 18:1's promised and prophesied global outpouring upon God's chosen ones, any more than he can shut up the windows of heaven. Good news—*both* the windows of heaven and the rain are under *God's* command! So shall we not passionately ask for the promised Gift?

THE LITTLE GIRL AND THE VASE

Ask the Lord for rain in the time of the latter rain. The Lord will make flashing clouds;
He will give them showers of rain, grass in the field for everyone. Zech. 10:1.

So is that it? Is that what God is waiting for from His chosen ones, simply that we ask for the rain? What's so complicated about that? Nothing, really. Except that asking is obviously more than simply mouthing the words. As every wife or husband knows, "I love you" on the lips is most powerfully corroborated with "I love you" in the life.

Ponder this invitation with me: "A revival of true godliness among us is the greatest and most urgent of all our needs. To seek this should be our first work. There must be earnest effort to obtain the blessing of the Lord, not because God is not willing to bestow His blessing upon us, but because we are unprepared to receive it. Our heavenly Father is more willing to give His Holy Spirit to them that ask Him, than are earthly parents to give good gifts to their children. But it is our work, by [1] confession, [2] humiliation, [3] repentance, and [4] earnest prayer, to fulfill the conditions upon which God has promised to grant us His blessing. A revival need be expected only in answer to prayer" (*Selected Messages*, book 1, p. 121). We all can handle prerequisite number 4—but what's up with numbers 1 through 3?

Reminds me of the little girl who was instructed by her mother not to play with the expensive vase in the living room. But later Mom caught the child with her hand literally inside the porcelain antique. And she couldn't get it out! Mother tried rubbing Vaseline on her girl's wrist, then cooking oil, still to no avail. In desperation she called the fire department. But even their industrial-strength petroleum jelly couldn't extricate the little girl's hand. Would they have to break the vase? The fire chief pondered for a moment, then gently asked the child what she had in her hand. "A penny," she innocently replied. "If you'll let it go, your hand will come right out." She did, and it did.

What is it we cling to that obstructs our hearts from God? A habit, a possession, a relationship, a penny or two? "Confession, humiliation, and repentance" aren't bad-news prerequisites—they're simply the act of the soul in letting go what obstructs our hearts from God. The little girl begged for the vase to be removed, but it wasn't until she let go of what was in her hand that her prayer was answered. Want a revival? Then let's help Jesus answer our prayer.

THE KINGDOM OF HEAVEN LIKE REALITY TV?

So he answered and said to me: "This is the word of the Lord to Zerubbabel: 'Not by might nor by power, but by My Spirit,' says the Lord of hosts." Zech. 4:6.

What if the kingdom of heaven were like reality television—one of those burgeoning talent programs whereby apparently everyone across the nation is watching simultaneously, and can call the toll-free number to cast a vote? What if heaven could organize every congregation in every time zone on earth to be simultaneously plugged in to a giant, global prayer meeting, all for the purpose of uniting behind a solitary prayer request? If we could pull it off, what do you suppose God would hope that prayer request would be? More faith, more grace, more power, more love, more victories, more satellites, more baptisms, more enrollment, more money, more volunteers, more time?

"Could there be a convocation of all the churches of earth, *the object of their united cry should be for the Holy Spirit.* When we have that, *Christ our sufficiency* is ever present. We shall have *every want supplied.* We shall have the mind of Christ" (Ellen G. White, *Manuscript Releases*, vol. 2, p. 24; italics supplied).

Talking about a blank check! When you pray for the Holy Spirit, you get *Jesus* plus "every want supplied." What more could we ask for!

Factor in the passionate mission of God's chosen—to communicate the truth about Jesus to every nation, kindred, tribe, and people in every time zone—and it really isn't rocket science to figure out why our community of faith ought to join together for this single prayer request.

Do the arithmetic. Every second on earth four babies are born and two humans die. That's a net growth to our population of two per second, or 1 million every six days, or 60 million every year. Which means that while we're still struggling to reach our next-door neighbors, the global population is exploding by a million a week! Who's going to reach them?

Let's face it. If we factor in our frail human realities, there is no way the chosen will ever be up to God's mission. Period. *Unless* the promise of our text today proves true—what human might and ecclesiastical power can never accomplish can in fact be done "'by My Spirit,' says the Lord of hosts!" No wonder the chosen are called to unite around a single prayer petition: "O God, have mercy on us in our weakness and fill us with the mighty Holy Spirit, so that *our* impossibilities might be transformed into *Your* glorious possibilities through Christ. Amen."

ASLEEP FOR 16 YEARS

Then the kingdom of heaven shall be likened to ten virgins who took their lamps and went out to meet the bridegroom. . . . But while the bridegroom was delayed, they all slumbered and slept. Matt. 25:1-5.

Dateline: Albuquerque, New Mexico. For 16 years 42-year-old Patricia White Bull had slept without a moment of consciousness. Doctors were unable to explain why she slipped into that catatonic state while delivering her fourth child. Over the ensuing years her husband and children came and went, but Patricia slept on. Until suddenly on Christmas Eve (true story) she awakened. You can imagine the wild joy of that reunion! We could write the headline: "Woman Asleep for Years Awakens and Comes Back to Life."

Isn't that the headline of Jesus' parable of the 10 virgins? As our text today indicates, all 10 of them fell asleep while awaiting the coming of the bridegroom. And so it wasn't the sleeping that determined whether they were wise or foolish. In Jesus' story it was the oil or the lack thereof that categorized the young women. The wise ones had carefully stored up the precious fuel, while the foolish ones had forgotten to bring extra. And when the Bridegroom suddenly returned, the foolish were left in the dark with no oil to light their way.

Middle East oil—the one precious commodity the whole world thirsts for! But oil in the Scriptures is often a graphic symbol of the Holy Spirit. He's the fuel of divine fire, the balm of divine anointing. And when your lamp—or life—is filled with Him, the bright flame of God's love radiates from you into the surrounding darkness.

The good news is we don't have to be caught without His oil as the foolish were. "The lapse of time has wrought no change in Christ's parting promise to send the Holy Spirit as His representative. It is not because of any restriction on the part of God that the riches of His grace do not flow earthward to [us]. . . . *If all were willing, all would be filled with the Spirit*" (*The Acts of the Apostles*, p. 50; italics supplied). There it is again—this Gift is ours for the *asking.* Even when the church around you seems sound asleep, don't despair. You don't have to wait until the final outpouring of the latter rain to be filled with the Spirit. Throw wide the doors to your heart and life right now, give yourself wholly to Jesus—the Gift is yours— you'll be filled. Who knows? *You* may be the Spirit-filled one God will use to awaken your church with *"The Bridegroom is coming!"*

PORCUPINES OR ROSE?

Peter was therefore kept in prison, but constant prayer was offered to God for him by the church. . . . Many were gathered together praying [for him]. Acts 12:5-12.

Someone has quipped that the church is like a pack of porcupines huddled for warmth in a blizzard. The closer we draw together, the more we keep pricking each other! Perhaps we ought to become like the Church of the Rose.

I love the story, the one about Peter sleeping away his last night on earth. Tomorrow morning King Herod is going to have him beheaded, yet Peter sleeps. Such is the faith of that friend of Jesus. Then suddenly an angel of God materializes inside the prison cell. Peter's guard snores on while the angel "strikes" Peter (no time for gentle tapping when you've got to go!). Now awake, and without chains, Peter jumps to his feet as the angel, with a finger to his lips, beckons him to follow. Past sleeping sentry after sentry after sentry they walk, while doors mysteriously open and close. *I must be dreaming,* Peter thinks. But the cool night air of the Jerusalem street convinces him that he really is free. Angel gone, Peter hurries to his friends.

He knocks as loudly as he dares. Finally a woman's voice. It's Rhoda ("rose" in Greek), the servant girl. But so flabbergasted is she that she leaves Peter in the dark while she races back to the church in prayer with the news their prayers are answered. Nobody believes her. But the knocking is persistent, until *finally* somebody opens the door! The End.

Do you know why the whole world knows about Rhoda? Because she was at a prayer meeting. Her only claim to fame, think about it, was that she was attending prayer meeting that Wednesday evening. Are you known for the same reason?

All this talk about praying for the Holy Spirit—but what's the point of praying alone? Sure, we're busy—on the job, at the school, around the house—who isn't? You don't think they were busy in Jerusalem? "Yes, but they had an urgent life-or-death need to be praying about." Don't we? Aren't we living on the edge of eternity right now, with tens of thousands of lives hovering between life and death? Doesn't our city, our little congregation need the collective praying of its men, women, young adults, teens, and children? What if the Church of the Rose had been too prickly to draw together and hadn't gathered to pray for Peter?

How much of history has been rewritten because God's people drew together to pray?

CANDLES IN THE DARK

And Jehoshaphat feared, and set himself to seek the Lord, and proclaimed a fast through-out all Judah. So Judah gathered together to ask help from the Lord; and from all the cities of Judah they came to seek the Lord. 2 Chron. 20:3, 4.

I was flying back from preaching in South Africa. Our plane was delayed in Johannesburg, so we didn't take off until 1:00 a.m. There are some barren stretches of midnight on that sub-Saharan part of the continent, pitch-black when you gaze down. But every now and then, from out of nowhere it seemed, there would suddenly appear the orange grid of a sprawling urban center somewhere in the African night. Black night, orange light.

You and I can attempt our pilgrimage to the Promised Land by ourselves, one lonely little candle to light up the night. But with a night as dark and foreboding as the midnight that now slowly steals across earth's last horizon, don't you think that this might be the right time for the chosen to bring their candles together, to become an orange grid of light in this dark?

"What is needed in this, our time of danger, is fervent prayer, mingled with earnest faith, a reliance upon God when Satan casts his shadow over God's people. Let everyone bear in mind that *God delights to listen to the supplications of His people*; for the prevailing iniquity calls for *more earnest prayer*" (*Selected Messages*, book 2, p. 372; italics supplied).

Can't get the whole church to come out to prayer meeting? Not to worry. There are surely seven or eight others like you who would be willing to band their candles together one night a week for a few minutes of singing, Bible studying, and praying. Can't sing? Then just study and pray. Can't study? But you can pray. And imagine the orange prayer grid that your collective candles will shine into the gathering darkness of this hour!

Jehoshaphat and Judah faced a fierce advancing enemy. What should they do in the face of the gathering darkness? As our text describes, the leader called his people to prayer meeting, and they came, young and aged, from far and wide. "We know [not] what to do," the king pleaded before God, "but our eyes are upon You" (verse 12). Who better to fasten our eyes upon in the night than the Almighty One? Twelve of you, seven of you, four of you, two of you—find somebody, won't you please, with whom to join candles? Let us band together to call upon the Light of the world on behalf of this night of the world.

THE BEST GIFT FOR YOUR PASTOR

Pray also for me, that whenever I open my mouth, words may be given me so that I will fearlessly make known the mystery of the gospel, for which I am an ambassador in chains. Pray that I may declare it fearlessly, as I should. Eph. 6:19, 20, NIV.

I discovered the secret quite by accident, and had it not been for that dear white-haired saint, I probably wouldn't be having this conversation with you. Her name was Ina Mae White, and one Sabbath after church she took my hands, looked into my eyes, and announced, "Pastor, I'm praying for you." As it turned out, she had been for some time. I'd never asked her to pray for me. It wasn't her ministry assignment at the church. Apparently the Spirit one day simply tapped her on the shoulder, and she obeyed by praying for her pastor.

Soon I began to call her (her phone number is still locked in my mind) with specific prayer needs. If I had an out-of-town preaching assignment, I called Ina Mae to request her prayer cover, telling her the time zone I'd be in and the times I'd be preaching.

And along the way, Ina Mae gathered a group of prayer partners together to pray for their pastor every Sabbath morning while he was preaching. And I could sense within me the power difference their intercessions were making. She was praying, they were praying, and all God was doing was answering their faith-filled prayers. And I tell you the truth—this pastor was all the better for their selfless ministry.

Trust me. Your pastor deeply needs your intercession. If you can't think of another human being in the world to put on your prayer list, please scribble down the name of your pastor. We are in a war, and the battle is only intensifying. For reasons known best by the enemy, it is more than apparent he has marked every spiritual leader for concerted attack. Take the leader, conquer the people—that diabolical strategy is as old as the world.

Which is why Paul was unapologetic about soliciting his congregations to pray for him. "Pray also for me [that is, you have much else to be praying for, but please include me], that whenever I open my mouth, words may be given me so that I will fearlessly make known the mystery of the gospel." For there is no more potent and influential a gift that a congregation can give to their shepherd than the pledge "I'm praying for you." Ina Mae sleeps in Jesus today. But He knows, and so do I, that the influence of her prayers will never perish.

"COVER ME AS I GO IN!"

For we are not fighting against flesh-and-blood enemies, but against evil rulers and authorities of the unseen world, against mighty powers in this dark world, and against evil spirits in the heavenly places. Eph. 6:12, NLT.

John Wayne was hardly the paragon of virtue. But that line he yelled over his back as he ducked and ran straight toward the outlaw's blazing hideout is the truth about praying for your pastor. "Cover me as I go in!"

The apostle, pastor, evangelist, and preacher Paul could hardly have been clearer. Bullets whizzing, ricocheting all around us, we are—all of us—pinned down in the crossfire and crosshairs of an unseen enemy, "evil spirits in the heavenly places," as our text describes them. But Paul knew there were those times when crossfire notwithstanding, it fell his lot to scramble to his feet and "go in" on behalf of the cause and the kingdom he served. "Pray for me" simply meant "Cover me as I go in." For in the fire power of collective prayer cover, Paul knew there was shielding protection and enabling power.

Garrie Williams, in his devotional book *Welcome, Holy Spirit*, tells the story of the great Scottish preacher James Stewart, who was in a large European city prior to World War II preaching a revival series. The meetings began with only seven people on a Friday evening, but in five days had skyrocketed to thousands in an auditorium, with large numbers being converted. Stewart was astounded! One evening before preaching, feeling utterly inadequate for the challenge of proclaiming the gospel to the huge crowd who had gathered, he went down to the basement to earnestly petition God. While praying in the darkness he sensed a presence of power, and realizing he was not alone, switched on the light. In the far corner, on their faces before God, were 12 women. And in an instant the preacher knew from whence came the supernatural outpouring.

There isn't a pastor or preacher alive who doesn't know from whence comes that power. And that is why on behalf of your pastor I earnestly appeal to you to keep on your knees for her, for him, for their spouses and children. Only eternity will fully disclose the shielding protection and enabling power that the Spirit unleashed, all because you took the time to daily pray for your pastor.

Thank you.

"ONE IS THE LONELIEST NUMBER"

And the Lord said, "Simon, Simon! Indeed, Satan has asked for you, that he may sift you as wheat. But I have prayed for you." Luke 22:31, 32.

Nobody should have to go through life all alone. Years ago an old song crooned, "One is the loneliest number that you'll ever do." And it's true, isn't it? While later this year we'll explore God's call to community among the chosen, right now ponder for a moment the joyful blessing of having and being a prayer partner. Do you have one?

More than a decade ago a professor of English, Joseph Warren, walked into my life uninvited, and I've thanked God ever since. He had taken it upon himself to pray for the preacher in a global satellite event called NET '98. And as those five weeks wore on, I began to find written prayers under my church office door. They were from Joe, who with Bible in hand would pound them out on his computer at the office or home. The very act of reading them lifted my spirits and energized my soul.

But it wasn't until after the evangelistic dust had settled that I got to know this prayer partner stranger. Turns out we were very different—different races, different careers, different congregations, different styles. But we also discovered that we shared much in common—same Savior, same faith community, same values, same gender, similar passions, similar kids and spouses (except for where they're different!). And thus was birthed a prayer partnership that has become a personal friendship. We've prayed for each other in times of joy and times of crisis. We've lifted up our voices in each other's presence (and while we're apart) for our kids, our wives, our university, our denomination, our leaders, our personal needs and private wrestlings.

I know of no book on how to be a prayer partner. But we have a divine-human example. When Jesus looked into Peter's eyes that late Thursday night and reminded him, "I'm praying for you," our Lord modeled the prevailing rule for prayer partners—*you pray for each other.* Good news for the soon-to-be-fallen Peter—he had Someone praying for him.

And good news for whoever it is that the Spirit of Jesus will lead you to. Can't think of anyone? Why don't you ask your heavenly Prayer Partner to lead you to someone with whom you can share the journey for a while. Not only will your own spiritual experience be enriched, but you may be the very answer somebody else has been praying for. Just like Jesus.

RULES OF ENGAGEMENT

I said to the Lord: "You are my God; hear the voice of my supplications, O Lord. O God the Lord, the strength of my salvation, You have covered my head in the day of battle." Ps. 140:6, 7.

Living as we do with the constant headlines of what they keep calling this "global war on terror," the whole notion of war (sadly enough) has become an everyday reality. And we don't need the military "talking heads" on television to tell us about "rules of engagement," those tacitly understood principles that guide "civilized" fighting (another sad oxymoron).

As it turns out, the cosmic spiritual war that has engulfed this planet and every one of us abides by apparent rules of engagement, too. One of them is crucial to an understanding of why we must persist in praying for others.

"The same compassionate Savior lives today, and He is as willing to listen to the prayer of faith as when He walked visibly among men. The natural cooperates with the supernatural. *It is a part of God's plan to grant us, in answer to the prayer of faith, that which He would not bestow did we not thus ask*" (*The Great Controversy*, p. 525; italics supplied). Or to put it another way: God can't intervene when He hasn't been invited.

In the conflict between the kingdoms of light and darkness, both forces honor human freedom of choice, or rather, one honors and the other complies, since the devil would in an instant attempt to force us against our choice were God not binding him to this rule of engagement. But because of free choice, God Himself may not intervene in a life that clearly has chosen to reject Him. Were He to do so, the guardian demon would immediately howl protest!

It is for that reason that intercessory prayer is so strategic for God's kingdom. For while it is true that God cannot answer a prayer that is not prayed—and clearly, the resistant one is *not* praying for intervention—He can certainly respond to someone else's prayer on behalf of that recalcitrant soul. To the demonic protest all God need reply is "I have come to this child at the behest of her mother, who is a friend of Mine." Free choice is still being guarded, but Love is now granted permission (as it were) through the prayerful intercessions of another.

The point? With prayer lists in hand, we must keep on our knees. *Do not quit.* Your intercessions may be the one green light God's been needing to win back that life for eternity.

THE LAW OF THE MIRROR

And all of us, with unveiled faces, seeing the glory of the Lord as though reflected in a mirror, are being transformed into the same image from one degree of glory to another.
2 Cor. 3:18, NRSV.

Before we leave the theme of the heart—or the prayer life—of the chosen, consider the law of the mirror.

I grew up a preacher's kid, which meant that we had to have worship every morning before racing off to school. (Nobody *has* to have morning family worship, of course, but looking back over the years, I'm now grateful we did.) My dad would often travel in Japan, and so Mom would be the one to gather us three kids together and read from a Morning Watch book (not unlike this one). But for a third grader even a short devotional can seem too long. Until the day I discovered my wristwatch could reflect the sun streaming through the window. Amazingly, if I positioned my wrist just right I could move a small golden ball of light all around the room—and straight into Greg's or Kari's eyes. No boredom now! Until Mother discovered my sudden enthusiasm and nixed all the fun.

Mirrors are that way, aren't they? A mirror reflects what you point it at—that's the law of the mirror. And that's the point of Paul's observation in our text today. Just like a mirror, we gaze into the glory of God and it reflects from our faces, our lives. "We all reflect as in a mirror the splendor of the Lord" is how *The New English Bible* renders it. The law of the mirror.

And where shall we go to seek God's glory? Just a few verses later Paul answers: "For God, who said, 'Let light shine out of darkness,' made his light shine in our hearts to give us the light of the knowledge of *the glory of God in the face of Christ*" (2 Cor. 4:6, NIV).

And that is where the chosen must go morning after morning, day after day—to the gospels, to the place where the face of Jesus shines bright with the glory of God. And there alone with Him in our prayer closets, we can get our mirrors readjusted (so sensitive and easily knocked from their focus by our sins), so that we might go forth into the day, by the grace of God, flooding our world with the glory of Jesus reflecting from our mirrors.

Just a tiny mirror, to be sure, but point it toward the Son, and the whole room lights up.

THAT OUR WIRES MIGHT BE CROSSED

My voice You shall hear in the morning,
O Lord; in the morning I will direct it to You, and I will look up. Ps. 5:3.

For one last reflection on prayer, consider this stirring paragraph: "Consecrate yourself to God in the morning; make this your very first work. Let your prayer be, 'Take me, O Lord, as wholly [Yours]. I lay all my plans at [Your] feet. Use me today in [Your] service. Abide with me, and let all my work be [shaped] in [You].' This is a daily matter. Each morning consecrate yourself to God for that day. Surrender all your plans to Him, to be carried out or given up as His providence shall indicate. Thus day by day you may be giving your life into the hands of God, and thus your life will be molded more and more after the life of Christ" (*Steps to Christ*, p. 70; italics supplied).

Why the morning? Because even if you're hopelessly a night owl, what better way to begin the new day than by drawing into God's presence the very first thing? And why that sample morning prayer about laying all our plans at His feet? Because what more significant commitment can we make than offering all of our waking hours and thoughts to His lordship?

Can you imagine a little community of God's chosen closeted with Jesus first thing in the day, and then fanning out over their village or city under His direct guidance through the Spirit? Imagine the town so blessed!

When we were pastoring in Salem, Oregon, something embarrassing happened to our telephone. We started getting the heavy metal rock station's music playing on our phone line. And I knew the saints calling were concluding they'd caught the pastor listening to such music, because no matter how I raised my voice, you could still hear the heart-thumping rock music in the background. I called the phone company. They tried everything. Then one day the music was gone. The technician reported that in laying new wires, the phone company had inadvertently placed them too close to the power lines of the radio station. So close, in fact, that the power of the one spilled over into the other, so that when they dialed our number they got the station, too.

Isn't that the secret to the heart of the chosen—getting so close to the Power that when people dial their numbers they get Jesus? "And they took note that these men and women had been with Jesus" (Acts 4:13, NIV). Then what do you say, we all get our wires crossed with Jesus!

A VIEW FROM OUTER SPACE

In the beginning God created the heavens and the earth. Gen. 1:1.

On Christmas Eve 1968 the three astronauts aboard the *Apollo 8* spacecraft peered out their cockpit windows onto the blue-green terrestrial ball in the far distance. And in a live transmission heard around the world they quoted the most recognized line in all of ancient Scripture: "In the beginning God created the heavens and the earth." Seven words in the Hebrew, 10 words in the English, this solitary line has become *the prologue to all divine revelation and the premise for all human faith.*

Richard Dawkins, the celebrated atheist biologist, is right. Either the heavens and the earth in the beginning were created by God or they were not. There is not a third option, a middle ground.

Hence there are only two worldviews when it comes to the origin of the universe. In one worldview random nature rules supreme. It is called *naturalism*. Charles Darwin's *Origin of Species* is its most widely circulated advocate, and atheism is its resulting philosophy. In the other worldview (the oldest) the divine Creator rules supreme. It is called *supernaturalism*. The Holy Scripture is its most widely circulated advocate, and theism is its resulting philosophy. There is no third worldview regarding origins. Either God created the universe or He did not—either He exists or He does not.

Genesis 1:1 declares that the worldview of a divine Creator is the *only* authentic expression of reality in this universe. That means the human saga is not the tale of humankind inventing God (as our atheist friends suggest), but rather the shining saga of God creating man and woman in His own rational image that together they might share the divine-human friendship on a very pristine and perfect garden planet.

"In the beginning God . . ." because when it comes to this planet you have to start somewhere. Not wanting to start there, Richard Dawkins entitled his bestseller *The God Delusion*. But in relegating God to a figment of the human imagination or longing, Dawkins leaves his readers with nothing but the sheer grit of human survival and the fickle luck of a random selection. Given the choice of Dawkins and Genesis, it's no wonder the majority of earth still chooses God.

GOD'S ELECTRIC BILL

Where were you when I laid the foundations of the earth . . . when the morning stars sang together, and all the sons of God shouted for joy? Job 38:4-7.

Penny Dawson, from Weatherford, Texas, knew that the utility bills had been going up. But this high? Yet there it was when she tore open the envelope, her bill for $24,200,700,004 (that's right, 24 *billion* plus)! Turns out 1,300 other utility customers also got bills for more than a billion dollars each. Turn off the lights!

What if God decided to bill us for living on *His* planet? After all, He's both the Creator and Sustainer. He keeps the lights on, the earth spinning, the air fresh, and the waters clean (except for where we've polluted them), the plants growing, the birds singing, and all creatures reproducing. What if we got a bill from our Creator? But who could pay it!

The truth is that this blue-green planet suspended in the solar system off to the edge of the Milky Way Galaxy is a gift from God to His earth children. No, not to exploit, ravage, and destroy. The planet and its delicate ecosystem are a divine gift for His human friends, a bestowal of love, an inheritance of grace, to cherish and nurture all our days.

"Upon all created things is seen the impress of the Deity. Nature testifies of God. The susceptible mind, brought in contact with the miracle and mystery of the universe, cannot but recognize the working of infinite power. Not by its own inherent energy does the earth produce its bounties, and year by year continue its motion around the sun. An unseen hand guides the planets in their circuit of the heavens. A mysterious life pervades all nature—a life that sustains the unnumbered worlds throughout immensity, that lives in the insect atom which floats in the summer breeze, that wings the flight of the swallow and feeds the young ravens which cry, that brings the bud to blossom and the flower to fruit" (*Education*, p. 99).

No wonder a meandering walk through a city park or a quiet pause beneath the midnight stars can become an act of worship. And with bowed heart we shall surely acknowledge, as Maltbie Babcock did: "This is my Father's world, and to my listening ears, all nature sings, and round me rings the music of the spheres. This is my Father's world; I rest me in the thought of rocks and trees, of skies and seas; His hand the wonders wrought" (*The SDA Hymnal*, no. 92).

"Worship Him who made heaven and earth, the sea and springs of waters" (Rev. 14:7).

A READER'S DIGEST CREATION

By the word of the Lord the heavens were made, and all the host of them by the breath of His mouth. . . . For He spoke, and it was done; He commanded, and it stood fast. Ps. 33:6-9.

Genesis 1 is the majestic narrative of the Creator moving closer and closer to His new earth children. So let's hurry to that glorious climax by sharing a *Reader's Digest*-type condensation of the Creation account (you can read the entire chapter at your leisure, of course). You remember each day ends with the Hebrew formula "evening was, morning was, day ___." The Hebrew word for "day" is *yôm*, which, when attached to a numeral (as it is 150 times in the Old Testament), *always* (except for Zech. 14.7) refers to a 24-hour period of time. So here goes:

24-hour Day One—God created light.
24-hour Day Two—God created atmosphere.
24-hour Day Three—God created land and vegetation.
24-hour Day Four—God created the sun and solar system.
24-hour Day Five—God created fish for the waters and birds for the air.
24-hour Day Six—God created mammals for the land.

And then in a climaxing act of very personal creation, the Creator stoops down and with His own divine hands shapes the first two of a new order of race, a male and a female human being, in whose combination is the very image of the Creator Himself.

And how did the reviews read at the end of those six days of Creation? "Then God saw everything that He had made, and indeed it was *very good*" (Gen. 1:31). You've done that, haven't you? Finished rebuilding an engine, completed a culinary masterpiece, or put the final brushstroke on that canvas—and then you stepped back with a big smile of satisfaction. "This is good—very good!"

Maybe the atheist astronomer Carl Sagan was right. "A religion, old or new, that stressed the magnificence of the Universe as revealed by modern science might be able to draw forth reserves of reverence and awe hardly tapped by the conventional faiths" (quoted in Richard Dawkins, *The God Delusion*, p. 33). Maybe we creationists *have* lost the awe of reverence for the Creator's breathtaking handiwork. But maybe if we recaptured it, those who do not believe might yet find in that shared reverence a step closer to the unnoticed Creator.

A PARENT'S VERY BEST GIFT

Thus the heavens and the earth, and all the host of them, were finished. And on the seventh day God ended His work which He had done, and He rested on the seventh day from all His work which He had done. Gen. 2:1, 2.

Think about it. God could have chosen a six-day week, couldn't He? And why not? In a perfect garden no one really gets tired, so who needs a rest? Or the Creator could have chosen an annual celebration of the world's birthday, just as we do for our own—"Let's have a party!" Or He could have chosen a monthly festival to commemorate His creation. But clearly there is a longing in the heart of the Creator that cannot be put off for a year or even a month. And so, for the human race, He celebrates the weekly seventh day as the divine gift day. Why?

Think about it some more. What is the most perfect gift that any loving parent can give his or her child? Isn't it the gift of uninterrupted, unhurried *time* together? Think back to when you were a kid. What is it you remember most? Some toy your dad gave you? Or the time your father gave to you?

My dad was a preacher. And when we were living on the west coast of Japan, at the foot of the Japan Alps, he was planting a church in a large city with hardly a Christian in it. That meant he was busy night and day. But one night he came home and announced to the family that he'd been thinking about it, and had decided that he was going to take every Tuesday off from henceforth. Since we were homeschooled, that meant that on Tuesdays in the spring, summer, and fall we'd pack a picnic lunch and head out to the beach or go for a bike ride or visit a museum. But in the winter it meant that every Tuesday we'd get up early, pack a lunch, travel by car and train high into the Alps and spend a glorious day skiing together. Now that my father is dead, I look back wistfully across the years that have passed and realize that he gave to us kids the very best gift of all. He didn't give money— he didn't have much. He didn't give toys—we were rather poor. He gave something even better—the gift of uninterrupted, unhurried time with him. The very same gift our Creator Father gives to you and me—24 hours of uninterrupted, unhurried time with Him—every seventh day.

Which leaves me with two questions: why would anyone ever want to get rid of the seventh-day Sabbath? And why would we ever want the Sabbath to be over?

THE THREE-ACT PLAY—1

Then God blessed the seventh day and sanctified it, because in it He rested from all His work which God had created and made. Gen. 2:3.

Act One—God *blessed* the seventh day.

Did you know that when God blesses something or someone, His posture assumes a very certain stance? You remember the famous benediction: "The Lord bless you and keep you; the Lord make his face shine upon you and be gracious to you; the Lord turn his face toward you and give you peace" (Num. 6:24-26, NIV). When God blesses you, what is His posture? "May God be gracious to us and bless us and make his face shine upon us" (Ps. 67:1, NIV). Clearly when God blesses something or someone, He turns *His face* toward it to give it His full attention.

You and I are the same way, aren't we? Remember your first car? Mine was a brand-new 11-year-old 1961 Volkswagen Beetle with a flaky green paint job, oversized rear tires, and a rusted, holey muffler. But I couldn't take my eyes off of it. Why? Because when something is of great value to you, you love to look at it. Husbands and wives know all about that: even after all those anniversaries, or especially *because* of all those anniversaries, you look across a crowded room and spot her, an epiphany of beauty that holds your gaze. Why? Because when someone is of great value to you, you love to look at her.

And "God blessed the seventh day." In those familiar words rich with meaning, He does something to that day that He does not do to any other day of the week. He turns His face toward the seventh day and with that divine benediction gives to the seventh day His full attention. It is the *only* day of the week that the Creator gazes upon with such rapt attention. For it is His gift to the chosen, and on it He and they will celebrate their friendship and love as on no other day of the week.

Which is why, for the life of me, I cannot imagine how anybody could come along and announce that this unique face-turning, gaze-holding blessing of God has been removed from the seventh day and transferred to another day. Especially since there is not a solitary hint of such a removal or transfer in all of Holy Scripture.

"*This* is the day the Lord has made; we will rejoice and be glad in it" (Ps. 118: 24).

THE THREE-ACT PLAY—2

Then God blessed the seventh day and sanctified it, because in it He rested from all His work which God had created and made. Gen. 2:3.

Act Two—God *sanctified* the seventh day.

Who doesn't love the story of the burning bush? The 80-year-old shepherd with that bleating flock at his heels thought he'd seen it all. But there in the middle of the rocky, barren wilderness is a fresh green bush enveloped in leaping orange flames—and still fresh and green! Moses strides over to that unsettling oddity and is about to thrust his staff into the crackling roar, when a Voice thunders: "Take off your shoes, for you are on *holy* ground!" Question: what made that burning bush holy? Answer: the very presence and glory of God.

Months later this same Moses, now the mighty deliverer of the children of Israel from Egypt, leads them back into this same wilderness. And the God of the burning bush took up residence, as it were, in a portable animal-skin tabernacle they called the sanctuary. On the day Israel dedicated their brand-new "church," a glory so bright and explosive filled that tent that not even Moses was able to enter the sanctuary. Question: what made that tent holy? Answer: the very presence and glory of God.

So when this same Moses describes this same God at the beginning of time "sanctifying" the seventh-day Sabbath, he uses the same Hebrew root word for "holy" at the burning bush and the sanctuary. Genesis 2:3 could literally read, "And God *holy-ized* the seventh day." In fact, *The Message* renders it "He made it a Holy Day." Thus the first object in Creation history that God declared holy was time. God made the seventh day a holy day (or "holi-day").

What makes something holy? It becomes infused with the very presence and glory of God. That means God is not only present *on* the Sabbath—He is also present *in* the Sabbath day. Which being interpreted means that on the seventh-day Sabbath, God is not the guest of the human race—the human race is the guest of God! God's very presence *in* the seventh day makes the Sabbath both *holy* and *wholly* His.

How then could anybody rise up and declare that God's holy presence has been removed from the seventh day and transferred to another day, without a solitary hint in all of Holy Scripture? "*This* is the day the Lord has made. We will rejoice and be glad in it!"

THE THREE-ACT PLAY—3

Then God blessed the seventh day and sanctified it, because in it He rested from all His work which God had created and made. Gen. 2:3.

Act Three—God *rested* on the seventh day.

Remember those nights when you were asleep before your head hit the pillow? It happened as a kid, it happens as an adult. Let's face it: sometimes we're so utterly spent there is nothing more glorious and satisfying than a feather pillow, a good warm comforter, and sleep!

Was it that way for God? Was He so fatigued and wearied after six long, grueling days of having to create this brand-new planet that He could hardly wait to crawl into the bed of the Sabbath to sleep? Hardly! "The everlasting God, the Lord, the Creator of the ends of the earth, neither faints nor is weary" (Isa. 40:28) reminds us that our infinite and omnipotent God doesn't need a snooze to recover from weariness. So why then would He have to have a Sabbath rest? (The Hebrew for "rest" is *shabbath,* from whence comes our word "Sabbath.")

On this weekend when the Christian world celebrates the death and resurrection of our Lord Jesus, let's go to the Passion story, because there are some remarkable parallels between earth's creation and Calvary's re-creation:

Parallel 1. Our Creator and our Redeemer are the same one. Genesis 1, John 1, Colossians 1, and Hebrews 1 declare the truth that the God who created us in the beginning is the same one who died for us in the end. No wonder He is such a friend!

Parallel 2. Christ ended both His creation of the world and His salvation of the world with the same triumphant conclusion: "It is finished!" (Gen. 2:1; John 19:30). Day 6 of Creation week and Day 6 of the Passion Week both end with the pronouncement of God's finished work. We cannot, we need not, add an iota to the completed gift of Christ's salvation. Hallelujah!

Parallel 3. And what did the Creator and Redeemer do when He finished His work on the sixth day? *He rested on the seventh day in a garden.* The Sacred Record could not be clearer. Christ, our Creator in life and our Savior in death, *rested* on His Sabbath day. He who is Lord of the Sabbath (Mark 2:28) became He who is Lord of salvation—and when He died on that Good Friday long ago, He kept the seventh-day Sabbath and rested. Proof enough that the Sabbath is a *forever* gift from our Forever *Friend.* Let us worship Him with joy!

THE MAN IN THE CASKET

On the evening of that first day of the week, when the disciples were together, with the doors locked for fear of the Jews, Jesus came and stood among them and said, "Peace be with you!" John 20:19, NIV.

In the little Chilean village of Angol, the family and friends of 81-year-old Feliberto Carrasco gathered for his wake. There in the mortuary memories and tears flowed freely over their beloved father, grandfather, and uncle, now dressed in his finest suit and lying still in his casket. One of his nephews sat to the side of the room as the crowd mingled. He looked to where his uncle was lying. And for some reason it seemed as if his uncle were looking back at him. "I couldn't believe it," he later told the local newspaper. "I thought I must be mistaken, and I shut my eyes. When I opened them again, my uncle was [still] looking at me. I started to cry and ran to get something to open the coffin to get him out."

And get him out they did! When the 81-year-old gentleman was helped out of the casket to the cheers and tears of his shocked family and friends, he quietly asked for a glass of *agua* (water). Later the local radio station announced a correction to Carrasco's death, saying the news had been premature!

Imagine the raw fear turned to wild joy in the upper room when Jesus suddenly materialized in the midst of His grieving friends! Though His first word was "Shalom," Luke's account is clear: "But they were terrified and frightened, and supposed they had seen a spirit" (Luke 24:37). Because earth's children know the bitter truth—dead people don't come back to life again. Hence we live with the numinous fear of our own impending demise.

But the God of creation became the Lord of salvation, and when He cried His expiring words—"It is finished!"—the universe knew, if not the world, that a permanent antidote to the satanic poison of death had at last been found. "Since the children have flesh and blood, he too shared in their humanity so that by his death he might destroy him who holds the power of death—that is, the devil—and free those who all their lives were held in slavery by their fear of death" (Heb. 2:14, 15, NIV). Because of Christ's resurrection—pass the word, will you?—death "is finished," really, truly finished, which can only mean that the ones we have deeply loved and tenderly buried will also come forth from their caskets and urns, just as Carrasco and Christ did.

THE TRUTH OF THE SKELETON

Remember the Sabbath day, to keep it holy. . . . For in six days the Lord made the heavens and the earth, the sea, and all that is in them, and rested the seventh day. Therefore the Lord blessed the Sabbath day and hallowed it. Ex. 20:8-11.

Imagine the human skeleton hanging in the biology class—all 206 bones of him or her. Do you know how many different ways 206 parts can be connected? If there were only one part, it would be $1 \times 1 = 1$. Two parts would be $1 \times 2 = 2$. Three parts, $1 \times 2 \times 3 = 6$. You get the picture. Do that for 206 different parts, and the answer is a gigantic 10^{388}, or a 1 followed by 388 zeroes! That's how many different ways a 206-part skeleton can be assembled, and only one of those ways is the correct way.

So what are the chances it all got assembled by random chance? Jerry Bergman, whose second Ph.D. is in human biology, explores that in an essay in *In Six Days* (ed. John Ashton). If we could randomly rearrange those 206 bones once every second "for every single second available in all of the estimated evolutionary view of astronomic time (about 10 to 20 billion years) . . . the chances that the correct general position will be obtained by random is *less than once in 10 billion years*" (p. 26). And that's just the skeleton. Factor in the 75 trillion cells we have in our bodies (10 billion of them in our cerebral cortex alone), keeping in mind that each cell is composed of myriad basic parts and multimillions of complex proteins and parts, and we are left with "a zero possibility" that the human skeleton, let alone the body, could have randomly evolved (p. 27). In other words, it is *statistically impossible* for a human being to be assembled through natural selection, even with a 20-billion-year lead time!

Carved into stone with the divine finger are these words of the fourth commandment: "For in six days the Lord made the heavens and the earth, the sea, and all that is in them, and rested the seventh day. Therefore the Lord blessed the Sabbath day and hallowed it."

The late Stephen Jay Gould concluded that humans are a "glorious evolutionary accident which required 60 trillion contingent events" (p. 28). No, declares the divine record in stone, we are no glorious accident at all. We are an order of beings personally created and chosen by the God of the universe, created and chosen to become His friends.

So that we would never forget, He gave us the Sabbath. No wonder He says "remember."

THE TWIN SISTER

For in six days the Lord made the heavens, the earth, the sea, and everything in them; but on the seventh day he rested. That is why the Lord blessed the Sabbath day and set it apart as holy. Ex. 20:11, NLT.

Have you ever known identical twins? Most of us have. What an amazing creation they are! You look at one, and you think of the other. You call for one, and you get them both. And when they're dressed alike? Help us all!

It may come as a surprise to you to learn that the Sabbath has a twin sister. And no, she's not Friday or Sunday. Who is she? In tracking time on this planet, we humans have turned to the skies for our clock. We calculated earth's long journey around the sun, and called that a year. We measured the moon's journey around the earth and we called it a "moonth," or month. We calibrated a single rotation of earth on its axis and declared that to be a 24-hour day. And what did we track, what celestial movement did we calibrate in order to devise our week? Nothing. There is no astronomical (or astrological) evidence for our septenary unit of time, the seven-day week.

As Robert Odom insightfully observed: "The week of seven days is not a natural division of time, and is not related to the movements of any of the heavenly bodies. The creation record of Genesis, the decalogue, and the Mosaic law clearly show that it was originally a divinely established institution and is *a twin sister of the Sabbath*" (*Sunday in Roman Paganism*, p. 241; italics supplied).

Both the Creation account in Genesis and the fourth commandment in Exodus reveal a sacred bond between the seven-day week and the seventh-day Sabbath. Logically, the only reason for the septenary week was so that the human race might keep track of the seventh-day Sabbath and their weekly appointment with their Creator. For "the seventh day is the Sabbath of the Lord your God" (Ex. 20:10). So it should come as no surprise that the serpent turned dragon would vent his diabolical fury against both divine gifts of time—no surprise that eventually the seven-day week became named after the gods of astrology, no surprise that his counterfeit sabbath would be named after the sun god. All because it's no surprise that the God of the chosen would choose a day just for them. And Him. At the end of every single week.

WHAT WOULD JESUS DO?

[Jesus] went to Nazareth, where he had been brought up, and on the Sabbath day he went into the synagogue, as was his custom. Luke 4:16, NIV.

Charles Sheldon's *In His Steps* is a century-old best-selling classic. It's the story about a pastor named Henry Maxwell and his congregation, the First Church of Raymond. One bright morning, just as the pastor concluded his sermon, a homeless man stumbled down the aisle of First Church, looked up at the pastor in his pulpit, and asked if he might address the congregation. The startled pastor deferred to the stranger with a nod. The man turned to face the worshippers, and with a halting voice he told of losing his job in another city 10 months earlier. For the past three days he had wandered the sidewalks of Raymond in search of employment. But he'd received not even a word of sympathy from some of the faces in church this morning. "I've been sitting in your balcony while your pastor preached about following Jesus. But what do you mean? What would Jesus do? Is that what it means to follow in His steps?"

The beggar staggered and then collapsed at the front of the church. A few days later, in the parsonage, he died. Charles Sheldon then weaves the inspiring story of a congregation that struggled to find and know the answer to the beggar's question, "What would Jesus do?"

These days people wear WWJD wristbands with that query. Nevertheless, it's still a fair question to ask when it comes to the seventh-day Sabbath, isn't it? What would Jesus do?

In today's text Luke observes that Jesus worshipped on the Sabbath "as was his custom." Everybody has personal customs or habits. We generally begin with the same foot when putting on our socks, sit in the same pew when worshipping in church, shake hands when introduced to a stranger—simple customs we adopt that have become a habitual way of life. The incarnate Creator was no different. And is anyone surprised that it would be so natural a custom for Him, this custom of keeping the seventh-day Sabbath and worshipping on it week after week after week? Wouldn't He keep the very gift He gave? He kept it in life, He kept it in death. "Therefore the Son of Man is also Lord of the Sabbath" (Mark 2:28).

Knowing what Jesus would do with the Sabbath, the more pertinent question is What should we do? "Come to Me, . . . and I will give you rest" (Matt. 11:28). What better custom for the chosen to embrace than to come to Jesus for His rest every seventh-day Sabbath!

IN PURSUIT OF THE THREE ANGELS — 1

Then I saw another angel flying in midair, and he had the eternal gospel to proclaim to those who live on the earth—to every nation, tribe, language and people. Rev. 14:6, NIV.

I believe the greatest spiritual contest in history is impending, and I fear (and I use that word advisedly) that it may well be much closer than any of us comprehends. This global spiritual crisis will be between two opposing religious communities—one leading the vast majority of the world in championing what has been her historic position through the centuries, and the other leading a minority opposition to the hegemony of the first power.

Three apocalyptic angels streaking across the midnight heavens make it clear that there will be only two positions, two ideologies, two camps in that final crisis. As peculiar as this sounds, the world will be divided—every religion, government, tribe, and nation—into two factions. This David and Goliath mismatch will settle once and for all the question of earth's loyalty to the Creator God of the universe . . . yea or nay? And if in that crisis you choose your allegiance based upon the numbers, it will be the easiest choice in the world.

Revelation 14:6-12 clearly portrays these three apocalyptic angels delivering their final warning to earth just before the return of Christ (see verse 14). Our text today portrays the first angel leaving his contrail high overhead with a message to the entire civilization. And be reminded that his is a message identified as "the eternal gospel," i.e., the quintessential good news that is as ancient as the throne of the Eternal. The month of January in this book was devoted to the gospel DNA of God's relentless love for all creation, all His children. Let it be clear that though the impending crisis is foreboding, the divine passion in this final warning flows from a heart already broken once at Calvary. It is good news for rebel sinners!

"Fear God and give glory to Him, for the hour of His judgment has come; and worship Him who made heaven and earth, the sea and springs of water" (verse 7). It is no accident that the actual wording of this first angel's cry to earth is taken verbatim from the Greek Old Testament language of the fourth commandment's call to remember the seventh-day Sabbath.

What does that mean for the world, for the chosen? It is compelling evidence that the Sabbath, as the Creator's memorial, will be at the heart of the final crisis. So? So right now in worship would be a perfect time to reaffirm our allegiance to our Creator, don't you think?

IN PURSUIT OF THE THREE ANGELS—2

Here is a call for the endurance of the saints, those who keep the commandments of God and hold fast to the faith of Jesus. Rev. 14:12, NRSV.

One of my father's favorite bedtime stories for us children was the Shadrach, Meshach, and Abednego saga. What's not to thrill over in that drama! You have the Jekyll-and-Hyde monarch of Babylon in a moment of insane pride ordering the construction of a towering golden image and commanding the world to worship it (him). And when the royal band strikes up the anthem, all the assembled political leaders from across the empire bow down, except for those three Hebrew young men. But when threatened with the rage of the king and his roaring fiery furnace, their loyalty to the Creator God is flintlike: "Let it be known to you, O king, that we do not serve your gods, nor will we worship the gold image which you have set up" (Dan. 3:18). And so with a howl, Nebuchadnezzar orders their immediate execution. But hallelujah, the Eternal One walks the flames with them and delivers them. The End.

It is that bedtime story that provides the apocalyptic clue to the urgent cries of the second and third angels streaking the night sky. One shouts that Babylon—the sum of spiritual confusion and rebellion against the Creator—is fallen. The other warns that any earth inhabitant that bows down to the rebel image will by that very act declare full and complete rebellion against the Creator. Without a doubt they are "the most solemn and fearful warnings ever sent by God to man" (*Last Day Events*, p. 45). And at the fiery heart of all three angels' messages is the worship of the Creator. The first angel calls the earth to worship Him on His Sabbath. And the third angel warns of bowing to the image of the Sabbath's counterfeit. Two competing loyalties, two conflicting days of worship, two global camps. But one choice: Shall I accept the authority of the Creator or the rule of the fallen coalition?

For the chosen the choice will not be easy, but it will be clear. Irrespective the numbers, the legislative coercions, the economic boycotts, and even the threat of death—as did the three Hebrew exiles (themselves chosen ones), the band of chosen in the final crisis will choose loyalty to Christ above all. Which makes the keeping of the Sabbath today more than an exercise in cultural heritage, doesn't it? When you celebrate the Sabbath this evening, you are declaring to any who asks and to all who witness that your supreme allegiance belongs to the Creator.

GOD'S PARTY

It is a sign between Me and the children of Israel forever; for in six days the Lord made the heavens and the earth, and on the seventh day He rested and was refreshed.
Ex. 31:17.

Have you noticed that nearly everything we own these days runs on a battery? Make a quick mental list of all the objects around your house that have to be recharged. Karen's and my lists will include: our iPods, cell phones, toothbrushes, flashlights, cameras, camcorders, laptops, Palm Pilots or PDAs, razors, drills, hedge trimmers, and now even cars. The list is practically endless! And is there anything more frustrating than a beeping cell phone warning you *while you're on it* that it's rapidly losing its charge? Battery-charging kiosks (for a price, of course) line our airports to make sure we don't lose a call.

So here's the question for all you high-techies: What's the purpose of a recharger? Simple—*to restore the power and energy of that which has become run down.*

And that's precisely what our text today declares about the Sabbath. It's the day of the week that "refreshes," or, as the Hebrew word *naphash* literally reads, allows you "to take a breath." When you come in from running, as I do each morning, you're sweaty, smelly, and generally a bit spent. And you "refresh" yourself by slowing down, sitting down, and catching your breath.

As James Richard Wibberding notes in *Sabbath Reflections,* the word *naphash* has a cousin, *nephesh,* which Moses used to describe the creation of Adam, "and man became a living being [or soul]" (Gen. 2:7). So when the Sabbath "re-freshes" you, it literally "re-souls" you, "re-breathes" you, i.e., it "re-charges" your very being. What a gift!

You know what my favorite part of a party is? Those mouthwatering delectable snacks that the hostess so carefully prepares. We call them "refreshments." Think Sabbath again!

The point? God didn't give us a day to be dreaded. After six long days of draining our emotional, mental, physical, and even spiritual batteries, isn't it good news that God offers a 24-hour recharger that can "re-soul" and "re-fresh" us to the core? Twenty-four hours to slow down, sit down, and catch our collective breath—the perfect gift for our high-tech lives.

No wonder God declares the Sabbath to be a "forever sign" between Him and the chosen. No wonder He calls it a "delight" (Isa. 58:13). Given all of that, is there any reason that we couldn't call this day God's Party? Then let us go out and celebrate with Him!

GOD'S MYSPACE DAY

Be still, and know that I am God; I will be exalted among the nations, I will be exalted in the earth! Ps. 46:10.

There was a time when more than 200 million human beings had space on MySpace. One out of every 33 people on earth had an account with that global social networking site. But then who's surprised, given that this is the most technologically savvy generation in the history of earth! Does God have space on MySpace, too?

The Hebrew word for rest, *shabbath*, is an interesting one, because it literally means "to cease or desist." And with that nuance, it certainly makes more sense out of the Genesis 2 declaration that God "rested" on the seventh day. The Creator of the cosmos was hardly worn out from issuing less than a dozen commands and hand-sculpting two human beings into existence. God didn't need to recharge His batteries or rest His body on the seventh day. So when the Bible declares that He rested, it means He simply *ceased doing what He had been doing all week long.*

And that's what He invites us to do in the fourth of the Ten Commandments: "Six days you shall labor and do all your work, but the seventh day is the Sabbath of the Lord your God. In it you shall do no work" (Ex. 20:9, 10). "I'm not against work," God declares. "I made you to work. But you need to take a break and come to Me and enjoy rest. Cease from all that has preoccupied you all week through." Why? Because it's the secret of lasting friendships—you unplug the distractions so that you can focus on the relationship.

So what would happen if on the Sabbath we unplugged all our gadgets? You know—the television, the radio, the high-speed Internet, Google, the e-mails, the chat rooms, the Blackberry, maybe even the laptop. You're probably wondering what kind of a fanatic I've become! But I'm afraid it's what we've all become—the most connected but addicted generation in history, addicted to our 24/7 information and technology glut. Nothing gets unplugged or turned off—not even in church—for fear we might miss a piece of information. But what if we agreed to "cease and desist" with some of our technology, and decided to give God back His MySpace Sabbath? Could it be that in unplugging from our gadgets, we might be more deeply plugged into our God? Getting unplugged in order to be plugged in is counterintuitive—but it's also peace.

GOD'S YAWNING FACEBOOK

Come to Me, all you who labor and are heavy laden, and I will give you rest. Take My yoke upon you and learn from Me, for I am gentle and lowly in heart, and you will find rest for your souls. Matt. 11:28, 29.

Do you know what everyone in Facebook does, what in fact is one of the most contagious of all human activities? According to howstuffworks.com, 55 percent of us will yawn within five minutes of seeing someone else yawn. In fact, just reading about yawning will make you yawn. And for a blind person all it takes is to hear someone yawning. But while yawning is a highly contagious act, scientists aren't quite sure why it is we yawn. Is it fatigue, boredom, drowsiness that cause a yawn? But then why do Olympic athletes yawn more just before competition? And why do 11-week-old fetuses yawn? Nobody knows for sure. We just do it!

Maybe we're born tired. One thing's for certain—God very much longs for every face in His book to find rest. The moving invitation of Jesus in our text for today certainly taps a felt need of our third-millennial society, doesn't it? Rest. Who doesn't yawn for more of that?

The word for "rest" here in Matthew 11 is actually a compound word in the Greek: "again" plus "to stop or cease," meaning "to stop again." It's what you do when you climb a mountain. Nobody I know climbs nonstop to the summit. To get to the top of Mount Fuji in Japan in time for sunrise is an all-night adventure. But dotting the ascending volcanic slope are little rest huts, orange glows in the night that offer a moment of thawing warmth and a nap on the straw mat floor. That's what Jesus is offering too. "In your ascent through life you've got to stop and rest—or you'll never make it to the top. So come to Me, and let Me be your rest stop again and again and again."

And what immediately follows Christ's invitation in Matthew 11 is a Sabbath story in Matthew 12, leaving no doubt that Matthew wanted his readers to link resting in Jesus with resting on the Sabbath. "For the Son of Man is Lord even of the Sabbath" (verse 8). And can you think of a more satisfying cure for our yawns than the 24 hours of His Sabbath rest?

"In these words Christ is speaking to every human being. Whether they know it or not, all are weary and heavy-laden. All are weighed down with burdens that only Christ can remove. . . . He will take the load from our weary shoulders. He will give us rest" (*The Desire of Ages*, pp. 328, 329).

GOD'S CURE FOR FOUR YAWNS — 1

He gives His beloved sleep. Ps. 127:2.

We are a tired nation. If you can't sleep tonight, just go to Google and type in "sleep studies" or "sleep research" or "sleep problems." There's enough reading and research there to cure any insomnia! Some say that more than 50 million Americans suffer from some sort of sleep deprivation. Nobody can quite agree on how much sleep on the average we're getting a night. But according to most, it isn't enough.

And it's not just adults now. Growing numbers of adolescents (one report suggested a quarter of its youthful participants) are complaining of insomnia. As a result, prescription sleep medication for children under the age of 19 is on the rise. I minister on a university campus. Young adults are notorious (and not only proverbially) for burning the midnight oil, or, if you prefer, burning the candle at both ends. We are a sleepy society!

That's why I love the one-line good news of our text for today. God gives those He loves—and that would be all of us earth children—sleep. Some would like to spiritualize away any notion of physical sleep or rest in this promise. But doing so does a disservice to the Creator. For surely the God who designed Adam and Eve in the beginning to enjoy a night of deeply satisfying sleep and rest is not displeased when His weary children come to the Sabbath eager for such refreshment. (Why else would God have created "evening" or "night" in Genesis 1?)

There was a time when the elders among us spoke disparagingly about sleeping on the Sabbath. But perhaps the point of their burden was that we ought not sleep away the entire gift day of God. And I'm sure we all would certainly concur. What's the point of running our minds and bodies ragged for six relentless days and nights, just so that we might collapse on the Sabbath, for the sake of recharging our batteries long enough to do the six-day rat race all over again? There's something obviously very wrong with that picture.

But the picture tucked away in our text today—"He gives His beloved sleep"—is a blessed reminder that a good, satisfying night of rest is indeed a gift from our Creator. Enjoy that sleep each night the rest of this week. And be blessed with His gift of sleep on the night of the coming Sabbath. After all, the Sabbath is God's cure for **yawn 1**—our physical fatigue.

"Come to Me, and I will give you rest."

GOD'S CURE FOR FOUR YAWNS—2

The Lord is close to the brokenhearted and saves those who are crushed in spirit.
Ps. 34:18, NIV.

The Sabbath is God's cure for **yawn 2**—emotional fatigue. Rebecca Brillhart wrote a beautiful piece in the *Adventist Review* a few years ago entitled "The Jade Belt Bridge" (Jan. 10, 2008, p. 10). In it she broods over the inner healing that the Sabbath can bring to us. She quotes the observation of a woman: "Now I understand that if I don't allow for this rhythm of rest in my busy life, illness becomes my Sabbath." Her point? Our bodies and spirits *are* going to get the rest they need, whether we give it voluntarily or not. Burn our bodies and hearts out, and the system will shut itself down on its own for the long-needed rest. Rebecca describes the Chinese character or pictogram for "too busy." It is the combination of two words, "heart" and "killing." "Too busy" is "heart killing." Would anybody disagree?

As a pastor I've observed that nothing kills our hearts and smothers our emotions more effectively and deeply than our mad scramble through the week. The price we're willing to pay for the accolades at the office, for the advancements in our careers, for the accumulations of our possessions! But what a heavy toll upon the human spirit!

The Sabbath is Christ's balm and cure for our "heart-killing" emotional fatigue. "Come to Me, and I will give you rest." How many marriages, how many families, how many lives might be spared emotional death were we to avail ourselves of the emotionally healing Sabbath rest?

"The Lord is close to the brokenhearted and saves those who are crushed in spirit." Isn't that a blessed assurance? The incarnated God who pitched His tent in the midst of our broken emotions, who grew up in a dysfunctional stepfamily, who surrounded himself with 12 emotionally challenged associates, who lived in the emotionally toxic environment of extreme legalism, who was a magnet to society's most emotionally dysfunctional (prostitutes and tax collectors)—this is the Lord of the Sabbath who calls to Him all of us who are broken and hurting; who invites us to find in the gift of His day the emotional rest that our spirits are dying for. How vital, how critical then is the cure of Jesus' Sabbath rest on the seventh day! Seek it this Sabbath.

"Come to me, and I will give you rest."

GOD'S CURE FOR FOUR YAWNS—3

Whom have I in heaven but You? And there is none upon earth that I desire besides You. My flesh and my heart fail; but God is the strength of my heart and my portion forever. Ps. 73:25, 26.

Aren't we something! Recently Americans spent $10 billion per year simply to change the ringtones on our cell phones. Half the world goes to sleep hungry at night, and we're changing our ring tones for a paltry $10 billion. Let's be honest—we in the West are driven to possess, aren't we? Never mind the economy (which, of course, we're all minding very much these days). If you've got to have it, you've got to have it. And so the world's largest collection of toys (for both children and adults), gadgets, tools, knickknacks (garage sale trophies), china, DVDs, clothing, ringtones, shoes, and lawn mowers keeps burgeoning bigger and bigger.

Perhaps that's why we've become the greatest debtor nation on earth. Credit cards maxed out beyond the limit, we've found a way to "keep up with the Joneses" and pay for our menagerie of possessions and expensive lifestyle. One commentator described it as our refusal to recognize natural limits. Is that it?

And then along comes the seventh-day Sabbath, the most nonmaterial of all gifts entrusted to the human race. You can't package it, cut it into small pieces, sell it to the highest bidder. You can't pick it or paint it. It is rather the stuff of the nonmaterial, the invisible, a temporal piece of eternal time sketched onto the calendars of human survival, offering us the *ultimate in the nonmaterial*, a personal friendship with our Creator.

The cry of the psalmist in our text today belongs to one who has come to the stark realization that earth's material possessions fade into banal insignificance in the light of the divine offer for us to possess God. "Whom *have* I in heaven but You?" Like a parent who joys in a child's sense of possession, "This is *my* daddy, *my* mommy," God longs to be so possessed. And in all honesty, next to Him, what really *do* we have in comparison in heaven or on earth? His Sabbath gift faithfully arrives with quiet release from our bone-wearying financial fatigue. Driven for more and more, we hear the Sabbath call to less and less—less and less of our wants, and more and more of our God. It is the freedom we've been longing for.

"Come to Me, and I will give you rest."

GOD'S CURE FOR FOUR YAWNS—4

Are you tired? Worn out? Burned out on religion? Come to me. Get away with me and you'll recover your life. I'll show you how to take a real rest. Walk with me and work with me—watch how I do it. Learn the unforced rhythms of grace. I won't lay anything heavy or ill-fitting on you. Keep company with me and you'll learn to live freely and lightly.
Matt. 11:28-30, Message.

Physical fatigue, emotional fatigue, financial fatigue, and now spiritual fatigue— the Sabbath is Jesus' offer to heal us of all four yawns, isn't it? And don't you like how Eugene Peterson's *The Message* renders Christ's invitation: "Keep company with me." What would happen if we began to think of every new Sabbath as "keeping company" with Jesus? A century ago Ellen White wrote a letter to an elderly friend who was about to die—and it contained this beautiful assurance: "Rest in [Christ's] arms, and know that He is your Savior, *and your very best Friend*, and that He will never leave you or forsake you. He has been your dependence for many years, and your soul may rest in hope" (*This Day With God*, p. 313; italics supplied).

So what would happen if we shifted our Sabbathkeeping paradigm from a day of obligatory rules and regulations (as the Pharisees viewed it), to a day of keeping special company with our very best Friend? Try this as Sabbath begins this evening. Read Matthew 11:28 and 29, then pray, "Dear Jesus, I receive Your Sabbath offer of rest. I wish to keep special company with You for these 24 hours. Let me see the face of my very best Friend. Amen."

Now spend the Sabbath looking for His face. You'll be absolutely amazed (and delighted) at where you see Him!

Then as Sabbath draws to an end, read the third verse of Jesus' invitation, Matthew 11:30. And pray something like this: "Lord, I want to be 'yoked' or partnered with You all through the new week ahead. Please keep company with me until we return together to Your Sabbath. Amen."

What are we doing by beginning and ending the Sabbath with our minds focused on our very best Friend? We make it simpler to keep special company with Him on the Sabbath, making it easier to keep company with Him all the new week through.

"Turn your eyes upon Jesus, Look full in His wonderful face; And the things of earth will grow strangely dim in the light of His glory and grace."

GOD'S YOUTUBE YOU-TOO DAY

And let us consider how we may spur one another on toward love and good deeds. Let us not give up meeting together, as some are in the habit of doing, but let us encourage one another—and all the more as you see the Day approaching. Heb. 10:24, 25, NIV.

What would we do without YouTube? The motto for Google's wildly popular Web site is Broadcast Yourself. It's open to anybody who has the ego strength to point a video camera at himself and then post it, making it the most frequented video swap shop in the universe! Laughing babies, jigging strangers—it's all there, plus more. And the more, the merrier.

That's true about God's own YouTube space—the YouTube You-Too Day He calls the Sabbath—where His passion is, the more, the merrier. Only the motto isn't "broadcast yourself," it's "bring yourself," as our text for today points out.

Don't see anything about the Sabbath in that text? Actually the phrase "meeting together" is a single word in the Greek, *episunagoge*, from which comes our word "synagogue," a place of Sabbath worship. In fact, throughout the book of Acts we find Christians and Jews worshipping together in synagogues on the Sabbath across the Roman Empire (Acts 13:14, 42, 44; 17:2; 18:4). Here in Hebrews 10 the author is simply admonishing his Christian readers *not to give up* coming together to worship God on the Sabbath day. And the key word is "together."

During the question-and-answer session after a public lecture, C. S. Lewis, the brilliant Christian apologist of the twentieth century, was asked if church attendance was necessary for a Christian. He replied: "That's a question which I cannot answer. My own experience is that when I first became a Christian . . . I thought that I could do it on my own, by retiring to my rooms and reading theology, and I wouldn't go to the churches and Gospel Halls" (*God in the Dock*, p. 61). Sound familiar? "Let me just be alone when I worship—me and God and a good book or the Good Book." Or: "I have my iPod, and I've downloaded several sermons—so I'll be just fine alone. Don't need this 'meeting together' thing." Or: "We plan to spend the day at the lake, maybe a hike, you know—enjoy the Creator's outdoors—why bother with this 'meeting together' business?" Lewis struggled as a new Christian over this "together" invitation, and came to a strong conclusion that we'll share tomorrow. But what do *you* think? Why did God put Hebrews 10 in our Bibles? There's got to be more to Sabbath worship than taking up an offering!

"TAKE ME OUT TO THE BALL GAME"

On the next Sabbath almost the whole city gathered to hear the word of the Lord.
Acts 13:44, NIV.

Before we go to the ball game, please note the rest of C. S. Lewis' reply to whether or not a Christian should go to church each week: "Then later [after worshipping alone in his room for a period] I found that . . . [if] there is anything in the teaching of the New Testament which is in the nature of a command, it is that you are obliged to [celebrate the Communion], and you can't do it without going to church. I disliked very much their hymns, which I considered to be fifth-rate poems set to sixth-rate music. But as I went on I saw the great merit of it. I came up against different people of quite different outlooks and different education, and then gradually my conceit just began peeling off. I realized that the hymns . . . were, nevertheless, being sung with devotion and benefit by an old saint in elastic-side boots in the opposite pew, and then you realize that you aren't fit to clean those boots. It gets you out of your solitary conceit" (*God in the Dock*, pp. 61, 62). C. S. Lewis discovered the divine value of "together" in worship.

It has become fashionable in some circles to demonstrate your intellectual prowess and artistic discernment by refusing to worship with those who sing "fifth-rate poems set to sixth-rate music" (students call it "praise music"). But Lewis realized such an attitude was "solitary conceit" masquerading as high taste. For in the communal "togetherness" of multigenerational, multisocioeconomic, multiethnic, multiliterate worshippers, the inclusive reality of God's family is best experienced.

Of course you can worship God alone—I do every day. But home alone is no substitute for the ball park! Since this is baseball season, notice how communal is this old favorite: "Take me out to the ball game; take me out to the *crowd*. Buy me some peanuts and Cracker Jack. I don't care if I never get back. Let me root, root, root for the *home team*. If they don't win, it's a shame. For it's one, two, three strikes, you're out, at the old ball game!" Community to the core! When you go to a ball park (read church), it strengthens your resolve ("Others share my passion!"); it reinforces your loyalty ("I'm not the only loyal one!"); and it emboldens your witness ("Others are willing to stand up and cheer, too!"). *We're in this together* is the subtext to every worship gathering. "For where two or three are gathered *together* in My name, I am there in the midst of *them*" (Matt. 18:20). Talk about a winning team!

THE FAMILY PORTRAIT

"For as the new heavens and the new earth which I will make shall remain before Me,"
says the Lord, "so shall your descendants and your name remain. And it shall come to pass
that from one New Moon to another, and from one Sabbath to another, all flesh shall come
to worship before Me," says the Lord. Isa. 66:22, 23.

For generations, one of the family rituals of our tribe has been taking a family portrait on Christmas before any gifts are opened. For the kids there's an element of expectation in the air, since once all the camera flashes are over, the presents can't be far behind. And for Mom and Dad, and any visiting family members, there's the joy of creating another full-color memory of our time together.

God's big on family portraits, too, which is why every Sabbath He gathers us to sit for His snapshot. Now, it's true that we don't gather in our congregations to look at one another. God is the object of our collective focus, the camera lenses of our souls all pointed upward in His direction. Nevertheless, in a very real sense, on Sabbath mornings we are as "family-portraited" as we ever get. Just as it's a disappointment when one of the kids or someone else in the family can't be there for our Christmas family photo, even so, in a very real sense, to have one of our spiritual family missing on Sabbath mornings creates a void, doesn't it? And if that family member is missing Sabbath after Sabbath, shall we simply pretend he or she no longer exists?

God is big on family portraits. Why, even in eternity, as our text today reminds us, God is going to gather His children from around the world for another unforgettable family portrait worship experience at the foot of His throne. "From one Sabbath to another" we'll come home to be with the family and the Father. And it will be a spiritual celebration—God's party, if you please—the likes of which you've never seen before!

So if God is that big on corporate, communal worship in His home above, shouldn't we be as big on it down here below? "Yes, but I don't really get anything out of worshipping in the little church near us." Could it be you've got the camera aimed at *you*? What if you worshipped God with His family, focusing on what you could bring to deepen the worship experience of the *others*? Do you suppose, like C. S. Lewis, you might discover a saint or two with "elastic-side boots" whose shoes you aren't really "fit to clean"? Family, after all, is *all* of us, isn't it?

THE FIREPLACE EMBER

Let us consider one another . . ., not forsaking the assembling of ourselves together, as is the manner of some, but exhorting one another, and so much the more as you see the Day approaching. . . . "For yet a little while, and He who is coming will come and will not tarry."
Heb. 10:24-37.

What's this capital-D Day that appears in our text? Read a little further in the chapter, and it's clear that the author is describing the second coming of Jesus. And his point? If you want to be in the portrait then, you've got to get in the group picture now. The closer the Day of Christ draws to us, the closer we must draw to each other on Christ's day, the Sabbath. You'll not find a stronger appeal for communal Sabbath worship anywhere else in Scripture!

Which being interpreted means that the days of skipping church and absenting ourselves from worship are over. We've been too laissez-faire about Sabbath worship, treating it too often as an optional choice based upon a personal whim. "I don't think I'll go today—I don't feel like it." But the passion of Hebrews 10 declares that "forsaking the assembling of ourselves together" must come to an end in the light of the soon-coming Savior. Corporate worship is linked to personal readiness for His return. Let it be repeated—if we want to be in the portrait then, we must get into the group picture now. How much further on the edge does this world need to teeter before we get it? Nobody needs to parse the headlines for us in order for us to affirm that we are living on the edge of eternity. Now more than ever we need each other every Sabbath!

Dwight L. Moody, the great American evangelist of the nineteenth century, was visiting one evening in the home of a successful businessman. Sitting by the fireplace, the man was waxing rather eloquently to his guest why it was that he didn't need to go to church for worship. After all, he found it much more satisfying to worship God alone, with a good book or a walk in nature, or some quiet Bible study. "Who needs the fuss and bother of crowded pews and inconvenient travel?" the man protested. Moody never said a word. Instead, when the gentleman was through, Moody quietly reached over to the fireplace, took up the tongs and pulled a red-hot piece of coal from the crackling fire. He slid the burning ember out onto the hearth away from the flames and left it there. The two men, in silence, stared at the bright piece of coal . . . that slowly but surely lost its fire and glow . . . until it eventually was nothing more than a wisp of smoke and a piece of cold, charred coal.

GOD'S GREEN EARTH DAY

Then God said, "Let Us make man in Our image, according to Our likeness; let them have dominion over the fish of the sea, over the birds of the air, and over the cattle, over all the earth and over every creeping thing that creeps on the earth." Gen. 1:26.

E. O. Wilson, the celebrated Harvard scientist and naturalist, caught my eye with his opening words in *The Creation*: "Pastor, we need your help. The Creation—living Nature—is in deep trouble. Scientists estimate that if habitat conversion and other destructive human activities continue at their present rates, half the species of plants and animals on Earth could be either gone or at least fated for early extinction by the end of the century. A full quarter will drop to this level during the next half century as a result of climate change alone. The ongoing extinction rate is calculated in the most conservative estimates to be about a hundred times above that prevailing before humans appeared on Earth [we would say, since the Fall], and it is expected to rise to at least a thousand times greater or more in the next few decades. If this rise continues unabated, the cost to humanity, in wealth, environmental security, and quality of life, will be catastrophic" (*The Creation*, pp. 4, 5).

How would you respond? The world these days is thinking, talking, and voting "green"—the conservation of nature and Mother Earth. But our text today reveals that God's been thinking green from the first week of Creation. So is it any surprise that the Sabbath is God's original Earth Day for His "green agenda" from the beginning? And given the passionate concern of scientists such as E. O. Wilson, shouldn't it follow that the people of the Sabbath, of all people on earth, would be on the leading edge of preserving God's creation?

As Seventh-day Adventists we choose to live by the following credos: (1) we are not products of natural selection's random chance, but are the creation of a loving, intelligent Creator; (2) as a memorial of His creation, God gave humanity the Sabbath, on which we rest in His friendship and celebrate His handiwork; (3) we therefore are reminded every seventh day that this world of nature is God's trust to us for our care; and (4) though we recognize that the Creation will never be fully healed of its obvious dysfunction until evil's final eradication, and though we eagerly *do* await the return of our Creator and Savior, nevertheless we believe our care of God's creation is required of all who are children of the Creator. Don't you agree?

PLANT A TREE

For the creation waits with eager longing for the revealing of the children of God. . . . We know that the whole creation has been groaning in labor pains until now.
Rom. 8:19-22, NRSV.

Paul Hawken, in *Blessed Unrest*, tells an old rabbinical teaching that if we hear that the world is ending and the Messiah is coming, we must first plant a tree and then go and determine if the story is true or not. For Seventh-day Adventists, who champion God's creation memorial and who celebrate the return of the Creator, planting a tree isn't such a bad idea, is it?

Our text reminds us that for millennia now our creation has suffered deeply under the effects of our very human rebellion. Can you imagine the latent longing within the natural world for the promised deliverance? But until then, how shall we live, we Sabbathkeepers of the Creator's flame?

We could begin by eating green. That's right, vegetarianism would diminish the number of animals raised and killed for consumption, and thus reduce the one fifth of earth's greenhouse gases that livestock produce. We can turn off the lights in the rooms we exit. We could inflate our tires and save 2 billion gallons of gas a year, some say. We could shorten our showers by two minutes, saving 12 gallons of water. We could recycle. We could save a few trees by skipping the receipts at ATMs and gas pumps, saving by one estimate 3 billion feet of paper. We could use our own thermos bottles and quit drinking bottled water, since a one-liter bottle requires five liters of water to cool the plastic, thus resulting in six liters of water for each bottle! Lists of "green" or environmentally friendly ways to live (like these from Ashleigh Burnette in the *Student Movement* here at the university) are all over the Web, and you can make your own.

The point? As Creator-worshipping, Sabbathkeeping, nature-preserving friends of Jesus, shouldn't we be at the forefront of ecological conservation and environmental care and protection? Truth be known, God Himself planted a tree once upon a time to save this creation. "To the death of Christ we owe even this earthly life. The bread [our farmland] we eat is the purchase of His broken body. The water [our rivers, streams] we drink is bought by His spilled blood. . . . The cross of Calvary is stamped on every loaf. It is reflected in every water spring" (*The Desire of Ages*, p. 660). Given the infinite cost of planting that tree, we must join Him in saving His creation.

HOW TO YAHOO! WITH GOD

There remains, then, a Sabbath-rest for the people of God; for anyone who enters God's rest also rests from his own work, just as God did from his. Heb. 4:9, 10, NIV.

Here are five simple strategies to keep God's presence alive with joy in your Sabbath:

1. Guard the doors. The doors to the Sabbath are the sundowns on Friday and Saturday evening. God initiated earth's creation with the darkness turned to light, and biblical reckoning ever since has kept time, "evening and morning" (see Gen. 1). So "from evening to evening, you shall celebrate your sabbath" (Lev. 23:32). Jesus did (Mark 1:21, 32), and so can we. How? Guarding the doors means to be at the door to welcome God into your Sabbath. Play your favorite religious CD. Sing (if you're the singing type), or play a hymn. Gather your family or join with some friends and claim Jesus' promise "Come to Me, and I will give you rest" (Matt. 11:28). Pick a psalm or Bible chapter to memorize. Then join in a prayer of welcome to the Lord of the Sabbath. Guard the back door by doing something similar as the Sabbath ends at sundown.

2. Get your rest. Here's a Chinese sage's three-word biography of the West: hurry, worry, bury. Who has time to slow down and rest? I read that politicians speak 50 percent faster than they did in the 1940s and that Beethoven's Fifth Symphony takes 20 percent less time to perform now than when it was first composed. No wonder we're worn out! My friend Larry Ulery, a faculty member here at Andrews, told me his favorite tombstone epitaph is "Got everything done. Still died!" Slow down and get your rest (in the *dark part* of the Sabbath).

3. Go to church. M. L. Andreasen describes God's chosen ones as "thrice blessed"—blessed to be chosen, worshipping in a place that is blessed, on a day that is blessed. "Surely, under such conditions God's richest blessing may be expected" (*The Sabbath*, pp. 47, 48). Share the Yahoo! joy of corporate worship.

4. Give of yourself. Isaiah 58, ending with the Sabbath, is actually an extended appeal to serve the needy (a call we'll examine later this year). Jesus' seven Sabbath miracles are evidence enough it is a day for serving others. Nursing homes, shut-ins, hospitals, inner-city tenements—the Sabbath isn't about serving yourself. It's about giving yourself.

5. Glory in your God. "Delight yourself also in the Lord, and He will give you the desires of your heart" (Ps. 37:4). Because there's only one word for a God like ours. Yahoo!

READING THE MIND OF THE ENEMY

And the dragon was enraged with the woman, and he went to make war with the rest of her offspring, who keep the commandments of God and have the testimony of Jesus Christ. Rev. 12:17.

So why all this fuss about the Sabbath? What's the big deal? Intelligence services jubilantly celebrated their incredible luck in locating and retrieving the laptop of the mastermind of terror. On it names, addresses, strategies, records—a veritable treasure trove exposing their antagonist's most secret plans. Neither is the truth about the seventh-day Sabbath some inconsequential option for God's chosen in this hour of history—it is central to the final showdown. For that reason, the following verbatim quote sheds light on the strategic thinking processes of heaven and earth's great dragon nemesis.

"Satan says, 'I will work at cross purposes with God. I will empower my followers to set aside God's memorial, the seventh-day Sabbath. Thus I will show the world that the day sanctified and blessed by God has been changed. That day shall not live in the minds of the people. I will obliterate the memory of it. I will place in its stead a day that does not bear the credentials of God, a day that cannot be a sign between God and His people. I will lead those who accept this day to place upon it the sanctity that God placed upon the seventh day. Through my vicegerent, I will exalt myself. The first day will be extolled, and the Protestant world will receive this spurious sabbath as genuine. Through the nonobservance of the Sabbath that God instituted, I will bring His law into contempt. . . . Thus the world will become mine. I will be the ruler of the earth, the prince of the world. I will so control the minds under my power that God's Sabbath shall be a special object of contempt. A sign? I will make the observance of the seventh day a sign of disloyalty to the authorities of earth. Human laws will be made so stringent that men and women will not dare to observe the seventh-day Sabbath'" (*Prophets and Kings*, pp. 183, 184).

In his rebellion against heaven, the dragon has declared the Sabbath a high-value target in a desperate strategy to obliterate the Creator from the minds of those on earth. Is it any surprise then that of all generations of the chosen, this last one is called to unfurl the flag of loyalty to the Creator through allegiance to His Sabbath? For to stand for Christ, even if to stand alone, is surely the highest honor of all for His friends.

A TALE OF TWO STORIES

Surely you have things turned around! Shall the potter be esteemed as the clay; for shall the thing made say of him who made it, "He did not make me"? Or shall the thing formed say of him who formed it, "He has no understanding"? Isa. 29:16.

Once upon a time in the middle of the nineteenth century, two competing stories were catapulted onto the stage of human awareness, two stories destined to become locked in a desperate struggle to the end of human time.

Both stories were birthed in the year 1844—the first out of an apocalyptic movement that ignited a revival in the exploration of the Word of God, the other in July of that same year when 189 pages of manuscript were written out longhand (though the world would not know of that birthing until the story was published in 1859). Both stories exploded with an implicit mission to every nation, kindred, tongue, and people. Knowing what we now know, it can hardly be mere coincidence that the two stories would be birthed at the same moment in history and compete for the same global allegiance.

The first story cries out from the midnight heavens, "Fear God and give glory to Him, for the hour of His judgment has come; and worship Him who made heaven and earth," in an unabashed appeal to earth to come to the Creator *now* (Rev. 14:7). The second story also cries from the dark sky, only it is the very antithesis of the first story, its shadowy opposite—there is *no* creator to worship, *no* judgment to heed, *no* God to obey save the god of your own making. Charles Darwin's theory of random evolutionary chance, too, has gone to the ends of the earth.

Two stories with two very opposite beginnings and two tragically opposite endings. It is *not* a choice between religion and science, as some would have you believe. Rather, it is the choice between two worldviews, two cosmic stories, two competing kingdoms. And at the head of one of them stands Jesus Christ, who still declares, "The sabbath was made for humankind, and . . . the Son of Man is lord even of the sabbath" (Mark 2:27, 28, NRSV).

And that is why, in the end, it really does come down to the choice between the two. Because no one can serve two kingdoms or two masters. The passionate appeal of Scripture is to choose the One who chose you "in the beginning." And frankly, how could our choice ever be wrong, if we choose the One who chose for us to live *for* Him and *with* Him *forever*?

SCHOOL'S OUT—ALMOST!

Here is the patience of the saints; here are those who keep the commandments of God and the faith of Jesus. Rev. 14:12.

Why is it that a perfectly good school year gets ruined with something like a final exam? Long ago those of us living in academic communities such as this campus had to make peace with the notion that final examinations are effective methods of measuring the grasp and retention of ideas and knowledge. (But it's certainly more pleasurable administering them than taking them!)

Not surprisingly, since the beginning of history God has proctored His share of final exams along the way. And you must admit that God's tests are (as Marvin Moore notes in *Could It Really Happen?*) *very simple and highly visible.* Take, for example, the tree in the middle of the garden—do not pluck fruit from it and eat it—a test very simple and highly visible. Cain and Abel—bring Me a sacrifice from your *flocks* when you come to worship—a test very simple and highly visible. And for the children of Israel—there will be no manna on the seventh day, the Sabbath, so collect twice as much on the sixth day—a test very simple and highly visible. Nebuchadnezzar's golden image—do not bow down to any image—a test very simple and highly visible. A command to worship no one but the king, and Daniel's choice to kneel down in front of an open window anyway—a test very simple and highly visible. The command at the end of time to reject the Sabbath of the Creator for the counterfeit day of another Babylon—a test very simple and highly visible.

Is the Sabbath a test too simple for the chosen? But what would be the point of making the final examination complicated? If the grand purpose of our human existence is to personally meet the Creator who chose us and destined us "in the beginning" to be born into this life, then why design a complicated examination that differentiates philosophical or ideological nuances, when at issue is a trusting relationship? Wouldn't the most effective and efficient test possible be one very simple (so no one need mistake the written instructions at the top of the exam sheet) and one very visible (so no one need become a mind reader to ascertain the choice and final answer of the student). The Sabbath isn't about a divine trick question on the final exam. From the beginning, at its heart it has always been and will always be about the gift of a friendship very simple and highly visible forever and ever. Amen.

THE ELEVENTH COMMANDMENT

A new commandment I give to you, that you love one another; as I have loved you, that you also love one another. By this all will know that you are My disciples, if you have love for one another. John 13:34, 35.

I got stuck in the last row of our commuter flight from South Bend, Indiana, to Chicago. So did a management consultant to Fortune 500 companies. We soon fell into conversation, making the best of the restrictive confines of our short flight across Lake Michigan. He was on the way to another company, and I to a preaching appointment across the country. He was a Jew; I, a Christian.

"And what will you be speaking on?" he queried.

"The eleventh commandment," I responded.

"The eleventh commandment?" he exclaimed incredulously. "We have a hard enough time with the ten! What would we ever do with an eleventh!"

An insightful question the Jewish gentleman raised. I wonder, What *will* we do with the eleventh?

Another Jew, and truly another gentleman (though this One is much younger), is about to speak. He will be dead in less than 24 hours—and He knows it. And when a man knows He's about to die, you can be sure that His final words will be fraught with that which He feels most deeply about. When you're counting down to death, every word counts.

"I give you a new commandment, that you love one another. Just as I have loved you, you also should love one another. By this everyone will know that you are my disciples, if you have love for one another" (John 13:34, 35, NRSV). In case you might be tempted to conclude that this command to love is simply an aside, an isolated passing thought by the Master, you need to know that here within these four upper-room walls Jesus will declare these words five times—love one another, love one another, love one another, love one another, love one another. And when you read the context for His Crucifixion-eve appeal, you can't help noticing that the word "love" or one of its derivatives appears 31 times on Jesus' death-row lips, 33 times in all here in John 13 through 17. Love is clearly, unequivocally on the Master's mind on the eve of His death.

"I give you a new commandment, that you love one another." An eleventh commandment for the chosen—for surely what was on His mind must be in our hearts—love for one another.

THE MAN IN THE FROZEN RIVER

You shall love your neighbor as yourself: I am the Lord. Lev. 19:18.

How could Jesus possibly call His command to "love one another" a new commandment? The disciples He first spoke it to had heard those words since they were knee-high to a grasshopper! Everybody knows that millennia earlier God had thundered those words from Sinai's rocky crag. And even Jesus Himself had reiterated those same ancient words in His own teaching and preaching during His ministry (Matt. 22:39; Mark 12:31).

But could it be that what made the eleventh commandment so dramatically "new" for the upper room disciples is that in less than 24 hours they would witness a bloody love so radical that it will forever rewrite the definition of "love" in the human language?

President Ronald Reagan, the grand communicator of the Oval Office years ago, touched the heart of the nation when he quoted the upper-room words of Jesus the night after the tragic Air Florida crash into the icy Potomac River just off the runway of National (now Ronald Reagan Washington National) Airport in Washington, D.C. Rescue helicopters and news cameras hovered over the frigid, windswept river as survivors of the crash fought to the surface amid ice and debris. A lifeline was lowered to one of the bobbing passengers, a bald-headed man. But instead of clinging to that line to safety, he tossed the life ring to another struggling victim, who was then dragged by the chopper to safety. Back came the life ring to the same bald-headed man, who again passed the ring to another floating survivor. Back and forth that drama of life and death played out. But when the helicopter returned one last time to rescue the unselfish stranger, he was not there, claimed at last by the frigid death waters. Intoning that stranger's unselfish bravery, President Reagan, in a national address, referred to Jesus', "Greater love hath no man than this, that a man lay down his life for his friends" (John 15:13, KJV).

Those were the crimson words of Christ spoken in that same upper room just moments after He declared His "new commandment, that you love one another." An old commandment that would become forever new on the morrow, when those 11 men would witness no "greater love" than the brutal glory of the Man on the center cross who "lay down His life for His friends." Calvary has forever rewritten the definition of love in the human language, rendering it fresh and new for all who would follow this same Jesus.

IT'S WHAT HE DIDN'T SAY

This is how everyone will recognize that you are my disciples—when they see the love you have for each other. John 13:35, Message.

I will be candid with you. As I brood over Jesus' upper-room command to love one another and recognize that He told His disciples what is to be *the ultimate defining and identifying characteristic of His true followers on earth*, what is painfully new and woefully evident to me is what He does *not* say. Please note that Jesus does *not* say, "By this all will know that you are My disciples—*if you keep the seventh-day Sabbath*." Make no mistake. He is addressing a roomful of Sabbatarian followers, who from their first breath to their last breath are Sabbathkeepers. It is the day of the chosen. But strangely, Jesus does not declare the seventh-day Sabbath to be the ultimate defining characteristic of His true followers.

Nor does He declare, "By this all will know that you are My disciples—*if your hope is in My second coming*." Though just moments later in the upper room Jesus will utter that most beloved of promises "Let not your heart be troubled. . . . I will come again" (John 14:1-3), He does not declare the Second Advent hope to be the ultimate defining characteristic of His true people. Though He neither denigrates nor denies either, obviously neither the "Seventh-day" nor the "Adventist" of Bible truth was how Jesus declared the world would recognize His chosen ones.

Not even the *cleansing of the Sanctuary and the final judgment* or the *28 fundamental beliefs* are the endings to Jesus' upper-room declaration, "By this all will know that you are My disciples . . ."

The truth that is so painfully obvious in Jesus' final injunction and command to His disciples is made all the more compelling by noting what Jesus does *not* declare to be the identifying mark of His true church on earth. Instead we read His unmistakable, unequivocal, unconditional declaration that night: "By this all—Red and Yellow, Black and White; rich and poor, educated, and illiterate; developed countries, developing countries—will know that you are My disciples—*if you have love for one another*."

Yes, you may celebrate the glad tidings of divine grace that you have been chosen. But let the record be clear that you have been chosen to love just the way Jesus did!

HIS NAME WAS JACK

Beloved, if God so loved us, we also ought to love one another. 1 John 4:11.

I'd like to share a letter with you I received from a woman across the country: "Dear Pastor Nelson: About five years ago another close friend of mine died of AIDS. His name was Jack, and he died at the age of 34. Jack was baptized as an Adventist about 15 months before he died, and I knew him mainly from the weekly prayer meetings. Jack was infected with HIV several years prior to his joining the church. . . . He never knew he had HIV until he got pneumonia. He survived the pneumonia, met some neighbors of his who were Adventists, and came into the truth through them. Unfortunately, a few members of the church couldn't accept Jack, because he had AIDS. Some stopped going to church and prayer meetings because he was there, and they feared catching AIDS from the air or sitting in the same room as him. My former pastor . . . tried very hard to educate these people—but they didn't want to hear it. When Pastor . . . spent time in the hospital with Jack every day before he passed away [good for you, Pastor!], they would say something like: 'I hope our pastor won't get AIDS in the hospital and then come back and give it to all of us!' How angels must weep in heaven for the hardness of hearts, even of professed Christians! Thank the Lord, Jack remained faithful until the end and even had a spirit of love and forgiveness toward those members who shunned him. Jack knew how much Jesus loved him, and that was enough."

But is it really? Is it enough to know that "Jesus loves me . . . for the Bible tells me so"? Apparently for Jesus it *isn't* enough that the world knows His love. Apparently for Him it is enough only when they know *our* love, too. "By this all will know that you are My disciples, if you have love for one another" (John 13:35).

May I ask an embarrassing question? Could it be that in our exuberance to help the world remember the fourth commandment, we have forgotten to remember the eleventh one? While we champion obedience to the Ten Commandments, do we disobey the eleventh commandment? It takes neither a theologian nor a sociologist to observe that humanity today isn't clamoring for the Ten Commandments. But the world over, human beings just like Jack are starving for the eleventh commandment. If God would win their minds, we must win their hearts. For that is what the love of the chosen is all about.

THE LIGHT UNDER THE DOOR

I am the vine, you are the branches. Those who abide in me and I in them bear much fruit, because apart from me you can do nothing. John 15:5, NRSV.

Edwina Humphrey Flynn, a gifted classical vocalist from New York City, was our guest at the Pioneer Memorial church for an evening concert, during which she related the following incident. It was her first day at the New York Conservatory, and early that morning she prayed that God would shine through her to all she met. Riding the crowded early-morning subway to downtown New York, she hurried to the conservatory and her music classes. Several weeks later on a day off (with the rest of the students away) Edwina was rehearsing her vocal routines in one of the conservatory practice rooms. Suddenly she seemed to hear distant voices, angry voices, drawing nearer and louder down the empty hallway. She held her breath until finally it seemed the fury was on the other side of her door. Then with a bang, her practice room door flew open and in they burst—four of them, as it turned out, fellow music students at the conservatory. "Ah, I knew you were here!" a young man triumphantly announced. Turns out they were having an argument over which was more powerful for good—"black magic" or "white magic." They were a group of young witches and warlocks (male witches), debating the "values" of the occult.

Edwina, recovering from their surprise entry, was nonplussed. "But what does that have to do with me? I know nothing about black or white magic!" To which the young spokesman reported that he'd spotted her disembarking from the subway on opening day of classes. "There was a glowing light that surrounded you and seemed to go ahead of you." Incredulous, she asked how they knew where to find her in the empty conservatory. "We were outside the building a few minutes ago, arguing, when I noticed an unusual light shining out from the under the door. I recognized it as the same light that surrounded you that day. I knew you had to be inside."

What a dramatic and compelling testimony of what can happen when a man or a woman chooses to live with a passion for Jesus Christ. Apparently the chosen can become so filled with the love of Christ that He chooses to shine through them even in getting off the subway! It's what happens when the promise "Abide in me and I in you" is united with the prayer "Out of my heart, shine out of my heart, Lord Jesus"—the right promise and prayer for the chosen today.

THE VINE AND THE BRANCHES

Abide in Me, and I in you. As the branch cannot bear fruit of itself, unless it abides in the vine, neither can you, unless you abide in Me. John 15:4.

One summer I traced their steps from the same Jerusalem upper room, up the alley, out the gate, and down the rather steep and bumpy stony pathway that descends from the wall to a notch in the valley below called the Kidron. Archaeologists tell us very few Roman pathways from the time of Christ still exist in modern Jerusalem. But this one has survived, and scholars believe it is the very path over which the sandals of Jesus and the 11 picked their way beneath the silver light of the full A.D. 31 Passover moon. Somewhere along that crooked pathway the Master Teacher stopped beside a moon-bathed trellis of grapes and spoke the words of today's text.

Through a solitary metaphor Jesus pours the secrets of eternity into a single teaching. He seizes a word He had used in the glow of the upper room torches, and now 10 times in a row He turns the noun into a verb. "In my Father's house are many *mansions*" (John 14:2, KJV) becomes "*abide* in me as I *abide* in you" (John 15:4, NRSV). Which means the translation could also read, "Mansion in me and I will mansion in you." Or, "Take up residence in Me, as I take up residence in you." That's why Eugene Peterson translates this line "Live in me. Make your home in me just as I do in you" (verse 4, Message).

However you wish to express it, Jesus' dynamic midnight teaching is clear—He is offering every friend and follower a union so close and intimate that it can be likened only to the bonded connection between a living branch and the life-giving vine. What could be closer! In the words of Oswald Chambers: "It is a joy to Jesus when a disciple takes time to step more intimately with Him. Fruit bearing is always mentioned as the manifestation of an intimate union with Jesus Christ" (*My Utmost for His Highest*, Jan. 7). What kind of fruit? "Love one another, even as I have loved you" (John 13:34, NASB).

It doesn't take a botanist or a horticulturist to know that the sole object of a branch's connection to the vine is for the sake of growing fruit. "For without Me you can do nothing" (John 15:5). It's no wonder then that the love of the chosen is nothing more than the fragrant, blossoming fruit of their union with Christ. No wonder the light shines under the door.

CHOKING ON A CAMEL—1

Woe to you, scribes and Pharisees, hypocrites! For you pay tithe of mint and anise and cummin, and have neglected the weightier matters of the law: justice and mercy and faith. These you ought to have done, without leaving the others undone. Matt. 23:23.

Are we choking on a camel? Before we answer, I wish Jesus hadn't called us hypocrites, don't you? I don't mind Him calling the Pharisees that, of course—they deserve it. But you and me? Please! It certainly isn't a compliment. While little Greek boys looked forward to growing up one day to become a *hypocrite*, the technical name for Greek actors (who could change their masks several times in a play—making them two-faced or even four-faced), nobody today wants to be called "two-faced"! What elicits such a strong dressing-down from the Master?

"You have neglected *the weightier matters of the law*: justice and mercy and faith." Did you catch that? Jesus clearly reveals here the existence of a hierarchy of values and truths within the corpus of God's revealed will, His law. And the weightiest of them all are justice, mercy, and faith. Two of those values are horizontal in focus—treating each other fairly (justice) and compassionately (mercy). And the other is vertical—trusting God (or as in Luke's parallel account, loving God—Luke 11:42). But note that Jesus identifies two out of the three weightier matters of the law having to do with our human-to-human interactions. Is Jesus somehow out of sync with the Law and the Prophets? Hardly. In fact, He has taken the grand Old Testament declaration of true religion and immersed it in the life of the Calvary community: "He has shown you, O man, what is good; and what does the Lord require of you but to do justly, to love mercy, and to walk humbly with your God?" (Micah 6:8). Justice, mercy, and faith.

How do you choke on a camel? Watch the Pharisees Jesus addresses. The smallest unclean creature listed in the dietary code of Leviticus 11 was the gnat, and the largest unclean creature was the camel. Jesus' stinging hyperbole was based on the practice of the Pharisees to filter their drinks with a piece of linen or gauze to avoid the ingestion of unclean bugs. But all the while, Jesus retorted, you are swallowing the hairy, big-lipped, humpbacked dromedary hiding in your cup. And we do the same, don't we? Majoring in the minors and minoring in the majors. Tithing our pennies, but ignoring our neighbors. Loving the truth, but not living the truth. Who can save the chosen from our two-faced, camel-swallowing lovelessness, if not Jesus!

CHOKING ON A CAMEL—2

Those who say, "I love God," and hate their brothers or sisters, are liars; for those who do not love a brother or sister whom they have seen, cannot love God whom they have not seen.
1 John 4:20, NRSV.

Are we swallowing the hairy, unclean camel of racism? "By this all will know that you are My disciples, if you have love for one another" (John 13:35).

Ever notice how Jesus spent His ministry desperately trying to break down the walls of prejudice, the racial and ethnic barriers that had grown up in hearts of the chosen? Witness His treatment of the hated Samaritans. He reserved for a lone woman of that race the most sublime truth He ever uttered—a woman who had three strikes against her, for she was a Samaritan, and a woman, and an adulteress. And when He struggled to break through the Jewish prejudice and pride by telling a story of merciful compassion, it took gall to make the hero a Samaritan; but it took *chutzpah* to make the Samaritan "good." Again and again—whether it was with the pleading Syrophoenician mother or with the demurring Roman centurion—Jesus cut across social prejudices in a passionate effort to break down the dividing walls.

Racism in all its forms is not only omitting "the weightier matters of the law"—it is a direct assault on the Lawgiver Himself! Ethnic jokes and racial slurs are easy to spot, and the Pharisee in all of us is quick to avow our distance from such sin. But what about our tendency to characterize or caricature the members of a race (whether we're Black or Brown or White or Yellow) on the basis of our experience with one member of that race? It's called racial profiling. How quick we are to prejudge (the root of "prejudice") a human being based upon our inbred or ingrained racial biases. It is still true that the most segregated hour of the week in America is Sunday or Sabbath morning. We pick our congregations, we choose our neighborhoods, we select our restaurants or shopping centers, we hire our employees, we decide our friends based upon an unspoken, sometimes even unconscious racial preference and bias.

Our text today raises an embarrassing but essential truth for the chosen. What's the point in extolling our love for God, whom we have never personally seen, all the while ignoring or pretending we don't see the brothers and sisters we'd have to be blind not to see? "Love one another as I have loved you" surely means to plead for both the eyes and the heart of Jesus.

CHOKING ON A CAMEL—3

We know what real love is because Christ gave up his life for us. So we also ought to give up our lives for our brothers and sisters. 1 John 3:16, NLT.

Some years ago *USA Weekend* ran a cover story on two Baptist churches in St. Paul, Minnesota—one Black, one White. It's the story of love triumphing over cultural and racial differences. It isn't a story about racial integration. Rather it is a wonderful narrative about racial reconciliation. And there is a difference: "Racial reconciliation is not the same as integration. The latter removes formal barriers, primarily laws, that keep people apart, but leaves intact the centuries-old images, beliefs and cultural barriers that divide people—the miles-high walls in our hearts and minds. In racial reconciliation, individuals consciously strive to overcome the legacy of racism, first by forging genuine bonds with at least one person of a different race" (September 10-12, 1999, p. 6).

Did you catch that? The calling of racial reconciliation is for each of us to become a committee of one and seek to forge "genuine bonds with at least one person of a different race." There must be somebody where you live, where you work, where you study, where you play that could be the one with whom you could forge a new and genuine friendship. Easy? No. Our text today goes so far as to suggest that sometimes it's a matter of laying down our lives for the sake of such radical love for a brother or a sister. Not easy, but utterly essential—Jesus' own brand of loving across the divide is proof enough.

Can we change an entire denomination? Perhaps not. Although if enough of the chosen wondered aloud about the need any more to have "separate but equal" congregations or conferences, don't you suppose the Spirit of Christ could repeat the St. Paul story again and again across the nation? For if there's no such thing as a Black Ford Motors and a White Ford Motors, then why such differentiation among the chosen? All it takes is a single change agent willing to forge genuine bonds of friendship "with at least one person of a different race." For while we may not be able to change an entire faith community or even a whole congregation, we can still become love's change agents one human being at a time, can't we?

Could that be the very reason you and I were chosen in the first place? Then let's live out our divine destiny with passion and love just as Jesus did!

ER—1

*Then Jesus went about all the cities and villages, teaching in their synagogues, preaching
the gospel of the kingdom, and healing every sickness and every disease among the people.
Matt. 9:35.*

Emergency room. You don't have to be an ER nurse or physician to know what takes place behind the swinging double doors and the hanging curtains of an emergency room. Thanks to television's preoccupation with the high-adrenaline drama and trauma of an ER, the whole world it seems knows the inner workings of an emergency room. Maybe you've done time in the crowded waiting room of a nearby ER, or perhaps you were the one they wheeled through those double doors. But whether or not you've personally experienced an emergency room, there is a simple truth about ERs that we all know intuitively: *emergency rooms are messy places.*

Do you know why? Because people come to them in the middle of a crisis. Step into an ER, and you might experience the coagulating odors of vomit, urine, blood, Lysol, antibacterial antiseptics, and exotic medicines—all wafting together in the frenetic air of that saving place. Just a few moments earlier those gurneys and beds had been draped with gloriously clean, white, sterile sheets, surrounded by septic walls and floors and drapes. But in a split second that sterile environment turned dirty, splattered, and contaminated. But that's OK, because everybody who works and lives in a hospital knows: "This is why we exist, this is why we are here—to get stained and exposed while we scramble as a team to save another life."

Isn't that the way it's supposed to be with the church of Jesus? Aren't we supposed to be soiled and stained, and at times smelly, saving places for people in the midst of a crisis, people who come just as they are in desperate hope of being saved and healed before it's too late? Doesn't the very example of Christ while He was here in our midst (as our text today portrays) define the church's emergency room mission as a hospital for sinners?

Then can you imagine an emergency room that requires its patients to get cleaned up *before* showing up? Are you kidding! There isn't a hospital or ER in the world that requires you to clean yourself and heal yourself before they'll admit you. You're supposed to *come as you are.* Because ERs and churches are *supposed* to be messy places, where people keep showing up in the middle of a life-threatening crisis. Where better to show up than the church of Jesus?

141

ER—2

When the Pharisees saw this, they asked his disciples, "Why does your teacher eat with tax collectors and 'sinners'?" On hearing this, Jesus said, "It is not the healthy who need a doctor, but the sick." Matt. 9:11, 12, NIV.

The neighborhood had never seen so many stretch limos in its life—limousines of every color, hue, size, and shape, lined up and down the sidewalks for blocks. (Everybody knows limousines are rented either for people who are important, or by people who think they are and are trying hard to prove a point.) And so they arrived in their rented status symbols, men with cheap wrinkled tuxedos and greasy slicked-back hair, pasty gaudy girlfriends clinging to their arms. Let the party begin! But where's the guest of honor? At last a battered old Dodge Caravan pulls into the driveway. And out He steps—no tux, no girl, just a bargain-basement suit and a van full of wrinkled but admiring disciples. The party host comes flying out of the noisy house, his Kodak camera flashing away—who needs the paparazzi! Jesus is here.

Matthew, Mark, and Luke all record that gala night, so profound the point Jesus made. You see, Matthew himself had been one of the hated tax collectors. And when Jesus called him to become one of the chosen, out of both profound gratitude to his Master and eager desire for his erstwhile colleagues to meet the Savior, Matthew threw Jesus the party. But the party poopers were not to be left out! Standing beneath one of Matthew's open windows, the spying Pharisees hiss to Jesus' nearby disciples the pointed barb of our text today, "What's the problem with your Master hanging around rejects like these?" And Jesus—like your mother who could track your conversations while engaged in one of her own—fired back an answer to a question that wasn't His! "It is not the healthy who need a doctor, but the sick. . . . I have not come to call the righteous, but sinners" (Matt. 9:12, 13, NIV). What kind of sinners? He doesn't say.

Heterosexual sinners and homosexual sinners, ethical sinners and unethical sinners, alcoholic and nonalcoholic sinners, Democrat and Republican sinners (and Independents, too), White and Black and Yellow sinners, rich and poor, young and old sinners, Adventist sinners and non-Adventist sinners. Apparently there are no limitations to the kinds of sinners that the church is to be an emergency room for, because Jesus simply said, "I have come to call sinners." *All sinners.* And aren't we all grateful and glad!

ER—3

Now the tax collectors and "sinners" were all gathering around to hear him. But the Pharisees and the teachers of the law muttered, "This man welcomes sinners and eats with them."
Luke 15:1, 2, NIV.

What a criticism to covet! "This man welcomes sinners and eats with them." Let's face it. That's the way Jesus was. He never met a sinner He didn't like or didn't love. And that's why the Pharisees hissed what we read in yesterday's and today's texts. Wouldn't it be wonderful if they said the same about you and me, too? "This man, this woman, welcomes sinners and eats with them." Better yet, what if they said that about our church? "This church welcomes sinners and eats with them." Sadly, I know some churches that welcome sinners and *eat them!* But there's a world of difference, isn't there?

As long as we're coveting the charges leveled against our Lord once upon a time, there's one more we might add to our list. On another occasion Jesus noted their criticism when He exposed the typical two-facedness of hypocritical religion, where—as they say—you're damned if you do and damned if you don't: "For John the Baptist came neither eating bread nor drinking wine, and you say, 'He has a demon.' The Son of Man came eating and drinking, and you say, 'Here is a glutton and a drunkard, *a friend of tax collectors and "sinners"* '" (Luke 7:33, 34, NIV). John lived separated from society in faithfulness to God, and they called him a friend of demons. Jesus lived in the midst of society in faithfulness to God, and they called Him a friend of sinners. You can't win with some people, can you?

"A friend of sinners!" What an indictment to covet, what a description to ponder, what a user-friendly example of who the chosen have been called to be! Just like Jesus. Just like a hospital emergency room.

Some worry that if the church of the chosen becomes too focused on less-respectable sinners, our church will somehow be diminished and marginalized. But quite to the contrary comes this observation a century ago: "If we would humble ourselves before God, and *be kind and courteous and tenderhearted and pitiful* [full of pity], there would be one hundred conversions to the truth where now there is only one" (*Welfare Ministry*, p. 86; italics supplied). Sounds like being a friend to sinners is Jesus' most effective way to grow His church! Then let's do it!

143

MUSEUM OR HOSPITAL?

Jesus said to him, "'You shall love the Lord your God with all your heart, with all your soul, and with all your mind.' This is the first and great commandment. And the second is like it: 'You shall love your neighbor as yourself.' On these two commandments hang all the Law and the Prophets." Matt. 22:37-40.

Do you enjoy a good museum? Chicago boasts one of the world's great collections of antiquities in its Field Museum of Natural History. And the towering *Tyrannosaurus rex* skeleton (named "Sue") near the entry is evidence enough that the museum majors in "old."

Is a museum a better metaphor for the church than a hospital? After all, isn't it the mission of the "remnant church" to preserve ancient truth and defend historic orthodoxy? "Here is a call for the endurance of the saints, those who keep the commandments of God and hold fast to the faith of Jesus" (Rev. 14:12, NRSV). You see, there it is—proof that we are to defend what is ancient, tried, and true. True—but be careful what you rule out.

An ecclesiastical lawyer once asked Jesus what was the greatest commandment of all. In today's text we see Jesus' reply, defining the *two greatest commandments* of all: first, supreme love for God, and second, impartial love for our neighbor. Which means that God's end-time chosen ones, defined by Revelation 14:12 as keeping the commandments of God, will be known as a community that loves God supremely and loves their neighbors impartially.

And when Revelation 12:17 defines the same "remnant" as having "the testimony of Jesus," wouldn't that testimony include Jesus' crucifixion-eve "eleventh commandment": "A new commandment I give to you, that you love one another; as I have loved you, that you also love one another. By this all will know that you are My disciples, if you have love for one another" (John 13:34, 35)? The point again—God's end-time chosen ones will be known the world over for their supreme love for Him, and their impartial love for their neighbors.

We have *not* been called to be a museum showcase of sainthood and orthodoxy. Rather the "orthodox saints" of the chosen have been called to live out Christ's messy, radical, healing, emergency room love for sinners of all casts and hues. Good news! You were destined to work in the ER, not dust a museum. There's a hurting sinner where you're headed today. So be the healing love God has always chosen you to be. Just like Jesus.

THE CHURCH OF THE RED CROSS

For to this you were called, because Christ also suffered for us, leaving us an example, that you should follow His steps . . . who Himself bore our sins in His own body on the tree, that we, having died to sins, might live for righteousness—by whose stripes you were healed. 1 Peter 2:21-24.

You may remember the daring rescue of guerrilla-held hostages several years ago in Colombia. It was hailed the world over as a brilliant ruse that fooled the captors into actually handing over the hostages to disguised government commandos aboard a helicopter. Unfortunately, a few days after the successful rescue a video clip revealed that as a part of the plot, one of the government soldiers was wearing a Red Cross armband as a disguise. The International Red Cross immediately lodged a formal protest, and you can understand why. If the Red Cross becomes an empty symbol commandeered as a disguise, who will trust it again?

On the eve of His own "red cross" death, Jesus quietly described how His community of followers would be known on earth. "By this everyone will know that you are my disciples, if you have love for one another" (John 13:35, NRSV). For us 2,000 years later it can mean only that an end-time community of faith must become an end-time community of love. A hospital for sinners—because there can be no more radical love and no more exalted calling for the church than to be like Jesus and become a hospital for sinners, can there?

Jim Cymbala, pastor of the Brooklyn Tabernacle, makes this appeal: "Christians often hesitate to reach out to those who are different. They want God to clean the fish before they catch them. If someone's gold ring is attached to an unusual body part, if [they] don't smell the best, or if the skin color is not the same, Christians tend to hesitate. But think for a moment about *God* reaching out to *us*. If ever there was a 'reach,' that was it: the holy, pure Deity extending himself to us who are soiled, evil-hearted, unholy" (*Fresh Wind, Fresh Fire*, p. 8).

Calvary became the divine ER for the entire human race, where the Physician sacrificed His life to save us all. Should we not then be willing to throw open to all sinners the doors of our own hearts and churches that we might love them and one another in the same way? For aren't the chosen the Church of the Red Cross? Not as a disguise, but as a genuine community of Calvary's healing love, an ER *for all*. Which is a universal coverage not even Blue Cross can match!

THE BROKEN GOBLET

For whoever keeps the whole law and yet stumbles at just one point is guilty of breaking all of it. James 2:10, NIV.

On my desk at church I keep the stem of a broken goblet. It's so that I won't forget the law of physics and the law of God. I was preaching on today's text and wanted to illustrate James's point that if you break one commandment you'll end up breaking them all. And so I decided to take a hammer and shatter a glass goblet during the sermon. I had done it once before. But since this time was live and on satellite camera, the director suggested we tape the goblet to the stand to make certain no glass would spray forward. Sorry, Isaac Newton—by taping the base, we ensured a law of physics that sent the glass exploding forward, all over the front row!

James's point is nonetheless true. Break the law at any point, and you'll shatter it all. For years I preached that text to reinforce the importance of observing the fourth commandment ("Remember the Sabbath day, to keep it holy") along with the other nine. But a few months after the broken-goblet sermon I revisited James 2 and discovered, to my surprise, that my previous application actually fell short of the radical point James is making! While the truth about God's seventh-day Sabbath is biblically incontrovertible, James in fact is *not* championing the *fourth* commandment, but is passionately appealing for the *eleventh* commandment.

James describes a congregation in which both a rich man and a poor man show up for worship. If you usher the rich man to a choice seat in the front and you motion the poor man to a pew in the back, "have you not shown partiality among yourselves, and become judges with evil thoughts?" (James 2:4). But of course! "If you really fulfill the royal law according to the Scripture, 'You shall love your neighbor as yourself,' you do well" (verse 8). God's "royal law" (impartial love for our neighbor) means we love all, regardless of economic station in life, in the same way.

To *not* love impartially, James goes on to say, is to break God's royal law in "one point" and thus shatter the whole goblet! Please note again that the breaking point he cites is not the fourth commandment, as critical as that is—but rather the eleventh, "Love one another, even as I have loved you" (John 13:34, NASB). Given His royal law, don't you suppose Calvary's King would be glad to answer our prayer today and fill us in advance with His love for those we'll meet?

THE CASTE SYSTEM

Let me not, I pray, show partiality to anyone. Job 32:21.

I was surrounded by worshippers in the towering, ornate, and colorful Hindu temple in Madurai, India. Trying to lock on to the sights and sounds and smells so unfamiliar to me, I flowed along with the river of humanity. But as we swept toward the inner sanctum, signs on the wall and signals from clerics made it clear I was to proceed no farther. Only the initiated of the proper caste pressed on. Makes you wonder, doesn't it? Even though we're not Hindus, do we, too, live with an unspoken but unsubtle caste system—arbitrary judgments whereby we (even unconsciously) classify people into neat (or not so neat) boxes marked "superior" or "inferior"?

Education or the lack of it can create caste. Some people mistake their academic achievement for personal or intellectual superiority (and insist their title be recognized), forgetting the brilliant God-man who never had formal education. *Economic status* quickly succumbs to caste thinking. But given the compelling precedent of God becoming dirt poor to save the likes of you and me, how could personal wealth ever be an accurate barometer of personal worth? *Position* (in the church or in the community) can atrophy into a caste value. The prelates in Jesus' day prayed in stained-glass voices, but Jesus' parable of the Pharisee and the publican painfully exposed the truth that being positioned and placed doesn't mean you go home from church declared right with God. *Personal opinions* can become candidates for caste. Congregations that have literally split over differences of worship preference ("You worship God in your way, and I'll worship Him in *His!*") reveal how destructively potent personal preference can become. And what about our subtle caste system of *theological differences*? Are we supposed to love people who differ from us theologically, or shall we publish and promote our criticisms and critiques, direct mailing or at least e-mailing them to every address we can unearth?

Let's be honest—the enemy of impartiality has devised an interminable catalog of ways and walls to devilishly divide us. "Let them go somewhere else—we don't need them around here!" Oh, but we do, both James and Jesus cry out. The royal law and the eleventh commandment and Calvary are utterly clear—God's outstretched arms are for all, and we must be, too. Which makes the prayer of Elihu the right prayer for the chosen, wouldn't you agree?

"Lord, let me not, I pray, show partiality to anyone." Amen.

THE GOOD SAM CLUB—1

The man wanted to justify his actions, so he asked Jesus, "And who is my neighbor?"
Luke 10:29, NLT.

Once upon a time a city-slicker lawyer stood up, cleared his throat, and set out to embarrass an itinerant country preacher in front of the whole crowd. "What do I have to do to get saved?" he asked. But the preacher was no country bumpkin and wisely answered the scholar's question with a question: "What do you read in the law?" To which the thoroughly schooled lawyer shot back, "Love God with all your heart and soul and strength and mind." It was the familiar Shema of Israel and had been a memory verse from kindergarten days. But for good measure the lawyer quickly threw in one more familiar line from the ancient law just to be safe—"And you should love your neighbor as yourself." Perfect!

But the self-congratulatory smile quickly vanished when the country preacher quietly congratulated the lawyer for having answered his own question. To the twitter of the crowd, the lawyer scrambled to regain the edge in his repartee with the Master. "But who is my neighbor?"

In response Jesus weaves a story straight out of the daily news with unsubtle racial overtones—about a Jewish victim, a Jewish clergyman, a Jewish elder, and a Samaritan businessman. As we noted earlier, it took *chutzpah* even to mention a Samaritan (the hated half-breeds of Palestine), but it is sheer daring to now elevate the Samaritan to hero before that Jewish audience! And when He gets to the end of the story, Jesus turns to the lawyer and recasts the lawyer's question: "Which one of these was the real neighbor?" And when the lawyer wouldn't even mention the name but instead mumbled, "The one who showed him mercy," Jesus was primed and ready with His revolutionary punch line: "Go and do likewise" (Luke 10:37).

Ponder this classic summation in *The Desire of Ages*: "Thus the question, 'Who is my neighbor?' is forever answered. Christ has shown that our neighbor does not mean merely one of the church or faith to which we belong. It has no reference to race, color, or class distinction. Our neighbor is every person who needs our help. Our neighbor is every soul who is wounded and bruised by the adversary. Our neighbor is everyone who is the property of God" (p. 503).

To whom shall I be a neighbor today? *To anyone in need.* That's why the chosen make the best neighbors of all, because just like Jesus they belong to the Good Sam Club.

THE GOOD SAM CLUB—2

But a certain Samaritan, as he journeyed, came where he was. And when he saw him, he had compassion. So he went to him and bandaged his wounds, pouring on oil and wine; and he set him on his own animal, brought him to an inn, and took care of him. On the next day, when he departed, he took out two denarii, gave them to the innkeeper, and said to him, "Take care of him; and whatever more you spend, when I come again, I will repay you." Luke 10:33-35.

The headline would catch anybody's eye: "Couple test faith by taking in sex offender—Neighborhood angry about ex-con moving in with family of four" (South Bend *Tribune*, Sept. 2, 1999). It's the true story about Nate Sims, a sex offender released from prison after 20 years, and Mark and Tammy LaPalme, "baby Christians" who decided to test their born-again faith and compassion by inviting Sims to share their home in Danville, Kentucky. "Instead of a jail cell, the 52-year-old Sims found himself living in . . . upscale Riverview Estates—with a couple who trusted him enough to bed him down across the hall from their children's playroom. 'I was in shock,' Sims said recently in a voice that seemed too soft to have come from his six-foot-four-inch frame. 'I ain't never had anyone lift a hand for me'" (*ibid.*). But the story isn't over. Because the neighbors found out, and bright-yellow flyers soon papered the neighborhood, warning of a sex offender in the LaPalme home. Anonymous letters followed. The press descended on that quiet street. It was more than Nate Sims could bear, and a few days later he fled.

So who was the neighbor in this modern good Samaritan tale? The irate Riverview Estates dwellers? The press? The LaPalme family? What if I told you the LaPalme family was Black and Nate Sims White? I'm not going to tell you. Jesus' radical point in the Good Sam parable is clear enough—*anyone in need is my neighbor.* And "thou shalt love thy neighbour as thyself" (Lev. 19:18, KJV). So do you? Do I?

What if we all joined the Good Sam Club? Sure, we could drive by or walk by and pretend we didn't see. But what if we acted on our conscience, and acted out our compassion? I have a friend who begins each day with this quiet prayer: "Lord, lead me today to someone to whom I can speak a word of kindness or lend a hand of assistance. Lead me to someone today who needs a good neighbor. I don't need to save the world today. Just let me make a small difference in one life, I pray. Amen."

THE PLEA OF THE DYING SOLDIER

Then Jesus said, "Father, forgive them, for they do not know what they do." Luke 23:34.

In his disturbing book *The Sunflower* the late Simon Wiesenthal relives the gripping, dark narrative of that moment when he was secretly removed one day from his work detail as a young Jewish prisoner in a Nazi concentration camp and led by an expressionless nurse up the stairs and down the hallway of a nearby Polish hospital. At last he found himself (despite his nervous fear and better judgment) standing by the bedside of a dying Nazi SS soldier, his face entirely bandaged except for four openings—one for the mouth, one for the nose, and two for the ears. Yellow stains oozed through the bandages where the eyes must have been. The nurse left, and the soldier groped for the hand of the boy. And when with hoarse whisper the man spoke, what tumbled forth was the surreal but tortured confession of an act of genocide against a house filled with 150 to 200 helpless Jews. Haunted by the nightmares of his complicity in that awful crime, the dying man's last desperate request to his nurse had been for a Jew, any Jew, to whom he might confess his sin. And so will you forgive me was the plea of the bandaged head. Wiesenthal describes the raging battle within his own young heart as he sat in the shadows beside that bed—shall I forgive him or shall I not? At last without a word he left the room.

Twenty-five years later, still haunted by that deathbed confession and his decision not to forgive, Simon Wiesenthal—who miraculously survived the Holocaust but lost 86 family members and loved ones to it—ends his narrative with these words: "You, who have just read this sad and tragic episode in my life, can mentally change places with me and ask yourself the crucial question, 'What would I have done?'" (p. 98).

Would you have forgiven him? If you were a Jew? If you were an African-American? If you were the victim of childhood abuse? If you were the target of workplace discrimination? If you were the sufferer in an extramarital affair? If you were a single parent? If you were the parent of a runaway? Would you forgive?

We know what Jesus of Nazareth would have done—we heard Him do it again in our text for today—"Father, forgive them, for they do not know what they do." But what would you do? What would I do? That God might forgive, all the great religions of the world allow. But that we should forgive each other? How far and how much? No wonder we need the cross of Jesus!

THE TWO LORD'S PRAYERS

In this manner, therefore, pray: Our Father in heaven, hallowed be Your name. Your kingdom come. Your will be done on earth as it is in heaven. Give us this day our daily bread. And forgive us our debts, as we forgive our debtors. Matt. 6:9-12.

One of the great stories of forgiveness in this modern age is the biography of Nelson Mandela, still a household name throughout the Republic of South Africa. I have stood in his very tiny home in Soweto, where the seeds of his vision for the freedom of his people and all peoples were first sown. The black-and-white picture of a young Mandela, peering through the bars of the infamous Robben Island prison, spread to the world when after 27 years of incarceration he forgave his jailer and rose up to lead his country into national reconciliation and forgiveness.

Two thousand years earlier the greatest of all forgiveness stories played out in excruciating, crimson drama atop the dusty knoll of Golgotha, when through tortured breath Jesus prayed for the forgiveness of not only His jailers but His prosecutors, His judges, His executioners: "Father, forgive them, for they do not know what they do" (Luke 23:34). Consider this profound commentary on the Lord's Prayer of Calvary from *The Desire of Ages*: "That prayer of Christ for His enemies embraced the world. *It took in every sinner that had lived or should live, from the beginning of the world to the end of time.* Upon all rests the guilt of crucifying the Son of God. To all, forgiveness is freely offered. 'Whosoever will' may have peace with God, and inherit eternal life" (p. 745; italics supplied). Did you catch that? You and I were forgiven that Friday long ago in the second Lord's Prayer.

No wonder the first Lord's Prayer reads the way it literally does in the Greek: "Forgive us our debts as we *forgave* our debtors." And that is why the only commentary Jesus ever gave on His model prayer immediately follows it: "For if you forgive others their trespasses, your heavenly Father will also forgive you; but if you do not forgive others, neither will your Father forgive your trespasses"(Matt. 6:14, 15, NRSV). Why such strong language in the first Lord's Prayer? Because of the profound promise in the second Lord's Prayer. If every sin of yours and mine was covered by Jesus' prayer for forgiveness on the cross, then shouldn't our hearts, so freely forgiven, forgive those who *have* sinned or *still* sin against us? Like Mandela, like Jesus?

WHEN THE DEBT RATIO
IS 600,000 TO ONE

Freely you have received, freely give. Matt. 10:8.

Once upon a time there was a man who owed so much money that if you changed his debt into dollar coins and stacked them on top of each other they would have stretched 142 miles into the heavens! And when the king found out about it, it wasn't a very pretty scene. But the desperate servant fell at the king's feet and pleaded for patience. (He should've pleaded for mercy—since his 10,000-talent debt was 1,250 times the combined annual taxes of the region of Palestine in Jesus' day!) As Jesus told the story: "Then [the king] was filled with pity for him, and he released him and forgave his debt" (Matt. 18:27, NLT). Can you believe it! The servant owes the king the equivalent of 60 million days of back wages, and the king forgives it all!

I wish the story ended there, but it doesn't. Because no sooner does the forgiven servant exit the palace (no doubt whistling, "Zip-a-dee-doo-dah, zip-a-dee-ay—my, oh my, what a wonderful day!") than does he run into one of his fellow servants, who happens to owe him 100 days of back wages. And when this second servant makes the same plea for patience, he gets neither patience nor mercy. Instead, the forgiven servant throws this hapless fellow in jail over a paltry debt 1/600,000th of what he had owed the king! And when the king hears the whole sorry story, guess who's livid! "You wicked slave, I forgave you all that debt because you pleaded with me. Should you not also have had mercy on your fellow slave, in the same way that I had mercy on you?" (verses 32, 33, NASB). And with that the king throws the now *un*forgiven servant into jail, until he pays off 60 million days or he dies, whichever comes first!

Jesus' punch line? "So my heavenly Father will also do to every one of you, if you do not forgive your brother or sister from your heart" (verse 35, NRSV). Twice in Matthew Jesus uses this very strong forgiveness language of quid pro quo. Where's our loving God in that! But think about it. How can God forgive me, when I withhold from Him the one area of my life that needs forgiveness, i.e., my unforgiving spirit? "Release me from my debt," I plead, when all the while I'm hanging on to it. What's a loving God to do? Hence, God's golden rule of forgiveness—whatever forgiveness you want from Me, you must offer to others—no forgiveness for them, no forgiveness for you.

Moral of the story? As freely you have been forgiven by God, freely forgive all others.

CONFUCIUS' PROVERB

For you know the grace of our Lord Jesus Christ, that though He was rich, yet for your sakes He became poor, that you through His poverty might become rich. 2 Cor. 8:9.

The ancient Chinese sage Confucius once taught: "If you devote your life to seeking revenge, first dig two graves." It's true, isn't it? When I refuse to forgive the one who has wronged me and instead spend my energies and my life seeking to get even, I end up destroying myself as well, do I not?

In his book *The Sunflower* Simon Wiesenthal not only relates the dark story of his youthful decision not to accept a dying Nazi soldier's plea for forgiveness (as we noted on May 19)—he also includes the responses of 53 distinguished men and women to his query, "What would *you* have done?" One of those respondents was best-selling author and rabbi Harold Kushner, who in his essay tells the story of a woman in his congregation: "She is a single mother, divorced, working to support herself and three young children. She says to me, 'Since my husband walked out on us, every month is a struggle to pay our bills. I have to tell my kids we have no money to go to the movies, while he's living it up with his new wife in another state. How can you tell me to forgive him?' I answer her, 'I'm not asking you to forgive him because what he did was acceptable. It wasn't; it was mean and selfish. I'm asking you to forgive because he doesn't deserve the power to live in your head and turn you into a bitter, angry woman. I'd like to see him out of your life emotionally as completely as he is out of it physically, but you keep holding on to him. You're not hurting him by holding on to that resentment, but you're hurting yourself' " (pp. 185, 186).

You may be one of those who have been severely wounded at the hands of another. The pain you have suffered is so sharp, so deep, so close to the surface that it now throbs into nearly every waking hour of your day. Something deep inside of you cries out for vengeance. And so you refuse to forgive so hurtful a wound and so evil a wounder. But is worth it in the end?

The rabbi and the sage are right. We destroy ourselves when we refuse to forgive.

The Man on the center cross not only forgave us in His prayer—He forgave our perpetrators, too. Perhaps then it will be His greatest healing when we learn not only to pray for our own forgiveness, but also to pray for the forgiveness of our enemies.

THE BEATITUDE IN THE MIDDLE AND AT THE END

Blessed are the merciful, for they shall obtain mercy. Matt. 5:7.

It was March 1935, and the 77-year-old gentleman lay dying of cancer in the Glendale Hospital of Los Angeles. A weary and worn warrior of the faith, his heart was troubled, for he knew that there had come an estrangement between him and another veteran leader of the faith. Before he died he must make it right. And so it was that the dying man, Arthur Grosvenor Daniells, president of the Seventh-day Adventist Church a century ago, hurriedly sent a message. Soon Willie White, the son of Ellen White and secretary of the White Estate, was seated at the bedside of A. G. Daniells.

The church archivist Bert Haloviak wrote up this portion of their ensuing conversation in the *Adventist Review* (Mar. 27, 1997): "White: 'I long for the time when we can sit down together as we used to do and talk over the progress of God's work.'

"Daniells: 'Brother White, let me have your hand. . . . I have not rendered you very good service.'

"White: 'Oh, don't think of that. Think of what we have done when we were working together.'

"Daniells: 'Yes, . . . we worked out some immortal principles, sitting on the deck of that old steamer. . . . I wanted my hand to clasp your hand as one of my truest friends on earth.'

"As the visit ended, Daniells told his colleague that he knew he had made mistakes in his leadership, but rejoiced that he had been 'bound up with the greatest character' to have lived in the modern era, Ellen White.

"Two days later Daniells died."

"Blessed are the merciful, for they shall obtain mercy." A little mercy can go a long way, can it not, even to the threshold of death? No wonder that of the nine beatitudes in Matthew's Sermon on the Mount, it is *this* beatitude that lies in the middle, a shining centerpiece to Jesus' portrayal of the chosen. For what could be more like their Master than the chosen having mercy upon each other?

Willie White's mother was right: "And in the hour of final need the merciful shall find refuge in the mercy of the compassionate Savior and shall be received into everlasting habitations" (*Thoughts From the Mount of Blessing*, p. 24). Mercy for the merciful even beyond death!

WHAT EVERY CARPENTER KNOWS

Judge not, that you be not judged. For with what judgment you judge, you will be judged; and with the measure you use, it will be measured back to you. Matt. 7:1, 2.

Having two carpenter aprons hanging on your garage wall doth not a carpenter make, as my wife and children will attest to you! But I know just enough about carpentry to realize that it can teach us an invariable law about human nature—a law that, if we get it and understand it and live it, will forever change the way we treat each other at home, at school, at work, at play. In fact, get this law straight and you'll never be the same again.

Every carpenter knows how to saw wood. But whether you've ever sawn a piece or not, you know that when the iron teeth of the saw cut against the wood very tiny pieces of residual wood fall to the floor. Sawdust. So here's the question: Which would you rather have stuck in your eye, that very, very tiny piece of sawdust . . . or the entire board?

Once upon a time there was a Carpenter who declared that the answer is a no-brainer! "Why do you look at the speck of sawdust in your brother's eye and pay no attention to the plank in your own eye? How can you say to your brother, 'Let me take the speck out of your eye,' when all the time there is a plank in your own eye?" (Matt. 7:3, 4, NIV). There it is—that great law of human nature: *what you criticize in others is invariably true about you.* That the little speck of sawdust that you see in somebody else's life, if the truth were known (as it is by God), happens to be a 10-foot two-by-four in your own life!

No wonder Jesus opens this teaching with the words of our text today, "Judge not, that you be not judged. For . . . with the measure you use, it will be measured back to you." Because the moment I open my mouth to point out *your* faults and weaknesses, I am very unsubtly and unmistakably identifying those as *my* faults and weaknesses, too! You see, the measure or skill with which I criticize you has been immeasurably enhanced by my own personal experience with those same sins and weaknesses. Why do you think I am so quick to spot them in you? For the same reason that once you drive a Ford Taurus you suddenly spot Tauruses everywhere. We all know the stories of televangelists who've thundered against the sins of others, only to be "outed" by the press. But let's not be too hard on them. Truth is, we all criticize in others what is true about ourselves. Which is why the Carpenter was so adamant: Do not judge!

THE THIN LINE

There is only one Lawgiver and Judge, the one who is able to save and destroy. But you—who are you to judge your neighbor? James 4:12, NIV.

Living in an academic community, I recognize that the lifeblood of educational institutions is "criticism." There are whole branches of knowledge based on criticism—literary criticism, historical criticism, higher and lower criticism, etc. That's why we have universities, so that the student's mental acuity can be developed in order to challenge theories, critique ideas, scrutinize evidence, and criticize conclusions. We must learn to "think critically" so that we don't fall for notions or assertions that fall far short of the truth. After all, our Creator fashioned our minds to carefully, prayerfully reason our way through life.

In His sermon on the mount Jesus does not challenge critical thinking, but does condemn critical acting. "Hypocrite! First remove the plank from your own eye, and then you will see clearly to remove the speck from your brother's eye" (Matt. 7:5). The Greek for "hypocrite," *hupokritēs*, is a word for the actor on a Greek stage—one who pretends to be what he is not—she wears a mask and fools her audience. When I fool everybody by acting or pretending to be what I am not, I am a hypocrite. And I have crossed the thin line between critical thinking and critical acting. And therein lies the danger, not only for academics but for all.

But is it a sin to criticize another? The English word "criticize" is based on the word "critic," which comes from the Greek *krites*, which is the word for a "judge." When we criticize someone, we in essence take the seat of a judge and pass judgment. But as our text today reminds us, there is only one Judge in the universe. So when I criticize you, I assume the sole prerogative of God Himself! And in any book, that is a sin—playing God by judging you.

Remember the Carpenter's law? What you criticize in others is invariably true about you. Oswald Chambers drives home that truth: "Every wrong thing that I see in you, God locates in me. Every time I judge, I condemn myself. . . . Stop having a measuring rod for other people. There is always one fact more in every man's case about which we know nothing. . . . I have never met the man I could despair of after discerning what lies in me apart from the grace of God" (*My Utmost for His Highest*, June 17). So why be the resident critic/criticizer in your marriage, your congregation, your office, your school? Let God be judge, and you be at peace.

THE GOLDEN RULER

So in everything, do to others what you would have them do to you, for this sums up the Law and the Prophets. Matt. 7:12, NIV.

Is there any mercy for the judgmental likes of you and me? Hallelujah, there is! And you'll find the secret in every carpenter's apron. It's a tape measure, or ruler, that every carpenter needs in order to be guided by an undeviating uniform standard. Use the ruler, and you'll get the identical dimensions and the same results every time. But as every carpenter knows, you must stick to the rule of this ruler. Deviate from it, and you'll ruin your work.

That was the Divine Carpenter's point, of course, in giving to us His guiding, uniform standard that we still call the golden rule, or ruler. We've memorized it from childhood: "Do unto others as you would have them do unto you." Plain and simple, treat others the way you want to be treated. It isn't rocket science. It's the golden ruler of character carpentry.

And as my friend and colleague Skip MacCarty observes, it has been the operative golden ruler of the Father, Son, and Holy Spirit from eternity past: "The Trinitarian covenant of love reveals itself in each treating the others as He would want to be treated were their roles reversed. . . . The 'golden rule' (Matt. 7:12) plumbs the depths of God's commitment inwardly within the Trinity and outwardly to His entire creation" (*In Granite or Ingrained?* pp. 4, 5). The Divine Carpenter has always lived by His own golden ruler. Which is why Jesus, who had every right to throw the book at His betrayer Judas in condemnation, quietly called him "Friend" (Matt. 26:50). Jesus was treating Judas the precise way He Himself longed to be treated, as a friend. Look at how He treated His taunting executioners. The Judge of all the earth (John 5:22)—who alone could justifiably call down invectives upon the entire sorry lot of them—refused to condemn them. Instead, when they stretched out the hands of the Divine Carpenter to nail them to the very wood He once crafted, with His last ounce of strength He reached into His broken heart and pulled out His ruler, the rule. And He treated His enemies the very way He would want them to treat Him were their positions reversed. He prayed for mercy to save them.

Do you suppose Jesus' example may be the simplest antidote to the spirit of criticism today? To intercede for her instead of criticizing her. To pray for him instead of judging him. Can you imagine what would happen if we lived by the golden ruler of Calvary's Carpenter?

WHAT WOULD BE THE MOST MERCIFUL THING TO DO?

For I desire mercy and not sacrifice, and the knowledge of God more than burnt offerings.
Hosea 6:6.

I love weddings! The glowing adoration, the shining affection that glistens in the nuptials' eyes as they breathlessly gaze into the other's face, hand in hand, hardly moving as the preacher drones on—is there a young man at that moment who wouldn't gladly give up half his kingdom were the damsel to ask it? For it is the joy of love to fulfill the longing of the other (at least it was on our wedding day!), isn't it?

Hosea 6:6 must have been a memory verse Jesus learned as a child—for He's the only one to quote it in the New Testament (twice in Matthew). It may be a dusty old line from an ancient prophet, but on Jesus' lips it becomes a powerful depiction of what it is that God, the unrelenting newlywed of His earth children, wants most of all. "I desire mercy." Could He have been clearer? The Hebrew *chesed* can be rendered "lovingkindness," "mercy," "unfailing love." In a single word it captures the deep covenantal commitment of newlyweds and lifelong lovers. It is the very essence of God, and clearly He longs for it to be lived out in the lives of His chosen. Jesus Himself declared, "Be merciful, even as your Father is merciful" (Luke 6:36, ESV).

As I've brooded over His call to mercy (to live "mercy-fully" or full of mercy), I've begun to experiment with a simple question. Perhaps it will be helpful for you: *What would be the most merciful response I could make in this instance?* For example, somebody calls me up and asks me for help—how should I respond? Or I want to give someone a piece of my mind for messing up—what would Mercy say? Or a colleague is in trouble, overloaded, burdened—what shall I do? Or two of us were gunning for the same gas pump or parking spot—what is the most merciful response? Or somebody's asked me for money? Or I have an acquaintance who is lost without Jesus? Or my pet dog needs to go out, but I'm late to an appointment? (Sounds trivial, perhaps, but "he who loves God will not only love his fellow men, but will regard with tender compassion the creatures God has made" [*Sons and Daughters of God*, p. 52].) Don't you suppose God could grow and guide us in seeking to make His mercy our default setting, so that instead of stewing with knotted stomachs, we can choose to live out the way of Mercy with an inner peace and quiet joy for the One who asked us to?

THE *VIA DOLOROSA*

From that time Jesus began to show to His disciples that He must go to Jerusalem, and suffer many things from the elders and chief priests and scribes, and be killed, and be raised the third day. Matt. 16:21.

Did you know that when Mercy comes a-runnin', she always takes the same road? The road is called the *Via Dolorosa*—Latin for "the way of grief" or "the way of sorrow" or "the way of suffering." In fact, a road today in Old Jerusalem is named the *Via Dolorosa*. I have traversed that sacred alley where tradition tells us the bloody footprints of Jesus stumbled. The *Via Dolorosa*, the way of suffering. Because without suffering, Mercy couldn't be mercy, could it?

"From that time Jesus began to show to His disciples that *He must . . . suffer many things*" (Matt. 16:21).

But that's just it, isn't it? It's that "must suffer" part that none of us wants. Goethe, the German philosopher poet, once remarked: "There are four things I hate—tobacco smoke, garlic, bedbugs, and the cross." Because nobody wants that "must suffer" part that the cross so nakedly portrays.

No wonder that no sooner had Jesus spoken this somber acknowledgment of impending suffering than Peter "took Him aside and began to rebuke Him" (verse 22). For just like Goethe, Peter had his own list of four things he hated—and "the cross" was one of them! "Far be it from You, Lord; this shall not happen to You!" (verse 22) No way, José—no way, Jesus—no *Via Dolorosa* for You, or (if we might read the subplot between the lines of Peter's vehement protest) for me!

And when Jesus twisted out of Peter's condescending grasp and looked His friend straight in the eye and uttered the most stinging rebuke ever to fall from His lips, we learned the truth that without suffering, Mercy couldn't be mercy. "Get away from me, Satan! You are a dangerous trap to me. You are seeing things merely from a human point of view, and not from God's" (verse 23, NLT).

Because from God's point of view the *Via Dolorosa* is the road Mercy always takes. The way of suffering is the way of mercy. So if it is you who is suffering today, your heart can know these two realities: you are on the road Mercy always takes, and Mercy is with you.

NIGHT

He cuts off every branch in me that bears no fruit, while every branch that does bear fruit he prunes so that it will be even more fruitful. John 15:2, NIV.

Elie Wiesel, the Nobel Peace Prize-winning author, in his classic book *Night*, recalls his survival as a boy in a concentration camp for Jews during World War II. He was in the prison long house alongside his father, who was wasting away with dysentery. Each night they were given a bowl of watery soup and a hard crust of bread. One night as 12-year-old Elie was feeding his father that crust of bread, one of the Jewish collaborators who supervised the prisoners snarled to the boy that he ought to eat that piece of bread himself and forget about his dying father. Wiesel describes the ensuing anguished struggle in his young heart, debating over whether to alleviate his own suffering by letting his father die.

Because nobody wants to suffer, do we? Do you think it was easy for Jesus?

And yet, could it be that the way of suffering is the only way Christ's chosen ones can be brought to the ultimate fullness of spiritual bloom, just like Him? What else could Jesus have meant when on the eve of His own death He spoke the words of our text today? "Every branch that does bear fruit [the Father] prunes so that it will be even more fruitful." In that single profound declaration Jesus makes clear that the painful cutting and pruning of the *Via Dolorosa*, "the way of suffering," is the divine pathway to the most exquisite blossom and fruitage possible in the human life! The way of suffering is the way of mercy.

Think about it for a moment. Who are the people who minister most to you in your pain? Those who have no inkling of what it is you're enduring? Or those who themselves have been through the same? When you've been fired from your job, who ministers most to you? When you've been flunked from your class? When you're battling cancer? When you're suffering divorce? When you're grieving over your child? When you're grieving over your sin? Who is it you want to come running but one who has journeyed that same *Via Dolorosa*, the same way of suffering?

How can that be? Ah, because when you suffer, Mercy grants you an heretofore-unavailable capacity to become empathetic mercy toward others. Because Mercy could not be mercy without suffering. And it is that reality that makes both Jesus and you so very special.

A NIAGARA FALLS
FOR YOUR OWN HEART

Now hope does not disappoint, because the love of God has been poured out in our hearts by the Holy Spirit who was given to us. Rom. 5:5.

Have you ever been to the Niagara Falls, ranked number three in the world in terms of water flow, with 600,000 gallons of water *per second* plunging over those precipices? Only two people have survived going over that watery edge without any stunt device for protection. A 7-year-old boy, wearing a life preserver, was thrown into the river in a boating accident and washed over the 180-foot plunge of the Horseshoe Falls and actually floated to one of the *Maid of the Mist* tour boats and was rescued. The other survivor was a daredevil who jumped into the waters with only shirt and pants, floated on his back over the edge (bystanders say with a smile on his face), and survived the free-fall height of a 20-story building, swimming to shore safely, where he was promptly arrested and fined $10,000. (There is no fine if you don't survive.)

Our text today has to be the Niagara Falls of Holy Scripture! Want to know where the love of the chosen comes from? It comes from the thundering cataracts described in Romans 5:5—"the love of God has been poured out in our hearts by the Holy Spirit who was given to us." More than 600,000 gallons a second, the truth is that in the gift of Jesus every last drop of God's love in the universe has been poured out!

Notice the theme of water in this stunning depiction: "All the paternal love which has come down from generation to generation through the channel of human hearts, all the springs of tenderness which have opened in the souls of men, are but as a tiny rill to the boundless ocean when compared with the infinite, exhaustless love of God. Tongue cannot utter it; pen cannot portray it. You may meditate upon it every day of your life; you may search the Scriptures diligently in order to understand it; you may summon every power and capability that God has given you, in the endeavor to comprehend the love and compassion of the heavenly Father; and yet there is an infinity beyond. You may study that love for ages; yet you can never fully comprehend the length and the breadth, the depth and the height, of the love of God in giving His Son to die for the world. Eternity itself can never fully reveal it" (*Testimonies,* vol. 5, p. 740).

Let the chosen be reminded that the very love Christ summons for this final generation is "but as a tiny rill" to the boundless Niagara Falls of the "infinite, exhaustless love of God."

BABY NUMBER 81

When we were utterly helpless, Christ came at just the right time and died for us sinners. Now, most people would not be willing to die for an upright person, though someone might perhaps be willing to die for a person who is especially good. But God showed his great love for us by sending Christ to die for us while we were still sinners. Rom. 5:6-8, NLT.

Baby Number 81" must have been the most loved and beloved baby on earth during those few days. The story behind his name was simple but sad—he was the eighty-first victim carried into that little Sri Lankan hospital after the devastating Christmas tsunami struck in 2004. No mother, no father, no siblings, this baby survived the tidal wave and was left at the hospital by a stranger who found him alive. The plot thickened, however, when in the subsequent days *nine mothers* came forward to claim him as their own tiny son! One of them was so distraught that in front of the news cameras she broke into the hospital nursery and snatched away the baby boy, only to be halted by nurses rushing to the ward to reclaim him. A judge ruled that the tearful pleadings of all nine mothers had to wait until DNA testing could determine the genetic bond and the rightful mother. Until then, Baby Number 81 was the most loved baby on earth.

And that is the gospel truth about you and me and the chosen, is it not? Given the stirring declaration of our text today, which one of us cannot go to bed at night, just like Baby Number 81, with the very certain assurance that we are loved, truly loved by the God and Father of us all? We don't need nine mothers claiming us, only one Father, who "showed his great love for us by sending Christ to die for us while we were still sinners" (Rom. 5:8, NLT).

Is there a "genetic bond" between the Father and you and me? Is the DNA of His love a match with the way you and I love the world around us? The good news about the eleventh commandment for the chosen is that Jesus doesn't command us to grit our teeth and scare up a love that is strangely unavailable or inaccessible. Rather His quiet command for us to love one another even as He has loved us is in reality simply an invitation to allow the love of God that has been poured *into* our hearts by the Holy Spirit to then be poured out *from* our hearts by the same Spirit. "Let My Spirit pour out of you what My love has poured into you."

Calvary is evidence enough that the chosen are chosen not because of *their* love, but because of *His*. And getting that straight is the first step in loving this world back to Him.

162

"IN THE CONFLUX OF ETERNITIES!"

Now all these things . . . were written for our admonition, upon whom the ends of the ages have come. 1 Cor. 10:11.

One evening Thomas Carlyle, the great English philosopher, found himself in a house full of guests at a New Year's Eve party in a home in northern England. As the evening dragged on, the idle chitchat and frivolous banter of the partygoers began to wear on his soul. Deciding to leave the crowd to its dance and song, Carlyle slipped out of the house and stepped into the black and ominous night, the silver stars shut away by angry storm clouds that spanned the dark horizon. A chill and moaning wind tore at his cloak. Through the darkness Carlyle found his way down to the pounding sea, until at last he stood on the English shore. As windswept breakers crashed at his feet, the midnight thunders roared overhead, and the black night spilled into the darkness of the deep. The old year was vanishing before the new, and the soul of the great philosopher, caught up in the enormity of it all, cried out: "I stand in the center of immensities, in the conflux of eternities!" (Llewellyn A. Wilcox, *Now Is the Time*, p. 15).

And so do we, for there has never been a generation on earth that has faced the accumulated critical "immensities" that we do. Ecologically, doomsayers predict the demise of our planet's delicately balanced ecosystem. Economically, the wisest sages on earth despair of ever reversing our free-falling global economies. Morally, society is hemorrhaging, and no power seems able to stanch evil's bloodletting. Politically, the governments of earth desperately look for some charismatic leader who might yet unite the world in peace. Spiritually, the religions of this civilization urgently seek a collaboration to save the planet's inhabitants.

And prophetically? The ancient prophets, to a man, prophesied the coalescing of these very forces on the eve of earth's destruction (read, deliverance). But after His own litany of end-time predictions (that read like our daily headlines of late), Jesus dramatically shifted the focus from doom to hope when He promised: "So when all these things begin to happen, stand and look up, for your salvation is near!" (Luke 21:28, NLT).

And that means that to this generation of the chosen, "upon whom the ends of the ages have come," is bequeathed the greatest "conflux of eternities," the greatest hope of all—the soon return of Christ. No wonder He commands us to stand tall with hope!

163

"IS THERE ANY H-O-P-E?"

We wait for the blessed hope—the glorious appearing of our great
God and Savior, Jesus Christ. Titus 2:13, NIV.

Years ago an experimental submarine turned turtle off the Eastern seaboard of the U.S., and with its crew encased within sank to the bottom of the sea. Rescue efforts began immediately. And eventually sonar readings picked up the Morse-code tapping of the survivors inside the upturned sub. Slowly their message was banged out against the hull of the sunken vessel: "I-s t-h-e-r-e a-n-y h-o-p-e?"

It is a collective question the world over, isn't it? "Is there any hope?" You can hear the Morse-code tapping coming through the urgent and clamoring questions of the press corps to that president or prime minister who stands before the gaggle of microphones to make another statement in the midst of yet another national crisis. "Is there any hope?" You hear its tapping behind the headlines of the financial Web sites that monitor 24/7 the gritty details of the monetary fluctuations in the economic meltdowns that now seem interminable. "Is there any hope?" The video news cams that zoom in to the anguished and distraught faces of those bombing survivors, interviewed for their dazed reaction to the mindless tragedy, pick up the tapping. "Is there any hope?" Stand at the edge of the huddled mourners at that graveside, and you can hear it in their muffled sobs. "Is there any hope?"

Why? Because hope is the stuff of human survival—that's why. The proverb could just as well be formulated, "Where there is no *hope*, the people perish."

So what is the hope of the chosen, the hope that can yet save this generation? "One of the most solemn and yet most glorious truths revealed in the Bible is that of Christ's second coming, to complete the great work of redemption. To God's pilgrim people, so long left to sojourn in 'the region and shadow of death,' *a precious, joy-inspiring hope* is given in the promise of His appearing, who is 'the resurrection and the life,' to 'bring home again His banished.' The doctrine of the second advent is *the very key-note* of the Sacred Scriptures" (*Maranatha*, p. 13; italics supplied).

That "very key-note" is the very message your world and mine desperately need right now. So let's go out today with hope—hope as it is in Jesus—which makes it "blessed" indeed!

THE BABY AND THE BATHWATER

Do not let your hearts be troubled. . . . I am going there to prepare a place for you. And if I go and prepare a place for you, I will come back and take you to be with me that you also may be where I am. John 14:1-3, NIV.

Philip Gulley, in his delightful book *Front Porch Tales*, recalls the day he and his four siblings, along with Mom and Dad, were on vacation and stopped to eat at a Stuckey's. When the family piled back into the car and drove off, young Philip was in the restroom. Twenty miles down the road someone counted heads and discovered the omission! As Gulley describes it, they "took a quick vote to come back for me. It was almost a tie, but at the last minute Mom changed her mind" (pp. 68, 69).

While that isn't quite like throwing out the baby with the bathwater, nevertheless it's a reminder that there are some things (or some ones) that we must never leave behind. Given the phenomenal best-selling success a few years ago of the evangelical novel series *Left Behind*—a fictionalized depiction of the secret rapture of Christ and the ensuing seven years of horrendous tribulation on earth—the return of Jesus is very obviously on the minds of at least this nation's Christians. For that, I for one am grateful. And while it is evident that the *Left Behind* novels left behind some critical truths of Scripture, nevertheless we mustn't throw out the Baby (of Bethlehem) with the bathwater. In our exuberance to defend the truth and correct the errors about the second and soon coming of Christ, we must not forget to affirm and celebrate the shining good news that's at the heart of it all—the return of Jesus!

After all, the most beloved promise in Holy Scripture (next to John 3:16) is found in the upper-room words of Jesus that are our text today. "Do not let your heart be troubled . . . I will come back."

And look what that promise means! "Long have we waited for our Savior's return. But nonetheless sure is the promise. Soon we shall be in our promised home. There Jesus will lead us beside the living stream flowing from the throne of God and will explain to us the dark providences through which on this earth He brought us in order to perfect our characters. There we shall behold with undimmed vision the beauties of Eden restored" (*Testimonies,* vol. 8, p. 254).

Is it any wonder they call the hope "blessed"!

GOOD NEWS, BAD NEWS?

Then they will see the Son of Man coming in the clouds with great power and glory. And then He will send His angels, and gather together His elect from the four winds, from the farthest part of earth to the farthest part of heaven. Mark 13:26, 27.

One wintry night Karen and I with some friends set out on a moonlight walk through the snow to the nearby Rose Hill Cemetery. The night sky was cloudless and crystalline, the air frigid and still. And awash as it was with the silver light of a full moon, the cemetery—at least for that night—shimmered as a place of frozen beauty. Stone crosses and granite headstones lifted through the snowy blanket atop their beds, casting long silver shadows upon the white. How many times have the heartbroken in my parish made their winding, mournful way to this village resting place? For them, for you and me, who cling to His promise that "I am the resurrection and the life," is the soon coming of Jesus to this world good news or bad news? Why bother even asking!

But coincidentally on that very same winter's night far to the south seven Texas penitentiary escapees were on the lam from the law. You can be assured that they had absolutely no desire to come face to face with the sheriff's posses that were hunting them down! Who wants to meet the Lawgiver when you're running from the law? The sixth chapter of the Apocalypse dramatically describes earth's inhabitants who cry to the rocks to hide them from the face of the returning Savior. Obviously, whether the soon return of Jesus Christ is good news or bad news depends entirely on your perspective.

So what is *your* perspective? If the God who is soon to return is not somebody to fear, but rather someone you know as a friend, then wouldn't the second coming of Jesus be the greatest news in the world, the most resplendent of all hopes? It all depends on your perspective.

For the next few pages and days I invite you to join me in revisiting some ancient, apocalyptic prophecies that have everything to do with the second coming of our Lord. Perhaps you've turned from them in the past, perhaps you've dismissed them as being too politically incorrect. But given these momentous times in which we live, isn't it high time we revisit the faith of our fathers and mothers? For how can we call the hope "blessed" if it remains a hope unexamined and a promise unclaimed?

GOOD VIBRATIONS

Blessed is the one who reads aloud the words of the prophecy, and blessed are those who hear and who keep what is written in it; for the time is near. Rev. 1:3, NRSV.

I could hardly believe her story! Young Evelyn Glennie, a graduate of London's prestigious Royal Academy of Music, became a percussion virtuoso—a career the doctors said was impossible. For Evelyn beats, shakes, rattles, or squeezes more than 600 musical instruments (from drums to marimbas, xylophones, cymbals, and tambourines), as the world's only full-time percussion soloist. With her lilting Scottish accent and perfect musical pitch, Evelyn made history when she gave the first solo percussion recital in the 95 years of the BBC's Promenade Concerts at Royal Albert Hall. Performances followed at the Kennedy Center and Hollywood Bowl. But the wild applause of her appreciative audiences literally falls on deaf ears, for since the age of 12 Evelyn Glennie has been unable to hear at all. She learned to "feel" the notes of the musical scale by placing her hand on the outside wall of the music room as her teacher struck the notes inside the room. The variations in the tingling vibrations became how she identified the notes. She now masters entire scores of complex music by playing a tape recorder between her knees. Her autobiography appropriately is entitled *Good Vibrations.*

John opens the Apocalypse (Greek, *apocalupsis*, "the revealing") with a benediction pronounced upon those who read its prophecies—"For the time is near." Even in John's day, the vibrations of apocalyptic fulfillment could be felt in the fingertips of those discerning hearts and minds that were open to Revelation's prophetic counsel. And while you and I live 2,000 years beyond John's handwritten parchment, the compelling reality for all who read the Apocalypse is that the same Christ who spoke with the lonely prophet banished there on Patmos speaks through His Spirit to every reader who comes in search of "the revealing."

"For the time is near." Vibrations unique to this hour of earth's history now tremble throughout the earth. It is a somber reality that we are closer to the return of Christ than any other generation that has lived. Of all people then, the chosen must seek and find in the Apocalypse a fresh revelation of Jesus Christ (read verse 1). For, "when we as a people understand what this book means . . . , there will be seen among us a great revival" (*Testimonies to Ministers*, p. 113). No wonder the reader is blessed!

BEAUTY AND THE BEAST—1

And I saw a beast coming out of the sea. He had ten horns and seven heads, with ten crowns on his horns, and on each head a blasphemous name. The beast I saw resembled a leopard, but had feet like those of a bear and a mouth like that of a lion. The dragon gave the beast his power and his throne and great authority. Rev. 13:1, 2, NIV.

When he was a boy, we took our son Kirk and some friends of his to the Studebaker Museum in South Bend, Indiana, for a trip into a surrealistic world of ancient beasts. Through carefully staged lighting and sound, these massive rubber-skinned prehistoric dinosaurs twisted and twitched, snarled and snapped with bloodcurdling roars. Though we kept telling ourselves they were all electronically controlled lifeless manikins, believe me when I confess that they looked and sounded frighteningly alive and utterly ferocious!

Imagine the horror of the aged apostle John as he saw in vision an amalgamated beast dripping with the brine of a windswept sea stalking toward him. What on earth is this ferocious amalgamation?

"And on each head a blasphemous name." Now, blasphemy (Greek, *blasphēmia*) we can all understand—taking the name of God in vain, of course. But notice how the dictionary expands the definition of blasphemy: "Impious or profane speaking of God, or of sacred persons or things." And then it adds this theological twist: "The act of claiming the attributes of God." So whatever else this beast power is, it is a power that, among other characteristics, claims the attributes and prerogatives of God.

Moreover, even a cursory reading of Revelation 13 makes clear that it is a *religious* power, for it receives worship (verse 4, "and they worshiped the beast"). It is also a *political* power, for only a political power has a throne and crowns and expansive dominion (verses 1, 2). And it is also a religio-political power that holds *global* sway (verse 3, "and all the world marveled and followed the beast"). So what is this geo-religio-political power that dominates history for 42 months (verse 5, or 1,260 days)? Using the interpretive key of a day for a year (Eze. 4:6; Num. 14:34), Bible scholars since Tichonius (fourth century) have described this beast as a powerful institution dominant in Christian history for more than 1,200 years.

No matter who this beast is, Revelation is clear. We must choose the beauty of the Lamb!

BEAUTY AND THE BEAST—2

They will make war against the Lamb, but the Lamb will overcome them because he is Lord of lords and King of kings—and with him will be his called, chosen and faithful followers.
Rev. 17:14, NIV.

Now, please note on whose side are the chosen. Today's text is unequivocal. The chosen are the followers of *the Lamb*. And who is "the Lamb slain from the foundation of the world" (Rev. 13:8)? The crucified, risen, and ascended Christ—the Beauty of heaven!

But before identifying the beast, we must note seven stunning imitations, compelling evidence that this beast power is an intentional counterfeit of the Lamb: (**1**) both the Lamb and the beast rise out of water to begin their influence on earth (one out of the Jordan River at His baptism, the other out of the apocalyptic sea); (**2**) both exercise power for three and a half years (one for a literal 3.5 years of ministry in Palestine, the other for a prophetic or symbolic 3.5 years [1,260 days/years]); (**3**) both are mortally wounded (in fact, the same Greek word in Revelation describes both their wounding—Revelation 5:6 and 13:8); (**4**) both come back to life (one as the divine Son of God—Revelation 1:18, the other as a revived global counterfeit—Revelation 13:3); (**5**) both have horns (the Lamb with seven—Revelation 5:6; the beast with 10—Revelation 13:1); (**6**) both of them receive honor and worship, to which only One of them is entitled (the language of global worship for the beast in Revelation 13:4 is the same language ascribed to divine worship in Exodus 15:11 and Psalm 35:10—hence, the "blasphemy" of this power); and (**7**) both seek to reach every nation, kindred, tongue, and people (one through His three angels—Revelation 14:6; the other through his tripartite coalition—Revelation 13:7).

There they are, seven intentional counterfeits between the Lamb (Beauty) and the beast—seven evidences that somebody is trying very hard to be like the Lamb, to look like the Lamb, to overtly take the place of the Lamb on this earth. In fact, the Greek word *anti* means "instead of"—so *anti*-Christ means "instead of Christ." Who then is this proud somebody who has had his jaded and jealous eye on the position of the Son of God from the beginning of the intergalactic rebellion called the great controversy? Could it be the dragon has created this beast front for his own nefarious, egotistical purposes?

Beauty or the beast? You see, even the chosen have to make that choice every single day.

BUT WHO IS THE BEAST?

And I saw one of his heads as if it had been mortally wounded, and his deadly wound was healed. And all the world marveled and followed the beast. Rev. 13:3.

In identifying this beast power, consider this important caveat: never forget that the Apocalypse describes a power and not a person or a people, an institution and not an individual. On the basis of this prophecy nobody has the right to point to a neighbor or friend or colleague and declare: "You must be what this is all about." The Lamb Himself taught us, "Judge not, that you be not judged" (Matt. 7:1). Theological pride is the child of Lucifer, not the Lamb.

Nevertheless, through the centuries there has been an amazing unanimity among Bible scholars in identifying this beast power. I have in my library LeRoy Froom's *Prophetic Faith of Our Fathers*—a four-volume compendium commended by Wilbur M. Smith of Fuller Theological Seminary as unparalleled "for exhaustiveness, freshness, and dependability in our language." In these volumes Froom has traced the history of Revelation 13's interpretation in the Christian church. Beginning with Eberhard II, the archbishop of Salzburg (1200-1246), there is a long line of scholars who believed and taught that this beast power in both Revelation and Daniel represents the institution of the Papacy in Rome.

As soon as one draws this conclusion, it is easy to dismiss such a conviction as nothing more than stereotypical antiquated Protestantism warmed over, an archaic appendage to medieval thinking. After all, the 1,260 years of the Dark and Middle Ages are past, and the world is enlightened now, and previous barbarities are no longer relevant. So what if in A.D. 538 the barbarian siege of Rome was broken, thus elevating the bishop of Rome to preeminent leader within the Catholic Church? So what if 1,260 years later the papacy was mortally wounded when Napoleon's general Berthier took the pope captive and proclaimed papal political rule at an end? So what if that politically crippling wound was healed last century when Mussolini's concordat restored Vatican land and began Rome's recovery of her geo-political dominion?

But for the chosen the question really isn't So what? but rather *So what's next?* Could it be that in Rome's breathtaking global dominance today we feel apocalyptic vibrations urgently warning that the end is near? And would this not then be the right time for the chosen to proactively, humbly share the truth as it is in Jesus with their Catholic neighbors and friends?

"HERE I STAND"

But hold fast what you have till I come. Rev. 2:25.

Holding fast has been the earmark of the chosen down through the millennia. On my wall I keep a picture of one who long ago stood alone against the geo-religio-political power of the Middle Ages church. It is a painting of Martin Luther summoned before the greatest personages of church and state in his day at the Diet of Worms on the evening of April 18, 1521.

The night before he was to return to the Diet (or Council) and defend his writings and faith in Holy Scripture, Luther suffered what we would call today a panic attack. Gripped by the icy paralysis of crippling fear, he crumbled to the floor of his tiny room, his anguished face pressed against the earth as he sobbed into that black night. "O God, do Thou help me against all the wisdom of the world. Do this, . . . Thou alone; . . . for this is not my work, but Thine. . . . O Lord, help me! Faithful and unchangeable God, in no man do I place my trust. . . . Thou hast chosen me for this work. . . . Stand at my side, for the sake of Thy well-beloved Jesus Christ, who is my defense, my shield, and my strong tower" (J. H. Merle D'Aubigné, *History of the Reformation of the Sixteenth Century*, p. 259).

Through the long night Luther poured out his soul to God. Finally ushered late in the day back into the judicial chambers of Emperor Charles V and the assembled prelates of the church, Luther was asked again if he would defend his books or did he wish to recant. Without a trace of fear or embarrassment this time the young pastor and professor firmly defended his faith in Holy Scripture and his humble efforts to publish the truth he had discovered therein. And when he had finished his defense in German, the magistrates requested that he repeat himself in Latin. Luther obeyed, until sweating and exhausted he ended his second defense: "Unless therefore I am convinced by the testimony of Scripture or by the clearest reasoning—unless I am persuaded by means of the passages I have quoted, and unless they thus render my conscience bound by the Word of God, *I cannot and I will not retract*, for it is unsafe for a Christian to speak against his conscience. Here I stand, I can do no other; may God help me. Amen" (*ibid.*, p. 265).

How did Jesus put it? "Hold fast what you have till I come." In the face of intensifying force, intensify your faith. And hold fast to Him. For the Christ who stood beside Martin Luther as he held fast will stand beside you, too. After all, isn't that why He chose you long ago?

"GOD BLESS AMERICA"

Then I saw another beast, coming out of the earth. He had two horns like a lamb, but he spoke like a dragon. Rev. 13:11, NIV.

Ever since the September 11, 2001, tragedies the Russian immigrant Irving Berlin's "God Bless America" has become the de facto national anthem of the U.S., hasn't it? What U.S. citizen doesn't sing with fervor the refrain, "God bless America, my home sweet home"!

And yet Revelation 13's enigmatic prophecy includes the story of a second beast as well—a power that rose up out of the earth at the very time the first (or sea) beast was being mortally wounded. Only this power would arise far away from the peopled crossroads of the Old World. In a desolate New World this two-horned lamblike creature would grow up, and eventually become the dominant political power on earth, as the ensuing prophecy describes.

So what lamblike (Christ- or Christian-like) global power of history sprang up (the Greek word describes the rapid growth of a weed) out of the desolate earth far away from the dominion of the first beast (Rome) at the time of her wounding (1790s) and subsequently rose to a position of global political dominance? There is only one international power today that fits the prophetic parameters of Revelation 13.

"God bless America"—and indeed He has. "The Lord has done more for the United States than for any other country upon which the sun shines" (*Maranatha*, p. 193). But tragically the somber prophecy depicts a future for this nation in which the divine blessings are squandered and its divine destiny abandoned.

How could this land of such unprecedented political and religious liberties—founded by settlers in search of a country without a king and a church without a pope—turn south so decisively in the end? Enter the destructive alliance between church and state. You may trace it in the annals of humanity, the baleful harvest that is reaped whenever the church turns to the state to enforce her precepts. Revelation 13 convincingly depicts this nation in the end mandating the worship and allegiance of the world for Rome, "telling those who dwell on the earth to make an image to the beast who was wounded by the sword and lived" (verse 14).

And whenever church and state collaborate, an innocent victim is sacrificed—as the crucifixion of Jesus more than aptly proves. No wonder the chosen must keep near the cross!

"BETTER TO LIGHT A CANDLE"

I urge you, first of all, to pray for all people. Ask God to help them; intercede on their behalf, and give thanks for them. Pray this way for kings and all who are in authority so that we can live peaceful and quiet lives marked by godliness and dignity. This is good and pleases God our Savior, who wants everyone to be saved and to understand the truth. 1 Tim. 2:1-4, NLT.

No one is sure who coined the phrase "It is better to light a candle than to curse the darkness." Nevertheless it is an appropriate proverb to consider as we brood over the apocalyptic prophecies of Revelation 13. The predicted global alliance between the two superpowers (one dominantly religious, the other dominantly political, but both an alliance of church and state) is reason enough for the chosen to light a candle of intercessory prayer on behalf of their governments and on behalf of the world. More than a call to spiritual arms, God's prophetic Word is surely a summons to prayer.

And whom shall we pray for? Paul is quick in our text today to call us to pray for our political leaders. Presidents, prime ministers, members of Parliament, members of Congress, governors, mayors—the list of political leaders is lengthy. But they are also needy. Truth be known, there are men and women in influential positions of leadership the world over who are being directed by the Holy Spirit to hold back the forces of darkness a little longer for the sake of God's final mission on earth. "The restraining influence of the Holy Spirit is felt by rulers and people. It still controls to some extent the laws of the land. . . . God also has His agents among the leading [men and women] of the nation. . . . Statesmen who fear the Lord are influenced by holy angels to oppose such propositions [the union of church and state] with unanswerable arguments. Thus a few [men and women] will hold in check a powerful current of evil" (*The Great Controversy,* pp. 610, 611).

Rather than rail against the gathering darkness of church and state union and bemoan this nation's abandonment of its constitutional liberties, let us light the candle of prayer in our homes. "God bless America" can still be a prayer for divine intervention in these uncertain times. Let the chosen be known throughout their communities as men, women, and children who love their land and who love their Lord, and who, on the basis of those twin devotions, are prayer warriors on behalf of their twin citizenships—their homeland and the kingdom of heaven.

There is more than enough darkness to go around. Instead let us lift up the light of Jesus.

THE THIRD RAIL

Then I saw three evil spirits that looked like frogs; they came out of the mouth of the dragon, out of the mouth of the beast and out of the mouth of the false prophet. They are spirits of demons performing miraculous signs, and they go out to the kings of the whole world, to gather them for the battle on the great day of God Almighty. Rev. 16:13, 14, NIV.

Watch out for the third rail! If you've ever traveled by subway or train, you know that along with the twin steel rails on which the train cars click and clack, there is between the rails a third rail. Warning signs posted up and down the platform remind travelers to stay off the tracks, for the third rail is a dangerous high-voltage power strip that hurls the trains down the tracks.

In the Apocalypse God warns us about the third rail that lies in between the two prophetic beast powers of Revelation 13. "The dragon gave him [them] his power, his throne, and great authority" (verse 2). And of course, the dragon is "that serpent of old, called the Devil and Satan, who deceives the whole world" (Rev. 12:9). He is the third rail of insidious deception and evil.

And as our text today reveals, he is the dark mastermind behind a final trilateral alliance, an end-time demonic counterfeit trinity that will seek to sweep the entire planet into a lockstep allegiance to the evil triumvirate. And as *The Great Controversy* warns, it will be a global coup d'état: "Through the two great errors, the immortality of the soul and Sunday sacredness, Satan will bring the people under his deceptions. While the former lays the foundation of spiritualism, the latter creates a bond of sympathy with Rome. The Protestants of the United States will be foremost in stretching their hands across the gulf to grasp the hand of spiritualism; they will reach over the abyss to clasp hands with the Roman power; and under the influence of this threefold union, this country will follow in the steps of Rome in trampling on the rights of conscience" (p. 588).

Watch out for the third rail! Tragically too many of even the chosen ignore the warnings and step onto his megavoltage ground. It isn't worth it, is it? Why attempt to inch near the third rail without stepping on it? Doesn't it make critical sense to stay as far away from him as possible?

Of all people on earth, surely the chosen in this hour of history will choose the divine Trinity as their closet Companions for the final journey. With our hopes pinned on the returning Savior, doesn't it make all the sense in the world to stay on board his one-way train?

THE GHOST INVASION

And no wonder, for Satan himself masquerades as an angel of light. It is not surprising, then, if his servants masquerade as servants of righteousness. 2 Cor. 11:14, 15, NIV.

Ghosts in church, ghosts in Hollywood, ghosts in college, ghosts in the boardroom, ghosts in the bedroom—they're everywhere! Where are they coming from? And why have they come in such droves? Are we being fattened for the day of slaughter?

An unusual category of ghosts are the "Marian apparitions," the reported appearances of Mary, the mother of Jesus. Today there is an International Marian Research Institute and Library at the University of Dayton. According to their statistics, 386 cases of Marian apparitions were recorded in the twentieth century, 87 of which have been examined by Rome. Hundreds of apparition reports go unreported and unexamined. Perhaps the apparitions can be explained by the title "Pontifex Maximus" that was adopted by the bishop of Rome 16 centuries ago. Latin for "the greatest bridge-builder," the title had once belonged to the high priest of the Roman pagan cult and occult. "The greatest bridge-builder"—didn't we read something yesterday about hands stretching across the gulf?

But the Word of God is clear. The "soul" and "spirit" of human beings are referred to more than 1,700 times in the Bible, but are never once said to be immortal or eternal. In fact, the Bible declares that only God is immortal (1 Tim. 6:14-16). The spirit that returns to God at death is not a conscious entity, but is the breath of life (Eccl. 12:7; Gen. 2:7). The words "spirit," "wind," and "breath" in our English translations come from the same original Hebrew and Greek words. Hence the only ghosts the Bible knows are the demonic impersonations of the dead (1 Sam. 28). Today's text warns about "angels of light" who are nothing more than masquerading demons of darkness.

The "supernatural" manifestations in worship services across the land, television's fascination with mediums and their "on camera" communications with the dead, Hollywood's fixation on the occult and spiritism, Marian apparitions—is this a concerted strategic effort to draw the entire civilization into the net of a massive end-time deception?

No wonder we hope! For the Jesus who predicted "great signs and wonders to deceive, if possible, even the elect" on the eve of His return *is* returning. Even the bad news is good!

THEY'RE WAITING

*For false christs and false prophets will arise and show great signs
and wonders, so as to deceive, if possible, even the elect. Matt. 24:24.*

We aren't the only ones waiting. A friend from India handed me a news clipping with the headline "India Awaits Vishnu's Return." Hindus believe we are living in the last age and that Vishnu, a member of the Hindu trinity, will return to this earth. We have company.

I stepped into a small sidewalk café in London to buy some chips from the Muslim proprietor. He asked why I was in town, and I told him I was at a church preaching about the soon coming of Christ. "Oh," he replied, "we too believe that Jesus is coming soon." Sure enough, a check of the Qur'an reveals that in fact Islam indeed teaches the Second Advent.

And of course our friends the Jews are awaiting the Messiah's coming too. One ultraorthodox Jewish sect in Israel notes that the Talmudic sages predicted that the Messiah's coming would be preceded by a time of great chaos and confusion. And thus His coming must be near, they have concluded. Even the Jains and Zoroastrians are expecting their gods.

The point? It doesn't take a doctorate to conclude that Lucifer has masterfully set the stage across the planet for his final and overmastering delusion. What more potent deception could there be than to suddenly appear before the gaping news cams of the international press and claim that he is the "angel of light" the heartsick masses of humanity have been longing for? "His voice is soft and subdued, yet full of melody. In gentle, compassionate tones he presents some of the same gracious, heavenly truths which the Saviour uttered; he heals the diseases of the people, and then, in his assumed character of Christ, he claims to have changed the Sabbath to Sunday, and commands all to hallow the day which he has blessed. . . . *This is the strong, almost overmastering delusion*" (*The Great Controversy,* p. 624; italics supplied).

And how will it be with the chosen? "Only those who have been diligent students of the Scriptures and who have received the love of the truth will be shielded from the powerful delusion that takes the world captive" (*The Great Controversy,* p. 625).

Yes, we must hope, and hope we shall. But it must be an informed, intelligent hope based upon a bedrock knowledge of the Bible. Now more than ever we must be alone with Jesus daily, immersed in His Word. True, the bad news is good news. But the best news is to walk with Him.

"DON'T BELIEVE IT!"

At that time if anyone says to you, "Look, here is the Christ!" or, "There he is!" do not believe it. . . . See, I have told you ahead of time. So if anyone tells you, "There he is, out in the desert," do not go out; or, "Here he is, in the inner rooms," do not believe it.
Matt. 24:23, 25, 26, NIV.

The most popular notion today of how Jesus will return is called the "secret rapture." The *Left Behind* series of novels made a fortune disseminating the idea that when Jesus comes back to earth He will do so secretly, quietly, like a "thief in the night." In the opening scene 747 pilot Rayford Steele rushes home to Chicago from his aborted trans-Atlantic flight (wherein passengers mysteriously disappeared at 35,000 feet), only to discover beneath the bedcovers his wife's nightie, her cross necklace, and her wedding ring—all that was left when she was secretly raptured in the night by Jesus. And now her distraught husband is "left behind," too.

Is that the way Jesus taught He would return one day? His warning in our text today is stark and clear—"If anyone tells you that I have come secretly, *do not believe it.*" In fact, He repeats Himself to make certain His followers get the point: *Don't believe it!* What could be clearer than "do not believe it"? To drive home His point, Jesus paints a picture.

Have you ever tried to sleep through a lightning storm? We have some humdinger springtime thunderstorms here in Michigan! Whenever Karen and I awaken to one of those rumbling midnight explosions, we commence the "one lollipop, two lollipop" count routine, as we nervously try to gauge the time span between the bedroom-illuminating white flash of light and the crashing thunder. What really gets your hair standing straight on end is when the white light and the exploding thunder are simultaneous! You've just been struck.

And that, Jesus declared, is how the second coming will be: "For as the lightning comes from the east and flashes to the west, so also will the coming of the Son of Man be" (verse 27). Nobody will wake up the next morning and wish he hadn't slept through Christ's return!

What difference does it make how Jesus comes as long as He comes? Follow the logic. If the Bible really taught that those who miss His secret coming have seven more years to get ready for the Big One, then why get ready now? The deceptive notion of a "second chance" lulled the antediluvians to sleep, too. No wonder "Don't believe it" is Jesus' appeal to be ready now.

THE APOCALYPTIC IMAX

At that time the sign of the Son of Man will appear in the sky, and all the nations of the earth will mourn. They will see the Son of Man coming on the clouds of the sky, with power and great glory. And he will send his angels with a loud trumpet call, and they will gather his elect from the four winds, from one end of the heavens to the other.
Matt. 24:30, 31, NIV.

Have you ever sat spellbound in a surround-sound, eight-stories-tall, giant-screen IMAX theater? The sound is so wall-vibratingly vibrant and the screen so massive, it's as if you were actually soaring through the Grand Canyon or inside that gyrating stunt plane or atop the roaring space shuttle. Because there's one reality about IMAX—it's the next-best thing to being there.

Matthew opens up a towering IMAX screen for us in our text today, as the heavens explode with "power and great glory" (the Greek word for "power" is the very one our word "dynamite" comes from)! Taller than eight stories, Matthew's canvas literally fills every millimeter of the fiery sky with the returning Jesus and a few trillion angels! And the sound effects? Why not even a million surround-sound speakers would do justice to that glorious event.

And what is more, Matthew records Jesus' stunning announcement that the entire globe will witness His return, "all the nations of earth"—or, as the Apocalypse describes it, "Every eye will see Him" (Rev. 1:7). Every man, woman, and child on this planet will see Him come back!

Then how in the world did the "secret rapture" teaching get such traction among Bible believers today? Two short phrases here in Matthew triggered the unbiblical conclusion. First, Jesus likened His return to a thief in the night (Matt. 24:43). "Aha—see, He's coming secretly!" But is that Jesus' point? Not at all. His very next words are: "Therefore you also be ready, for the Son of Man is coming at an hour when *you do not expect Him*" (verse 44). The effectiveness of thieves is not their silence or their secrecy, but rather their unexpectedness. They never send a postcard announcing the time of their planned arrival. Second, Jesus described two people together at His coming—"one will be taken and the other left" (verses 40, 41). *Left Behind* concluded that being left behind means a second chance, but Jesus is utterly clear: those left behind are *not* left to go on, for *they are not left alive*, as His retelling of the stories of the Flood and Sodom and Gomorrah makes amply clear (verses 37, 38; Luke 17:28-30).

His point? *Now is the only time to follow Jesus.* And that is what it means to be ready.

DEATH POSTPONEMENT

For the Lord Himself will descend from heaven with a shout, with the voice of an archangel, and with the trumpet of God. And the dead in Christ will rise first. Then we who are alive and remain shall be caught up together with them in the clouds to meet the Lord in the air. And thus we shall always be with the Lord. Therefore comfort one another with these words. 1 Thess. 4:16-18.

How can we talk of hope without pondering death or its glorious antithesis? Did you know that medical research has shown that we humans are able to postpone our death? Doctors long have surmised it, but empirical studies now confirm the truth. A famous case of death postponement was the death of Thomas Jefferson, the author of the Declaration of Independence, who lingered until the fiftieth anniversary of the document's signing, and then died on July 4, 1826. The death patterns of Jewish men and Chinese women living in California reveal a significantly measurable drop in their mortality rates before the Passover (25 percent drop) and before the Harvest Moon Festival (35 percent drop), leading researchers to conclude that some people are able to briefly postpone their death in order to reach a psychologically significant occasion for them.

But forget that word "briefly." How would you like to postpone your death forever?

Without a doubt the most compelling truth about the blessed hope of Jesus' second coming is the divine pronouncement that death (our mortal enemy and unrelenting nemesis) will not only be postponed, but will in fact be eternally eradicated for every man, woman, and child who trusts in God for salvation. In fact, not only will death be eternally "postponed" for His friends who are alive and waiting for Him when He returns, death will also be eternally eradicated for that "great multitude which no one could number" that will be resurrected at His second coming (Rev. 7:9). Scripture's triumphant pronouncement is that the day is coming when "death" will be forever eliminated from the human vocabulary.

No wonder the hope is called "blessed"! Blessed hope for our heartbroken families who in tears finally tear themselves away from that fresh mound of graveyard earth and return to a lonely house and life vacated by one so dearly loved. "Because I live, you shall live also" is the one promise that can carry us through the darkest night until He returns—postponed no longer.

"A LITTLE LONGER"

Soon afterward Jesus went with his disciples to the village of Nain, and a large crowd followed him. A funeral procession was coming out as he approached the village gate. The young man who had died was a widow's only son, and a large crowd from the village was with her. When the Lord saw her, his heart overflowed with compassion. "Don't cry!" he said.
Luke 7:11-13, NLT.

How many times have I stood in a quiet cemetery beside a devastated husband or wife, a heartbroken father or mother, or stunned and grieving children—my heart aching with the longing that this Jesus of Nain might suddenly walk into our village and touch the cold casket and summon back to life the one so tragically taken in death! There is much joy in the life of a pastor, but there are so many tears. And the tears over death are the most painful of all.

Just weeks from graduation and on the cusp of a new career, her death left the campus stunned. At the conclusion of her funeral, I stood beside her casket, as the mourners walked by her still form. Just a few feet from the casket, her family was seated on the front row of the church. And it seemed that with every mourner, young or old, who stooped over them with a hug or kiss of condolence, the parents' grief was only compounded. How can even a pastor hide his tears when they flow so freely around him?

But even more bitter would be the tears if only for this life we hoped. No, refracted through our crystalline grief is that resplendent hope we still call blessed. And I love the way *The Desire of Ages* frames its promise: "Christ is coming with clouds and with great glory. A multitude of shining angels will attend Him. He will come to raise the dead, and to change the living saints from glory to glory. He will come to honor those who have loved Him, and kept His commandments, and to take them to Himself. He has not forgotten them nor His promise. *There will be a relinking of the family chain.* When we look upon our dead, we may think of the morning when the trump of God shall sound, when 'the dead shall be raised incorruptible, and we shall be changed.' 1 Cor. 15:52. A little longer, and we shall see the King in His beauty. A little longer, and He will wipe all tears from our eyes. A little longer, and He will present us 'faultless before the presence of His glory with exceeding joy' " (p. 632; italics supplied). A little longer, my friend, let us cling to hope.

THE LEGEND OF SAMARA

Jesus said to her, "I am the resurrection and the life. Those who believe in me, even though they die, will live, and everyone who lives and believes in me will never die. Do you believe this?" John 11:25, 26, NRSV.

On the streets of Baghdad a merchant sent his servant to the market, so the legend goes. But soon the man returned, ashen-faced and trembling. "O Master," he said, "down in the marketplace I was jostled by a woman, and when I turned I saw it was Death. She looked at me and made a threatening gesture. Please, Master, lend me a horse. I will flee to Samara. Death will not find me there!"

Later the merchant walked to the market, where he saw Death in the crowd. "Why did you frighten my servant this morning with that threatening gesture?" he asked.

Death replied, "Oh, that was not a threatening gesture—it was a start of surprise. I was astonished to see him here in Baghdad, for I have an appointment with him tonight in Samara."

Are you afraid of death, afraid of that inevitable, inescapable moment when you and she shall meet? Alan Seeger, who died in World War I at the age of 28, wrote the famous lines: "I have a rendezvous with Death at some disputed barricade when Spring comes back with rustling shade and apple-blossoms fill the air." We all have that rendezvous, do we not?

Even the friends of Jesus got sick and died. Lazarus did. And amazingly, Christ waited four days before hurrying to the side of Martha and Mary. "Our friend Lazarus sleeps," Jesus informed His band of followers. "Then let him rest, Lord," they unanimously advised. "Then Jesus said to them plainly, 'Lazarus is dead'" (John 11:14).

You see, for the Lifegiver, death is but a sleep from which we can be awakened. "I am the resurrection, and the life," He told the brokenhearted Martha. "He that believeth in me, though he were dead, yet shall he live" (verse 25, KJV). And then to demonstrate His credentials that would be triumphantly certified at His own death and resurrection just weeks away, Jesus stepped before the tomb of Lazarus and commanded His friend to come back to life. And when the Lifegiver gives the command, even the dead obey!

Yes, if Jesus doesn't come soon enough or you and I don't live long enough, there will be a gravestone with our names chiseled into its granite. But never mind, because in Christ our rendezvous with death is but a peaceful sleep until He comes! And that is no legend at all.

A TALE OF TWIN TENSIONS

Very early in the morning, on the first day of the week, they came to the tomb when the sun had risen. And they said among themselves, "Who will roll away the stone from the door of the tomb for us?" Mark 16:2, 3.

The world knows Charles Dickens' opening salvo to his classic *A Tale of Two Cities*—"It was the best of times, it was the worst of times." Someone printed a T-shirt with these words: "I wish you would make up your mind, Mr. Dickens. Was it the best of times or the worst of times? It could scarcely have been both."

But of course, it really can be both, can't it? Living as we do in a world of such blatant contrasts—wealth and poverty, education and illiteracy, East and West, creation and evolution, hope and hopelessness, faith and unbelief, life and death—don't we all struggle with the sometimes-suffocating tension of trying to harmonize, or at least bring a semblance of sanity, to our disequilibrium? "It was the best of times, it was the worst of times." It really was for the women on the way to the tomb that early Sunday morning—He is dead, He is not. And it really is for us who journey the inevitable way to the tomb too—He is coming soon, He is not.

How then shall we live, we who are jammed somewhere between the time of the end and the end of time? The American writer F. Scott Fitzgerald once concluded: "The test of a first-rate intelligence is the ability to hold two opposed ideas in the mind at the same time, and still retain the ability to function." What if we adjusted that sentence this way: *The test of a lasting faith is the ability to hold two opposed ideas in mind at the same time, and still retain the ability to trust.* Life is difficult . . . God is love. I have fear . . . I have faith. I doubt . . . I trust. I sin . . . Christ saves. I shall descend to the grave . . . He shall return for me. Lasting faith is the necessity of holding two opposed ideas in mind at the same time and yet retaining our trust in God.

"For as in Adam all die, even so in Christ all shall be made alive" (1 Cor. 15:22). Two opposing ideas, one trust—yes, we will die; but yes, in Christ we can all be made alive again. And that is why we do not "sorrow as others who have no hope" (1 Thess. 4:13). For we trust Him. *Trust.* Without it the chosen have no hope and no choice. But because of the resurrection of Christ we can hope, we can trust, we can choose. "It was the best of times, it was the worst of times." But choose Jesus afresh today, and the promise sure—the stone will be rolled away.

CROCHETING HOPE

Now to Him who is able to do exceedingly abundantly above all that we ask or think, according to the power that works in us, to Him be glory in the church by Christ Jesus throughout all ages, would without end. Amen. Eph. 3:20, 21.

As the London *Guardian* wryly observed: "Whatever faults Maria D'Antuono may have, wasting time is not among them." The 98-year-old woman was one of the few survivors to be pulled from the rubble of the 6.3 magnitude earthquake that struck central Italy. For 30 dark and interminable hours she lay trapped beneath the ruins of her home, not far from the L'Aquila epicenter. But they found her! And as the elderly woman was carried to safety amid the cheers of the onlooking crowd, someone asked her what she had done to pass the hours while waiting and hoping for rescue. "Why, crochet, of course!" Her world came down around her—but the 98-year-old matriarch survived with a hook, a ball of yarn, and a heart full of hope.

Not even an earthquake can bury hope. "There was a violent earthquake, for an angel of the Lord came down from heaven and, going to the tomb, rolled back the stone and sat on it" (Matt. 28:2, NIV). His enemies could have piled a thousand Mount Everests on top of the garden tomb of Jesus—but it would have made no difference, for not even an earthquake can bury hope. And when Christ came striding out of that quake-shattered crypt and declared over the predawn rubble, "I am the resurrection and the life!" then humankind's last hope was made forever secure. Death may bury us, but in the power of the risen Savior hope can still be resurrected.

And is it any different for the myriad of crises that come crashing in upon us, burying us under their crushing weight, leaving both life and hope entombed? Emotionally, financially, socially, physically, spiritually you may feel buried right now in the rubble. No way out of the collapse, no hope of rescue, no promise of resurrection. But don't repeat the computation error of the 11 disciples who neglected to calculate the power of divine omnipotence into their crisis. For only afterward did they discover that no matter how heavy the stone that entombs us, the risen Christ can yet roll it away.

So put your finger on this resurrection promise and crochet your future with new hope: "God can do anything, you know—far more than you could ever imagine or guess or request in your wildest dreams" (Eph. 3:20, Message).

THE UNMAGIC KINGDOM—1

These all died in faith, not having received the promises, but having seen them afar off were assured of them, embraced them, and confessed that they were strangers and pilgrims on the earth. Heb. 11:13.

What is there about Disneyland that captures the fancy of young and old alike? I remember the first time I ever laid eyes on that theme park. I was a 5-year-old missionary's kid who'd never been to America in his life, and whose uncle and aunt announced, "Welcome to America—we're going to take you to Disneyland!" Today Disney World is the largest amusement park on earth, driven (since 1987) by a marketing campaign second to none. After the Super Bowl's most valuable player is announced and he's surrounded by that gang of reporters and cameras, one of Disney's planted agents calls out a question heard on live TV around the world: "Hey, you've just won the Super Bowl—what are you going to do now?" And the MVP (all the players are coached by Disney before the game) knows to reply: "I'm going to Disney World!" (if the team is from the East) or "I'm going to Disneyland!" (if it's from the West). Pretty clever marketing—this capitalizing on kids' great sports heroes.

But did you know that Disney simply tore a page out of God's own playbook? He's been doing it for millennia—using His heroes to market his Unmagic Kingdom. Just read the Bible's Hall of Fame/Hall of Faith chapter! Our text today sums up the lives of earth's greatest citizens—Abel, Enoch, Noah, Abraham and Sarah, Isaac, Jacob, Joseph, Moses, Rahab, Gideon, Samson, David (to name some of them)—with the reminder that to a man and woman they all considered themselves "strangers and pilgrims" on the earth. Why? Because they had their hopes pinned on another land, on another kingdom. And it was that hope that fueled their lives.

I love to travel. But the best part for me is the journey home. When you land in a foreign country, it isn't the country that's foreign—it's you! And you're reminded of that at passport control: "Foreigners/aliens queue here." But when I come home, the cheery (sometimes) "Welcome home!" from the agent matches my own glad spirit. I'm home at last.

Just like God's friends throughout sacred history, you and I are strangers, aliens in this land, pilgrims passing through, counting the days until our Savior returns. So when you're asked what you're doing now, you can shout it out with joyful hope: "I'm getting ready to go home!"

THE UNMAGIC KINGDOM—2

But they were looking for a better place, a heavenly homeland. That is why God is not ashamed to be called their God, for he has prepared a heavenly city for them. Heb. 11:16, NLT.

Ted Dekker, in *The Slumber of Christianity: Awakening a Passion for Heaven on Earth*, makes an insightful observation about hope. "What elevates our emotions, and what dashes them to the ground? What makes us jump for joy, and what sends us into a pit of deep discouragement? The answers are surprisingly simple: Hope. And hopelessness. . . . If you think about what changes your mood from one of happiness to one of sadness, you will always find hopelessness." And then he describes hope: "Hope is the primary force that drives human beings from hour to hour. Hope for a simple pleasure, a hug, a kiss. . . . The renewed health of an ill child or aging mother. These are among the many hopes that motivate our daily lives. Everything we do is driven by hope or hopelessness in one form or another" (pp. 34, 35).

If that's true—and I have a feeling we'd agree—then what would happen if we spent time every day meditating on the hope of heaven—through a song, a poem, some music, a scriptural promise or two? What if we intentionally turned our minds away from the incessant bad news of a broken economy, a messed-up world, a struggling ecosystem, a morally bankrupted culture—turned away from the daily hopeless fare of the media and focused our minds instead on that "heavenly homeland," as our text today phrases it, that eternal city and land that God has promised His friends? Talking about an injection of hope! Not for hours but for a few moments each new morning during worship, what if we dreamed of heaven?

"Paul had a view of heaven, and in discoursing on the glories there, the very best thing he could do was to not try to describe them. He tells us that eye had not seen nor ear heard, neither hath it entered into the heart of man the things which God hath prepared for those that love Him. So you may *put your imagination to the stretch*, you may try to the very best of your abilities to take in and consider the eternal weight of glory, and yet your finite senses, faint and weary with the effort, cannot grasp it, for there is an infinity beyond. It takes all of eternity to unfold the glories and bring out the precious treasures of the Word of God" (*The Seventh-day Adventist Bible Commentary*, Ellen G. White Comments, vol. 6, p. 1107; italics supplied). It takes all of eternity, but that doesn't mean we can't start today! So stretch your imagination of heaven right now, and let the Spirit inject you with a fresh dose of hope.

"IMAGINE"

*Behold, I will create new heavens and a new earth. The former things will
not be remembered, nor will they come to mind. Isa. 65:17, NIV.*

Even John Lennon dreamed of heaven before he died in a pool of his own blood
on a cold New York City sidewalk. Months before he was tragically gunned
down, Lennon wrote, composed, and sang what became his most popular solo
work, "Imagine." In between the lines of his composition, can you hear a wistful
plea for a heaven on earth? "Imagine there's no heaven/It's easy if you try/No hell
below us/Above us only sky/Imagine all the people/Living for today/Imagine
there's no countries/It isn't hard to do/Nothing to kill or die for/And no religion,
too/Imagine all the people living life in peace/You may say I'm a dreamer/But I'm
not the only one/I hope someday you'll join us/And the world will live as one."

If only John Lennon could have known that the very heaven on earth he
dreamed of had already in fact been promised long, long ago. In today's text God
declares that what Lennon wished for so wistfully, God has longed for, too—a
brand-new world where the old ways are gone forever and ever. Amen.

But did you notice that so new will be the new earth that God announces,
"The former things will not be remembered, nor will they come to mind." Once
I was studying the Bible with a man who read this text and wanted to know why
God was going to blank out our memories. But actually Isaiah is employing a fig-
ure of speech that Jeremiah does a few pages later where the prophet writes, "It
shall not come to mind, or be remembered, or missed" (Jer. 3:16, NRSV).

In other words, when God re-creates new heavens and a new earth with its
new society, nobody is going to be wistfully singing the very opposite of Lennon's
wish: "Imagine there is cancer—it's easy if you try. Imagine there are murders—
and rapes and robberies on the sly. Imagine there're more killing, wars, and
morgues, and courts. You may say I'm a dreamer, but I'm not the only one. I hope
someday we can go back, to when the world was ruined."

That old diseased, decrepit, dysfunctional, dead earth will never be missed, or
longingly remembered again! So utterly, thoroughly thrilled will we be with God's
pristine new creation that not a single redeemed friend of God's will ever even
imagine walking up to Jesus and asking if we might repeat the wretched rebellion
that gave Him His scars. Can you imagine that!

"GOING HOME"

And I saw a new heaven and a new earth, for the first heaven and the first earth had passed away. Also there was no more sea. . . . And God will wipe away every tear from their eyes; there shall be no more death, nor sorrow, nor crying; and there shall be no more pain, for the former things have passed away. Rev. 21:1-4.

One of my favorite classical compositions is by Antonin Dvorak, his Symphony No. 9 in E Minor that he named "From the New World." Today it's remembered simply as "The New World Symphony." Most are especially familiar with the Largo portion, and I admit that it's the Largo that I love to hum. Especially since a lyricist wrote these accompanying words: "Going home, going home, Lord, I'm going home. Going home, going home, Lord, I'm going home."

Do you suppose that deep within every human heart there is a God-planted instinct, a haunting longing to go home? Could it be that "Going home" are the lyrics to that wordless melody sung in every language and village of earth? After all, didn't the wise man observe, "[God] has put eternity in their hearts" (Eccl. 3:11)? And the heart—oh, how the heart longs and dreams of a better place to call home than this, doesn't it?

For that reason John's description of the new earth in our text today is so beloved, and so often quoted when we gather in sorrow to bury our dead. But did you notice that John has to turn to the negative in order for us to grasp the positive? "Let me tell you what won't be there!" No more tears, no more death, no more sorrow, no more crying, no more pain. No more hospitals, no more divorce courts, no more jails, no more slums, no more crime, no more war. No, no, no.

Harry Blamires poignantly reflects: "If only we could have the positives of earthly life without the negatives. But that is precisely what heaven has to offer—the removal of the negatives. . . . [In heaven] both [human sin and the dominion of time] will be swept away. Here below, time withers flowers and human beauty, it encourages good intentions to evaporate, it deprives us of our loved ones. Within the universe ruled by time, the happiest marriage ends in death, the loveliest woman becomes a skeleton. Fading and aging, losing and failing, being deprived and being frustrated—these are the negative aspects of life in time. Life in eternity will liberate us from all loss, all deprivation" ("The Eternal Weight of Glory," *Christianity Today,* May 27, 1991, p. 30). No wonder the distant melody "Going home" still plays in our hearts.

"FAR TOO EASILY PLEASED"

As it is written: "No eye has seen, no ear has heard, no mind has conceived what God has prepared for those who love him." 1 Cor. 2:9, NIV.

In the village where I live, he's one of our favorite citizens! After all, who doesn't like having as a neighbor a man who can take a paintbrush and turn a palette of sticky colors into a breathtaking panorama? Just ask the folks at the Smithsonian's National Air and Space Museum in Washington, D.C., where Nathan Greene's towering canvass of the lunar landscape graces one of their exhibit walls. I've been privileged to have Nathan's gifted artistry grace the covers of four books I've written. And hanging beside the door of my church office is his moving depiction of Jesus (titled *Ever Interceding*) prostrate in prayer atop the curvature of earth.

But one of Nathan Greene's most popular pieces of art is his work *The Lion and the Lamb.* One of my parishioners selected that canvass as a memorial gift for her husband, and now it hangs where all can see it beside a busy thoroughfare at Pioneer Memorial church. Nathan has imagined a future scene from heaven, where the friendly Jesus is surrounded by children, a little girl seated in His arms and leaning against His chest. At the Savior's feet lies a giant pussycat of a lion. And beside that king of the forest stands a curly black lamb. "They shall not hurt nor destroy in all My holy mountain" (Isa. 11:9).

Heaven. As our text today reminds us, it is simply impossible for our finite and fallen minds to comprehend, let alone visualize, the glories of that paradise that God has waiting for His chosen, His friends of this earth. But though it puts to the stretch our highest imaginings, we must never allow ourselves to become so jaded by this world's broken landscapes and tinny amusements that we end up exchanging the hope of heaven for their paltry immediacy.

C. S. Lewis wondered why we aren't more preoccupied with the utterly glorious hope of heaven one day: "If we consider the unblushing promises of reward and the staggering nature of the rewards promised in the Gospels, it would seem that our Lord finds our desires not too strong, but too weak. We are halfhearted creatures, fooling about with drink and sex and ambition when infinite joy is offered us, like an ignorant child who wants to go on making mud pies in a slum because he cannot imagine what is meant by the offer of a holiday at the sea. We are far too easily pleased" (*The Weight of Glory,* p. 4). Aren't we?

CHRONIC ENTROPY

These things I have spoken to you, that in Me you may have peace. In the world you will have tribulation; but be of good cheer, I have overcome the world. John 16:33.

I was out walking in the Michigan chill before sunrise, mulling over the spate of nonstop headlines we've become accustomed to of late. And as I brooded over it all, two words came to mind. "Chronic" (as in chronic cough or headache)—because how else can you explain the incessant, seemingly interminable march of bad news that's become our daily fare? And then alongside "chronic" popped the word "entropy"—a word scientists have tucked into the second law of thermodynamics to describe the gradual disintegration our universe experiences, slowly but surely degrading toward disorder. "Chronic entropy" then becomes a fitting description of life on the planet these days, incessantly marching toward disintegration. Wouldn't you agree?

It's not a very cheery notion, I understand. Which is why alongside this couplet we need to quickly affix another. Because if we read the apocalyptic portions of Holy Scripture correctly (Matthew 24, Mark 13, and Luke 21, along with Daniel and Revelation), the chronic entropy that they all describe is but the harbinger of the second advent of Christ and the eventual restoration of an entire cosmos previously destined for disintegration. And that means that the most broken of the headlines we're living with these days—from the economic and moral meltdown of society, to the ecological and ecclesiastical disintegration of the world—all of it is prophetic assurance that on the heels of the "baddest" news comes the promise of the greatest news of all, the soon return of Jesus. "Chronic entropy," meet another couplet: "blessed hope!"

No wonder, on the very eve of His own death, Jesus could call us to such buoyant confidence: "In the world you're going to face one debilitating headline after another—but never mind, be of good cheer, for I have overcome the chronic entropy of this age; and I am coming back for you" (see John 14:1-3; 16:33).

Ponder this reflection of Jesus' promise: "Whatever may be the tribulation that shall come upon us in the world, we are to be of good cheer, knowing that Christ has overcome the world. We will have tribulation in the world, but peace in Jesus Christ. Turn your eyes from within, and look to Jesus, who is your only helper" (*Review and Herald*, May 19, 1896).

"Chronic entropy," meet the Savior, and be of good cheer!

WHO'S IN THE SADDLE?

Blessed be the name of God forever and ever, for wisdom and might are His. And He changes the times and the seasons; He removes kings and raises up kings; He gives wisdom to the wise and knowledge to those who have understanding. He reveals deep and secret things; He knows what is in the darkness, and light dwells with Him. Dan. 2:20-22.

It was the nineteenth-century sage Ralph Waldo Emerson who quipped: "Events are in the saddle and tend to ride mankind." While that may have been true back then, is it proving true in our twenty-first century? The next time you listen to the president at a news conference, note the checklist of events he and the reporters will tick off one by one, the immense challenges everyone knows our nation and world are facing. "Events in the saddle" indeed!

But the ancient prophets perennially reminded their audiences and readers to remember the Someone else who is also in the saddle. Stepping into that midnight palace of inebriated orgy, the elderly prophet Daniel interpreted to the petrified (and now cold sober) King Belshazzar the mysterious handwriting on the wall: "The Most High God rules in the kingdom of men, and appoints over it whomever He chooses. . . . The God who holds your breath in His hand and owns all your ways, you have not glorified" (Dan. 5:21-23). Hardly had those words been uttered when the mighty empire of Babylon collapsed in the wee hours of that very morning. "Events are in the saddle"—but so is God!

And that is why I'm convinced we can face the future with confident hope and quiet assurance. The economic meltdown that is draining away the financial might of this civilization isn't worth fearing. If God chooses to restore our financial viability for the sake of His kingdom and His mission on earth, then He will. If, on the other hand, He chooses to allow the monetary hemorrhaging to bleed away our economic vitality for the sake of advancing His kingdom and mission on earth, then "all the king's horses and all the king's men" won't be able to put Humpty together again. Knowing His will is done on earth "even as it is in heaven" assures the one who trusts God that in our very present circumstances God is still achieving His ultimate purpose, and that all things are working together for good—"the complicated play of human events ['in the saddle'] is under divine control. Amidst the strife and tumult of nations, He . . . still guides the affairs of the earth" (*Education,* p. 178). There is room in the saddle for hope!

"TODAY, TODAY, AND TODAY"

But the day of the Lord will come like a thief. The heavens will disappear with a roar; the elements will be destroyed by fire, and the earth and everything in it will be laid bare. Since everything will be destroyed in this way, what kind of people ought you to be? You ought to live holy and godly lives as you look forward to the day of God and speed its coming.
2 Peter 3:10-12, NIV.

On November 10, 1844, a Baptist farmer-turned-preacher reached for his pen and with a heartbroken sigh scribbled the following words. But when we read them today, though they still shine with a reflected hope, it is not possible for us to fathom the keen and bitter disappointment cloaked inside his careful penmanship. After all, how could you and I possibly know what it was like to have believed with such utter confidence and then to have declared it to all with such absolute certainty that Christ could come back to earth on October 22? Declaring the prediction in advance would be one matter. But having to live in the aftermath of its unfulfilled reality would be quite another. Disappointed? No wonder they called it the "great disappointment"!

Nineteen days after his hopes had been dashed, William Miller picked up his pen there in his quiet farmhouse in Low Hampton, New York, and wrote the following words to his colleague in ministry, Joshua Himes: "Although I have been twice disappointed, I am not yet cast down or discouraged. God has been with me in spirit, and has comforted me. I have now much more evidence that I do believe in God's Word; and . . . my mind is perfectly calm, and my hope in the coming of Christ is as strong as ever. I have done only what after years of sober consideration I felt to be my solemn duty to do. If I have erred, it has been on the side of charity, the love of my fellow men, and my conviction of duty to God."

And then Miller pens the new date to which he has affixed his hope: "*Brethren*, hold fast; let no man take your crown. I have fixed my mind upon another time, and here I mean to stand until God gives me more light.—And that is *Today*, TODAY, and TODAY, until He comes, and I see HIM for whom my soul yearns" (quoted in F. D. Nichol, *The Midnight Cry,* pp. 266, 267).

There it is, the handwriting of hope upon the wall of God's chosen, the very hope that ignited the movement you and I have joined. "*Today,* TODAY, and TODAY." But then, can you think of a better day in which to expect Jesus to come . . . than today?

THE FACE OF THE FATHER

God is our refuge and strength, a very present help in trouble. Therefore we will not fear,
though the earth be removed, and though the mountains be carried into the midst of the sea;
though its waters roar and be troubled, though the mountains shake with its swelling. . . .
The Lord of hosts is with us; the God of Jacob is our refuge. Ps. 46:1-7.

These were the words that inspired Martin Luther to write, "*Ein' feste Burg ist unser Gott*"—"A Mighty Fortress Is Our God"—the stirring battle hymn of the Reformation. And when we sing that hymn today, we sing out our hope, our faith, our confidence in "the God of Jacob" who is our refuge, "Lord Sabaoth His name, from age to age the same." No wonder the psalmist exclaims, "Therefore we will not fear!"

In *Now Is the Hour* Llewellyn Wilcox told the World War II story of a father and his little girl who fled into their backyard air-raid shelter during the blitzkrieg over London. Above them death and destruction rained down. The little girl was frightened. Hoping they both might fall asleep and forget their danger for a night, the father tucked his daughter into one of the small cots, turned off the light and lay down on the cot against the other wall.

But the little girl couldn't sleep. The rumble overhead, the strangeness of the shelter with its black shadows, and her mommy gone—it was more than she could stand. "Daddy," she whispered across the room, "are you there?"

"Yes, dear, I am here. Now go to sleep," he quietly responded. And she tried to. But she just couldn't. And before long that tiny voice spoke again, "Daddy, are you *still* there?" Quick was his answer: "Yes, darling, I'm here. Don't be afraid; just go to sleep. It's all right." And for some time there was only silence, each lost in their thoughts.

But finally, when the stillness and darkness were no longer bearable, the voice of the little one, craving reassurance, spoke the third time. "Daddy," she called out, "please tell me just one more thing: *Is your face turned this way?*" And through the dark quickly there came the voice of her father in reply, "Yes, darling. Daddy is right here, and his face is turned your way." In an instant the girl fell asleep, in the perfect trust of a little child.

"God is our refuge and strength . . . therefore we will not fear." Good news for the chosen in earth's impending crisis—no matter what lies ahead, *the face of our Father is turned our way.*

AM I MY BROTHER'S KEEPER? — 1

Adam made love to his wife Eve, and she became pregnant and gave birth to Cain. She said, "With the help of the Lord I have brought forth a man." Later she gave birth to his brother Abel. Now Abel kept flocks, and Cain worked the soil. Gen. 4:1, 2, TNIV.

A few years ago the United States Postal Service issued a commemorative stamp honoring the famed Boys Town USA, outside of Omaha, Nebraska. Begun in 1917 by Father Flanagan for a group of five vagabond runaway boys the priest had taken in, Boys Town USA has grown from that humble beginning into an internationally acclaimed center for compassion and care for delinquent and disenfranchised boys . . . and today, girls as well. The commemorative stamp depicts a young "urchin" (as my dad's generation called them), a ragamuffin street kid standing at the door of Boys Town. Apparently he's been asked a question about what it is that's on his back, and isn't it awfully heavy? Because underneath that celebrated picture are inscribed the older boy's response, "He ain't heavy, Mister—he's my brother." In search of help the boy had carried his little brother all the way to the gates of Boys Town.

"He ain't heavy—he's my brother." If only we had heard those words at another set of gates long, long ago. You can't read the very first "family story" in all the Bible and not be hoping against hope that maybe this time the story will turn out different. But it never does.

Once upon a time long, long ago, after a terrible moral meltdown, there was a father and mother who gave birth to two boys. Their eldest son they named "Acquired"—since mother was almost sure that this was "the Man" God had promised to send into the human line to deliver them all from Eden's awful fall. (The Hebrew literally reads, "I have acquired a man Lord," suggesting Eve hoped against hope Cain might be the Deliverer of Genesis 3:15.) But as time dragged by and a second boy was born, the grim reality of a perhaps very long wait is reflected in Adam and Eve's naming of their second child "Vanity/nothingness."

How quickly in the human family (even today) we quietly, painfully at times, downgrade our fondest hopes and dreams from the promise of deliverance to the vanity of nothingness . . . just a few steps from the garden marriage altar. But how reassuring the promise that the God who made us family will carry us on His lash-scarred back to the gates of eternity. "He ain't heavy, she ain't heavy, they ain't heavy—they're My children."

AM I MY BROTHER'S KEEPER? — 2

And in the process of time it came to pass that Cain brought an offering of the fruit of the ground to the Lord. Abel also brought of the firstlings of his flock and of their fat. And the Lord respected Abel and his offering, but He did not respect Cain and his offering. And Cain was very angry, and his countenance fell. Gen. 4:3-5.

I love to stand by the produce section in the Apple Valley Market here in our village. What could be more pleasing to the eye than those tiered and glistening rows (thanks to the automatic sprayers that gently mist the vegetables beneath the fluorescent lights) of purple eggplants, scarlet beets, white rutabagas, green leafy lettuce and spinach and asparagus and broccoli, yellow squash, orange carrots, and red tomatoes? No wonder they call it garden delight!

So please don't misunderstand God. He has absolutely nothing against all that shimmering produce. After all, he's the vegetarian Creator who invented them all! So Cain was simply being a young man after God's own heart by loving the fruitage of the rich brown soil as God did. There was and is nothing wrong with bringing "the firstfruits" of the soil to the Creator.

But it is clear from the narrative that this wasn't a "taking up the offering" time. This was a divinely prescribed worship service at the family altar whereon the promise of God's sacrifice one day was to be reenacted in the slaying of an innocent lamb. The ancient creed was crystal clear: "Without the shedding of blood there is no forgiveness" (Heb. 9:22, NIV; see Lev. 17:11). It must be clear that sin always results in death. Cain knew that, and knew it well. But Cain's full name may as well have been Frank Cain Sinatra—for "I did it my way" was his mantra too. And he heaped onto *his* stoney altar his choicest mangos, pineapples, avocados, and eggplants.

But Abel came to his altar "by faith" in the promised Lamb of God and "offered God a better sacrifice than Cain did" (Heb. 11:4, NIV). And "the Lord looked with favor on Abel and his offering" (Gen. 4:4, NIV). All four worshippers saw it—the orange flame that bolted from heaven, consuming Abel's sacrifice but leaving untouched both Cain's proud, cold altar and his proud, cold heart. It was a critical moment for God's fledgling community of chosen. Would faith, hope, and love keep them bound to God and each other? Or would disobedience rend His family forever? When it comes to the community of the chosen, have you noticed the stakes are always high?

AM I MY BROTHER'S KEEPER? — 3

Now Cain talked with Abel his brother; and it came to pass, when they were in the field, that Cain rose up against Abel his brother and killed him. Then the Lord said to Cain, "Where is Abel your brother?" And he said, "I do not know. Am I my brother's keeper?" And [God] said, "What have you done? The voice of your brother's blood cries out to Me from the ground." Gen. 4:8-10.

The heartbreaking story of history's first family is proof enough that the Book we hold sacred is hardly a collection of whitewashed "happily-ever-after" myths. The breathtaking speed with which sin guts the human community and plunges it into familial (and familiar) dysfunction is stunning.

Seven times in this tragic narrative Moses, the author of Genesis, intentionally describes Abel as the "brother" of Cain, so that we might never forget that this nefarious deed was perpetrated against a brother. And for the story's climax, the final three references to "brother" are possessive: "brother's keeper," "brother's blood," and "brother's blood."

Who can fathom the fainting horror that felled those dear parents when later they wonder where both sons are and go out into the fields in search of them, "Cain? Abel? Where are you?" How long before they discovered the truth, who knows? But when Adam and Eve collapsed over the mangled form of their younger son and mingled their tears with the first spilled human blood on earth, surely their broken hearts knew that they had lost both sons in one day.

And when God catches up with Cain (dreamed to be earth's Deliverer but instead is earth's first murderer), on the lam and out of breath, the young man's confession is painfully instructive for the community of the chosen today. "Where is your brother?" Feigning innocence, Cain shrugs off the divine query: "How am I to know? *Am I my brother's keeper?*" But God is not fooled: "I hear your brother's blood crying out to Me from the ground."

Two stunning truths in one tragic tale, and God is unequivocal in both. First, you and I are God's surrogate keepers for every human we know—not only within our families, but within our communities. There is no human exception. Second, the cries of those we refuse to care for may be muffled in our own hearts but are heard in the Father's. Twin truths that are reason enough for one prayer right now: O God, please make me the keeper of those You send today.

DEPENDENCE DAY

The God who made the world and everything in it is the Lord of heaven and earth and does not live in temples built by hands. And he is not served by human hands, as if he needed anything. Rather, he himself gives everyone life and breath and everything else. From one man he made all the nations, that they should inhabit the whole earth. Acts 17:24-26, TNIV.

The United States calls this day Independence Day, but given the following statistics, perhaps we might think of it as Dependence Day.

Someone sent me an e-mail (you know the kind—forwarded for the fifty-seventh time) that opened my eyes to the realities of this civilization you and I belong to. They say that if we could shrink the earth's population to a village of precisely 100 people and keep all the demographic ratios the same, our world would look something like this: there would be 57 Asians, 21 Europeans, 14 from the Western Hemisphere (north and south), and eight from Africa. Fifty-two would be female, and 48 male; 70 non-White, and 30 White. Seventy would be non-Christian, and 30 Christian. Six out of the 100 would possess 59 percent of the entire world's wealth, and all six would be from the United States. Eighty would live in substandard housing; 70 would be unable to read; 50 would suffer from malnutrition; one would be near death, and one would be near birth; one would have a college education; and one (yes, only one) would own a computer.

"Am I my brother's and sister's keeper?" And would they include all of these? Obviously it is impossible for us mentally and emotionally to carry the whole world on our hearts, let alone on our shoulders. Our text today reminds us that only God has "got the whole world in His hands." But in a world that through communication technology has been reduced to a global village, and yet remains so dramatically divided between those who have and those who have not, how can we possibly be each other's keepers? Perhaps we ought to at least begin at home.

Norman Mailer, the American writer, put his finger on our pulse when he observed: "Something has been stolen from us that we can't quite name." Could it be what Richard Swenson in his book *Margin* calls the "one-anothering" of each other? Have we lost our sense of community? Have we abandoned our divine "familyhood" for our twenty-first-century high-tech cubicles of private isolation? Instead of our independence, maybe we need to be declaring our dependence on each other. Maybe the first cubicle to enlarge is my own. Will you come in?

"ONE-ANOTHERING"

And the Lord God said, "It is not good for the man to be alone. I will make a companion who will help him." Gen. 2:18, NLT.

Richard Swenson, the physician author of *Margin*, makes a point, doesn't he? "Nearly all the indices of the scripturally prescribed relational life have suffered major setbacks over the last three decades. Marriage—worse; parenting—worse; the extended family—worse; the sense of community—worse; social-support system—worse; church commitment—worse; church unity—worse; and one-anothering in church—worse. And it happened seemingly overnight. Little wonder our pains are so acute" (p. 55).

Could it be that God's musing there in the Garden of Eden over Adam's need of a companion is in fact the truth of all humanity, married or not? Namely, could it be we have all been created to need the community of one another?

A study in Alameda County, California, highlights the effects of this "aloneness" from which our generation suffers. Richard Swenson reports on it: "*Study after study* confirms that a healthy marriage, family, or community support structure yields better health and increased longevity—a kind of buffering system against the pain of distress. One of the largest surveys followed five thousand residents of Alameda County, California, for nine years. The conclusion? After correcting for variables: 'Those who were unmarried had few friends or relatives, and shunned community organizations were more than twice as likely to die during that time than people who had these social relationships' " (*Margin*, p. 62).

If all I experience is "aloneness" in the workplace, in the study place, in the worship place—and I am without community—my mortality suffers! "It is not good for My children to be alone." God could hardly have been clearer, could He?

Then what will it take to transform our churches into communities where we practice "one-anothering"? Who will be the one to turn our worshipping places into caring places? Wouldn't it be logical to conclude that the chosen, of all people on earth, would offer the most compassionate and caring experiences and environments for genuine community? Are we our brothers' and sisters' keepers? And if not, why not? The statistics are in. Without God's communal "one-anothering," will the chosen die just like the rest of the world—alone and lonely?

IS JOY THERE? — 1

They devoted themselves to the apostles' teaching and to the fellowship, to the breaking of bread and to prayer. . . . All the believers were together and had everything in common. Selling their possessions and goods, they gave to anyone as he had need. Every day they continued to meet together in the temple courts. They broke bread in their homes and ate together with glad and sincere hearts, praising God and enjoying the favor of all the people. Acts 2:42-47, NIV.

Kathleen Piper shared her story on the Give and Take page of the *Adventist Review:* "One evening while I was attending a church board meeting in the basement of our church, the phone in an adjoining room kept ringing. Being the closest to the door, I got up to answer it. A voice on the other end of the line asked, 'Is Joy there?' Without thinking, I replied: 'No, sir, there is no Joy here; this is a church.' I often wondered if the caller got the full import of my reply."

How about in your church, in mine—is joy there? It certainly was in the infant church of Acts! Three thousand new believers crowd into that brand-new spiritual community "with glad hearts." The Greek word for "glad" can be translated "extreme joy." So much so, that they "did" church seven days a week, or "every day," as Dr. Luke phrased it. Now, that's church!

And what was it they did? Here's how *The Message* renders our text: "They committed themselves to the teaching of the apostles, the life together, the common meal, and the prayers" (Acts 2:42). There they are—the four vital ingredients for community-building among the chosen. In fact, if you decide today that you want to grow community among five or six brothers and sisters in your church, these four keys will be the secret to experiencing the "one-anothering" kind of community of Acts: the Word (no Gideon Bibles back then—just the apostles' teaching from Scripture); the group (the gathering of a few in their homes—just a handful, since you can't pack all 3,000 into one room!); the bread (they shared a meal—not every day and every time—but enough to build a strong social bond); and the prayers (they talked to God together—no fancy language or elaborate prayers, just a small community of brothers and sisters talking out loud to Jesus with each other). The early church didn't need doctorates in community building. All the Spirit needed was a handful of men and women, eager and willing to love God supremely and to love each other impartially.

And that's all He needs today, whenever somebody calls your church looking for joy.

IS JOY THERE?—2

They followed a daily discipline of worship in the Temple followed by meals at home, every meal a celebration, exuberant and joyful, as they praised God. People in general liked what they saw. Every day their number grew as God added those who were saved.
Acts 2:46, 47, Message.

Who wouldn't want to join a church as joyful and exuberant as that! Reflecting on the "one-anothering" kind of community demonstrated in Acts 2, the church historian Stephen Neill drew this conclusion: "Within the fellowship of those who are bound together by personal loyalty to Jesus Christ, the relationship of love reaches an intimacy and intensity unknown elsewhere. Friendship between the friends of Jesus of Nazareth is unlike any other friendship. . . . That in existing Christian congregations it is so rare is a measure of the failure of the church as a whole to live up to the purpose of its Founder for it. Where it is experienced, especially across the barriers of race, nationality and language, it is one of the most convincing evidences of the continuing activity of Jesus among men" (*Christian Faith Today,* p. 174).

I received an anonymous letter from a survivor of divorce, who described the depression he was suffering and how, outside of the church community, he actually experienced more "community" among his secular colleagues than he did in his own congregation. "God loves me. Why can't someone here?" So how shall we answer him, you and I who are his church?

Do you suppose God is waiting for you and me to take the initiative, to seek out five or six others willing to share the journey once a week? Could it be as simple as embracing yesterday's four ingredients (the Word, the group, the bread, the prayers) and humbly, even fumblingly setting out to grow that "one-anothering" kind of community of loving care?

"Things will go wrong with every one; sadness and discouragement press every soul; then a personal presence, a friend who will comfort and impart strength, will turn back the darts of the enemy that are aimed to destroy. Christian friends are not half as plentiful as they should be. In hours of temptation, in a crisis, what a value is a true friend! . . . True friends who will counsel, who will impart magnetic hopefulness, the calming faith that uplifts the soul—oh, such help is worth more than precious pearls" (*The Seventh-day Adventist Bible Commentary,* Ellen G. White Comments, vol. 3, p. 1163).

So the next time they call asking for joy, why don't you be the friend who answers?

THE COMMUNITY OF THE TWISTED KISS

Bear one another's burdens, and so fulfill the law of Christ. Gal. 6:2.

Surgeon Richard Seltzer tells the unforgettable story in his *Mortal Lessons*: "I stand by the bed where a young woman lies, her face postoperative, her mouth twisted in palsy, clownish. A tiny twig of the facial nerve, the one to the muscles of her mouth, has been severed. She will be thus from now on. The surgeon had followed with religious fervor the curve of her flesh; I promise you that. Nevertheless, to remove the tumor in her cheek, I had to cut that little nerve.

"Her young husband is in the room. He stands on the opposite side of the bed, and together they seem to dwell in the evening lamplight, isolated from me. Who are they, I ask myself, he and this wry-mouth I have made, who gaze at and touch each other so generously, greedily? The young woman speaks. 'Will my mouth always be like this?' she asks. 'Yes,' I say, 'it will. It is because the nerve was cut.' She nods, and is silent. But the young man smiles. 'I like it,' he says, 'It is kind of cute.'

"All at once I *know* who he is. I understand, and I lower my gaze. One is not bold in an encounter with a god. Unmindful, he bends to kiss her crooked mouth, and I [am] so close I can see how he twists his own lips to accommodate to hers, to show her that their kiss still works" (in Brennan Manning, *The Ragamuffin Gospel*, pp. 105, 106).

Isn't that a glorious story? Could it be that it is what we have been called to be—the community of the twisted kiss? Twisting our lives, adjusting our hearts, shaping our embraces in order to draw near to those who in their bentness long to be noticed and held and loved?

"Bear one another's burdens, and so fulfill the law of Christ." What law? Surely Paul recalls the Savior's second great commandment, "You shall love your neighbor as yourself" (Matt. 22:39). For in the end, what else can it mean to bear each other's burdens? Isn't it the law of Christ to become your brother's and sister's keeper? Isn't it the will of Christ that we become a real live community known far and wide (or at least across town) for the way we choose to love the morally twisted, the socially, spiritually bent? Doesn't fulfilling Jesus' law in fact mean that the chosen must become *more* than simply a community of *faith*—that we must also become a flesh-and-blood *community* of flesh-and-blood *love* lived out in the twisted world where God has placed us? The community of the twisted kiss. After all, that's the way He first loved us.

THE LESSON OF THE SWEDES

Share each other's troubles and problems, and in this way obey the law of Christ.
Gal. 6:2, NLT.

The Swedes have a saying: "Shared joy is double joy, and shared sorrow is half a sorrow." When I share my joy with you, I double it—and when I share my sorrow with you, I cut it in half. Because life was meant to be shared, wasn't it? God never made us to be Lone Rangers. So how can we "share each other's troubles and problems"? How about these three simple steps?

1. I must break out of my *comfort* zone. Of course, it's never comfortable for me to move beyond a surface contact with you (you know, the weather, the news) and ask how you're really doing and if I can help. Because once I ask, I'm obligated to respond. But the truth is that until we do what doesn't come naturally to us—take that deep breath, screw up our courage, and ask, "Is there anything I can do to help you?"—we'll never break out of our safe sterility and become the compassionate community the chosen were raised up to be.

2. I must step into your *burden* zone. Because if I don't step in, you can't break out. The burdened heart longs for somebody to lift that emotionally or spiritually or financially heavy load. Nobody truly desires to suffer alone. You want to tell me about your burden, but you're afraid to burden me, which is why you need me to take the initiative and come to you.

3. I must draw you into my *friendship* zone. While that doesn't mean we become bosom buddies, it does mean that I draw you into my own community. I may call a few more friends who will join me in providing a new, small community for you. Because when community is larger than just the two of us, you realize that I'm not an aberration or an exception, that God really does have a "one-anothering" family of brothers and sisters for you.

Where did these three steps come from? Simple—they're the three steps Jesus took to carry our burdens. He broke out of His comfort zone in heaven. He stepped deeply into our burden zone of earth and sin. And then He drew all He met into His friendship zone: "With lovingkindness I have drawn you"—"come to Me"—for "I have called you friends" (Jer. 31:3; Matt. 11:28; John 15:15). No wonder they said of Him, "This man receives sinners and eats with them" (Luke 15:2). Truth is—Jesus built community out of sinners. And the truth also is—we will never have community until and unless we do the same.

THE LONELIEST DAY

Now there is in Jerusalem near the Sheep Gate a pool, which in Aramaic is called Bethesda and which is surrounded by five covered colonnades. Here a great number of disabled people used to lie—the blind, the lame, the paralyzed. One who was there had been an invalid for thirty-eight years. When Jesus saw him lying there and learned that he had been in this condition for a long time, he asked him, "Do you want to get well?" "Sir," the invalid replied, "I have no one to help me." John 5:2-7, NIV.

What a sad admission: "I have no one to help me." But do you really believe that invalid shriveled beside the Pool of Bethesda was the only one on earth to have made that mournful confession? Beside how many apartments, mobile homes, houses, dormitories, parked cars, and underpasses will Jesus pass tonight, only to hear the same muffled sob, "I have no one to help me"? How many church pews are crowded on Sabbath with that very heart cry? Or perhaps we should ask how many church pews will be left empty this coming Sabbath because of that cry?

May I share a secret with you? For too many of the chosen, *the most lonely day of the week is the Sabbath.* Oh sure, they will buck up their courage, paste on their smile, get in their car, and walk through our door, sit in our class (though they mostly come only for worship), sing from our hymnal, and listen to our sermon. But the most painful part of their faithful Sabbathkeeping ritual is still ahead. Because after the benediction has been pronounced and the postlude played, that's when they must stand to their feet and walk right past us, knowing there will be no one to return their smile, nobody to grab their hand and ask, "How was your week?" or "Why don't you come to our home for dinner today?" Only in their dreams do such conversations ever take place. But this Sabbath they must once again pass unnoticed through our noisy foyer, out into the sunshine or rain or snow, and bravely crawl back into their car and leave our church and premises to return home. Alone again. And again. And again.

"And that day was the Sabbath" (John 5:9). Had Jesus not taken the personal initiative with that invalid that Sabbath, we'd have no clue what He's been waiting a very long time for us to do for the men, women, and children who keep coming to us on the Sabbath with the heartbreaking confession: "I have no one to help me." In the name of Christ, why can't we help them?

"THE GIFT OF FAILURE, THE GIFT OF FEELING FLOPPIER"

Now the multitude of those who believed were of one heart and one soul. . . . And great grace was upon them all. Acts 4:32, 33.

Why are we so hard on ourselves when we fail? Do we really believe that one can navigate this life without repeated and painful failures? Anne Lamott, in her book *Traveling Mercies,* tells of her invitation as a novice writer to share the stage with a world-class author. Meant to be an evening of repartee between this author and her, it ended in disaster, with Anne mangling her comments and embarrassing her guest in front of a large audience. Much later she wrote in reflection: "My fear of failure has been lifelong and deep. If you are what you do—and I think my parents may have accidentally given me this idea—and you do poorly, what then? It's over; you're wiped out. All those prophecies you heard in the dark have come true, and people can see the real you" (p. 142). But as she brooded over grace, her paradigm for failure shifted until it became a gift. "The gift of failure," she concluded, "breaks through all that held breath and isometric tension about needing to look good: it's the gift of feeling floppier" (p. 143).

Could it be the chosen need that "gift of feeling floppier"? Holding our breath and striking our spiritual poses might make us look good for a moment, but it's the death of community! Because put the word on the street that to join our community you have to be a muscular spiritual giant (no floppy failures admitted), we not only kid ourselves—we keep our community empty. Truth is—just like the church in Acts, we need "great grace" to be upon us all.

"Grace is nothing more or less than the face that love wears when it meets imperfection, weakness, failure, sin" (Joseph Cooke, *Celebration of Grace,* p. 13). And oh, how the chosen need that face! Think of all the people God could heal and restore if grace were the face love wore around our church! A community of "great grace"? Why, we couldn't keep them away!

Martin Luther was right: "The Kingdom [read community] is to be in the midst of your enemies. And he who will not suffer this does not want to be of the Kingdom [community] of Christ; he wants to be among friends, to sit among roses and lilies, not with the bad people but the devout people. O you blasphemers and betrayers of Christ! If Christ had done what you are doing, who would ever have been spared?"

Truth is—freely we have received such "great grace"—now freely let us give it to all.

BOWLING ALONE

The body is a unit, though it is made up of many parts; and though all its parts are many, they form one body. So it is with Christ. . . . If one part suffers, every part suffers with it; if one part is honored, every part rejoices with it. Now you are the body of Christ, and each one of you is a part of it. 1 Cor. 12:12, 26, 27, NIV.

Back in the mid-nineties a rather obscure academic suddenly found himself catapulted onto the stage of public attention. He was invited to Camp David to spend a weekend with the U.S. president. His picture appeared on the cover of *People* magazine. A major publishing house offered to publish his research. All because of Robert Putnam's provocative thesis that America is suffering from a "growing social capital deficit." He argues that civil society itself is breaking down as more and more Americans become disconnected from their families, their communities, and the republic itself—all of this precipitated by television, two-career families, suburban sprawl, generational changes in values, etc. We've become a nation of loners. And bowling is his metaphor of proof. While years ago thousands of Americans bowled in leagues, today people tend to bowl alone (if at all). "Bowling alone" has become the American way of life.

What a stark contrast to Acts' portrayal of communal life in the early church! "They had all things in common" (Acts 4:32). Men and women, Jews and Gentiles, the haves and the have-nots, saints and sinners—the infant church was a menagerie of community! Some have fretted that the church in Acts was a grand experiment in Christian socialism, where the goods of all where thrown into a pot for all. But a careful reading reveals that there was no compulsion (as the story of Ananias and Sapphira makes clear), all liquidated and gave their assets freely, and the recipients of the offerings were those in need, not the entire church. What is also clear is that nobody was "bowling alone." Nobody had to.

Why? As Paul championed in our text today, the church of Christ is the very body of Christ. Can you imagine one of your organs succumbing to "growing social-capital deficit," and choosing to live and function alone? The very notion is ludicrous, since the health of the organism is dependent upon the collective health of the organs. No heart can bowl or beat alone and survive. It is the collective nature of community that keeps health optimum for your personal body, and for your local church. And that's why you need the church, and the church needs you!

"COME UNITY"

Holy Father, protect them by the power of your name—the name you gave me—so that they may be one as we are one. John 17:11, NIV.

I was in our House of Prayer service one Wednesday evening, pondering the prayer card handed out at the door, when it suddenly struck me that the word "community" combines the sounds of two words: "come" and "unity." The more I ruminated on it, the more appropriate it seemed to conclude that any call to "community" is in reality a call to "come unity." In fact, if we take the "unity" out of "community" there is no "community" left.

That's why Jesus' high priestly prayer in John 17 is so profound. He had much He could have been interceding to the Father about—the safety of His disciples in the impending clandestine arrest and kangaroo trial He was facing, the global expansion of the fledgling movement He was leaving behind, the triumph of the new theology that would burst the seams of Judaism. But instead, four times in that single prayer Christ pleads with the Father "that they may be one" (John 17:11, 21-23). Our unity was very much on the suffering heart of the Savior.

Why? Ponder these words, from more than a century ago, with our "community" focus: "[Community] in diversity among God's children—the manifestation of love and forbearance in spite of difference of disposition—this is the testimony that God sent His Son into the world to save sinners. . . . This [community] is the most convincing proof to the world of the majesty and virtue of Christ, and of His power to take away sin. The powers of darkness stand a poor chance against believers who love one another as Christ has loved them, who refuse to create alienation and strife, who stand together, who are kind, courteous, and tender-hearted, cherishing the faith that works by love and purifies the soul. . . . In [community] there is a life, a power, that can be obtained in no other way" (*Sons and Daughters of God*, p. 286).

Did you catch that? Only through community can we obtain the life power of Christ! His call to unity—"come to unity"—is a summons to the "most convincing proof" available to this secular world of the Savior's power. Why? Because when people as diverse as you and I are, are bound together in community by a radical love for one another, what could be more convincing of the gospel's power to transform and elevate fallen humanity than that? For this reason alone community is not an option for the chosen. It is Christ's mandate, His passionate prayer.

THE MASK

[Jesus] said to them, "Watch yourselves carefully so you don't get contaminated with Pharisee yeast, Pharisee phoniness. You can't keep your true self hidden forever; before long you'll be exposed. You can't hide behind a religious mask forever; sooner or later the mask will slip and your true face will be known." Luke 12:1, 2, Message.

Once upon a time a team of pastors I belonged to went on a retreat. One evening in one of our motel rooms, three of us rather innocently wandered into a rather painful (for me) conversation about transparency and vulnerability. And since I was the leader, my two colleagues began to gently, kindly probe why I wasn't more personally transparent with the group. Why didn't I share with them some of the painful struggles I was experiencing as a parent? Why did I have to project an image of having it all together, when in fact I didn't? Why didn't I model failure more, giving permission for others to do the same?

When the evening was over, I and my two friends knew that what we'd just shared needed to be experienced by the entire team. And so the next day we huddled as a small community and plunged into a collective soul searching. There were tears, naturally. And confessions, too. And prayers—a lot of them. But looking back on that moment, I now realize it was a vital catalyst, a necessary (and even necessarily painful) step for a small group in search of the community Jesus came to build. "You can't hide behind a mask forever," He warned.

A few weeks later I came across these words of Henri Nouwen:"The best cure for hypocrisy is community." In fact, is there any other cure for our proclivity to two-facedness? What can keep us more honest *with* ourselves, *about* ourselves, than a circle of fellow sinners saved by grace? If you and I can make the commitment to love each other in Christ, no matter what we might discover about each other, what a liberating openness and transparency we discover! No more pretending around each other, for we learn we can trust each other.

And how is it in the circles where you live and move and work and study? Could it be that the others are waiting for you to take the first step and make the move toward vulnerability and transparency? Too painful a step? But for the sake of pain avoidance, are you really willing to sacrifice the joy-filled freedom of a community of genuine "one-anothering"? Not if you knew how truly blessed is the gift of "come unity" Jesus died to secure. Trust me—it's worth it all!

THE FRONT PORCH—1

Look! Here I stand at the door and knock. If you hear my voice and open the door, I will come in, and we will share a meal together as friends. Rev. 3:20, NLT.

Maybe what this generation needs is an old front porch! Drive through our little village of Berrien Springs, and it is quickly evident that only the old, old houses—the ones that creak with memories from a century ago—offer that piece of Americana architecture we still call the front porch. Black-and-white memories of lanky Andy Griffith and aproned Aunt Bea and little Opie on their Mayberry front porch, whiling away the twilight hours with friends and neighbors, are locked in our national psyche.

Actually, social observers such as Joseph Myers are suggesting that our twenty-first-century lives have already created new "front porches" for this generation—from cyberspace social networks (MySpace, Facebook, et al.) to the ubiquitous Starbucks cafés that now dot the globe—"front porch" meeting places for social connecting and community. It's all about what Myers calls "median space," that in-between space between the privacy of my own little world and home and the rough-and-tumble workaday world of survival, an in-between space where we can meet and connect socially without intruding on each other's private worlds. "It is the experience of social connection that draws people to stop in for a moment" (*The Search to Belong,* p. 127).

So how can we build front porches onto (and into) our churches? Whatever happened to our old-fashioned potlucks? Before you slam this book shut, let me be quick to remind you as our text reminds us all, when God wants to get up close and personal with us, He describes Himself knocking on our door, hoping to enter and "share a meal as friends." Maybe God enjoys a good potluck, too! We've struggled at Pioneer to keep a weekly fellowship dinner for family and visiting friends viable. I know—it takes a lot of work. But we've finally concluded that the social, "front porch" benefits—visitors feel welcomed, members feel needed—make the labor a worthwhile labor of love. So what if you organized a few members into a dinner team once a month or quarter or even year? Better yet, what if your Sabbath school classes took turns hosting a "front porch" dinner? If this generation is hungry for front porch community, even our smallest congregations could help satisfy that hunger, couldn't we?

THE FRONT PORCH—2

Therefore if you have any encouragement from being united with Christ, if any comfort from his love, if any common sharing in the Spirit, if any tenderness and compassion, then make my joy complete by being like-minded, having the same love, being one in spirit and of one mind. Phil. 2:1, 2, TNIV.

Wouldn't it be something if the best way to close the back door of our church is to build a front porch? Her letter wasn't anonymous, though I'll keep it so: "Dear Pastor Nelson: I must tell you why I resorted to listening to the sermon on the radio this morning. I have been an active member at PMC for seven years. Although I sit among 3,000 people each Sabbath, the worship experience is usually painfully lonely for me. There have been times when I have skipped church for several weeks at a time. Last week I submitted a request to have my membership transferred. I am hoping [another] church will provide the sense of community I am seeking." Maybe we need a new front porch.

Joseph Myers reports on research that has defined four spaces we as humans utilize in our development of personality and sense of belonging: *public space* (12 feet and beyond)—joining noisy fans in a stadium; *social space* (four to 12 feet)—belonging to a civic club or service organization; *personal space* (18 inches to four feet)—meeting in a weekly small group; *intimate space* (zero to 18 inches)—my spouse. Myers concludes: "All belonging [in all four spaces] is significant. Healthy community—the goal humankind has sought since the beginning—is achieved when we hold harmonious connections in all four spaces. Harmony means more public belongings than social. More social than personal. And very few intimate. A healthy strategy for those working to build community entails allowing people to grow significant relationships in all four spaces" (*The Search to Belong*, p. 51).

So how can we build a new front porch for the church? What did the church in Acts do? They took 3,000 members and immediately broke the numbers down into small groups of *koinonia* (Greek, "fellowship"), by building front porches "from house of house" (Acts 2:46). Crowd 100 people into a church—that's celebration. Put 10 of them together in a living room—that's community. The chosen have spent decades practicing the celebration. But people still leave us. Proof enough it's time to build front porch communities. How? Please keep reading.

THE FRONT PORCH—3

So it is with Christ's body. We are many parts of one body, and we all belong to each other. In his grace, God has given us different gifts for doing certain things well.
Rom. 12:5, 6, NLT.

OK. I'm willing to be open to this idea of forming or joining a small group. But where in the world do I begin?" Good question. What do you say we begin with a few of the questions/objections typically raised whenever small groups are being considered?

"Nobody's ever invited me to join a small group." One of the realities we've learned about small groups is that you can't program or decree them from up front. But the good news is that small groups don't have to be a congregational program in order for a friend of Jesus (you) to be able to invite a group of members (friends, colleagues, neighbors, even strangers) together to pray and study His Word and grow community. If no one comes to you, why don't you ask the Holy Spirit to direct you to five or six individuals who'd be interested in joining you for this new venture? You may be the very one God is needing to grow new community in your church!

"But I don't have a clue as to what to do in a small group." That's the adventure the Spirit is leading you into. We all begin as novices. The good news is that there are some excellent resource books available. A classic is Kim Johnson's *Spiritual Body Building.* Your pastor may have other suggestions, or may know an experienced leader to mentor you. You may simply choose a book of the Bible to study through together. Don't forget the four ingredients to Acts 2's community: the Word, the group, the bread, and the prayers. You can do it!

"But I'm not into cooking and bringing food." Fair enough. Nobody says small groups have to eat in order to grow community. (Too much eating can grow something else!) But if you're in a group where some are willing to bring some food, I say, be blessed!

"I don't like strangers." All of us are more comfortable with our friends, of course. But in a group committed to us spiritually and socially, you're not going to be a stranger for long.

"I prefer my own kind for community building." Who doesn't? But if the body of Christ is God's strategy to grow the kingdom of heaven in the hearts of all of His earth children through their diversity, then where better than a small group to reflect God's wide-open embrace?

Two more important questions and four incredible blessings—let's share them tomorrow.

THE FRONT PORCH—4

Don't just pretend to love others. Really love them. Hate what is wrong.
Hold tightly to what is good. Love each other with genuine affection,
and take delight in honoring each other. Rom. 12:9, 10, NLT.

Here are a couple more objections we hear whenever small groups are being considered.

"I don't want to sign my life away." One of the fears people have is joining a group that will last forever and ever. Amen. No one wants that. That's why at the beginning of a new small group, a "sunset clause" needs to be voted. There's nothing wrong with agreeing to meet for three or four months, and renegotiating your "contract" after that. If a group chooses to meet for a longer period, that's fine. But having a cutoff/renegotiate date keeps everybody comfortable.

"Actually, I'm just not the small groups kind of guy. I don't have this huge need to belong. I'm not lonely. I'm not a misfit. I've got friends. So I don't think I'd get much out of it." Well, at least you're honest! And you may be right, initially. But may I gently suggest that the power of Christian community is about giving more than getting? Jesus hardly needed us either, this planet of misfits. But His irrepressible joy arose not out of His joining our group to get, but rather to give. Did you ever think that maybe a significant reason for your joining a small "front porch" group is because that little community needs what you will bring? After all, it's that way in families, isn't it? Nobody gets to pick their family—but the miracle of love means that your bratty sister and pesky brother are near and dear to you, "'cause we're family!"

But that isn't to suggest there aren't some very significant blessings that come to you when you join a small group. Here are four of them: **1.** We find **strength** for life's storms. I enjoy sailing, but I don't want to be out there alone when a storm strikes! **2.** We receive **wisdom** for making important decisions. Solomon knew: "As iron sharpens iron, so a friend sharpens a friend" (Prov. 27:17, NLT). **3.** We experience **accountability**, which is vital to spiritual growth. Remember, "lone rangers are alone rangers." And **4.** We find **acceptance** that helps us repair our wounds. I have watched the most secure and successful people go through crises. It's inevitable. Having a "front porch" community you belong to (besides your spouse or usual work colleagues) can be a godsend for your needy heart. People will draw their wagons around you, and stand your ground beside you. And as I've learned, that is priceless.

THE LESSON OF THE MOONIES

All the believers were one in heart and mind. Acts 4:32, TNIV.

In case you're still wondering about the value of growing spiritual and social community within our faith community, consider this study of the Moonies (members of Reverend Sun Myung Moon's Unification Church). Rodney Stark reports the study's fascinating conclusions in his book *The Rise of Christianity*. Back in the early sixties he and John Lofland became the first social scientists to observe people convert to a new religious movement. After hundreds of interviews with Moonies, the researchers noted that Moonie conversions were similar to conversions to Christianity in the first century—namely, conversion came in the face of strong disapproval from nonmembers (i.e., family, friends). The lasting conversions were those in which "interpersonal attachments to members [of the new community] overbalanced their attachments to nonmembers" (p. 17). That is, strong interpersonal attachment within the new community of faith is what keeps new members from reverting to their former attachments. "Attachments lie at the heart of conversion, and therefore that conversion tends to proceed along social networks formed by interpersonal attachments" (p. 18). Thus Stark concludes: "The basis for successful conversionist movements is growth through social networks, through a structure of direct and intimate interpersonal attachments" (p. 20).

The point is inescapable, isn't it? One of the significant factors for the explosive growth of the early church was its brilliant, obviously Spirit-directed emphasis on building small "front porch" groups of community within the movement. It wasn't the only factor, but as Stark's research with the Moonies shows, it was a very strategic factor.

No wonder a century before Stark and Lofland, Ellen White came to the same conclusion: "The formation of small companies as a basis of Christian effort has been presented to me by One who cannot err" (*Christian Service*, p. 72).

Turns out we don't need the Moonies to conclude that interpersonal attachment has ever been the strength and strategy of God's community-building on earth. The stories of early Acts and early Adventism are narratives woven with the strong thread of small group interpersonal communities. Given the cubicled isolation of life and society today, can you think of a more critical time for you and me to embrace the counsel of "One who cannot err"?

A PERSONAL TESTIMONY

Therefore encourage one another and build each other up, just as in fact you are doing.
1 Thess. 5:11, NIV.

Let's end our "front porch" and "one-anothering" reflections with Rob Thomas's personal testimony that my friend Kay Kuzma shared in her devotional book *Fit Forever:*

"My mom's suicide rocked my life. My first reaction was shock. Then denial. Then anger. *(How could she do this to me? to my kids?)* Then guilt. *(Why didn't I do something more?)* As I tried to put the pieces of my life together, I questioned God's role in Mom's suffering (she was manic-depressive) and her subsequent choice to end her life. Blindly, I saw only two options: (1) God didn't fulfill His promise to not allow any temptation beyond what Mom could bear; or (2) Mom just blew it! Either way, it was a losing situation. Either God or Mom screwed up, and that conclusion almost destroyed my relationship with God.

"Over the next year or two I really struggled with my spiritual life. In retrospect, I think it was a combination of my relatively sterile spiritual life before Mom's death, her suicide itself, and the subsequent questions it raised in my mind about God's role in our lives. Also, I attended a large, impersonal church where I had no support group to listen, encourage, and reinforce to me the truth that God loves and Satan destroys. I'm embarrassed to say that I almost gave up on God. I kept going to church, but mainly for the kids' sake. Even though I was struggling, I still believed in a God to whom I wanted my kids to relate. I didn't want them to grow up not going to church because of me.

"Before making a final choice to bail out on God, I committed to do some reading and investigating. I read a book by Philip Yancey, *Where Is God When It Hurts?* That really helped me to 'wake up and smell the roses!' My family also began attending a smaller church where I became involved and made friends who loved me, regardless—and I began therapy.

"Over the past five years I've really come alive spiritually! I've benefited from four small groups (one secular recovery group and three spiritually based groups). I've had a much more meaningful devotional and prayer life, and I've been much more active in my church. It's been wonderful—like my own spiritual resurrection! I wonder why it took me so long (30 years) to get connected with God" (p. 216; italics supplied).

REQUIEM FOR A
FALLEN BROTHER—1

*On the evening of that first day of the week, when the disciples were together,
with the doors locked for fear of the Jews, Jesus came and stood among them and said,
"Peace be with you!" After he said this, he showed them his hands and side. The
disciples were overjoyed when they saw the Lord. John 20:19, 20, NIV.*

Who knows how many bars and padlocks the panicked disciples have slapped onto that upper room door! One thing's for sure—they aren't convened for a grand worship celebration. The record is embarrassingly clear. The doors are locked "for fear of the Jews." The 11 are utterly convinced that the same authorities that brutally executed their Master on Friday are now with bloodhounds on their own trail. The doors are locked and the windows shuttered.

But hallelujah, the great truth of the empty tomb is invincible: all the master locks in the world can never lock the Master out! For there He stands in their gaping midst, the Dead One now risen. And the place goes berserk. How would you react if one you knew was dead suddenly was standing beside you? "Shalom to you." Jesus smiles with beckoning hands that invite them to approach. But nobody moves or breathes. The disciples are frozen. "Look, it's Me!" Jesus pushes up His sleeves and draws aside His mantle, exposing His hands, His chest, His feet. In plain sight are the still-ugly, scabbed wounds of Calvary. When that glorious reality finally breaks through their numb shock, the upper room explodes with "I can't believe it" joy and worship and gratitude. Jesus is alive!

But that this is more than a Sunday evening show-and-tell report becomes clear when Jesus speaks the provocative words: "Receive the Holy Spirit. If you forgive anyone his sins, they are forgiven; if you do not forgive them, they are not forgiven" (John 20:22, 23, NIV). Too often we have hurried past these words, letting our Protestant rejection of the confessional distract us from Christ's compelling point. For in a single sentence He declares the birth of a resurrection community: a community that resurrects and restores—a community that restores and forgives. That's why there are actually *two resurrections* in John's narrative. For there is someone else in the upper room who has already died a thousand deaths. And unless he, too, is resurrected, the fledgling church that Christ is founding will never become community at all.

Makes you wonder—could there be a resurrection awaiting in your church, too?

REQUIEM FOR A
FALLEN BROTHER—2

About an hour later, someone else spoke up, really adamant: "He's got to have been with him!
He's got 'Galilean' written all over him." Peter said, "Man, I don't know what you're talking
about." At that very moment, the last word hardly off his lips, a rooster crowed. Just then, the
Master turned and looked at Peter. Peter remembered what the Master had said to him: "Before
the rooster crows, you will deny me three times." He went out and cried and cried and cried.
Luke 22:59-62, Message.

I have looked upon brothers and sisters who have fallen in our community. The
shame, the stigma, the sorrow. I send personal birthday letters to my parishioners,
and waiting to be signed one afternoon was a birthday letter to a brother who, in
humiliation after a moral fall, fled our community, practically under the cover of
darkness. I'm embarrassed to tell you that as I stared at his letter with an out-of-
town address, I wondered what I should inscribe at the bottom? Wouldn't it be easier to scribble nothing, just a signature? Or maybe not even send the letter at all,
for surely he'd simply conclude, "I guess I'm not on their list anymore."

Requiem for a fallen brother. Requiem is Latin for "rest." But is there any rest
for a fallen brother or fallen sister in our community? "Am I my brother's keeper?"
How easy it is to dismiss him. But how hard it is to forgive.

After all, Peter had fallen in as public a way as is possible. Ground the name of
Jesus like a cigarette butt beneath his cursing heel in front of everybody that night.
Why, even Jesus heard him turn the air blue with his fisherman's thesaurus of ob-
scenities. You can't fall any lower than publicly repudiating your Savior by your
words, your life, your very lifestyle, can you? "I . . . do . . . not . . . know . . . that
. . . blankety-blank-blank Man!"

How long would a brother like Peter last in a community like ours? It is a shining testimony to the love of his brothers that Simon Peter didn't have to go fishing
all alone several weeks later. "We'll go with you" (John 21:3, NIV). But as is so often
the case, the morally fallen become the professionally failing. That dark night on
Galilee, Peter caught not a single fish. He was not only fallen—he was a failure. And
only the fallen can tell you what that double blow really feels like. But don't you
give up, Peter. For standing there in the guilty shadows of your long night is
Someone who is about to resurrect you to a brand-new life. Don't give up!

RESURRECTION OF A
FALLEN BROTHER—1

The third time he said to him, "Simon son of John, do you love me?" Peter was hurt because Jesus asked him the third time, "Do you love me?" He said, "Lord, you know all things; you know that I love you." Jesus said, "Feed my sheep." . . . Then he said to him, "Follow me!" John 21:17-19, NIV.

It happened so quickly! No fish all night. The command of a stranger on the shore. Nets suddenly bursting with silver. "It's Jesus!" Peter in the water splashing toward Him. Skiffs beached. Fishermen squatting wide-eyed around a campfire. Breakfast with the Risen One. Who interrogates Peter in front of the rest—gentle, but pointed—"Do you love me?" Three public probings to match Peter's three public denials. And in response a heartbroken young man confesses—quietly, contritely—"You know that I love you." Then before their very eyes, with the stunning speed of the Divine, Mercy triumphs over judgment. The Savior declares the resurrection of Simon Peter complete, and the fallen one is restored. It happened so quickly!

What does a *fallen* man, a *failing* woman have to go through to be resurrected and restored in a community like ours? And how long do they remain fallen? By that I mean How long does the adjective "fallen" remain attached to their memory? I'm not thinking of God's record—I'm wondering about ours. Moreover, these fallen ones—do they remain our brothers and sisters in the meantime, during their fallenness? You say, "Well, that depends on whether they really repent of their moral failure or not." Does it? Does there come a time when I am no longer my brother's keeper? "But what are you suggesting—that it really doesn't matter whether they repent of their sinful, shameful public fall or not?" I'm not suggesting that at all. In fact, I'm not even thinking of *their* response right now. I'm wondering about *ours*. When does the adjective "fallen" get dropped from their memory—meaning, *our* memory of them?

Could it be the reason we're so hard on the fallen is because the fallen remind us of us? And so we pretend piety in ourselves, and we demand piety in others, so that no one discovers the sinner inside? Dietrich Bonhoeffer astutely observed: "The pious fellowship permits no one to be a sinner" (*Life Together*, p. 110). But tragically, it is by that very pretending that we inadvertently choke off any possible community. For how can I get close to you if I won't let you get close to me? Perhaps it isn't only the "fallen" that are in need of Jesus' resurrection.

RESURRECTION OF A FALLEN BROTHER—2

I, even I, am he who blots out your transgressions,
for my own sake, and remembers your sins no more. Isa. 43:25, NIV.

A woman was having visions of Jesus. When church authorities learned of her claims, a bishop was commissioned to examine both the woman and her revelations. Brennan Manning tells the story. "'Is it true, ma'am, that you have visions of Jesus?' asked the cleric. 'Yes,' the woman replied simply. 'Well, the next time you have a vision, I want you to ask Jesus to tell you the sins that I confessed. . . .' The woman was stunned. '. . . You actually want me to ask Jesus to tell me the sins of your past?' 'Exactly. Please call me if anything happens.' Ten days later the woman notified her spiritual leader. . . . 'Please come,' she said. . . . 'Did you do what I asked?' 'Yes, bishop. . . .' The bishop leaned forward with anticipation. His eyes narrowed. 'What did Jesus say?' She took his hand and gazed deep into his eyes. 'Bishop,' she said, 'these are His exact words: I CAN'T REMEMBER'" (*The Ragamuffin Gospel,* pp. 116, 117).

Apocryphal? Perhaps. Truth? Indeed. For a century ago these words were written: "If you give yourself to [Jesus], and accept Him as your Savior, then, sinful as your life may have been, for His sake you are accounted righteous . . . and you are accepted before God *just as if you had not sinned*" (*Steps to Christ*, p. 62; italics supplied).

"I am he who remembers your sins no more." So speaks God. So speaks grace. And so we must speak and act if we would experience genuine community. For you see, a "graceless" community is an oxymoron. For it is no community at all. A "pious fellowship," perhaps—but it is not community, genuine community. For only grace can resurrect community.

And that is why the chosen must keep returning to the foot of the cross. For the truth about grace is that I will never extend it to you, fallen as you are, until I experience it in me, fallen as I am. The cross always precedes the Resurrection. I can't resurrect you until grace has restored me. "Peter, do you love Me?" "Oh, Lord, you know that I love You." "Good. Now go and love the fallen back to Me."

And they will come back to Him when you and I extend to them the forgiveness He has already extended to us. "I can't remember." Great news—for it is when we say the same to each other that we resurrect our brother, we restore our sister, and we revive our community!

THE GOOD OLE DAYS

All these faithful ones died without receiving what God had promised them, but they saw it all from a distance and welcomed the promises of God. They agreed that they were no more than foreigners and nomads here on earth. Heb. 11:13, NLT.

Don't you wish we lived in "the good ole days," when parents were loving, kids were obedient, and families were happy? What do you say we make a tally of the model homes among the great "First Families" of sacred history? To help us spot the model families, let's give them letter grades—A for model/ideal, C for average, and F for failing. Here we go.

Adam and Eve. We all want to give them an A for being our brave progenitors, but not even a perfect home can keep you from messing up, can it? C. How about **Cain and Abel**? That would be a big F—no sibling harmony there. And the pre-Flood families? Cain ran away from home, Lamech introduced polygamy, Enoch did fine, but the intermarrying of the lines of the faithful and rebellious melted down society—C or F or in between for the whole family tree of them. **Noah and Mrs. Noah** and the boys. An embarrassing ending to the family, but let's be generous—C (all right, all right—B+).

Abraham and Sarah. A happy childless couple, but they lied to their neighbors to keep hubby alive. Then the Hagar meltdown was one pretty mess, wasn't it? One husband and father, two wives and mothers, and a couple bratty stepbrothers. A charitable grade would have to be C, wouldn't it? Were **Isaac and Rebekah** any better? They certainly seemed happy, though they were also childless and liars. But they spoiled God's gift of twins Esau and Jacob by choosing favorites. It was all downhill from there. Grades? C for the parents and an F for sibling rivalry. Was it any better for **Jacob** and sister wives, **Leah and Rachel**, two concubines and 12 sons, one of whom slept with Jacob's daughter-in-law and 10 of whom plunged the internecine conflict to shameful depths in selling their half brother as a slave! Grade for Jacob and company? F-minus! I could find only one marriage without stain—**Joseph and Asenath**. Give them an A!

The "good ole days"? Are you kidding! The community of the chosen was in family meltdown from the beginning. If misery loves company, we ought to all be happy! Because it's good news: the God of the chosen takes us as we are—dysfunctional, vulnerable, and weak—and still loves us and still leads us, broken families and all, until we reach the Promised Land.

THE ACHILLES' HEEL OF THE AVERAGE HOME

Behold, I will send you Elijah the prophet before the coming of the great and dreadful day of the Lord. And he will turn the hearts of the fathers to the children, and the hearts of the children to their fathers. Mal. 4:5, 6.

There was one family we left out of our "first families" review yesterday. And while it might sound sacrilegious even to suggest it, the family that our Lord Jesus grew up in needs to come under the same scrutiny we gave the others. What letter grade would you give to Jesus and His mother, Mary; His stepfather, Joseph; and all His stepbrothers and stepsisters? After all, wouldn't they be considered the ultimate "first family"?

You do remember that Jesus grew up in a preexisting family (and I don't mean the one in heaven). After beginning His ministry, when Jesus returned to His hometown of Nazareth, the villagers whispered to one another, "Is this not the carpenter, the Son of Mary, and brother of James, Joses, Judas, and Simon? And are not His sisters here with us?" (Mark 6:3). Were these the sons and daughters of Joseph and Mary? We could conclude that were it not for the fact that in His dying agony Jesus commended His mother to His closest disciple John (see John 19:26, 27). If Mary had had other children, there would have been no need to make provision for her loving care. Thus we can conclude from the Gospel record that Joseph had children by a previous marriage before he, the older widower, and his young bride were joined in holy wedlock.

So how was it in the childhood home of our Lord? Loving parents? Yes. Happy siblings? Perhaps not. The haughty and bossy way Jesus' older stepbrothers treated Him as an adult is a huge clue to how they must have treated Him when He was a boy (see John 7:3-5; Mark 3:31-35). "His brothers felt that [Jesus'] influence went far to counteract theirs. He possessed a tact which none of them had, or desired to have. . . . Being older than Jesus, they felt that He should be under their dictation. . . . Often they threatened and tried to intimidate Him. . . . They were jealous of Him, and manifested the most decided unbelief and contempt" (*The Desire of Ages,* p. 87).

Amazing! God got to choose His own family, and the family He chose was crippled with the same Achilles' heel as ours—vulnerable and weak at the heart of the most sacred, covenanted of all relationships. So if God chose them, surely He can choose us, too. To be unhappy forever? No. God dreams of healing our families here even before we join His family above (Mal. 4:6).

HIS NEEDS, HER NEEDS — 1

Love suffers long and is kind; love does not envy; love does not parade itself, is not puffed up; does not behave rudely, does not seek its own, is not provoked, thinks no evil.
1 Cor. 13:4, 5.

Karen and I once decided to preach a sermon together, at the end of a series on covenantal relationships (sexuality and marriage). Every preacher knows his or her spouse is taking notes whenever marriage is the theme. Someone sent me a cartoon of a pastor and his wife driving home after church. She's jauntily gazing out the window, her arm draped over the car seat, a picture of nonchalance. He's clutching the steering wheel, tie loosened, glaring straight ahead, consternation all over his countenance. He speaks: "Have you stopped to consider how much more effective my sermon would have been if you hadn't yelled 'Ha!'?" That's why I knew we had to preach that sermon *together*. We shared five secrets from a book that has blessed us immensely—Willard F. Harley, Jr.'s *His Needs, Her Needs: Building an Affair-proof Marriage.* Consider for yourself these top five needs in the community of marriage.

Harley identifies the number one need of a wife: *affection.* "When a husband shows his wife affection, he sends the following messages: I'll take care of you and protect you. You are important to me, and I don't want anything to happen to you. I'm concerned about the problems you face, and I am with you. I think you've done a good job, and I'm proud of you" (p. 33). I've read that how a couple relates to each other in the first four minutes of the morning and the evening sets the agenda for their entire time together.

Harley's number one need for a husband: *sexual fulfillment.* No surprise—men are sexual creatures. Read the Pentateuch! "When a man chooses a wife, he promises to remain faithful to her for life. This means that he believes his wife will be his only sexual partner 'until death do us part.' He makes this commitment because he trusts her to be sexually interested in him as he is in her" (p. 43).

From years of ministry to couples, Harley identifies the number two needs as *conversation* for the wife and *recreational companionship* for the husband. Talk together, play together. It's how we courted each other—it's how we keep each other. It isn't rocket science, these lists of Harley's. It's love in everyday clothes, celebrating God's gift of your closest friend.

HIS NEEDS, HER NEEDS—2

[Love] keeps no record of being wronged. It does not rejoice about injustice but rejoices whenever the truth wins out. Love never gives up, never loses faith, is always hopeful, and endures through every circumstance. . . . Love will last forever! 1 Cor. 13:5-8, NLT.

From a quarter century of marriage counseling Willard Harley says that the number three need he's heard most from wives is *honesty and openness.* Harley tells husbands, "Your mate should know you better than anyone else in the world." But unless we open up our hearts, gentlemen, she'll never know. "A sense of security is the bright golden thread woven through all of a woman's five basic needs. If a husband does not keep up honest and open communication with his wife, he undermines her trust and eventually destroys her security" (p. 91).

The number three need for husbands? *An attractive spouse.* That "simply means that your appearance makes someone feel good." Obviously beauty is more than skin-deep, but physical attraction is often what ignited the first flame. And while some husbands have emotional needs more important than their need for an attractive wife, Harley counsels: "She should resemble the woman he married" (p. 108). Her number four need is *financial support,* and his is *domestic support.* In today's economy most homes need two incomes, but Harley suggests that wives prefer the family budget set up on his income alone. She may choose to work, or have to work, but she looks to her husband for financial security, while it is a source of security for him when she's the domestic manager of his life, family, house, and home. Clearly the strongest and happiest marriages are a mutually embraced partnership on every front they share.

The wife's number five need: *family commitment.* It is Harley's ninth law of marriage: the best husband is a good father. Do it together: meals, worship, church, outings, bike rides, beach, board games, sporting events, bedtime stories, family projects, etc. Quantity edges out quality on this front. Spend time together! And the husband's number five need? *Admiration.* "Biographies of great men prove it, and the lives of all men show it: A man simply thrives on a woman's admiration" (p. 158). Why tear him down in public or in private—he becomes what you make him. "Love one another; as I have loved you" (John 13:34). When a man and woman pledge to love each other just as God has loved them, you have the makings of a love story that will last forever!

"SEX AND THE CITY" AND COUNTRY AND OTHER VIRTUAL PLACES

Now Joseph was well-built and handsome, and after a while his master's wife took notice of Joseph and said, "Come to bed with me!" Gen. 39:6, 7, NIV.

Malcolm Muggeridge, the celebrated English journalist, once wrote: "Today people have sex on their minds, which, if you think about it, is a strange place to have sex." But today's culture is utterly saturated with it. America has sex on its media mind around the clock. In the city, in the country, in outer space, in cyber space, sex is virtually everywhere.

It's even in the Bible. Our text today is from one of the greatest sex-on-your-mind stories in all of Scripture. Everybody knows the tale of Joseph and Mrs. Potiphar's attempted seduction of the virile young slave in her husband's employ. Don't think her perfumed amorous advance wasn't a temptation to Joseph. It could be his ticket to freedom. But remember, "Come lie with me" always requires two lies: to *lie* with her, and then to *lie* about it with her.

It is the most critical line in the plot and the most important line to memorize in your battle against sexual temptation—Joseph's response: "How then can I do this great wickedness, and sin against God?" (verse 9). Not against Potiphar, not against her, not even against himself—the sin of sexual temptation is always against God.

So it is with porn, the greatest moral killer in the world today. An equal-opportunity slayer, it preys on every category of men *and* women. Its insidious online accessibility, anonymity, and affordability ("the three A's of cybersex") brook no survivors. I have heard grown men weep over the power of their sexual addiction! What can spare you the same anguish? The answer lies in Joseph's and David's radically opposite responses to the identical sexual temptation: Joseph *fled*—David *fed*. And therein still lies the fatal difference. Kill the "mouse," shut off the computer, turn off the DVD, get out of the car, walk out of the office, get off the phone, toss out the magazine. And run! Flee as if your life depended on it, for it does.

"Call upon Me in the day of trouble; I will deliver you" (Ps. 50:15). There is a God who can set you free from temptation, from addiction. Having withstood the sexual battle when He was here, Christ promises that you can be "free indeed" (John 8:36). Too late for you? No it is not! "Create in me a clean heart, O God" (Ps. 51:10). "Wash me, and I shall be whiter than snow" (verse 7). Because of Calvary, like David you can become a new creation, pure and clean again.

HOW CAN YOU MEND A BROKEN HEART?

Have mercy on me, O God, according to your unfailing love; according to your great compassion blot out my transgressions. Wash away all my iniquity and cleanse me from my sin. Ps. 51:1, 2, NIV.

The note was under my windshield wiper after church. *Thank you for your sermon on how to choose the right partner in marriage. My husband and I will be in divorce court on Monday. I had an affair two years ago, and it seems we have never been able to get over it.*

Lewis Smedes wrote: "The most creative power given to the human spirit is the power to heal the wounds of a past it cannot change" (*The Art of Forgiving*, p. 176). Can a heart, can a home, be mended? Can a family, can a community, be saved? Let's brood over forgiveness for a moment.

Forgiveness is indeed possible. Adultery isn't so much the grounds for divorce as it is the grounds for forgiveness. The Bible offers no catalog for sins easiest to forgive. It simply assures us God forgives sin, and friends of God can do the same.

Forgiveness, in fact, is necessary. "When we forgive we set a prisoner free and discover that the prisoner we set free is us" (p. 178). If I hold on to my woundedness and pain, I do not punish you—I punish me.

Forgiveness is in reality tough. When you've been hurt that deeply and you long for revenge or retribution at best, it isn't easy to let go.

Forgiveness is a choice. And nobody, not even God, can make that choice but you. It is the choice to release the one who wounded you into the care and love of God. You may need to stand alone in your house and repeat out loud, "I forgive him, I forgive him, I forgive him." It is a choice of the will, but the feelings will eventually follow.

Forgiveness is not forgetting. As Smedes puts it: "A healed memory is not a deleted memory." Of course you will remember the deed! But "forgiving what we cannot forget creates a new way to remember. We change the memory of our past into a hope for our future" (p. 171).

Forgiveness is offered. The prayer on the center cross was for us all. "Father, forgive them, for they do not know what they do" (Luke 23:34) is a prayer offered to us all, so that we too might pray it and offer it. Christ gave it to us—forgiveness, full and free and forever. And we must pass it on. "Freely you have received; freely give" (Matt. 10:8). For how else shall we mend a broken heart?

THE FARMER'S WIFE

For I have chosen him, so that he will direct his children and his household after him to keep the way of the Lord by doing what is right and just, so that the Lord will bring about for Abraham what he has promised him. Gen. 18:19, NIV.

Don't you suppose it went into their memory book as the most unforgettable day of their lives—the day Abraham and Sarah not only "entertained angels unawares" (Heb. 13:2) but entertained God Himself! It had started out simply enough as an act of Middle Eastern hospitality, three mantled strangers passing by, followed by Abraham's insistence that they pause under his tree for some refreshment and rest. And halfway through that dinner of curds and veal the Leader of the three announced that the centenarian parents were going to have a child! You know the story. Sarah stifled a laugh. God heard it. She denied it. God begged to differ. And dinner finished, the three Strangers left.

But not before the Leader announced why the couple had been chosen. His words in our text are a stunning pronouncement that the chosen are chosen in order *that they might grow God's community on earth*—among their children, among themselves, among God's family. So powerful is His summons to grow community that our acceptance of His calling and our commitment to His community must remain unrelenting (as the rest of Genesis describes), not only when we feel like family at home or at church, but when we don't as well.

We are called to be in God's family for life, as this story told by Fred Smith, Christian author and business leader, so poignantly portrays: "One of my treasured memories comes from a doughnut shop in Grand Saline, Texas. There was a young farm couple sitting at the table next to mine. He was wearing overalls and she a gingham dress. After finishing their doughnuts, he got up to pay the bill, and I noticed she didn't get up to follow him. But then he came back and stood in front of her. She put her arms around his neck, and he lifted her up, revealing that she was wearing a full-body brace. He lifted her out of her chair and backed out the front door to the pickup truck, with her hanging from his neck. As he gently put her into the truck, everyone in the shop watched. No one said anything until a waitress remarked, almost reverently, 'He took his vows seriously.' "

And so must the chosen.

THE "DAVIDIC" CODE—1

Oh, how I love Your law! It is my meditation all the day. Ps. 119:97.

May I place three pictures on the screen of your mind for a moment? Two won't be hard to imagine, but I wonder what picture the third one will be. Picture 1—you see a classroom full of young Muslim boys, kneeling on mats, their garments wrapped around their bended knees. It is a *madras,* a conservative Islamic school that indoctrinates their young. The boys are all reading the Qur'an, the holy book of their religion, their capped heads bobbing back and forth in rhythm to their rote memory and recitation.

Picture 2—a heartbroken, curly-bearded rabbi is surrounded by soldiers as he is forced out of his synagogue in a Jewish settlement in the Gaza Strip. Deported now from that occupied Palestinian territory, what is it the rabbi carries so tenderly in his arms? Look closely. They are the sacred scrolls of the holiest book of Judaism—the ancient Torah and Prophets and Writings. Congregants wail as the rabbi and their holy book are escorted away.

Pictures of the three great monotheistic religions of earth—and what shall we play upon the screen of our minds for Christianity? How do Christians regard their holy Book? I was stunned with a survey I read that while most Americans regard themselves as Christians, barely half of them claimed to make moral choices based upon specific principles or standards. And of those, only three in 10 named the Bible as the source of their principles!

Would picture 3 be one of you and me carrying our Bibles under our arms to worship every Sabbath? I'd like to think so. But one Sabbath we stationed Pathfinders at every entrance to our sanctuary to count how many worshippers arrived without their Bibles. Never mind the numbers, but suffice it to say that a group photo of you and me at worship wouldn't exactly be a portrait of our Holy Book front and center.

So can picture 3 be changed? I believe it can. Psalm 119, the longest chapter in the Bible, can rightly be called "An Ode to God's Word." An acrostic poem, its 22 stanzas begin with successive letters of the Hebrew alphabet, and every verse contains either "law" or "word" or one of their synonyms. Psalm 119 is David's passionate love song for God's Word.

A love song for our Holy Book? But why not? After all, given life today, shouldn't the chosen be as passionate about their Holy Book as the other religions are? Just read Psalm 119.

THE "DAVIDIC" CODE—2

Your word is a lamp to my feet and a light to my path. Ps. 119:105.

Everybody's heard of *The Da Vinci Code*, that runaway best seller that sold un-substantiated histrionic fiction for entertainment and profit. But it has been a long, long time since very many paid much attention to the "DaVidic" Code of Psalm 119—the longest poem and chapter in Scripture, an unabashed love song to the Word of God. But would you like to know what distinguishes our Holy Book from the other holy books of the world?

The Bible supersedes all other holy books. I gleaned three major evidences of this from James MacDonald's *God Wrote a Book*. **Evidence 1. External.** The Bible is preeminent in literature, standing head and shoulders above every other piece of human literature throughout history. It is preeminent in circulation, having been read by more people in more languages than any other book in history. (It is now translated into 400 languages, with portions of it in 2,500 languages. Recently Gideons International placed an average of 1 million Bibles a week, or 113 copies a minute!) The Bible is preeminent in influence. More books have been written about the Bible than any other subject, and more authors have quoted from the Bible than any other source.

Further external evidence includes the Bible's preservation. People have devoted their lives to destroying God's Word. No other book has been so burned, banned, and banished as the Bible. Voltaire, the great French infidel, predicted that Christianity would be destroyed within 100 years of his lifetime, and the Bible would be found only in a museum. Today you can find Voltaire only in a museum, and the Bible continues as the world's fastest-selling book.

Some charge that the Book is simply too old to be reliable. Really? Today we have more than 5,600 ancient manuscripts of the Greek New Testament, 10,000 Latin manuscripts, and 9,300 early versions—a total of nearly 25,000 early manuscripts of the Bible. The next most commonly copied document is Homer's *Iliad*, with 643 manuscripts. The Bible outnumbers Homer by nearly 40 to one! Want archaeological proof of the Bible's veracity? Just go to the Web and Google the words "Bible" and "archaeology."

When David sings of God's Word as a bright light shining into the darkness, he isn't extolling a piece of fiction. The evidence is simply too compelling. So let the light shine in!

THE "DAVIDIC" CODE—3

The entrance of Your words gives light; it gives understanding to the simple. Ps. 119:130.

Having examined external evidence that corroborates the veracity of Holy Scripture, consider now: **Evidence 2. Internal.** The Bible is a collection of 40 authors who wrote across a period of 1,500 years. And as James MacDonald observes, they wrote about the two subjects nobody can agree upon—religion and politics! And yet the Word of God is the most internally consistent piece of accumulated human writing in history. How can we explain it? God wrote the Book. No, He didn't pen it or dictate it. Human beings did—which is why, like four witnesses to a single car accident, you get four varying accounts. But the only explanation for the Bible's compelling internal consistency regarding human morality and divine truth is its divine authorship or inspiration.

Take fulfilled prophecy, for example. There are 61 major prophecies concerning the life of Jesus Christ written centuries before His birth. MacDonald notes that statisticians tell us that the statistical probability of just eight of those prophecies being fulfilled is 10^{17} (one out of 100,000,000,000,000,000 chances). That is the same likelihood as covering the state of Texas with silver dollars two feet deep, and then blindfolding you and telling you to wade out into all those coins across Texas and pick out the one silver dollar that has a red dot on it! And yet, not eight, but all 61 prophecies regarding Jesus were fulfilled.

But beyond the external and internal evidence, there is also: **Evidence 3. Experiential.** As a pastor I must testify that over the years of my ministry I have witnessed the profound, supernatural effects both the hearing and the reading of Holy Scripture have had on parishioners. I have watched men die at peace because of this Book. I have watched women live in hell with peace because of this Book. I have witnessed young adults become set free from life-shackling, body-addicting habits because of this Book. I have listened to children sing their little hearts out about this Book, and have watched them grow up to become mighty champions of the faith of Jesus Christ because of this Book. And I have personally discovered the supernatural power of a personal friendship with the Author of this Book.

Which is why, like those children, I still sing: "The B-I-B-L-E, yes, that's the Book for me; I stand alone on the Word of God, the B-I-B-L-E!"

SHOWDOWN IN THE DESERT—1

Your word I have hidden in my heart, that I might not sin against You. Ps. 119:11.

The Middle East has tragically been the blistering-sanded hotbed of some of the world's greatest conflicts and showdowns. But there never has been a showdown in the desert like the one we are about to witness all over again.

The solitary figure moves into the blinding light of the desert sun. Stretched before him beneath the withering blaze is a vast expanse of cracked and wrinkled earth. Brown and barren, it offers for his solace not a single tree or a solitary blade. The lone figure trudges on, his lips cracked and parched, his eyes bloodshot and tired, his face burned by the sun and beaten by the wind. But there is nothing to slake his dusty thirst here, nothing to feed his gnawing hunger. And so he turns. Back to the sweltering shade of that hillside's rocky outcropping, back to where he has prayed these nearly six weeks without food. Forty days ago the heavens had been rent with a shaft of light and the echo of a Voice that declared the dripping baptismal candidate to be the beloved Son of God. But that was 40 days ago. Now the voice of God seems but the mirage of a faraway memory as the solitary Man suffers alone in the desert fire.

Suddenly another voice breaks the hot, oppressive calm. The Man whirls around to face the intruder. What a comedy of contrasts, this portrait of these two beings! One face emaciated and haggard, eyes sunken, cheekbones protruding like a black-and-white photograph from the Holocaust. But the other face—smooth, clear, noble, proud—as if bathed with a celestial glow. Antagonists, the two of them are in a war that is still galactic. The masquerading angel who is the fallen rebel is the first to speak: "If You are the Son of God, command that these stones become bread" (Matt. 4:3).

The emaciated One slowly rubs His dry tongue over salty, cracked lips. The truth is that He not only had divine power *at* His fingertips—He had divine power *in* His fingertips—for He is God made flesh, and with a single command He could indeed turn that rocky floor into a bakery. But He answered and said, "It is written . . ." (verse 4).

Three times the enemy of heaven and humanity will strafe the weakened Savior on that desert floor. And three times with just three words Jesus will drive him back. "It is written."

But how can you know it is written in the Word, if it isn't memorized in the heart?

SHOWDOWN IN THE DESERT—2

Jesus answered, "It is written: 'People do not live on bread alone, but on every word that comes from the mouth of God.'" Matt. 4:4, TNIV.

It is written," "It is written," "It is written"—three times that was His only weapon under demonic attack. But what will be our defense today? In all candor I tremble for this generation of the chosen that now must traverse the same desert and face this same antagonist.

For we have raised a generation that no longer turns to the written page, but rather to the electronic screen. To be sure, technology is not our enemy. But when the screens of our laptops and PDAs and office computers and TVs and movie theaters are the only places we will pause long enough to read, it is no wonder that the dusty onionskin page of a Bible can hardly compete.

The devil was defeated in that desert showdown by an unshakable "It is written." He has spent the rest of history making certain he would not repeat the same mistake and be bested in the same way. And so he has methodically gone about obliterating the "It is written" from our lives and from our world. We live today in a world with more Bibles per capita than at any time in history, but a world that may go down as the most biblically illiterate generation of modern time, one that believes Joan of Arc was Noah's wife.

Seriously, outside of required reading, who seriously reads much of anything anymore? John Grisham, Stephen King, and Dan Brown thrillers don't count. Nor do the tabloids or sports extras. Outside of professionally necessitated or academically mandated reading, who reads anymore? "It is written." Oh, really? *Where?*

Jesus' showdown reply to Satan was a direct quotation from Deuteronomy 8:3. In fact, for all three temptations His calculated response was to quote from Deuteronomy. No pocket Bible, no PDA or laptop with the Scriptures, He simply quoted them by memory. So how did He learn? "The child Jesus did not receive instruction in the synagogue schools. His mother was His first human teacher. . . . His intimate acquaintance with the Scriptures shows how diligently His early years were given to the study of God's Word" (*The Desire of Ages,* p. 70). Memorizing Scripture. You can't be too young; you can't be too old. And from the simple steps we'll learn tomorrow, turning "It is written" into "It is memorized" doesn't have to be too difficult either.

SHOWDOWN IN THE DESERT—3

Your words were found, and I ate them, and Your word was to me the joy and rejoicing of my heart; for I am called by Your name, O Lord God of hosts. Jer. 15:16.

What was Jesus' modus operandi in the desert? How did He defeat the devil? Peter Gomes in his *The Good Book* makes the point well: "[Jesus] recalled in every instance the instruction of scripture, the teachings of an inherited faith to which he subordinated himself in his debates with the tempter. He didn't outfox or even outmaneuver Satan; he simply relied on those things he knew to be true . . ." (pp. 280, 281). "Your word I have hidden in my heart, that I might not sin against You" (Ps. 119:11). How then shall we memorize the Word of God?

My friends at FAST (www.fast.st) have devised a simple strategy for memorizing Scripture that we've shared with hundreds of our members. Go online and order their study guides. Here's an abbreviated synopsis: **1.** Determine the version of the Bible you're going to memorize and stay with that translation (be it KJV, NKJV, NIV, et al.). **2.** Like good food, start with small portions. There's no point in memorizing Psalm 119 initially—but verses 11, 97, and 105 are keepers. Start with short texts. **3.** Use small blank cards or a small notebook for transcribing your verse to paper. **4.** Write the text reference on one side. **5.** Lock in the reference to the text by writing it twice: (one side) Psalm 119:11; (the other side) "Thy word have I hid in mine heart, that I might not sin against thee" (Ps. 119:11, KJV).

6. Learn one word and then one phrase at a time. The quip—"inch by inch, anything's a cinch"—is true. **7.** Practice being "word perfect" with whatever translation you use; otherwise lack of precision will result in lack of retention. **8.** Review your texts every day—and even throughout the day. Those small cards fit in a pocket, a purse, a backpack. **9.** Review your verses once a week with a partner who is using the same translation. Here's where family members and friends can be a great encouragement and help. **10.** With daily review, in two months your texts will be "locked" on your hard disk memory.

Think of it—with just two texts a week, in a year you'd have a hundred texts stored in your memory, a hundred powerful promises the Holy Spirit can bring to mind night or day. Why, in six years you could memorize the Gospel of Mark! And what better words to memorize than the words of the One who taught us by His example to do just that? So why wait? Start now!

AUDIENCE WITH THE ETERNAL—1

Come, let us bow down in worship, let us kneel before the Lord our Maker; for he is our God and we are the people of his pasture, the flock under his care. Today, if only you would hear his voice . . . Ps. 95:6, 7, TNIV.

The next time I'm in London I'd love to have an audience with Queen Elizabeth II. "Audiences" are what you have with powerful personages, a private conversation and moment with someone very famous. But the problem with an "audience" is that you can't invite yourself to have one with the queen by simply showing up at Buckingham Palace or knocking on the Windsor Castle door— "Thought I'd drop by to have a cup of tea with Her Majesty. Might she be available?" It doesn't work that way. *She does the inviting.*

"The Bible is God's voice speaking to us, just as surely as if we could hear it with our ears. If we realized this, with what awe we would open God's Word and with what earnestness we would search its precepts. The reading and contemplation of the Scriptures would be regarded as *an audience with the Infinite One*" (*My Life Today,* p. 283; italics supplied). What an awesome thought! The Book Jesus taught us to memorize—when we open it, we are granted a personal audience with the most powerful, famous, and influential Being in the universe!

No wonder "we are to open the Word of God with reverence and with a sincere desire to know the will of God concerning us. . . . The heavenly angels [the highest created intelligences in the universe] will direct our search. God speaks to us in His Word. We are *in the audience chamber of the Most High, in the very presence of God*. Christ enters the heart" (*ibid.*; italics supplied). Forget the queen of England, the prime minister of Canada, and the president of the United States. The audience chamber we can be ushered into *daily* belongs to the Almighty Himself.

If we remembered that reality, I have a feeling we would read the Book a whole lot more than we do, don't you? And surely we would read it so much more carefully, prayerfully. When I was in college I wrote a letter to then-president Richard Nixon. I can't remember what I wrote, but the whole dormitory knew I'd received his reply on White House stationery! How could you possibly keep secret an audience with the Eternal? Why would you even want to? The supernal blessings that overflow from a daily audience with God in His Word are impossible to conceal. You can't help being changed—in phenomenal ways—as we will note tomorrow.

AUDIENCE WITH THE ETERNAL—2

At the end of the ten days they looked healthier and better nourished than any of the young men who ate the royal food. . . . In every matter of wisdom and understanding about which the king questioned them, he found them ten times better than all the magicians and enchanters in his whole kingdom. Dan. 1:15-20, NIV.

Every time you enter the pages of Scripture and the audience chamber of the Eternal, the Author of the Book will phenomenally bless you in the following seven realms of your life.

1. Physically. Today's text recalls the story of the four Hebrew students—Daniel, Shadrach, Meshach, and Abednego—who, exiled in Babylon, had no pocket Bibles to consult and no flash cards to review, only their memories of what they had learned from the Word of God back home. But in just 10 days the Eternal honored their obedience to the health principles of His Word and physically blessed His four young friends beyond all the others. Why? "Prayer and a study of the word bring *life and health* to the soul," for "the study of the Bible in our schools will give the students special advantages. Those who receive into their hearts the holy principles of truth will work *with increasing energy*" (*Testimonies,* vol. 6, p. 253; *Counsels to Parents, Teachers, and Students,* p. 450; italics supplied). You will be abundantly blessed physically by the Author of the Word you meditate upon daily.

2. Academically. Not just the body, but the scholastic itself is benefited. Nebuchadnezzar personally examined the four Hebrew young adults and found them "ten times better than all" the court professionals he had. Why did they score the highest on their entrance exams? "As an educating power, the Bible is without rival. Nothing will so impart vigor to all the faculties as an effort to grasp the stupendous truths of revelation," for "the Word of God is the most perfect educational book in our world" (*My Life Today,* p. 23; *Fundamentals of Christian Education,* p. 394). The Book isn't magic. But remember, when you read from its pages, you are in the audience chamber of the Eternal.

A young freshman came up to me after our House of Prayer service one Wednesday and commented: "I feel like I'm not cutting it academically. I'm feeling overwhelmed with my classes. What can I do?" My reply was simple: "First of all, welcome to being a freshman! And second, begin memorizing Scripture. It will deepen your grasp." Because it's true: "The Bible will do for mind and morals what cannot be done by books of science and philosophy" (*Counsels to Parents, Teachers, and Students,* p. 422). It's the most powerful Book on earth. Trust me—its Author will take care of you.

AUDIENCE WITH THE ETERNAL—3

I have more insight than all my teachers, for I meditate on your statutes. I have more understanding than the elders, for I obey your precepts. Ps. 119:99, 100, NIV.

Let's continue with the third, fourth, and fifth realms. **3. Mentally.** According to the *Journal of the American Medical Association* the National Institute of Aging found that "adults who regularly participate in intellectually stimulating activities [such as memorization] may reduce their risk of developing dementia such as Alzheimer's disease by as much as 47 percent" (http://jama.ama-assn.org/cgi/content/abstract/287/6/742). While David isn't discussing gerontology in today's text or describing a 47 percent edge, he makes the phenomenal claim that meditating on God's Word increases your mental grasp no matter your age! "The Bible, just as it reads, is to be our guide. Nothing is so calculated to enlarge the mind and strengthen the intellect as the study of the Bible" (*Mind, Character, and Personality*, vol. 1, p. 93). But there's more: "Let the more important passages of Scripture . . . be committed to memory, not as a task, but as a privilege. Though at first the memory [may] be defective, *it will gain strength by exercise*" (*Child Guidance*, p. 512; italics supplied). It is incontrovertible that God promises to bless you mentally as you interact with Him in Holy Scripture.

4. Socially. There is no level of life God cannot bless. Surprising as it may seem, the Bible can guide those who seek a life companion. If you follow the advice of godly parents (Prov. 6:20-22), the leading of the Holy Spirit (Rom. 8:4), and the counsel of God (Ps. 32:8), "He shall give you the desires of your heart" (Ps. 37:4). The love story of Isaac and Rebekah is a beautiful example (Gen. 24). But not only *find* your life companion, the Bible can help you *keep* your life companion. Read the book of Proverbs and Ephesians 5 sometime. God promises to bless you socially, as you seek Him in His Word.

5. Financially. Another phenomenal promise is the one God makes in Malachi 3:10, NIV: "'Bring the whole tithe into the storehouse, that there may be food in my house. Test me in this,' says the Lord Almighty, 'and see if I will not throw open the floodgates of heaven and pour out so much blessing that you will not have room enough for it." Isn't it a promise? "Whenever God's people, in any period of the world, have . . . acknowledged the claims of God, and complied with His requirements, honoring Him with their substance, their barns were filled with plenty" (*Counsels on Stewardship*, p. 347). What if God really means what He promises? Why wouldn't He?

AUDIENCE WITH THE ETERNAL—4

God can do anything, you know—far more than you could ever imagine or guess or request in your wildest dreams! He does it not by pushing us around but by working within us, his Spirit deeply and gently within us. Eph. 3:20, Message.

Today we'll look at the final two ways in which you'll be blessed as a result of studying the Scriptures.

6. Professionally. Would it be inappropriate for God to bless His friends in their careers as well? Ask Joseph, whom God promoted from prison counselor to prime minister in the space of three hours (allowing time for his post-incarceration haircut and shave)! Ask David, whom God elevated from lowly sheepherder to national ruler. Ask Esther, whom God raised from adopted orphan to queen of the Persian Empire. God's Word impacts the lives of His friends professionally. "Let the youth take the Bible as their guide, and stand like a rock for principle, and they can *aspire to any height of attainment.* There is *no limit* to the knowledge that they may reach. You may aspire as you wish, but there will always be *an infinity beyond*" (*Signs of the Times,* Mar. 4, 1889; italics supplied). And why not? When you're friends with the Eternal, infinity is your limit! Isn't that Paul's very point in our text today?

7. Spiritually. "Your word I have hidden in my heart, that I might not sin against You" (Ps. 119:11). Because the realm and level of life that matters most to us all is the spiritual, isn't it? Success on this front is life's greatest victory. And David's promise is that the memorized Word of God is "a mighty barricade against temptation" (*Education,* p. 190). Read on: "You can fight against the enemy, not in your own strength, but in the strength God is ever ready to give you. Trusting in His Word, you will never say, 'I can't'" (*The Adventist Home,* p. 357). Never say "I can't"? Why not? Because "I can do all things through Christ who strengthens me" (Phil. 4:13). Have you read a more dynamic promise of victory than this? "In [the Bible's] power, men and women have broken the chains of sinful habit. They have renounced selfishness. The profane have become reverent, the drunken sober, the profligate pure. Souls that have borne the likeness of Satan have been transformed into the image of God. This change is itself the miracle of miracles. A change wrought by the word, it is one of the deepest mysteries of the word" (*Education,* p. 171).

"Miracle of miracles"—who doesn't desire it! Knowing that Christ has promised to open wide heaven's windows and pour out His blessings unmatched and unexcelled, can you give me one good reason you and I shouldn't seek His friendship in His Word every day of our lives?

233

THE LUCKY ROYAL TURTLE

I delight to do Your will, O my God, and Your law is within my heart. Ps. 40:8.

In Vietnam they were calling him "the lucky royal turtle." For he could've ended up in a savory Chinese soup somewhere, had it not been for a stroke of good fortune. Wildlife officers raided a smuggler's house in southern Vietnam's Tay Ninh province and discovered a cache of live contraband—more than 30 turtles destined for sale in China, where turtle meat is considered a delicacy. But "Lucky" stood out big-time, a 33-pound giant among the small reptiles. They'd never seen a turtle so large! A consultation with an Asian turtle specialist determined that the "big one" was a *Batagur baska*, an Asian river terrapin, a species from Cambodia thought to have disappeared but recently rediscovered and subsequently declared protected by King Norodom Sihamoni. Hence its name, the "royal turtle." But the clinching identification for "Lucky" came when there beneath his wrinkled skin was discovered a tiny microchip, proof positive he was both rare and protected . . . and now saved!

Like a microchip hidden under the skin, our text today declares the Word of God hidden in the heart as the clinching identification. It certainly was for Jesus. According to Hebrews 10:5-7 the words of Psalm 40 are His own testimony: "I delight to do Your will, O my God, and Your law is within my heart" (verse 8). The Hebrew word here for "law" is *torah*, which narrowly describes the divine law and broadly includes the entire written corpus of divine revelation. When a new chief justice of the U.S. Supreme Court places his or her hand upon the Bible and swears to uphold the Constitution, in a limited sense that word describes the original document that is the bedrock for American jurisprudence and governance. But the oath is also understood to include the laws of the land that have expanded from that original document. Even so when Christ declared, "Your law is within my heart," He was declaring not only His allegiance to the *torah* Law of God, but also to the *torah* Word of God—both treasured and hidden in His heart.

So is it a surprise to discover that this same "microchip" is embedded in the hearts of His friends? God calls to His chosen ones: "Listen to Me, you who know righteousness, you people in whose heart is My law" (Isa. 51:7)—or as the New Living Translation renders it, "you who cherish my law in your hearts." Cherishing the law in their hearts just like Jesus—that doesn't make His friends lucky. Luck is for turtles. But it does make them blessed, very blessed indeed.

"MY WARMEST THOUGHTS ENGAGE"

Jesus said to them, "Have you never read in the Scriptures: 'The stone the builders rejected has become the capstone; the Lord has done this, and it is marvelous in our eyes'?"
Matt. 21:42, NIV.

One accusation you could never make of Jesus was that He was wishy-washy regarding both the authority and the veracity of Holy Scripture. Ten times in the Gospels He probes His listeners with either "Haven't you read?" or "Have you never read?" And all 10 of those interrogative challenges concerned the reading of the Bible. You can almost hear His nonplussed astonishment that His hearers hadn't read those passages.

Twenty times in the same Gospels the words "It is written" are on Christ's lips. No wonder Rene Pache could declare: "We can say with all reverence that Jesus Christ was practically saturated with the Scriptures, which He knew 'having never learned' (John 7:15, KJV). One tenth of His words were taken from the Old Testament. In the four Gospels, 180 of 1,800 verses which report His discourses are either quotations of the written revelation or else direct allusions to it" (quoted in Norman Gulley, *Systematic Theology: Prolegomena*, p. 381).

But Christ not only quoted from and alluded to the Old Testament, the only Bible of His day. He was unequivocal in maintaining its historical reliability as well. Norman Gulley lists 23 Old Testament incidents, whose historicity Jesus confirmed, from the creation of Adam and Eve, to the murder of Abel, to Noah and the Flood, to the destruction of Sodom, to the Decalogue, to the prophecy of Daniel, et al.—23 Old Testament events He confirmed as historically accurate and true. Gulley concludes, "Because Jesus Christ is the infallible authority, His estimate of Scripture must be a part of that infallible authority" (*ibid.*).

For that reason it is imperative that the chosen not be beguiled into concluding that God's Word is not the reliable, authoritative, bedrock of divine truth for humanity that Jesus declared it to be. "It was Christ's view that the Word of God is as enduring as the God of the Word" (*ibid.*, p. 379). Faith's embrace need never be overruled by science nor overturned by the academy. The hymn of Isaac Watts is still the prayer of the chosen (*The SDA Hymnal*, no. 273):

"Lord, I have made Thy word my choice, my lasting heritage;
There shall my noblest powers rejoice, my warmest thoughts engage."

TORAH, TORAH, TORAH

Happy are those who do not follow the advice of the wicked, or take the path that sinners tread, or sit in the seat of scoffers; but their delight is in the law of the Lord, and on his law they meditate day and night. They are like trees planted by streams of water, which yield their fruit in its season, and their leaves do not wither. In all that they do, they prosper.
Ps. 1:1-3, NRSV.

How would you like to live in a world where a stop sign simply meant, "We wish you'd slow down a bit," where speed limits were cheerful suggestions, where green meant "go" and yellow, "go faster," and red meant "fly"? While we all drive that way on "rare" occasions, the fact is nobody wants to live in a world in which protective laws and legal standards are abandoned.

And yet once upon a time that was their world: "In those days . . . everyone did what was right in his own eyes" (Judges 21:25). A world not unlike what Fyodor Dostoevsky described in *The Brothers Karamazov*: "If there is no God, everything is permitted." Which, of course, is not very different from the world we live in today, is it? "Everyone did what was right in his own eyes."

Against this secular, postmodern backdrop—where there is no such thing as capital T Truth, or "true truth," as Francis Schaeffer put it—it feels a bit quaint, doesn't it, to read aloud the first three verses of the Psalter in our text today. Go ahead and read them aloud this time. It's almost embarrassing, isn't it? To *delight* in God's law? Please! When was the last time any of us did that! But remember, *torah,* the Hebrew word for "law," can be as specific as the Decalogue and as expansive as the entire Scriptures. While Psalm 1 isn't a divine call for "legalists," it is a bold depiction of the friends of God who delight to immerse themselves in His *torah* night and day, who have discovered in both the divine law and divine Word their protection from wickedness and their promise for prosperous success. Their daily spiritual discipline acknowledges the observation of Jean-Paul Sarte: "No finite point has meaning without an infinite reference point." They have found in their God and His Word an infinite reference point to guide them.

Hasn't the time then come for the chosen to no longer allow fear of the charge of "legalism" to restrain their immersion into the heart of the divine *torah*? "Let no one yield to the temptation and become less fervent in his attachment to God's law because of the contempt placed upon it. . . . It is time to fight when champions are most needed" (*Review and Herald*, June 8, 1897). When Christ is your infinite reference point, why not defend His law in an age of lawlessness?

BETWEEN THE WINGS
OF THE CHERUBIM

And Hezekiah prayed to the Lord: "O Lord, God of Israel, enthroned between the cherubim,
you alone are God over all the kingdoms of the earth. You have made heaven and earth."
2 Kings 19:15, NIV.

When the news is really, really bad—when the phone rings at 2:00 a.m., when the doctor sits down with your test results, when the lawyer calls, when the police call—what then?

Just ask Hezekiah, who faced a death sentence the next morning. The king had just received a FedExed threat from the commander of the 185,000 Assyrian warriors that had his city in a choke hold. "Surrender or you're dead." Clutching the letter, Hezekiah rushed to the House of God. Falling to the Temple floor in anguish, the king spread out the written threat before God, with this desperate prayer: "O Lord, God of Israel, enthroned between the cherubim, save us!" It is a unique depiction of God used seven times in Scripture, "enthroned between the cherubim," and harkens back to the rumbling Mount Sinai, where alone with Moses God designed the golden ark that was to be placed inside the Most Holy Place of Israel's new portable "church." "And you shall make two cherubim of gold. . . . And there I will meet with you, and I will speak with you from above the mercy seat, from between the two cherubim" (Ex. 25:18-22). The ark was to be a sacred and graphic portrayal on earth of the very throne of God in heaven! And the chamber would be perennially filled with the white fire of divine glory between the cherubim.

"O Lord, God of Israel, enthroned between the cherubim, save us!" It is a "Daniel 8:14 prayer," for only once a year on Yom Kippur, the Day of Atonement, would the high priest dare to enter the fiery glory of the Most Holy Place in the "cleansing of the sanctuary," a ritual symbolic of the final cleansing in the heavenly sanctuary, prophesied by Daniel, before the cataclysmic end of the world. Living as we do in this hour of the final cleansing, how compelling the prayer of the king for whatever crisis we face: "O God, enthroned between the cherubim, save me. Save us!" Even at 2:00 a.m. is Christ not "able to save completely those who come to God through him, because he always lives to intercede for" us? (Heb. 7:25, NIV). He did so for the desperate king, and the next morning 185,000 Assyrian soldiers "woke up" dead.

And God will answer your "Daniel 8:14 prayer" for help, too, no matter the crisis. So pray. And take hope. For He is still between the cherubim. And it is still the mercy seat.

MORAL GIANTS IN AN AGE OF PYGMIES

Shadrach, Meshach and Abednego replied to the king, "O Nebuchadnezzar, we do not need to defend ourselves before you in this matter. If we are thrown into the blazing furnace, the God we serve is able to save us from it, and he will rescue us from your hand, O king. But even if he does not, we want you to know, O king, that we will not serve your gods or worship the image of gold you have set up." Dan. 3:16-18, NIV.

You have to admire the moral courage of these three Hebrew court officials, don't you? Talk about countercultural! Shadrach, Meshach, and Abednego (not to mention Daniel) have stood out in the profligate court of the king of Babylon like sore thumbs more than once. And now they absolutely decry Nebuchadnezzar's command and refuse to even nod the head, let alone bend the knee, to his golden image. What would you have done? What would I do?

Do you know why they passed their final exam with flying colors? It's one of the surest and oldest laws of academia: *In order to pass the final, you need to be passing the quizzes.* The purpose of the quiz is to prepare you for the final. Flunk the quizzes, and you'll not pass the final. It's not rocket science; it's the simple truth of life and learning.

Remember the quiz these three young adults had in chapter one of Daniel? A one-question quiz: Shall we obey the health code of God's Word, or not? It wasn't even a multiple-choice question. Just yes or no. They had to answer. A lot of people think that healthful living is no big deal. But if those boys had failed the quiz in chapter one, there'd have been no final exam in chapter three—trust me! Living in a community that gives a lot of lip service to healthful living—even making the cover of a national magazine now and then—we forget that the purpose of God's health code is not so much to elongate our lives as it is to enervate our minds and embolden our hearts to live radically obedient lives in allegiance to God, no matter what society or the world might say or command. Of course, the quizzes aren't all on health. Some are on sex and finances and integrity and pride. But the purpose is the same—to prepare you for the final.

"Day by day God instructs His children. By the circumstances of the daily life He is preparing them to act their part upon that wider stage to which His providence has appointed them. It is the issue of the daily test that determines their victory or defeat in life's great crisis" (*The Desire of Ages,* p. 382).

God's daily quizzes shape His moral giants. That's why He chose you.

TWIN PEAKS: A TALE OF TWO MOUNTAINS AND TWO HANDS

Can a mother forget the baby at her breast and have no compassion on the child she has borne? Though she may forget, I will not forget you! See, I have engraved you on the palms of my hands; your walls are ever before me. Isa. 49:15, 16, NIV.

When you hold a person's hand, there is something special in that bonding, isn't there? When a timid boy holds the hand of a blushing girl for the first time, when an elderly couple clasps their wrinkled hands for the last time, it is something special. When I held the hand of my dad before he died, a hand both tender and manly, even in his weakness, the bonding was sacred. Then what would it be like to hold the hand of God for even a moment?

Consider the two most powerful portrayals of God's hand in all of literature, and both of them upon a summit. On the first summit in an explosion of light and glory we witness that Cecil B. DeMille moment when the fiery hand of the Divine stretches forth to carve flaming letters into the tablets of the Ten Commandments. "And when He had made an end of speaking with him on Mount Sinai, He gave Moses two tablets of the Testimony, tablets of stone, written with the finger of God" (Ex 31:18). This much we know for certain—the only autograph of God, directly attributable to Him in all of Holy Scripture, are these Ten Commandments. His hand wrote all 10 of them, which surely must say something about the incontrovertible authority of the Decalogue for the entire human race. As Ted Koppel once remarked, Moses did not bring down from Sinai "the Ten Suggestions." They are the Ten Commandments written by God.

On the second summit appeared His hand again. "The assembly of the wicked has enclosed Me. They pierced My hands and My feet" (Ps. 22:16). No burst of light and glory now. Instead we witness that Mel Gibson moment when the hand of Jesus is callously pinned against the wooden beam, the Roman spike jammed into His palm, the mallet blows clinking metal on metal atop Golgotha, pounding through hand and beam until blood drips off the protruding point.

Never forget that hand. For it is the same hand that wrote the law. Sinai's finger is Calvary's hand. The hand that wrote in stone was nailed to wood. The Lawgiver atop the one mountain became the Lifegiver atop the other. So why play the mountains against each other, and reject Sinai in favor of Calvary? Yes, two mountains. Yes, two hands. But only one God. And one love. So deep that it engraved all of us sinners upon the palms of His hands—forever.

THY WORD HAVE I SUNG IN MY HEART

But at midnight Paul and Silas were praying and singing hymns to God, and the prisoners were listening to them. Acts 16:25.

I can't imagine the burning, bruising pain of being beaten with rods on your bare back. I had my share of spankings as a boy. But stripped naked for a public flogging? Poor Paul and Silas—their backs a palette of black and blue and red all over, forced to sit on their bruised and bleeding buttocks, their swollen ankles and feet jammed into wooden stocks, and all the while unable to lean against the damp prison wall, so painful were their backs to the touch. So what's a follower of Christ supposed to do?

Paul and Silas begin singing. Probably not one of those blow-out-your-speakers, stomp-your-feet, high-fiving-God praise songs. Maybe one of them begins to hum. And the other recognizes the tune and joins in. Because have you noticed, even a hum can be contagious!

Even at midnight. Even when you're suffering. *Especially* when you're suffering. Because life *does* hurt, and pain *is* real. And midnights can last for days, even years sometimes. Which is why we need to take a page from the playbook of Paul and Silas, who had no choice, and couldn't sleep, and so they sang. Because it's true—praise is contagious, even for yourself.

Brood over this insightful observation: "It is a law of nature that our thoughts and feelings are encouraged and strengthened as we give them utterance. While words express thoughts, it is also true that thoughts follow words. If we would give more expression to our faith, rejoice more in the blessings that we know we have—the great mercy and love of God—we should have more faith and greater joy. . . . Let praise and thanksgiving be expressed in song. When tempted, instead of giving utterance to our feelings, let us by faith lift up a song of thanksgiving to God. . . . *Song is a weapon that we can always use against discouragement.* As we thus open the heart to the sunlight of the Saviour's presence, we shall have health and His blessing" (*The Ministry of Healing,* pp. 251-254; italics supplied).

So what if we memorized Psalm 34:1, set it to music, and hummed it whenever we stubbed our little toe, or were cut off in traffic, or felt the dark cloud of discouragement descending, or were hurt deeply by one we loved. What if we memorized and sang this praise instead: "I will bless the Lord at all times; His praise shall continually be in my mouth."

STORM BREWING

Therefore everyone who hears these words of mine and puts them into practice is like a wise man who built his house on the rock. . . . But everyone who hears these words of mine and does not put them into practice is like a foolish man who built his house on sand.
Matt. 7:24-26, NIV.

Once upon a time Jesus told a parable. And I predict you know it by heart. Not because you can recite it, but because you can still sing it. Go ahead: "The wise man built his house upon the rock . . . and the rains came a-tumblin' down. Oh, the rains came down and the floods came up. . . . And the house on the rock stood firm!" And the second stanza was like unto it, but different. It was a very short parable, but it packed a very sharp truth: *The only ones who will stand in the final storm are the ones who both hear and heed the Word of God.*

A storm is brewing across this planet. You'd have to be Rip Van Winkle not to know. And by the millions (is it billions?), unthinking men and women and young adults are building and betting their future on quicksand. They've been sold a bill of goods by a demonic realtor who has convinced them that a piece of marshy quicksand is the most beautiful spot on earth upon which to construct their lives. Poor fool, to quote the Master. Why? Because the only ones who will survive the final storm are those who built their lives on the rock of God's Word. "Only those who have been diligent students of the Scriptures and who have received the love of the truth will be shielded from the powerful delusion that takes the world captive. By the Bible testimony these will detect the deceiver in his disguise. To all the testing time will come. By the sifting of temptation the genuine Christian will be revealed. Are the people of God now so firmly established upon His word that they would not yield to the evidence of their senses? Would they, in such a crisis, *cling to the Bible and the Bible only?*" (*The Great Controversy*, p. 625; italics supplied).

So let me earnestly appeal to you right now. There really is a storm brewing. And it really is high time for the chosen to choose "the Bible and the Bible only" as our only bedrock. It isn't the Bible that is our rock, of course. But there is no other Book on earth that can sink our foundations deep into the Rock, Christ Jesus. The time has come for the chosen to reclaim their destiny as the people of the Book. Going deep with Christ, let us choose the Rock over sand, wise over foolish, and life over death. "Rock of Ages, cleft for me, let me hide myself in Thee."

"BRIDEGROOM OF BLOOD"

Christ loved the church and gave himself up for her to make her holy, cleansing her by the washing with water through the word, and to present her to himself as a radiant church, without stain or wrinkle or any other blemish, but holy and blameless. Eph. 5:25-27, NIV.

It is one of the most bizarre tales in all of Scripture. Four weary travelers collapse in a heap upon the hard floor of a seemingly godforsaken wilderness. Their tired, aching muscles refuse one more step, and before night falls all are fast asleep. Suddenly the darkness explodes with light—a Being, a drawn sword in his hand. Straddling one of the sleepers, he raises his weapon high into the night sky. In that instant two of the sleepers awaken, the one straddled and his wide-eyed wife. Sensing imminent death for her husband, she leaps across the shadows to a third sleeper, rips open his garment, and in a flash circumcises her boy. And when she throws that tiny piece of boy flesh upon her husband, the menacing Being vanishes into the night. The End.

This brief narrative of Moses and Zipporah and the hasty midnight circumcision of their younger son in the face of the divine threatening is stunning. But even more stunning is its razor-sharp point for spiritual leaders: *Beware the whisper, "It doesn't matter."*

Because for those whom God has called to lead His people to the Promised Land, it really *does* matter. It is an occupational hazard for preachers and teachers, the dangerous inoculation that can numb pastors' hearts to the very Book that is their occupation and profession and life calling. Familiarity can breed contempt, or at least carelessness. Moses knew the covenant sign of circumcision. He wrote the Genesis 17 story himself. But he and his wife decided the ritual really didn't matter for their second boy. However, "such a neglect on the part of their chosen leader could not but lessen the force of the divine precepts upon the people [he was about to lead]" (*Patriarchs and Prophets,* p. 256). When we no longer practice what we preach, we jeopardize the entire community of the chosen. And we abdicate our moral authority to lead.

Where is the gospel of hope for spiritual leaders? "You are a bridgegroom of blood to me!" Zipporah cried out (Ex. 4:25, NIV). Therein lies our deliverance, too. For on Calvary Christ became the Bridegroom of blood for His bride, the church—His sacrifice not only cleansing spiritual leaders, but also granting us new moral authority to lead again without compromise.

JOURNEYING WITH THE JEWS—1

By the rivers of Babylon, there we sat down, yea, we wept when we remembered Zion. We hung our harps upon the willows in the midst of it. . . . How shall we sing the Lord's song in a foreign land? Ps. 137:1-4.

Reflect with me for a moment on that retching of human history we still remember as the Holocaust. I once stood in the haunted silence of Auschwitz on the day after Easter. And I pondered the muted message its cold, dusty crematoriums yet speak to a world that still survives. But I did not cry. I once stood with my family in the sobbing stillness of Dachau. We trudged the long pathway from the black-and-white museum with its pictures of utter horror and numbing tragedy to the small brick crematorium on the edge of that death camp. This time somebody did cry. We heard her sobs as we rounded the lush foliage that now surrounds that place of death. She was a student with a group of classmates on some proscribed field trip. They were Jews, and she a young Jewish girl. There beside the memorial statue she wept, a classmate's consoling arm about her trembling shoulders. To my shame I confess that I did not cry.

But beyond the colossal proportions of this epic human tragedy, why should we cry and why should we weep, we who call ourselves Seventh-day Adventists? In the years that have passed since standing inside those death camps, I now realize there is reason to weep. When the brief history of time is written, I believe it will show that like two matching bookends upon the shelf of sacred history are two communities of truth that occupied the beginning and the end of salvation history's story, two communities of faith that are inextricably bound together by a shared fate—their divine calling to become the chosen ones. These two communities will bear the epitaph "the remnant." And both shall know the meaning of the very high cost of truth.

It is a curious calling—that name, "the remnant"—and you can trace its history back to earth's pristine beginnings. For in the lives and deaths of Eve's two sons, Cain and Abel, are birthed two separate strands of history—the community of the remnant and the community of rebellion. The die was cast, and "the dragon was wroth with the woman, and went to make war with the remnant of her seed" (Rev. 12:17, KJV). And no wonder, for hadn't God promised that out of the woman would come a Seed that would crush the serpent and save the race?

JOURNEYING WITH THE JEWS—2

The Lord saw how great the wickedness of the human race had become on the earth, and that every inclination of the thoughts of the human heart was only evil all the time. The Lord regretted that he had made human beings on the earth, and his heart was deeply troubled. Gen. 6:5, 6, TNIV.

Eight survivors in a floating ark isn't exactly a grand launching of the remnant. And neither is the fact that the captain of the vessel got drunk after disembarking to dry land. The remnant has never been large or perfect. As sacred history has shown, whenever God has called out His remnant it has never been on the basis of their innate holiness or advanced sainthood. There's a kernel of truth to the bumper sticker "I'm not perfect—just forgiven." Just like Noah and Abraham, who as progenitors of the remnant, were called and chosen by God to a radical faith in Him despite their human weaknesses. "Come out of Babel, come out of Ur, come out of her, my people" has been God's passionate cry to His remnant from the beginning. And they have come, "enfeebled and defective" though they were (and still are).

And over them has raged the great cosmic battle between Christ and Satan, the battleground ever centered upon these communities of truth, seeking to remain faithful to the Creator God. But have you noticed, just when it appeared the people of God were about to be exterminated, God would supernaturally intervene and deliver a remnant from destruction? Thus Joseph could announce to his still-in-shock brothers who moments earlier learned that he was their kid brother they sold into slavery: "But God sent me ahead of you [here in Egypt] *to preserve for you a remnant on earth* and to save your lives by a great deliverance" (Gen. 45:7, NIV). To save His remnant, God keeps intervening.

As He did in the mighty Exodus, when that horde of liberated slaves fled Egypt under the cover of darkness. Who but God could have known that fateful night it was the birthing of the great faith and truth movement that like a bookend would line one side of salvation history's shelf? And what was the raison d'être of that movement? "For you are a people holy to the Lord your God. The Lord your God has chosen you out of all the peoples on the face of the earth to be his people, his treasured possession . . . because the Lord loved you" (Deut. 7:6-8, NIV). The chosen are the remnant. And the remnant are chosen simply because of the love of God.

JOURNEYING WITH THE JEWS—3

Jesus declared, "Believe me, woman, a time is coming when you will worship the Father neither on this mountain nor in Jerusalem. You Samaritans worship what you do not know; we worship what we do know, for salvation is from the Jews." John 4:21, 22, NIV.

The celebrated author and pastor Henri Nouwen wrote his book *Life of the Beloved* in the first person as a letter to a young Jewish professional living with his wife in New York City. Nouwen and he had become acquainted when Nouwen taught at Yale, and a deep and abiding friendship developed between the two. The book is a response to the young agnostic's plea for Nouwen to try to put religion in terms he and his friends of the city could understand. Along the way to making his point, Nouwen shares a profound insight into the meaning of being chosen by God: "I hope that the word 'chosen' speaks to you. It must be for you a word with very special connotations. As a Jew, you know the positive and negative associations in being considered one of God's chosen people. . . . From all eternity, long before you were born and became a part of history, you existed in God's heart. Long before your parents admired you or your friends acknowledged your gifts or your teachers, colleagues and employers encouraged you, you were already 'chosen.' The eyes of love had seen you as precious, as of infinite beauty, as of eternal value. When love chooses, it chooses with a perfect sensitivity for the unique beauty of the chosen one, and it chooses without making anyone else feel excluded" (pp. 45-47).

And so it has been for the chosen remnant from the beginning, not a divine calling to be exclusive but a divine summons to be inclusive. It is the heart of God's loving strategy to save the entire planet. How can we know? Note carefully the provocative claim Jesus made to the Samaritan woman by the well in our text today: "Salvation is from the Jews." He could have flimflammed around (as much religion does today) and declared that all that matters is that God loves you—so "not to worry" over such inconsequential particulars as truth, doctrine, and revelation. But He didn't. You want to know who has the truth of salvation? Looking her straight in the eye, He announced: the remnant community of the Jews does. Period. Christ was not being arrogant, but He was being honest. God cannot save the world through an ecumenical stew of teachings. He has always entrusted His corpus of truth to His chosen remnant, whose solitary mission is to share it with the world. And that is why there is a remnant—and there is you.

JOURNEYING WITH THE JEWS—4

You have known the Holy Scriptures, which are able to make you wise for salvation through faith in Christ Jesus. All Scripture is God-breathed and is useful for teaching, rebuking, correcting and training in righteousness, so that all God's people may be thoroughly equipped for every good work. 2 Tim. 3:15, 16, TNIV.

If Jesus was right, and "salvation is from the Jews," then whatever truth God entrusted to them at the beginning of the salvation story, wouldn't it follow that the matching bookend at the end of the story would espouse the same truth? So what did they believe?

My friend Cliff Goldstein, an American Jew who became a Seventh-day Adventist, identifies (in his book *The Remnant: Biblical Reality or Wishful Thinking?*) 10 tenets of the Jews—let's make them 11. **Tenet 1—monotheism.** In the pagan world of polytheism, it was a radical confession: "Hear, O Israel: the Lord our God, the Lord is one!" (Deut. 6:4). A new truth? No, as old as Creation, but a truth that desperately needed to be restored. **Tenet 2—the seventh-day Sabbath.** Another truth that stretched all the way back to earth's primal beginning, but a lost and forgotten truth the Creator needed a people to champion once again. **Tenet 3—the Ten Commandments.** Sure, Israel's surrounding nations possessed civil and religious codes and laws, but nothing like the profound simplicity and breadth of God's Decalogue. **Tenet 4—the truth about creation.** Their neighbors propagated absurd and silly myths about how the world came into existence. God's chosen ones were raised up to tell the truth about a loving Creator who seeks a relationship with all His earth children. **Tenet 5—the sanctuary.** The pagan neighbors had their temples, but along with them came cult prostitution and human sacrifices. Israel told the ancient truth of a divine sacrifice, a Lamb of God to take away the sins of the world. No religion confronted the sin problem and the salvation gift like the chosen remnant. **Tenet 6—the truth about death.** Of all peoples, only the Hebrews taught death as an unconscious sleep and the Creator God the only immortal Source of life. **Tenet 7—healthful living.** In a world that knew nothing about cholesterol and fat, heart disease, and cancer, God instilled in His remnant the teaching of clean and unclean foods, principles of dietary health founded upon the natural diet of Eden.

No wonder Paul could be so unequivocal to the chosen in our text today. The tenets of the Holy Book of the Jews "are able to make you wise for salvation through faith in Christ Jesus."

JOURNEYING WITH THE JEWS—5

It is by the name of Jesus Christ of Nazareth, whom you crucified but whom God raised from the dead, that this man stands before you healed. . . . Salvation is found in no one else, for there is no other name given under heaven by which we must be saved. Acts 4:10-12, TNIV.

Our list of tenets embraced by God's chosen remnant at the beginning of salvation history continues. **Tenet 8—the great controversy between God and Satan.** In fact, Job, the oldest book of the Old Testament, graphically introduced the great cosmic theme of a battle between God and Satan for the loyalty of humankind. Their pagan neighbors offered a pantheon of myths, but only the Hebrews championed the truth. **Tenet 9—the spirit of prophecy.** It is to the Hebrews we still turn for the rich legacy of their prophets, both canonical and noncanonical, male and female. Their divinely inspired messages formed the very basis of all Judeo-Christian faith today. False prophets abounded in the world around them, but God raised up a remnant with the true spirit of prophecy to be a shining light in a dark, dark night. **Tenet 10—the truth about the great Day of Atonement.** No other religion even faintly captured this truth about a final judgment of the human race and the cleansing of a heavenly sanctuary. But it was truth nonetheless, and God raised up a people who would proclaim it to the world. Judgment is coming—turn to the Savior God! And finally, **Tenet 11—the truth of the coming Redeemer Messiah.** They had the truth about both advents of the Messiah, but they particularly embraced the promised first advent. Theirs was the unique and divinely entrusted privilege of announcing the coming of the Messiah to the world, and they themselves were to prepare for it. Israel alone possessed the great messianic prophecies of Isaiah 53, Daniel 9, and Psalm 22. A new truth? Certainly not! All the way back to the gates of Eden could be traced the promise that God would provide a Deliverer from sin. He simply needed a remnant community to proclaim those glad tidings to all the world.

If only Israel had embraced the Messiah when He came to them, there would have been no need of a further remnant. They wouldn't have become a bookend—they could have been the entire shelf of God's salvation history. But alas, having it all, they missed it all in Jesus Christ. But they didn't all miss it! For to a Jew named Peter we owe the majestic declaration of our text today, the shining heart of all remnant truth: Jesus and only Jesus saves!

JOURNEYING WITH THE JEWS—6

He came to His own, and His own did not receive Him. But as many as received Him, to them He gave the right to become children of God, to those who believe in His name.
John 1:11, 12.

There is a question that begs to be asked: If there were a remnant community to preserve and propagate God's corpus of truth at the beginning of the salvation story, would it not follow that the same God who raised up the first remnant would also raise up a last remnant community to preserve and propagate those very same truths at the end of the story?

The Apocalypse is clear: "And the dragon was wroth with the woman, and went to make war with the remnant of her seed, which keep the commandments of God, and have the testimony of Jesus Christ" (Rev. 12:17, KJV). God will have a remnant to end the story! Who are they? Portions of all 11 of the tenets of divine truth can be found in communities of faith the world over. But there is only one faith community that embraces all 11, centering them all in Jesus Christ, the great summation of all divine revelation. They, too, are His chosen people. Not because they are greater than the rest—Israel wasn't, nor will they be. But God, in His sovereign grace and providence, raised them up as inheritors of ancient Israel's remnant legacy, to share the glad and urgent tidings of these divine truths with an end-time world.

The bookends match. But that reality is a two-edged sword. For while there is cause to rejoice in the legacy of divine truth and reason enough to be grateful for its possession (if truth indeed can be possessed), there is an inherent warning as well. Our text declares that Christ was rejected by "His own" remnant community. Apparently, intellectual possession of "truth" is no guarantee of salvation or validation of the chosen. It is only to those who "receive" Him personally that membership in the family of God is extended. Personal relationship trumps all.

In one of his last games Babe Ruth was having a terrible day on the field. In one inning alone his errors were responsible for five runs by their opponents. The fickle crowd booed the aging star as he walked off the field, head down. Suddenly a small boy leaped onto the field and with tears ran to hug his hero. The Babe scooped up the boy, tossed him in the air, and ruffled his hair, and the two walked hand in hand to the dugout. Suddenly the booing stopped and a hush fell over the park. Why? Because they saw a hero who in spite of a dismal day still cared for a little boy. In the end, you see, it is a relationship that makes all the difference in the world.

JOURNEYING WITH THE JEWS—7

Brothers and sisters, my heart's desire and prayer to God
for the Israelites is that they may be saved. Rom. 10:1, TNIV.

Consider one final word, while the Jews and the remnant are on our hearts. My friend Jacques Doukhan, himself a French Jew and a Seventh-day Adventist, has written a book appealing to Jews and Christians alike. In it is a provocative statement written by Jewish historian Jules Isaac: "The Jewish rejection of Christ was triggered by the Christian rejection of the Law. . . . The rejection of the Law was enough; to ask of the Jewish people that they accept this rejection . . . was like asking them to tear out their heart. History records no example of such a collective suicide" (quoted in *Drinking at the Sources*, p. 25).

Remember the bookends? They match. While faithful Jews see in much of contemporary Christianity a rejection of the law and a repudiation of the seventh-day Sabbath, it is a very different portrait they see in Seventh-day Adventists. Can you see there is a divinely intended kinship between Adventists and Jews? Ellen White urged: "There are among the Jews *many who will be converted*, and through whom we shall see the salvation of God go forth as a lamp that burneth. There are Jews everywhere, and to them the light of present truth is to be brought. There are among them *many who will come to the light*, and who will proclaim the immutability of the law of God with wonderful power" (*Evangelism,* p. 578; italics supplied). Could it be that of all people on earth we are to be the most open-hearted to our Jewish neighbors, classmates, and colleagues? Remember the bookends? "Converted Jews are to have an important part to act in the great preparations to be made in the future to receive Christ, our Prince. A nation shall be born in a day" (*Evangelism,* p. 579). That cryptic line intimates that one day the bookends will be united, does it not?

Will it be the final holocaust that will make the chosen ones one? Could it be, then, that the God-fearing of both major Sabbatarian communities of faith will be bound together in a sacred affinity never before witnessed? At the end, will the shared chalice of suffering become the catalyst for a uniting of the chosen? And, if Christ, the God of the universe, Himself became a Jew in order to face His own holocaust and become Savior of the world, should not His followers today pray and work passionately for His own kindred, "that they may be saved," too?

NO GREATER PROPHET BORN
OF A WOMAN

Assuredly, I say to you, among those born of women there has not risen one greater than John the Baptist; but he who is least in the kingdom of heaven is greater than he. Matt. 11:11.

How would you like to become a prophet? For $450 you can. And I've got the brochure to prove it. A gentleman named Kent Simpson, who refers to himself as "Prophetic Minister in the School of the Prophets," sells a set of 10 videos to train you. MasterCard, Visa, Discover, and American Express are accepted. It makes you wonder if that school isn't more about profits than prophets. But back to our question—how would you like to become a prophet?

Be careful how you answer. The occupational hazards of being a prophet are extremely high, the track record is abysmally discouraging, and many of their retirement plans paid out through martyrdom. Oh, it's true—the people will venerate you and love you after you're dead and gone. But they'll tar and feather you and ride you out of town on a rail while you're alive.

So why on earth would any prophet choose to be a prophet of God? They didn't, of course. It got chosen for them—by God. And it's a tough challenge to argue with Him—as Jonah quickly discovered! You can run, but you can't hide. Why? "For the gifts and the calling of God are irrevocable" (Rom. 11:29).

But "irrevocable" notwithstanding, exercising your gifts and calling doesn't mean you're impervious to discouragement and depression. Exhibit A—depressed Elijah, who finally begged God to take his life and let him die, so miserable a failure he felt himself. Exhibit B—discouraged John the Baptist, who after six months in Herod's fortress dungeon began to question not only himself but the God whose voice thundered that Jesus was His beloved Son.

And how did Jesus respond that sunny afternoon when the also-discouraged disciples of John showed up at one of His public rallies and point-blank queried, "Are you the Messiah or aren't you?" He quietly answered, "Go tell John what you've seen here today." And then turning to the crowd, Jesus paid the discouraged prophet the most sweeping compliment ever given to any mortal. "Of all who have been born, there is no one greater than John!" The world will never bow and call "great" those who've been called to prepare for the Messiah's advent. But Jesus' compliment is stunningly clear—Heaven reserves its highest accolades for those whose success is measured, not by applause, but rather by faithfulness. Good news for the least in the kingdom!

IT'S HIS CHOICE

Then what did you go out to see? A prophet? Yes, I tell you, and more than a prophet. This is the one about whom it is written: "I will send my messenger ahead of you, who will prepare your way before you." Matt. 11:9, 10, NIV.

Let's parse Jesus' compliment. When He declared John the Baptist to be the greatest human being who had ever exited a mother's womb, He elevated John above every prophet who preceded the Baptist. Amos, Micah, Jeremiah, Isaiah, Moses, Elijah—the list of John's renowned predecessors is a prophetic Hall of Fame! Why did Jesus reserve His superlatives for John? Because he was the one prophet appointed by God to be the great herald of the coming Messiah. He was raised up "to make ready a people prepared for the Lord" (Luke 1:17).

Jesus' compliment of John proves two points, doesn't it? First, you don't have to be canonical (have your prophetic writings placed in Scripture) to be a prophet. No writings of John's are in our Scriptures today. But then again, no writings of these predecessors of John were canonical either: Nathan (2 Sam. 7:2), Elijah (2 Chron. 21:12), Gad (1 Sam. 22:5), Ahijah (1 Kings 11:29), Shemaiah (2 Chron. 12:5), Iddo (2 Chron. 13:22), Obed (2 Chron. 15:8), Elisha (2 Kings 6:12), Deborah (Judges 4:4), Huldah (2 Kings 22:14) or even Anna, the prophet of the Christmas story (Luke 2:36). And second, Jesus' compliment of John the Baptist proves that you don't have to be canonical to be considered a great prophet.

And while you can't draw this from Jesus' compliment, that list of John's prophetic predecessors also reveals that you don't have to be a man to be a prophet. Deborah, Anna, Huldah, and the daughters of Philip the evangelist (Acts 21:9) were all prophets of God.

Apparently God can choose anybody He wishes to reveal "His secrets" to (Amos 3:7), especially to prepare His people for the seismic events in salvation history: the Flood (Noah), a new remnant (Abraham), the Exodus (Moses), the Exile (Jeremiah), the Messiah's first coming (John). Based on that divine track record, wouldn't it be logical to conclude that before the Messiah returns the second time God would raise up another prophet—a prophet like John to make ready a people prepared for the Lord's return, a prophet like John who would not have written a single word in Scripture? Since God has amply shown He can choose whomever He wishes to prepare His chosen, couldn't He choose that prophet to be a woman?

THE PROOF IS IN THE PUDDING

Likewise every good tree bears good fruit, but a bad tree bears bad fruit.
A good tree cannot bear bad fruit, and a bad tree cannot bear good fruit. . . .
Thus, by their fruit you will recognize them. Matt. 7:17-20, NIV.

She was a woman of remarkable spiritual gifts, who lived most of her life in the
nineteenth century. Yet through her writings and public ministry she has made
a revolutionary impact on millions of people into the twenty-first century, including my own life. From the age of 17 until she died 70 years later, Ellen White received nearly 2,000 visions and dreams, varying in length from a few moments to
nearly four hours. It was those revelations that resulted in her prodigious literary
output that includes 100 books available in English, 5,000 periodical articles, and
55,000 pages of manuscript. She is one of the most translated authors in history; her
life-changing masterpiece, *Steps to Christ,* has been published in more than 135 languages.

As a further consequence of that prophetic gift, she helped raise up a Christian
movement that today offers the largest Protestant educational system in the world,
and the most extensive Protestant health system on earth. *National Geographic* magazine carried a cover story extolling the longevity benefits of the health message
Ellen White received and championed during her lifetime, a message far ahead of
the medical and nutritional knowledge of her day, but validated in our generation
by extensive scientific research and study. And as the result of her visionary leadership, the Seventh-day Adventist Church she helped found is in more countries
today than any other Protestant denomination on earth.

Why? I don't believe there is a human explanation for so prolific and fruitful a
life and ministry. The words of Christ in today's text direct us to evaluate the fruit of
the life of one with the prophetic gift. The fruitage of Ellen White's ministry, I believe, can be explained only by the divine ministry of the Holy Spirit through this
humble, very human woman. Do her writings take the place of Holy Scripture in
my life or the life of the church I serve? Hardly! She herself described her writings
as the "lesser light" of the moon, humbly but faithfully reflecting the "greater light"
of the Sun of righteousness. That her writings reflect the glory of Jesus as no other
author I have ever read is for me the greatest fruit of all. *But taste the fruit for yourself.*

TASTE THEM AGAIN
FOR THE FIRST TIME—1

Good people bring good things out of the good stored up in their heart, and evil people bring evil things out of the evil stored up in their heart. For out of the overflow of the heart the mouth speaks. Luke 6:45, TNIV.

Some years ago Kellogg's Corn Flakes came out with a clever marketing slogan to draw back an aging demographic market slice of consumers who'd been weaned on the trademark taste of their cornflakes but had moved to more exotic breakfast cuisine: "Taste them again . . . for the first time." How can you do something again, for the first time? You can't, of course—but then again you can, if you're coming back for a fresh experience with something that's been a part of your long-ago story. "Taste them again for the first time."

That isn't too bad a marketing slogan for the "red books," is it? Because of the characteristic publishing house book covers, they used to call Ellen White's writings the "red books." Though for this generation perhaps the more accurate title would be "the unread" books. After all, who reads them anymore? Who needs our grandparents' cornflakes for breakfast?

Two friends of mine, Roger Dudley and Des Cummings, Jr., researched the correlation between spiritual development and the reading of Ellen White's writings, with some astounding results. In a survey of more than 8,200 members in 193 Adventist churches in North America, 20 categories of spiritual life were measured, including a single question whether those surveyed were regular readers of the writings of Ellen White or not. Note these stunning numbers: 82 percent of the regular readers of Ellen White's writings assessed their relationship with Jesus as "intimate," in comparison with 56 percent for the nonreaders of Ellen White. Eighty-two percent of regular readers of Ellen White indicated a high degree of assurance of being right with God, compared to 59 percent of the nonreaders. Readers of Ellen White were 24 percent more involved in Christian outreach and service activities than were nonreaders. And 82 percent of those who read Ellen White regularly also have daily personal Bible study, compared with 47 percent of the nonreaders (exactly the opposite effect, by the way, false prophets have on their followers). *In fact, in every one of the 20 spiritual life categories surveyed, the regular readers of Ellen White scored higher than the nonreaders.* "By their fruits you will know them." Jesus was right. So why don't you "taste them again for the first time" and grow in Christ?

TASTE THEM AGAIN
FOR THE FIRST TIME—2

Have faith in the Lord your God and you will be upheld; have faith in his prophets and you will be successful. 2 Chron. 20:20, NIV.

I grew up a fifth-generation Seventh-day Adventist and became a fourth-generation preacher in this community of faith. So it may sound a bit incongruous to tell you that I didn't meet Jesus Christ in a lasting way until I was a graduate student in the seminary. God used the teachings of one of my professors to convict my heart of a desperate spiritual need I'd been ignoring through my early young adult years. With anguished guilt I sought out that professor in a stairwell in the seminary building. As I began to pour out my heart, his immediate response was brusque but Spirit-directed: "Go read *Steps to Christ*. Go read *Steps to Christ*." I had hoped for a listening ear, but he sent me to a book instead. But today I am very grateful he did. Because back in our apartment was an old Army-Navy edition of a *Steps to Christ* I'd had to read in the eighth grade in order to be baptized. I pulled it off my shelf and slowly began to reread that old classic. And in tasting it again for the first time, I discovered that the title to the book was a self-fulfilling prophecy. It really did become for me fresh, new steps to Christ.

Out of that spiritual rebirthing, as it were, God began to guide my journey into a relationally focused devotional/worship/prayer life that we've already shared in this book. And out of that journey there was awakened in my heart a new and deeper appreciation for the ministry of Ellen White. That's why I wanted to share with you what we have these past few days. There truly is an empirical, spiritual correlation between reading the writings of this messenger to the chosen at this time in history and our walk with God. Roger Dudley and Des Cummings, Jr., ended their research (noted yesterday) with this compelling conclusion: "Seldom does a research study find the evidence so heavily weighted toward one conclusion. In the church growth survey, on *every single item* that deals with personal attitudes or practices [of spiritual life], the [church] member who regularly studies Ellen White's books tends to rank higher than does the member who reads them only occasionally or never" (*Ministry*, October 1982, p. 12).

Is all of this, then, about who among us ranks the highest? Hardly! But given the urgent times in which we're living and the promise of our text today, why wouldn't the chosen want the one gift God personally chose for our spiritual success and our end-time mission?

GENERAL DOUGLAS MACARTHUR ISN'T ON OUR SIDE!

And Jesus came and spoke to them, saying, "All authority has been given to Me in heaven and on earth. Go therefore and make disciples of all the nations." Matt. 28:18, 19.

Can you remember the first time you took Jesus' Great Commission seriously? How well I remember. It happened on the shores of the beautiful mountain Lake Nojiri in Japan, a favorite summer escape for missionaries of all denominations. My little brother, Greg, and I were best of friends with two other Adventist brothers, Doug and Dave Clark. And in between our two hillside cabins were the Kellys, a Southern Baptist family with two boys our ages. And that transformed six little American boys into a summertime cadre of fun.

Except for one small fly in the ointment. The Kelly brothers found out that we Adventists were vegetarians. Their young Baptist fervor knew no limits: "You're vegetarians—you eat rabbits' food—ha ha ha ha ha ha." We four Adventist boys were stumped! That was back in the late fifties, before a whole lot of scientific corroboration of the organic, natural diet. And so we'd just gulp and have to take it from our Baptist pals. Again and again. Until that unforgettable day when Doug Clark, the oldest of us Adventist guys, came prepared and primed for rebuttal. When the Kelly brothers brought it up again, Doug threw his little shoulders back and declared, "Did you know that General Douglas MacArthur is a Seventh-day Adventist?" Those Southern Baptist eyes about popped out! (MacArthur was a household name on both sides of the Pacific back then.) "And what is more," Doug went on, "*He is a vegetarian!*" You should've seen their faces. Why, even my own parents had failed to inform me of that great fact! But it was all I needed to jump on the gospel bandwagon: "Ha ha ha ha ha ha—MacArthur is an Adventist, and he's a VEGETARIAN!" I never knew witnessing could be so exhilarating! And so successful. Because those little Baptist chums of ours never brought it up again. It felt so good to win one for Jesus.

I have since learned our great victory for the gospel was based upon a small but rather significant error. General MacArthur was *never* an Adventist—or a vegetarian. Doug had gotten him mixed up with our favorite Uncle Arthur of the *Bedtime Stories!*

But while the Great Commission isn't a co-mission with that great but deceased general, it is indeed a co-mission partnership with the greatest Being in the universe who has all the authority and power we need to gladly embrace His mission. And win one for Jesus!

YOU *CAN* LEARN SOMETHING FROM A 12-YEAR-OLD

And He said to them, "Why did you seek Me? Did you not know that I must be about My Father's business?" Luke 2:49.

I've got a book in my library by New Testament scholar Conrad Gempf, *Jesus Asked.* Did you know that of the 67 episodes in the Gospel of Mark in which there is any conversation at all, in 50 of them Jesus asks a question? Even when other people asked Him a question, He replied with one of His own. "Good Teacher, what must I do to inherit eternal life?" Jesus replies, "Why do you call me 'good'?" Or how about "Is it lawful to pay taxes to Caesar or not?" Jesus' answer: "Whose picture is on this coin?" Jesus was big on questions.

And that may explain how a thoughtful and inquisitive 12-year-old could hold the rapt attention of Jerusalem's brightest minds and most revered clerics. He was asking questions. You remember the story, don't you? For his bar mitzvah Jesus traveled with Joseph and Mary from Nazareth to the holy city. But on their return trip with the post-Passover throngs, His parents failed to notice that He wasn't with them. That evening their neglect became clear. Racing back to Jerusalem the next day, Joseph and Mary spent yet another day frantically searching for their "lost" child. And where did they find Him? "They found Him in the temple, sitting in the midst of the teachers, both listening to them and asking them questions" (Luke 2:46). *The Desire of Ages* describes those questions: "Jesus presented Himself as one thirsting for a knowledge of God. His questions were suggestive of deep truths which had long been obscured, yet which were vital to the salvation of souls" (p. 78). With chiding relief Mary rushed to the side of her Boy. "Son, why have You done this to us? Look, Your father and I have sought You anxiously" (verse 48). The 12-year-old Jesus gazed into the loving but scolding face of His mother, and when He spoke the first red-letter words in Luke's Gospel, sure enough—it's a question. Actually, two questions. "Why did you seek Me?" He asked. "Did you not know that I must be about My Father's business?" Mary cried out, "*Your father* and I," and the lad replied, "No, *My Father* and I." Because isn't it that relationship that is the defining one for all of us?

"I must be about My Father's business." After all, isn't that why the chosen were chosen in the first place, to join their Father in His passionate business and solitary mission to seek and save the rest of His lost children? Isn't it time we, too, were about our Father's business?

HOW TO BE A NONANXIOUS FARMER

While a large crowd was gathering and people were coming to Jesus from town after town, he told this parable: "A farmer went out to sow his seed." Luke 8:4, 5, NIV.

Did you know that Labor Day is supposed to be the best day of the year to plant a new lawn? And so even though it was raining that September Monday, my daughter Kristin and I headed out to the front yard to do just that in a 10' x 12' bare patch of earth that covered a now-buried culvert. We did what every farmer from time immemorial has done—we scattered our seed. And sure enough, it turned out just the way Jesus said it would.

Remember His parable? One early morning a farmer traversed his rolling fields, grabbing from his bag of seed fistfuls of potential grain and "broadcasting" them to the right and to the left. It didn't matter the soil—rocky, trampled, weedy, or rich—the farmer's solitary mission was simply to keep on hurling his seed. No pausing to fret over the outcome of his sowing, he depends on the Creator for the germination and growth of the seed. He is a nonanxious farmer.

And so must the chosen be, too. Nonanxious. Which is usually what we aren't, isn't it, when it comes to the mission of evangelizing and witnessing? I have a young friend who pines because he feels he hasn't had very much measurable success in sharing the Word of God with his neighbors and colleagues and friends. Ask him, "Well, aren't you sharing the seed?" and he'll reply, "Sure I am—everywhere—but nobody ever gets baptized from all the sharing that I've done. I can't seem to get a harvest." Truth is, he isn't the only farmer in the church who feels that way, is he? Nonanxious really isn't how we feel when it comes to witnessing.

But read Jesus' opening line again: "A farmer went out to sow his seed." Period. And it's that period that's the good news! No paralysis of analysis for that farmer. Because he knows it is his task to *sow* the seed—and it is God's task to *grow* the seed. The farmer sows, God grows. You sow, God grows. It's not ours to worry about where the seed lands or how the seed grows or when the seed gets harvested. All we farmers must do, who want to be about our Farmer Father's business, is take the seed by the handful and sow it everywhere we go. A handful of gospel pamphlets, some Web site cards for the Discover Bible School (www.discover online.org), a gift subscription to *Signs of the Times*—the sky's the limit, and so are the seeds. So why be anxious? Instead, simply be God's farmer and go out to sow the seed—today.

QUIT FISHING IN THE AQUARIUM—1

Jesus replied to Simon, "Don't be afraid! From now on you'll be fishing for people!" And as soon as they landed, they left everything and followed Jesus. Luke 5:10, 11, NLT.

Here is a story we could very well entitle *The Complete Idiot's Guide to Fishing*. You've seen those bright-orange how-to manuals, haven't you? I have *The Complete Idiot's Guide to PCs* in my library. Sometimes all we need is a very basic how-to manual to get going.

Once upon a time Jesus stepped into the fishing skiff of the big fisherman (that would be Peter) and asked if he might shove away from the shore so the Master could teach the sprawling crowd that had gathered that bright Galilee morning. When the teaching was ended, the Teacher got down to the real teaching of the day. "He said to Simon, 'Launch out into the deep and let down your nets for a catch'" (Luke 5:4). Peter didn't need an idiot's guide to fishing—he'd been doing it all his life. And anybody who knows anything about fishing knows you don't cast your net in the middle of the day when the fish can spot the net on the surface. But bless his soul, Peter sighs, shrugs, and complies with Jesus' command. Have you ever water-skied and felt the boat's tow rope nearly yank your arms out? With eyes wide and mouth gaping, Peter's biceps strain to hang on to a net suddenly exploding with fish. Frantically he yells for his fishing partners. And now both boats start to sink beneath the haul of fish! In that instant Peter realizes he is in the presence of divinity. Knee-deep in floppy, silvery fish, Peter drops to his knees crying, "Depart from me, for I am a sinful man, O Lord" (verse 8). It is then that Jesus speaks the words of today's text: "Don't be afraid! From now on you'll be fishing for people!"

What's the Teacher's people-fishing lesson for the day? Simple, really. If you really want to catch fish, quit hanging around the aquarium and "launch out into the deep." And yet how many of the chosen have chosen to spend their lives where the fish are already "found"? Why go fishing when we have our nifty little home-church aquarium where a few prized fish are kept on display? But that aquarium mentality will never reach this generation, which swims in the deeps of inner cities, secular campuses, corporate high rises, and community playgrounds far away from our quaint aquariums and beyond our comfort zones. The truth is that until we obey Jesus' command to move out into the dark depths of society, we will never be more than a gurgling aquarium with a few bored fish. And nobody needs a manual for that.

QUIT FISHING IN THE AQUARIUM—2

Once again, the kingdom of heaven is like a net that was let down into the lake and caught all kinds of fish. When it was full, the fishermen pulled it up on the shore. Then they sat down and collected the good fish in baskets, but threw the bad away. Matt. 13:47, 48, NIV.

It can be dangerous to fish in the deep. Some mean storms roil up out there that can threaten your little skiff; raging waters that a sterile, tranquil, oxygenated aquarium never experiences. But such is the price of real fishing! And besides, what was that song we sang so loudly so long ago: "I will make you fishers of men . . . if you follow Me."

It is because we want to be about our Fisherman Father's business and follow Him that Jesus told us the fish story we see in today's text. It's not very long, this parable about fishers dropping their dragnet into the sea and hauling in every imaginable kind of fish in their catch. But it's just long enough to remind us that a boatload of deep-water fish can be messy, slimy, and stinky. Because the fish you catch out in the deep may not be at all like the fish we find in the aquarium of the church. You know, *clean* fish (with fins and scales, à la Leviticus 11)—sweet little shore-hugging minnows like you and me. Let's be honest. If you take Jesus' admonition seriously and throw your net out into deep waters, you could end up with fish that are *unclean*. Because when you're out "finding Nemo," you may net more than a clown fish. Unclean, unkept fish with alcohol on the breath or at least in the back seat of their car—drunk as a fish. You'll catch fish with sexual dysfunctions, deviancies, and even transmittable diseases. Some will be like the catch Jesus made at a well in Samaria and be on their fourth or fifth marriage. Other fish from the deep will be covered with glittering lures or alluring tattoos.

"Oh, don't worry—as soon as we get 'em into our aquarium, we'll skin 'em and scale 'em and clean 'em up just like us. And if we don't like 'em, we'll toss 'em out!" Jesus was afraid of that, which is why His parable punch line declares that the cleaning, sorting, and judging is done by the angels "at the end of the age" (verse 49). The angels will do the sorting—it is *our* mission to do the fishing. Why? Because fish are our Father's business—clean *and* unclean. We do the deep-sea fishing—He does the in-house cleaning. If we get that straight, I have a feeling we'll spend less time critiquing the fish in the aquarium and more time on the high seas fishing for the lost.

PRIME TIME—1

When the day of Pentecost came, they were all together in one place.
Suddenly a sound like the blowing of a violent wind came from heaven and filled the
whole house where they were sitting. Acts 2:1, 2, NIV.

What if while we are on our knees in church this Sabbath, we hear—as if in the distance—the low-decibel moaning of a faraway wind? Our eyes still closed in prayer, we can hear it distinctly now, a crescendoing, windy moaning and groaning. Suddenly whatever it is becomes the rumble of an approaching freight train. (In the Midwest we've been taught to recognize that as the audible warning of a tornado.) But before we can react, the howling wind seems to explode into our sanctuary. But the light fixtures that you'd expect to be blowing at a crazy angle hang limp and motionless. No wind, no movement of air, just the roar of a furious tornado inside the church. That's when we see it, suspended in midair halfway up to the ceiling: a roiling, orange ball of fire, like a cauldron of seething melted steel without an iron pot to contain it—liquid fire suspended in midair. Then as if by invisible hands, thin strips of flame peel away from the fiery ball and dart through the air, up and down every aisle and pew, until a flickering tongue of fire burns above every worshipper's head. Pentecost! What would happen if it happened right now and right here?

There are some who have been praying for Pentecost for a long time. I know—I have met them. Two young adults were in my church office sharing their earnest longing for it to happen again, and why not here, they wondered. Shall I tell them it can't happen yet? This isn't the right time? We aren't the right generation for Pentecost? And besides, what would it look like?

The answer lies in the Greek word *pentecoste,* which means "fiftieth day." Add 50 days to Passover, and you get Pentecost. Both symbolic holy days were predicated on a solitary divine passion. From the gates of Eden to the cross of Christ—even to this very day—every act of God, without exception, has been driven by His passionate love for fallen human sinners. Bethlehem, Calvary, Pentecost—all because of His crimson passion. And so when you pray for Pentecost, you are asking for more than simply to be filled with God's Spirit—you are, in fact, pleading for the infilling of God's fiery passion for lost people. For how could you be filled with the Spirit of God if you were not filled with the passion of God?

PRIME TIME — 2

So when they met together, they asked him, "Lord, are you at this time going to restore the kingdom to Israel?" He said to them: "It is not for you to know the times or dates the Father has set by his own authority. But you will receive power when the Holy Spirit comes on you; and you will be my witnesses in Jerusalem, and in all Judea and Samaria, and to the ends of the earth." Acts 1:6-8, NIV.

What an "Adventist" question: "Is this the end?" But what an "un-Adventist" answer: "Don't worry about it—you've got a lot of work yet to do!" Jesus is clear. His disciples' most pressing need isn't to know the date of His return, but to claim the promise of His Spirit. For "you will receive power [Greek—*dunamis*— "dynamite"] when the Holy Spirit comes on you; and you will be my witnesses [Greek—*martus*—"martyr," one who witnesses through life and even death] to the ends of the earth." It was because of this "dynamite" promise that the 120 men, women, and young adults were crowded into that upper room (see Acts 2).

And for what were they praying? Listen to *The Acts of the Apostles* describe their pleading: "The disciples prayed with intense earnestness for a fitness to meet [people] and in their daily [conversations] to speak words that would lead sinners to Christ. . . . They did not ask for a blessing for themselves merely. *They were weighted with the burden of [the divine passion for] the salvation of souls.* They realized that the gospel was to be carried to the world, and they claimed the power that Christ had promised" (p. 37; italics supplied). They prayed for the Holy Spirit—not for the sake of warm spiritual fuzzies, not for the possession of an ecstatic spiritual high, but so that lost people might be found and saved.

What would happen if the chosen began to earnestly pray that pre-Pentecost prayer? What if today we asked Jesus to fulfill His Acts 1:8 promise and fill us with the Holy Spirit, that we too might be ignited with His passionate love for lost people? One thing I've learned is that no preacher can preach into me a passion for lost souls. No book can create in your heart a new longing to reach lost people for Christ. Not even the Bible can instill such a passionate love for lost sinners. For there is only one Source for that passion—and that is the heart of God Himself. So what if we went straight to Him right now and began pleading for His gift? For a prime-time generation in earth's prime-time history, what could be a more prime-time prayer and passion?

THE KINGDOM ADVANCES
AMONG FRIENDS—1

Then those who gladly received his word were baptized; and that day about three thousand souls were added to them. Acts 2:41.

Their picture went global thanks to the Internet. Born identical twins and 12 weeks premature in Worcester, Massachusetts, the tiny sisters, Kyrie and Brielle Jackson, barely weighed two pounds each. Kyrie quickly began gaining weight, but little Brielle had breathing and heart-rate problems, her blood oxygen level low, her weight gain very slow. Then suddenly four weeks into her journey, Brielle began gasping for air, her tiny face and stick arms turning bluish-gray, her heart rate shooting high, and dangerous hiccups putting her body under stress. Neonatal-intensive-care-unit nurse Gayle Kasparian desperately tried to stabilize her, but to no avail. Then the nurse recalled a "double bedding multiple birth babies" procedure common in Europe but forbidden in this country for fear of passing infection. Kasparian scooped up Brielle and placed her in the incubator beside sister Kyrie. And according to news reports, in that very moment Brielle's oxygen levels suddenly soared, her breathing became less labored, her crying stopped, and a normal pinkish complexion spread. Someone snapped a picture of the preemie sisters in their shared incubator. *Life* magazine and *Reader's Digest* picked it up, and it is all over the Internet today. So famous did this photo become, in fact, that the parents of these twin sisters had to get an unlisted phone number! The twins are doing fine today. The picture? Lying on their tummies side by side in the incubator and sound asleep, Kyrie has her little arm draped around the shoulders of Brielle, tiny friends in repose. They call the picture "The Rescuing Hug."

Many people end the story of Pentecost with that glorious baptism of 3,000. But the story goes on. For there is a "rescuing hug" depicted in what follows that clearly is vitally essential for the newborns. "And they [the spiritual newborns] continued steadfastly in . . . fellowship" (Acts 2:42). The "rescuing hug" is in the Greek word *koinonia*, for "fellowship" or warm relational interaction. Isn't that amazing? Vital in God's salvation strategy is the power of arm-around-the-shoulders friendship. My friend Ruthie Jacobsen in her delightful book *Bridges 101* is absolutely right: "The kingdom advances among friends." The kingdom of God grows not only through public rallies (Acts 2:41), but also through private relationships (verses 42, 47). And that's why the mission of the chosen is to make new friends for Jesus. So why not do it today!

THE KINGDOM ADVANCES
AMONG FRIENDS—2

And the Lord added to the church daily those who were being saved. Acts 2:47.

Praise God for the 3,000 who joined the fledgling new Christian community in a single day! But no less significant are the countless numbers of men, women, and children who were quietly being added, as our text today notes, "daily" through interpersonal interaction. The kingdom really does advance among friends.

How can we live by this strategic primetime principle? Here are a handful of methods you and I can implement right away to take advantage of God's friendship strategy.

Method 1. Enlarge your circle of friends. So who are the friends that God is hoping and praying you'll reach for Him? You can picture the faces, can't you? But so that you won't forget, why not grab a piece of paper right now and scribble down their names? (I'll wait.) Who are the people we know who don't know Jesus, i.e., if Jesus were to return tonight, your heart worries that they'd be lost? Jot down their names in a "My Friends Who Need Jesus" list.

The sad reality for most of us is that the longer we've been members of the church, the shorter has grown our list of lost friends and acquaintances. Why's that true? Because it's human nature to seek security and acceptance with those who are spiritually and socially "kin" to us. That way I don't have to explain my very countercultural habit of setting aside the final 24 hours of the week (from sundown Friday to sundown Saturday) when I hang around fellow Sabbatarians. And when I have only the "saved" in my friendship circle, I don't have to explain why I don't drink that or I don't eat this. Nobody likes living outside their comfort zone. We all enjoy nonthreatening security with people who think and act like us. But it doesn't take rocket science to realize that if communities embrace "us only" friendship circles, they are on the sure path to eventual extinction. Remember the Amish.

To proactively enlarge our circle of friends to include lost people is simply to begin focusing and growing friendships with the people around us. Neighbors are immediate candidates, aren't they? And so are classmates and colleagues and business contacts. You can grow your "friends who need Jesus" list as boldly as you like. You don't need 100—but you can concentrate on a handful. How else shall we explain Jesus' proactive, winsome, "outside the comfort zone" friendships? He looked for new friends. So just like Him, why can't we?

THE KINGDOM ADVANCES
AMONG FRIENDS—3

And if anyone gives even a cup of cold water to one of these little ones because he is my disciple, I tell you the truth, he will certainly not lose his reward. Matt. 10:42, NIV.

Method 2. Engage in low-risk/high-grace activities. That's how Ruthie Jacobsen describes "any kingdom witnessing activity that is comfortable for the timid but has the muscle to make a powerful grace statement. It's a love-sharing activity that is doable even for those who have never seen themselves as members of the God Squad" (*Bridges 101*, p. 19). Her book is chock-full of stories of activities as simple as giving away bottles of cold water at a county fair (with a church name tag and phone number on the back), or sponsoring a 50-cent gasoline price reduction at the local station for a couple hours, while a team of friends washes windshields and hands out welcome cards and granola bars. The point is that low-risk/high-grace kinds of activities, in which you can build bridges as an avenue to building friendships, abound.

My favorite story is about the grocery bag guy who decided his witness would be a short, pithy pick-me-up saying on a slip of paper tucked inside every bag he stuffed. Within days the manager couldn't figure out why the lane where the young man served had a line snaking throughout the supermarket—and nobody would switch lanes! All you need is a heart that is praying for God's passion to open your eyes to new bridges for new friends.

Method 3. Spread your warmth. Ruthie's husband, Don (who was my preaching professor in seminary), was traveling in Japan and on the plane was thumbing through a Japanese magazine he couldn't read. He came to a very unusual ad—a gray, rather drab picture of a butterfly with some Japanese words underneath it. The Japanese businessman beside him noticed Don's quandary and explained that he was supposed to put his hand over the butterfly. Don did, and a few moments later the warming of special ink in the ad turned into all the beautiful colors of a butterfly. Ruthie asks, "Who in the world needs a warm hand to help them blossom and come alive?" (p. 35). Spread your warmth, my friend. And discover how the Spirit will lead you to people who for right now simply need your warm touch. Stop and talk with that stranger. Give a helping hand to an elderly woman. Spread your warmth in the cafeteria or the Laundromat or the library (quietly). Who knows? It may be your "rescuing hug" that God will use to save one more life for His kingdom.

THE KINGDOM ADVANCES
AMONG FRIENDS—4

The woman answered and said, "I have no husband." Jesus said to her, "You have well said, 'I have no husband,' for you have had five husbands, and the one whom you now have is not your husband; in that you spoke truly." John 4:17, 18.

There is one more method you and I can implement right away to take advantage of God's friendship strategy and mission. **Method 4. Practice radical inclusiveness.** Bill Hybels describes radical inclusiveness this way: "You have new eyes to see things as Jesus saw them. You allow people's foibles and failings and faults to fall away, instead seeing them in their potential, Spirit-infused state. You see filthy-mouthed, party-loving, woman-chasing Joe, and you say, 'What would Joe—even a guy like Joe—be like if God ruled and reigned in his heart? Joe would be incredible if Christ invaded his world'" (*Just Walk Across the Room*, p. 69).

The point? Quit walking past the Joes and Jills of your world. Quit writing off the "hopeless" and the "helpless." Instead, begin to vision what that man, that woman, that teenager might become if only Jesus could invade their world. So grab your "My Friends Who Need Jesus" list and scribble down their names.

In fact, why don't you take a page from Jesus' own playbook? Can you imagine a more helpless and hopeless prospect to cross His path that hot and thirsty noon hour than the Samaritan woman at the well? I mean, please! If you're going to concentrate on "winnable" and "worthy" strangers as potential prospects for the kingdom, she hardly makes the cut. And yet in the eyes of Him who once said, "I have called you friends" (John 15:15), nobody is too bad or too lost to become His new friend. And you guessed it—His winning her trust and friendship in a single noontime conversation became God's winning strategy in saving an entire Samaritan town!

"Christ's method alone will give true success in reaching the people. The Saviour mingled with [them] as one who desired their good. He showed His sympathy for them, ministered to their needs, and won their confidence. Then He bade them, 'Follow Me'" (*The Ministry of Healing*, p. 143).

The life of our Lord is proof enough that the kingdom advances among friends. Can you think of a more winsome way to be like your Savior than to make a new friend for Him today?

DOWN ON ALL FOURS—1

One day Peter and John were going up to the temple at the time of prayer—at three in the afternoon. Now a man crippled from birth was being carried to the temple gate called Beautiful, where he was put every day to beg from those going into the temple courts. . . . Then Peter said, "Silver or gold I do not have, but what I have I give you. In the name of Jesus Christ of Nazareth, walk." Acts 3:1-6, NIV.

One day Thomas Aquinas, the great philosopher of the Middle Ages, was visiting Pope Innocent IV. The pope was giving Aquinas a guided tour through the amassed wealth of the church, piled high on tables in the treasury. "You see, Thomas," the pope smiled, "the church can no longer say, 'Silver and gold have I none.'" "Yes, Holy Father," Aquinas replied, "but neither can she say, 'In the name of Jesus Christ of Nazareth, rise up and walk!'"

I suppose by any standard today, the church is wealthy. But where is the power of the risen Christ in our midst? "Silver and gold I do not have"—didn't we have to memorize Peter's famous exclamation when we were kids in Sabbath school? "But what I do have I give you: In the name of Jesus Christ of Nazareth, rise up and walk!" (verse 6). From whence came the power behind that explosive command that healed a beggar lame from birth?

The secret to the church in the beginning and at its ending remains the same. It is the "time of prayer" that unleashes the time of power. Peter and John were on their way to prayer meeting—that's right, read the text again—when the lame man was healed. He would not have been healed had the men not been headed to prayer. They were no different than us. They had a dozen pressing duties, I'm sure. But there is nothing more essential for our mission than prayer.

It makes you wonder, doesn't it? If we really believed that ourselves, wouldn't we be praying all the time? "Prayer is the mightiest power on earth. Enough of us, if we prayed enough, could save the world—if we prayed enough" (Wesley Duewel, *Mighty Prevailing Prayer*, p. 153). But do we pray enough? Do we even pray much at all for lost people? Could it be John Dawson is right: "The prayer of a human being can alter history by releasing legions of angels into the earth. If we really grasped this truth, we would pray with intensity, and we would pray constantly" (*Taking Our Cities for God*, p. 140). Intensely, constantly—just look at the church in the beginning.

DOWN ON ALL FOURS—2

And when they had prayed, the place where they were assembled together was shaken; and they were all filled with the Holy Spirit, and they spoke the word of God with boldness.
Acts 4:31.

Chicago teacher Natalie Meilinger heard male voices when she went to check her baby's video monitor. Quickly scanning the screen, she saw men on it. But what were they doing in her baby's room! By a technological fluke her video baby monitor was receiving live images from the space shuttle *Atlantis*! Messages from outer space—Acts records 25 instances of praying and prayer. They were down on all fours often, weren't they, in communion with heaven?

In today's episode Peter and John have just been released from prison, held overnight and interrogated for their faith. In response to the crisis, the church gathers in the familiar upper room to pour out their collective heart in earnest petition to God for deliverance. It is the longest prayer recorded in Acts. And it climaxes with their pleading, "Now, Lord, look on their threats, and grant to Your servants that with all boldness they may speak Your word" (Acts 4:29). What is so stirring is to note the immediate divine response to their intercessions, as recorded in our text today. John Franklin's book *And the Place Was Shaken* keys off this dramatic prayer moment to address the church of the third millennium. "The first secret that unlocked the resources of heaven for [the church in Acts] was this: they went from being on their own agenda to being on God's agenda" (p. 33). And that is the secret that can unlock the resources of heaven for us, too.

So is God's agenda your agenda, my agenda, our agenda? Have we, like Jesus in the Garden of Gethsemane, learned to passionately pray, "Not what I want, but what You want: I want to embrace Your agenda, O God, for my agenda—not my will but Yours be done"? The fact that it was "with loud cries and tears" that Jesus sobbed that prayer is proof enough that there are times that our deepest wants can fiercely clash against the wants and will of God. It isn't always easy to pray, "Thy will be done on earth as it is in heaven." But unless heaven's agenda is ours in this critical prime time of earth's history, what's the point of being church, of being the chosen?

Are there others in your congregation you could invite to join you in Acts 4's collective prayer for God's outpouring power? Isn't this the hour for the chosen to be shaken with a fresh anointing, that we might speak God's Word with a new boldness to this generation? Then pray!

DOWN ON ALL FOURS—3

I urge, then, first of all, that petitions, prayers, intercession and thanksgiving be made for everyone. . . . This is good, and pleases God our Savior, who wants all people to be saved and to come to a knowledge of the truth. 1 Tim. 2:1, 3, 4, TNIV.

Wesley Duewel is right: "You can love more people through prayer than any other way" (*Mighty Prevailing Prayer*, p. 116). If this is earth's primetime hour, and the kingdom advances among friends, then what more potent way can there be to love our lost friends than through prayer? After all, as Paul notes in our text today, "this is good, and pleases God our Savior."

So here are five ways for you to love lost people through prayer.

1. Make a list. This can include, but isn't necessarily limited to, your "My Friends Who Need Jesus" list. I've chosen to combine all my prayer lists into a single one that I keep separately in my daily prayer journal. This list will grow to be a long one, because here you're going to jot down the names of everybody God has impressed you to pray for, friend or not, acquaintance or stranger. Lost family members, lost friends, lost golfing buddies, lost students, lost teachers—anyone you care about who needs to know Christ and His truth—that's who goes on this intercessory prayer list. I include strangers I've met on planes, and some well-known preachers I've never met at all. After all, Paul is adamant: "I urge that intercessions be made *for everyone*. . . . This is good, and pleases God our Savior."

2. Pray the list. Should you pray this list every day? You can, but you don't have to. I've chosen to pray through my list once a week on Friday mornings. But the point is that there's no point in a prayer list if you don't pray it! Ellen White notes how this kind of intercessory praying impacts our own lives. "As we seek to win others to Christ, bearing the burden of souls in our prayers, our own hearts will throb with the quickening influence of God's grace; our own affections will glow with more divine fervor; our whole Christian life will be more of a reality, more earnest, more prayerful" (*Christ's Object Lessons*, p. 354). Note how closely spiritual vitality and personal growth are bound up with tapping into God's passion to seek and save lost people through intercessory praying. Why? Because when you pray for lost people by name, you are putting into practice God's Calvary passion and tapping into its crimson power. Hands down (and knees, too), God's love for lost earth children is the greatest power in the universe!

DOWN ON ALL FOURS — 4

Therefore he is able to save completely those who come to God through him, because he always lives to intercede for them. Heb. 7:25, NIV.

Let's continue with the third way to love lost people through prayer. **3. Work the list.** For some time I've had the name of a college professor on my prayer list (he teaches at another college in our vicinity). We studied the Bible together, and the Spirit seemed to be leading us deeper and deeper into the Word. Then suddenly he was plunged into a personal crisis, and our studies came to a halt. Every attempt of mine to later reconnect with him was rebuffed. So I concluded that this was one of those instances that you follow the Spirit into a witnessing relationship, you give it your best energies and fervent prayers, but you accept the reality that not every effort to lead a person to Christ and His truth ends in success. And besides, what may appear as failure to us can actually turn out to be strategic in the Holy Spirit's ministry to that individual long after we are off the scene and can end with a win-win for God.

I kept the college teacher on my prayer list and continued every Friday to lift him before God, asking that God would be at work where I couldn't. Then one Friday morning I was out on a prayer walk. (While I run daily, I've found including a weekly early morning walk can be a refreshing and quiet time to review your intercessory list with God.) That morning this professor's name was particularly impressed on my heart, and so I said, "God—I don't know if I should even try anymore to make contact with him—so, if it's Your will for us to reconnect in studying Your Word, please have him contact me." Two hours later I received an e-mail from this teacher, saying, "I've missed our time together—when can we start studying the Bible again—and you pick the subject this time." Praise God! And I did.

The point? You've got to be willing to work your list on God's behalf. Yes, we must pray for those who are lost. But we must in the same breath be open to the possibility that God needs to use us to answer our own prayers. You say, "There's no way I could ever study the Bible with anyone!" But don't be too quick to dismiss what the Spirit can do through you. First, you have the promise "I can do all things through Christ who strengthens me" (Phil. 4:13). And second, there are a host of materials and seminars God can use to equip you (including the Pioneer Memorial church's "Contagious Adventist" seminar). Pray your list. Work your list.

DOWN ON ALL FOURS—5

Every time I think of you, I give thanks to my God. Whenever I pray,
I make my requests for all of you with joy. Phil. 1:3, 4, NLT.

How can we love lost people through prayer? We're sharing five simple ways to use our prayer lists to grow in us God's passion for lost people. Here are the last two:

4. Grow the list. You watch—God will keep bringing new names to you, as you faithfully intercede for the names you already have. So don't be afraid to keep adding names as the Spirit brings them to mind. You'll be surprised, by the way, at how your *prayers* for the lost will actually grow your *passion* for the lost. It's the law of returns on Wall Street—the more you invest in a stock, the more fervently you long for its success. The more you pray for the lost, the more fervently you will long for their salvation. After all, praying for them is about changing God's heart for them, isn't it? Calvary is unassailable proof God needed no incentive or encouragement to empty His treasury for us sinners. Truth is, praying for the lost changes the intercessors ourselves. The more we pray, the deeper our passion. "Oh, that the earnest prayer of faith may arise everywhere, Give me souls buried now in . . . error, or I die! Bring them to the knowledge of the truth as it is in Jesus" (*This Day With God*, p. 171). That's passion with a purpose!

5. Keep the list. Keep on praying, no matter what happens (or doesn't happen). Don't quit bringing that lost heart to Jesus. George Mueller—who through sheer faith and prayer raised up the equivalent of $180 million to found orphanages across England in the nineteenth century—early on began praying for five unsaved friends. After five years one came to Christ. After 10 more years two more friends were converted. Mueller once testified, "I have prayed for two men by name every day for 35 years; on land or sea, sick or well, I have remembered them before God by name, and I shall continue to pray for them daily, by name, until they are saved, or die." After 35 years of prayer the fourth friend was saved. Mueller went on praying for a total of 52 years for the fifth friend. But Mueller died. And three days after his funeral, the fifth friend was saved.

Who needs to be on your prayer list for lost people? It is prime time in earth's history to be praying for them. So make the list, pray the list, work the list, grow the list, and keep the list. There may be somebody on earth nobody else is praying for. No wonder God needs you!

TURNING YOUR STORY
INTO HIS-STORY—1

But they have conquered him by the blood of the Lamb and by the word of their testimony, for they did not cling to life even in the face of death. Rev. 12:11, NRSV.

Do you know what the one truth is that nobody—and I mean nobody—will be able to contradict or defeat? It is a single, simple truth that can make you the most effective witness for Christ on earth. Exhibit A: the apostle Paul, formerly Saul of Tarsus.

Every reader of Acts knows the explosive story of the showdown between young Stephen, the mighty Christian apologist of Jerusalem, and young Saul, the up-and-coming bright star in the orbit of the Sanhedrin. A careful reading of Acts 6 indicates that in a public debate Stephen bested Saul in his defense of Jesus as the Messiah. In retaliation, Stephen is arraigned before the Sanhedrin on trumped-up charges. His eloquent defense of his faith in Christ seals his fate. The executioners heap their coats at Saul's feet, as he stands a mute accomplice in Stephen's stoning. Desperate to efface the memory of Stephen's apologetic, Saul ravenously persecutes the fledgling Christian community. Hurrying northward to Damascus to root out any followers of Christ, in a blinding flash Saul comes face to face with the risen Messiah. Led blinded into the city, for three long days and nights Saul struggles with the compelling truth about Jesus. But out of that blinding, his eyes are opened. Now, his heart broken and converted to the Savior, Saul is baptized as a disciple of the Master, and plunges into an ardent and passionate life of testifying to all who will listen to his undying faith in the living Christ.

It is in Dr. Luke's retelling of the story of this intrepid convert and witness to Jesus that we discover just what truth it is that cannot be contradicted or defeated. If we will master that simple truth, we, too, might yet be as effective a witness for Christ as Paul was. What is that truth? *It is the personal testimony of the follower of Christ.* We know that because of the repetitive way Luke records three occasions in which Paul recounts the story of his personal encounter with Jesus on the Damascus road. How many times Paul actually repeated that testimony we, of course, do not know. But Luke chose to record three of those occasions for us, so his readers would be impressed with how significantly influential and powerfully effective a personal testimony can be. It is no wonder that the Apocalypse in our text today portrays God's chosen ones overcoming their mortal enemy through Calvary's victory *"by the word of their testimony."*

TURNING YOUR STORY
INTO HIS-STORY—2

Now it happened, as I journeyed and came near Damascus at about noon, suddenly a great light from heaven shone around me. And I fell to the ground and heard a voice saying to me, "Saul, Saul, why are you persecuting Me?" So I answered, "Who are You, Lord?" And He said to me, "I am Jesus of Nazareth, whom you are persecuting." Acts 22:6-8.

As they say, whenever Paul came to town, there was either a revival or a riot! In each of the three recorded instances in which Paul shared his personal testimony, he was in chains. And the first instance began with a riot. But putting the three testimonies together, we find simple instructions for how we can effectively share our story, too. **Testimony 1. Acts 22:1-21. Keep it simple.** Paul's testimony on the heels of that riot went like this: here's how I grew up; here's what I believed; and then I met Jesus; and here's what He has done for my life. Not very complicated, is it? And yet so powerful was this first-person account of meeting Christ that a second riot erupted! But forget about the riot and remember these three simple components for telling your story: (1) your life before you met Jesus; (2) how you met Jesus; and (3) your life after meeting Jesus. If you've met Jesus, then you have all three of these simple components ready to be shared. How? Keep reading.

Testimony 2. Acts 23:6. Keep it short. You won't find a shorter testimony than this one. In a brilliant move to defend his faith, Paul here takes his life story and reduces it to a single sentence. Truth is, you don't need a long testimony. Some suggest about 100 words will do just fine. **Testimony 3. Acts 26:4-23. Keep it suitable.** Notice how Paul adapts his testimony on each of these occasions, adjusting the story to fit his listeners. As you do with your clothing—changing your "suits" to fit the occasion—even so make your story "suit-able" for the occasion you're in. You're on a plane visiting with a stranger—your story wears one suit to fit. You're visiting with a classmate after class—the same story puts on a different suit to match that moment. You're writing an e-mail, and you want to share how you met Jesus—the suit you put on for your story will match the needs of the one you're writing to.

Keep it simple, keep it short, and keep it suitable. And remember that turning your story into His story is what your personal testimony is all about. But as we'll note tomorrow, there are ways to do it best.

TURNING YOUR STORY
INTO HIS-STORY—3

That which was from the beginning, which we have heard, which we have seen with our eyes, which we have looked at and our hands have touched—this we proclaim concerning the Word of life . . . so that you also may have fellowship with us. And our fellowship is with the Father and with his Son, Jesus Christ. 1 John 1:1, 3, NIV.

The old maxim is true, isn't it? "Anything worth saying is worth saying well." That's why writing out your personal testimony is so helpful—not only in order to refine it, but also to memorize it. While no one wants to sound like a third grader's reading report, "In my own words . . .," nevertheless taking the time to prayerfully shape your testimony can make it not only "rememberable" but also memorable.

What should you keep in mind as you turn your story into not only history but His story? Bill Hybels, in his book *Just Walk Across the Room,* offers four suggestions. **1. Don't be long-winded.** Your testimony should be no longer than three minutes. Pay attention to the other person's body language. Keep your story short enough to allow them to ask questions. **2. Watch out for fuzziness.** "The only thing worse than a long story is a long story that is incoherent" (p. 120). Hybels' point is to keep your testimony simple with a clear story line that "conveys the heartbeat of your faith journey." **3. Avoid religionese.** Cut out the spiritual or churchy jargon we insiders use: "When I came to the truth" might better be "When I discovered what the Bible was teaching"; "When the Holy Spirit set my heart on fire" (Are you serious? How did they put it out?) might better be "In Jesus I've discovered a brand-new reason for living!" **4. Abandon superiority.** Nothing turns a non-Christian off more quickly than a holier-than-thou spirit. If my story becomes a recitation of my spiritual superiority over those who "don't have the truth," then it's best that I keep my story to myself.

To sell products, Madison Avenue thrives on before-and-after photos. Because when you share the same "before" and you're seeking the same "after," nothing is more persuasive than the testimony "It worked for me!" It's that way with Jesus. Our "before" pictures—fear, guilt, self-destructive behavior, ego—are amazingly similar. That's why people everywhere are longing for a new "after" picture—peace, forgiveness, self-control, humility. And that's why they need your testimony. Because your story is a very attractive, winsome before-and-after picture for Jesus.

WHY THE BAD NEWS IS GOOD NEWS

The people who walked in darkness have seen a great light; those who dwelt in the land of the shadow of death, upon them a light has shined. Isa. 9:2.

In 1967 two researchers at the University of Washington School of Medicine—Thomas H. Holmes and Richard H. Rahe—designed an instrument called "the social readjustment rating scale" (SRRS). It gives point values to 43 different life experiences. Their premise was that the good and bad events in our lives can increase our stress levels and thus make us more vulnerable to physical and mental illnesses; that certain of our life experiences cause enough stress to create disequilibrium in our lives, opening us up to the possibility of major paradigm shifts, not only physically but mentally.

The number one stressor? Death of a child, followed by death of a spouse, a divorce, marital separation, jail term, etc. But it isn't only bad news that creates stress. Good life experiences, such as marriage, pregnancy, outstanding personal achievements, do too. And given the economic roller coaster we're on globally today, I was intrigued to note that of these 43 life experiences, 12 of them have to do with our personal financial state.

That means that times of economic uncertainty and financial crisis open us up wide to the possibility of experiencing a major paradigm shift, a major change in our lives, the very change the gospel of Christ seeks in every human heart. Think about it. In this season of bad news the world over, the good news is that the bad news actually opens people up as never before to a receptivity to the good news, which can turn this time of bad news into a time of great news indeed!

Come to think of it, in this season before the Messiah's second coming, conditions aren't unlike those that existed when He came the first time, are they? Economic instability, political uncertainty, moral decadence, social collapse, racial/ethnic conflict, religious strife—but then wouldn't you expect the God of the universe to select the most opportune and productive time to announce the major paradigm shift of His everlasting gospel? When the bad news is the "baddest," the good news is the greatest! All of which means that there couldn't be a more opportune time to be praying for lost people than today. But not only praying for them—today is the perfect time to begin effectively sharing our faith with them. How? Let's explore the ways.

JUST DO IT—1

Then an angel of the Lord said to Philip, "Get up and go toward the south to the road that goes down from Jerusalem to Gaza." (This is a wilderness road.) So he got up and went. Now there was an Ethiopian eunuch, a court official of the Candace, queen of the Ethiopians, in charge of her entire treasury. Acts 8:26, 27, NRSV.

It was Nike that came up with the marketing slogan "Just do it!" Not a bad admonition either, when it comes to sharing your faith with someone. That's what hitchhiking Philip did. You can do it too, when you practice the seven witnessing principles tucked away in his story.

How would you like to get your orders from an angel? As today's text notes, Philip did. But then, who's surprised? After all, of our unseen guardian companions the Bible teaches: "Are not all angels ministering spirits sent to serve those who will inherit salvation?" (Heb. 1:14, NIV). That means there is no witnessing experience in which you're alone. I like the way John Stott put it—never forget that the other person's conscience is on your side. In other words, as you share your faith in Jesus or your belief in a Bible truth with others, remember that their guardian angel is affirming that very truth inside their minds or conscience. You'll always have a partner in your mission for God!

What's the first principle of witnessing that emerges from the story of Philip and the Ethiopian eunuch? It's found in the words "So he got up and went." **Principle 1. Be open to the Spirit's impressions and promptings.** Whether it's your angel or the Holy Spirit doesn't matter. There are crucial moments in your life when your witness to another human being will be strategic for the kingdom of heaven. "But how can I know for sure whether right now is one of those moments?" Ask yourself what you think Jesus wants for this individual—to be saved or lost? Duh! "At the foot of the cross, remembering that for one sinner Christ would have laid down His life, you may estimate the value of a soul" (*Christ's Object Lessons*, p. 196). "Yes, but is this the right time?" You may be one of a long line of witnesses God will use to slowly but surely open up that person to the Spirit's influence. "But how do I know witnessing is really my gift?" It may not be your gift, but it certainly is your role. Remember Acts 1:8? God hasn't made us all evangelists, but He has called us all to be witnesses. And bashful, shy, introverted—still you may be the most strategic link in God's golden chain of salvation for that person.

JUST DO IT—2

The Spirit told Philip, "Go to that chariot and stay near it." Then Philip ran up to the chariot and heard the man reading Isaiah the prophet. "Do you understand what you are reading?" Philip asked. Acts 8:29, 30, NIV.

Based on our text for today, here is the next principle from this favorite story. **Principle 2. Be willing to walk across the road or the room.** Do as Philip did. Put yourself in proximity to engage in a conversation. Make yourself available to the individual the Spirit is impressing you about. You have no idea where this will go, but if you don't go, you'll never know.

Bill Hybels tells the story of how a tall African-American Muslim came to know Christ because of the action of a stranger at a social engagement one evening. The two were in the same room of noisy conversation, but the Muslim, obviously feeling awkward as a minority in the group, stood off by himself, and a stranger observed him across the room alone. "The Spirit living inside him caused him to feel such compassion for the man standing alone that he excused himself from his Circle of Comfort, made the turn to the other side of the room, and started walking in the direction of a place I call the 'Zone of the Unknown.' . . . He had resolved in his heart, probably praying every step of the way, to enter into the Zone . . . and see what God might do. (In my opinion, it's within this zone that God does His very *best* work)" (*Just Walk Across the Room*, p. 23).

Do as that stranger did. Do as Philip did. Obey the promptings of the Spirit and take a walk (sometimes it will feel like a *long* walk) across the room or across the road. Step out of your Circle of Comfort and step into the Zone of the Unknown. For that is precisely what our Lord Jesus did once upon a long-ago time. Walking across the universe, He stepped into this rebel planet's Zone of the Unknown for the sake of saving the likes of you and me. We must be willing to do the same: "The same devotion, the same self-sacrifice, the same subjection to the claims of the Word of God, that were manifest in the life of Christ, must be seen in the lives of His [witnesses]. He left His home of security and peace, left the glory He had with the Father, left His position on the throne of the universe. He went forth . . . in solitude, to sow in tears, to water with His blood, the seed of life for a lost world. In like manner His [witnesses] are to go forth to sow" (*Review and Herald*, Nov. 23, 1905). Just like Philip. Just like Jesus.

JUST DO IT—3

Then Philip ran up to the chariot and heard the man reading Isaiah the prophet. "Do you understand what you are reading?" Philip asked. "How can I," he said, "unless someone explains it to me?" So he invited Philip to come up and sit with him. Acts 8:30, 31, NIV.

Have you noticed that questions are a very effective way to gain someone's attention and open up a conversation? "Do you understand what you are reading?" the hitchhiker asked the Ethiopian. "Can you believe the economy these days?" "What do you do for a living?" "Who's going to win the World Series?" "Can I borrow your ladder?" "What's your major?" Flying on a plane one day, I was sitting beside an engineer. He had a stack of scholarly journal articles on photons and nanoseconds (from what I could see): "What are you reading?" The point is, you don't have to look for a clever or original entrance into a conversation. Just ask a question.

Philip does, and we are reminded of **Principle 3** for effective witnessing. **Be ready to take the initiative.** "But I'm not an expert on any of this." You don't have to be. Witnessing is not about your *ability*—it's about your *availability*. Be available and ready to take the initiative when the Spirit prompts you.

Principle 4. Be prepared to answer a question. The court official was perplexed with the meaning of Isaiah 53. "What person is this passage talking about?" The story reads, "Then Philip began with that very passage of Scripture and told him the good news about Jesus" (Acts 8:35, NIV). Be ready to answer a question. "Oh, great! Now I've got to become a Bible answer expert!" Not at all. But remember Peter's appeal: "Always be prepared to give an answer to everyone who asks you to give the reason for the hope that you have" (1 Peter 3:15). "But I'm just a student." Just a student? Listen, "Christ desires to use every student as His agent" (*Ye Shall Receive Power,* p. 215). "But I won't know what to say." Hang on to this dynamite promise from Jesus for that very concern: "Don't worry about what to say in your defense, for the Holy Spirit will teach you what needs to be said *even as you are standing there*" (Luke 12:11, 12, NLT). Isn't that incredible! On the spot, while you and I are standing there or sitting there with that individual, we can dash a brief "Help!" prayer to heaven, and Jesus promises that in that split second His Spirit will bring to us the very thoughts and words we need to respond to a seeking heart. It really is true—when it comes to sharing your faith, you are *never* alone!

JUST DO IT—4

Be ready to speak up and tell anyone who asks why you're living the way you are, and always with the utmost courtesy. 1 Peter 3:15, Message.

Don't be like a presidential candidate. Have you noticed that politicians have a knack for answering any question you might raise? They'll smile, briefly acknowledge your specific query, and then launch into a recitation of another one of their memorized campaign slogans or speeches. Not so for those who seek to share their faith in Christ. Philip had a hundred stock answers he could have hauled out that hot desert afternoon sitting in the chariot beside the Ethiopian court official. But he was sensitive to the spiritual interests of the official.

Principle 5. Be mindful of the context of that moment and conversation. If he's asking about Isaiah 53, then focus on Jesus and Isaiah 53. If she's asking about the Sabbath, then share your witness about Jesus and the Sabbath. If they're wondering what you believe about death, then let your response be about Jesus and the Bible truth about death. Don't be like the politician and turn the conversation to your favorite doctrine. Philip began with the Ethiopian's point of interest, but then expanded the biblical witness to the truth as it is in Jesus.

Principle 6. Be focused on the ultimate goal of every witness—the salvation of the individual through baptism into Christ. An important leadership maxim states: "Begin with the end in mind." That simply means that as you plunge into a new project, keep fresh in your mind a picture of the desired outcome. Reminding yourself often of what the finished product is going to look like can turn the necessary routine and even daily drudgery into essential steps toward that shining dream. When it comes to sharing your faith, don't be timid about envisioning in your mind the glad day when your heart will thrill and your eyes will glisten as you witness that man, that woman, that young adult, that teenager baptized in Christ. Trust me. There is no greater joy in this life! "God might have committed the message of the gospel, and all the work of loving ministry, to the heavenly angels. He might have employed other means for accomplishing His purpose. But in His infinite love He chose to make us coworkers with Himself, with Christ and the angels, that we might share the blessing, the joy, the spiritual uplifting, which results from this unselfish ministry" (*Steps to Christ*, p. 79). So begin your witness with that glorious end in mind.

JUST DO IT—5

When they came up out of the water, the Spirit of the Lord suddenly took Philip away, and the eunuch did not see him again, but went on his way rejoicing. Philip, however, appeared at Azotus and traveled about, preaching the gospel in all the towns. Acts 8:39, 40, NIV.

What's the final principle for effectively sharing your faith learned in the story of Phillip and the Ethiopian eunuch? **Principle 7. Be ready to turn around and do it all over again.**

In fact, Philip's story makes clear the teaching of Jesus, "To everyone who has, more will be given" (Luke 19:26, NIV). That explains why some people keep finding new witnessing opportunities wherever they go. It's not that they're somehow better than the rest of us. It's simply that they keep making themselves available to the Spirit, who like a good businessman chooses to invest His treasure with those who keep bringing returns, rather than with those who refuse to invest what they have.

So what if we began every day with this humble, simple prayer: "O God, today I offer You my life and my witness. Send to me, or send me to, someone who needs to know Jesus and His truth. Amen." Remember—sharing your faith isn't about your ability—it's about your availability. This quiet prayer at the beginning of the day is simply an announcement to the God of the universe that if there is any one of His earth children who needs to know Jesus and His truth, you are declaring, "Here am I—send me" (Isa. 6:8, NIV). "I have no idea who they are or what they need, but I have Jesus' promise that Your Spirit will bring to me instantly the words You need for me to say at that moment. And so on the authority of Your calling and His promise, I am making myself available to You today."

When I go into the day remembering to pray this prayer—and let me hit the pause button here: I confess that there are days when it's the furthest thing from my mind, when all I want to do is get a plane seat to myself without any interruptions or all I'm thinking about is getting my own agenda accomplished by nighttime. But when I remember to offer myself to God for His witness, the people I meet and the stories that unfold surprise even me! Early the other morning I prayed that prayer, and on a snow-delayed flight from Chicago to Los Angeles, I sat beside a stranger who unburdened her faith journey to me. When our conversation was over, she remarked, "Somebody made sure I missed my flight so we could talk." Because of that prayer, I knew who it was.

GEOMETRIC PROGRESSION

A little one shall become a thousand, and a small one a strong nation. I, the Lord, will hasten it in its time. Isa. 60:22.

I used to fret about the future. How in the world is God going to reach the whole world? Do you understand how quickly the human race is growing? Every second four babies are born and two people die somewhere on earth. With a net growth of two per second, that means that every six days our population increases by 1 million. We can't even reach the people who are here right now, let alone all those who keep getting born in the meantime! And then I came across two uncommon phrases that have infused me with a new breath of fresh hope for the future. And both phrases are hinted at in our text today.

Phrase 1. Geometric progression. It's a mathematical reality that works like this. Let's say that you're a fervent, passionate Seventh-day Adventist (I'm sure you are) and that you're committed to reproducing yourself once every year (I hope you are). Every year you will invest enough energy to lead one more human being to become an Adventist who shares your same fervor and passion. How long will it take you to reach the entire world? In year one you'd become two (you plus the one you won). In year two you both go out and each win one, which makes four. Year three you'd become eight. Year four you'd become 16. By year 10 you'd become 1,024 fervent passionate Adventists. In 20 years you'd become 1 million. In 30 years there would be 1 billion fervent, passionate Adventists just like you. And in 35 years you would become five times earth's population! So in less than half a lifetime you could reach this entire planet five times. Naturally, for our example of geometric progression to work you and those you reach would need to embrace two commitments: (1) a fervent, passionate commitment to your Lord; and (2) a fervent, passionate commitment to reproduce yourself once every year. But that is precisely Isaiah's point: "A little one shall become a thousand, and a small one a strong nation." What I once dismissed as practically impossible now at least mathematically seems doable. The entire planet can be reached for God in less than a lifetime.

That means God hasn't given the chosen a "mission impossible." Your fervent commitment to Christ and His mission coupled with the reality behind the *second* uncommon phrase (tomorrow's reading) can truly make the numbers really work.

THE DIVINE PASSIVE

For He will finish the work and cut it short in righteousness,
because the Lord will make a short work upon the earth. Rom. 9:28.

My friend Ranko Stefanovic in his commentary on Revelation introduced me to the second uncommon phrase that is reflected in yesterday's text, Isaiah 60:22.

Phrase 2. Divine passive. You remember that a passive verb is a verb that acts back on the subject. I hit the ball—that's active. I was hit by the ball—that's passive. The "Hebrew divine passive" is a grammatical device in which, when no actor is delineated in a sentence, the action of the passive verb is understood to be accomplished by God Himself. Genesis 2:1 reads: "Thus the heavens and the earth, and all the host of them, were finished." "Were finished" is a passive verb that reflects back on the subject, "the heavens and the earth." Though we're not told who did the finishing, it certainly is understood that in fact God did. When Jesus cried out on the cross, "It is finished" (John 19:30), we are not told who did the finishing, but the passive there (in the Greek) suggests once again that God Himself completed the action.

But why all this grammar technicality? Consider another familiar text that suddenly radiates with hope when we factor in the divine passive: "And this gospel of the kingdom will be preached in all the world . . . and then the end will come" (Matt. 24:14). The verb "will be preached" is passive. But why the passive here? In giving this sign of His second coming, Jesus could very clearly have declared: "And you shall preach [active] the gospel in all the world." But He didn't. Instead He chose a passive verb without any actor delineated for the action described. And what does the divine passive signify? That the action will ultimately be accomplished by God Himself! Which is precisely what Isaiah 60:22 declares: "I, the Lord, will hasten it in its time." Today's text announces the same—God Himself will finish the work and cut it short. No wonder a century ago this prediction was made: "Let me tell you that the Lord will work in this last work in a manner very much out of the common order of things. . . . God will use ways and means by which it will be seen that He is taking the reins into His own hands" (*Testimonies to Ministers,* p. 300). Yes, *geometric progression* means that mathematically our mission is doable. But factor in the *divine passive,* and suddenly we are confronted with the stunning truth that God Himself completes it! All He asks is that we share His mission until it is finished.

WHERE THE LIGHT IS "WORSER"

In the land of Zebulun and of Naphtali, beside the sea, beyond the Jordan River, in Galilee where so many Gentiles live, the people who sat in darkness have seen a great light. And for those who lived in the land where death casts its shadow, a light has shined. Matt. 4:15, 16, NLT.

Gary Krause tells the story of two men searching for a lost watch under a lamppost one dark night. "Are you sure you dropped it here?" one asked. "Well, not exactly—it's 20 yards out there," the other said, pointing to the darkness. "Then why are we looking *here*?" To which the man replied, "Because the light is better!" Foolish man, we smile. But it's no laughing matter to recognize that too many of the chosen have congregated with pockets of other chosen, where "the light is better." What a sad contrast with the example of our Lord Jesus.

For a year Christ ministered in Judea and Jerusalem—a region that boasted more "saved" people per square foot than any other place on earth. Holy Temple, religion headquarters, seminary, kosher markets—what an ideal place to spend your life and mission. But in the terse announcement "He departed to Galilee" (Matt. 4:12) we realize that Jesus chose to walk away from it all. Why? Because in Galilee were more "lost" people per square foot than anywhere else in Palestine. The people there "sat in darkness." Leaving the light behind, Jesus moved His messianic mission from religious Jerusalem to godless Galilee.

Is Jesus an example for the chosen today? Postmodern seculars dominate the West. And while we rightfully acknowledge the "10/40 window of the East"—that swath of geography where 60 percent of the world lives but only 1 percent believes in Jesus—our mission can no longer afford to avoid the "10/40 window of the West." The church has struggled to bridge to this secular generation. We who rightfully champion "the truth" have a difficult time connecting with these who reject any notion of a singular truth, but rather embrace a pluralism that suggests that everybody possesses truth. What is our mission to this secular generation?

What would Jesus do (WWJD)? We already know. He moved into the most pagan neighborhood of His land, where the light was "worser," not "better." He didn't set up a think tank or open an institute. He simply mingled among them, as one who sought their friendship. And the people saw "a great light." Could that be what it means to let our light shine, too?

THE COMMUNIST AND
THE MISSIONARY

Go therefore and make disciples of all the nations, baptizing them in the name of the Father and of the Son and of the Holy Spirit, teaching them to observe all things that I have commanded you; and lo, I am with you always, even to the end of the age. Matt. 28:19, 20.

It's true. One of the intellectual founders of Communism and one of the intellectual founders of Adventism were contemporaries! Both men lived and died impoverished and in the same year, 1883. And both men left behind a corpus of writings, carving indelible marks on the movements they helped found. The men: Karl Marx and John Nevins Andrews—one a Communist, the other a missionary. Marx wrote: "The philosophers hitherto have only interpreted the world . . . ; the thing, however, is to change it." And while he was wrong about much, he was right about that, for the call to radically change the world is needed more today than ever in history. But how shall we change our world? Andrews wrote: "I know of but one way: Find a field of labor, ask God to help, take off your coat, and pitch into the work." And therein lies the mission of the chosen. It is high time we take off our coats, roll up our sleeves, and do something, anything really, for the sake of God's passion and mission to save lost people.

The Great Commission Jesus gave us on the eve of His ascension is in itself a profound call, not to interpret the world, but to change it. How? Take off your coat, roll up your sleeves, and *move out into the darkness* in search of the lost. For that reason we've spent this month focusing on simple but practical ways to translate our divine mission into very human and user-friendly strategies. But reading God's invitation is no longer enough—it's time to move out!

In *Out of This World* Nancy Irland and Peter Beck tell how the Reuben Donnelly Company in Chicago, one of the world's largest magazine printers, once mailed—thanks to a tiny spring that snapped in a giant printer—the same subscription notification 9,734 times to the same recipient. Overwhelmed with those 9,734 reminders that his *National Geographic* subscription was expiring, the hapless Colorado rancher drove the 10 miles into town and mailed his subscription money along with this note: "Send me the magazine. I give up!"

Wherever we turn in Scripture, we run headlong into Calvary's relentless passion for lost people. Again and again God keeps inviting us to share that passion and His mission. It's time to scribble the note: "I give up. Your love has convinced me. Let me join You in seeking the lost!"

NOBODY SAID IT WAS GOING TO BE EASY

And when they had preached the gospel to that city and made many disciples, they returned to Lystra, . . . strengthening the souls of the disciples, exhorting them to continue in the faith, and saying, "We must through many tribulations enter the kingdom of God." Acts 14:21, 22.

What dawns on you when you read the book of Acts is that even the friends of Jesus suffer. Or perhaps "truth in advertising" means we must admit that *especially* the friends of Jesus suffer. I wish Dr. Luke had left that line about "tribulations" out of our text today. But he didn't. Because being entrusted with the greatest mission on earth exacts a price, a very high price.

In an airport in Denver I noticed two men in clerical garb. I thought I'd join them, but I soon realized they were speaking an unfamiliar tongue. Finally the rabbi left. "What language was that?" I asked the man with the clerical collar.

"We're both from Romania," he replied.

"Well, I'm a minister too," I said.

He nodded. "What church?" Now when people ask you your church you take a deep breath, look them in the eye, and say, "Seventh-day Adventist."

The man smiled, "Oh, I know Seventh-day Adventists. I knew them when they were in prison." My heart fell—just my luck to meet a prison chaplain who knew some Adventist crooks! "Actually, we were in prison together." Turns out I was conversing with the well-known Lutheran pastor and author Richard Wurmbrand, who had been incarcerated for his faith in Communist Romania. I had his book *Sermons in Solitary Confinement* in my library.

"Oh yes, I knew you Adventists in prison. Why, your people tithed there!" I thought it a bit strange that they'd announce their tithing to the prisoners. "Every day we received a crusty piece of bread. But every tenth day the Adventists would give up their bread to another hungry prisoner." Could it be? "Yes," he went on, "and we always knew when the seventh day had come when we heard you Adventists calling out." I thought it odd that Adventists would be yelling "Sabbath's here" to all the prisoners. "No, we knew it was the Sabbath, as we listened to the Adventists screaming through their beatings for refusing to work on that day."

Tithing their bread crusts and screaming through their Sabbath beatings—nobody said the mission of the chosen was going to be easy. But now that I know their story, God help me be as faithful to my witness as my brothers and sisters were to theirs. After all, isn't it our mission?

THE MACEDONIAN MATRIX—1

Now when they had gone through Phrygia and the region of Galatia, they were forbidden by the Holy Spirit to preach the word in Asia. After they had come to Mysia, they tried to go into Bithynia, but the Spirit did not permit them. Acts 16:6, 7.

What are you supposed to do when it seems God keeps slamming the door in your face? How many of us right now are doing our best to bravely carry on with our noses pressed against a closed door? Could it be that the very best way to an open door is through a closed one?

I saw a list once of all the closed doors Abraham Lincoln, arguably the greatest president of the United States, experienced: 1832—he lost his job; 1832—he was defeated in his race for the Illinois legislature; 1833—he failed in business; 1834—he was elected to the state legislature; 1835—his sweetheart died; 1836—he had a nervous breakdown; 1838—he was defeated for speaker of the Illinois legislature; 1843—he was defeated for election to Congress; 1846—he was elected to Congress; 1848—he lost his reelection to Congress; 1849—he was rejected for land officer; 1854—he was defeated in a race for the U. S. Senate; 1856—he was defeated in a race for vice president; 1858—he was again defeated for the Senate; 1860—Abraham Lincoln was elected president of the United States. Could it be that the very best way to an open door is through a closed one?

Classic case study number two is our text for today. The intrepid apostle Paul and his traveling evangelistic team have concluded their gospel commission work in Lystra and Derbe and decide to press westward in obedience to Jesus' command to "go into all the world." But while we're not told how or why, the record reads that the door was shut in their face. The Spirit said No! Undaunted by that closed door, Paul and his companions revised their plans and pressed northward with the gospel instead. But when they tried to enter Bithynia, another giant closed door and a No! from God was waiting for them. So where was Paul to go now? He wasn't sure. Because when God closes a door in your life, you're never quite sure, are you? Joseph the slave had no clue. Neither did Moses the shepherd. Not even Abraham Lincoln did. So if your nose is pressed against the cold surface of another closed door, don't feel bad—you're not alone.

Just remember the truth Paul is about to discover—when you walk with God, the very best way to an open door very often is through a closed one.

THE MACEDONIAN MATRIX—2

Proceeding on through Mysia, they went down to the seaport Troas. That night Paul had a dream. A Macedonian stood on the far shore and called across the sea, "Come over to Macedonia and help us!" The dream gave Paul his map. We went to work at once getting things ready to cross over to Macedonia. All the pieces had come together. We knew now for sure that God had called us to preach the good news to the Europeans. Acts 16:8-10, Message.

Did you catch that? *"We knew for sure."* Proof enough that the best way to an open door is through a closed one. That's the anomaly and mystery of divine guidance. We think that because the door is closed it means there's no way to get through. But God responds, "No, no—it's precisely because the door *is* closed that you're going to get through . . . another door." Must be why He keeps allowing our closed doors—so that one day we'll discover His open one.

Could it be that the open door for Paul is an open door for you and me, too? Jim Collins, in his classic *Good to Great: Why Some Companies Make the Leap . . . and Others Don't,* describes how the most successful companies and organizations are driven by what he calls a BHAG: big, hairy, audacious goal. That's a huge, daunting goal or vision so compelling that it drives the entire organization in its unique mission and destiny. In the Macedonian cry, God gave Paul a compelling BHAG! Heretofore, Paul and the others had been content to wander around Asia Minor for the gospel of Christ, a laudable mission to be sure. But all of heaven was ready for a BHAG, and in that single vision, "Come into Macedonia and help us," God blew the borders off Paul's mission. "You're dreaming too small for Me, Paul. You're asking for a province, but I want to give you a continent that one day will become the entire West!"

So where is *our* Macedonia? It is an entire planet of lost men, women, and children, isn't it? The secular West, the pagan East, and the cities of both—for this generation Macedonia is the world! "To show a liberal, self-denying spirit for the success of foreign missions [global] is a sure way to advance home missionary work [local]; for the prosperity of the home work [local] depends largely, under God, upon the reflex influence of the evangelical work done in countries afar off [global]. It is in working to supply the necessities of others that we bring our souls into touch with the Source of all power" (*Gospel Workers,* pp. 465, 466). Isn't it time to let God's BHAG Macedonian call mobilize our offerings, our volunteerings, and our goings for Jesus?

A WHALE OF A MOBILIZATION — 1

Arise, go to Nineveh, that great city, and cry out against it;
for their wickedness has come up before Me. Jonah 1:2.

On most Sabbaths four generations gather to worship. The GI generation (those born in the 1920s and 1930s), the baby boomers (those born in the 1940s and 1950s), the GenX generation (those born in the 1960s and 1970s), and the millennials (those born in the 1980s and 1990s). Three of these generations have already conquered new frontiers: the GI generation with their "inner" space (not very high up into the stratosphere); the boomers with their "outer" space; and the GenXers with their "cyber" space. But what "space" is left for today's generation to conquer for God? There's a very short book in the Bible that is filled with questions—13 of them. It even ends with a question. And if that last question will become our first question, we'll discover the one "space" on earth that's still left to conquer for the kingdom of heaven.

That very first question in the book of Jonah hurls us into the drama: "How can you sleep? Get up and call on your god! Maybe he will take notice of us, and we will not perish" (Jonah 1:6, NIV). But sleepy Jonah isn't in any mood for praying. He knows from whence comes the howling winds and pitching sea—the God he disobeyed has come after him, and all hell has broken loose on the Mediterranean! How could he sleep at all? Haddon Robinson in an essay observed: "If ever there was a man who lived in direct disobedience to God, it was the prophet Jonah. God directed him to preach to the citizens of Nineveh, but he boarded a ship and sailed away from God rather than do what God had commanded him to do. During his flight a violent storm arose that terrified the pagan sailors, but Jonah was below deck in the boat asleep. Evidently Jonah had peace about the decision he made. On the other hand, if ever there was someone who was doing God's will, it was Jesus going to the cross. Yet, in the Garden of Gethsemane He was in anguish, and His sweat was like drops of blood falling to earth (Luke 22:44). Peace is not evidence we have made a godly decision" (in *Preaching to a Shifting Culture*, pp. 85, 86).

Just because the chosen are at peace about leaving the last frontier and "space" unconquered for God doesn't mean we have made a godly decision. So are you ready to reverse course and help God conquer the final frontier?

A WHALE OF A MOBILIZATION—2

But I, with a song of thanksgiving, will sacrifice to you.
What I have vowed I will make good. Salvation comes from the Lord. Jonah 2:9, NIV.

In rapid-fire sequence, the sea-drenched pagan sailors in Jonah's epic narrative shout above the howling winds questions two through eight straight into the heart of the runaway prophet. And gripping the rails of that heaving Phoenician vessel, Jonah licks the salt from his lips and responds with his mea culpa. "Pick me up and throw me into the sea," he replied, "and it will become calm. I know that it is my fault that this great storm has come upon you" (Jonah 1:12, NIV). The men believe him and hurl him into the sea, and in that instant the sea is calm.

Not for Jonah, who is sucked out of the gurgling depths into the retching environs of a monstrous sea creature. But in that pitch-black sea-born roller coaster Jonah amazingly neither dies nor vomits. He prays in abject repentance and confession. And apparently our God can hear us no matter where on earth (or in the sea) we happen to be, for the runaway prophet is pardoned. With joy Jonah exclaims the words of today's text: "Salvation comes from the Lord." The pagans discovered that truth. The prophet discovers it. And eventually an entire city will, too. How does that old gospel hymn go? "We have heard a joyful sound, Jesus saves, Jesus saves!"

But the sound that followed wasn't quite as joyful. When our dog Sadie Hawkins begins to vomit, she makes a distinctive retching sound that throws whoever's closest to her into an adrenalin rush, scooping hapless Sadie up and flying her to linoleum or outdoors! Jonah doesn't mind the sound—he is vomited up onto dry ground. Hallelujah! And when God commands "Go" the second time, Jonah immediately goes—mobilized into God's mission for that lost city.

And lo and behold, in one of the greatest evangelistic campaigns in the history of earth, the remobilized one becomes God's agent in effecting a citywide revival that brings divine salvation to the wickedest city on earth (so Jonah believed and thus had fled)! "When God saw what they did and how they turned from their evil ways, he had compassion and did not bring upon them the destruction he had threatened" (Jonah 3:10, NIV).

And Jonah? He was so angry that the end didn't come, he actually (true story) begged God to kill him! Apparently it is possible for the chosen to long more for the end of the world than for the salvation of the lost, as if their reputation mattered more than God's. Do we? Does it?

A WHALE OF A MOBILIZATION—3

*But Nineveh has more than a hundred and twenty thousand people
who cannot tell their right hand from their left, and many cattle as well.
Should I not be concerned about that great city? Jonah 4:11, NIV.*

That's the last line of Jonah's epic narrative. The story ends with a single question (number 13) from the lips of God: "Should I not be concerned about that great city?" The End.

Hasn't the time come in history when God's last question must become our first? Of this planet's nearly 7 *billion inhabitants*, it is now estimated that 47 percent of them live in a city (not a suburb, town, village, or the country). In fact, earth's cities have become so large that 438 of them are now being called "agglomerations," defined as contiguous spreads of inhabited buildings and streets. Among the world's largest agglomerations are: Tokyo, Mexico City, Seoul, New York, São Paulo, Mumbai, Delhi, Shanghai, Los Angeles, and Osaka. Just these 10 cities contain more human beings than half the U.S. population. If the cry of God that ends the book of Jonah was for only one city, can you imagine the depth of the divine cry today?

Want to know how God really feels about cities?

"As [Jesus] came near and saw the city, he wept over it" (Luke 19:41, NRSV). There are only two instances in the Gospel record where Jesus is described as weeping—once over a dead friend, and once over a lost city. Bob Pierce, the founder of World Vision, used to say, "We must come to the place where what breaks the heart of God breaks our hearts, too." Maybe that's why these words were written more than a century ago: "Work the cities without delay, for time is short. . . . At such a time as this, every hand is to be employed. . . . *The burden of the needs of our cities has rested so heavily upon me that it has sometimes seemed that I should die*" (*Evangelism,* pp. 33, 34; italics supplied).

But rather than being discouraged by this immense urban challenge, we need to recognize how God has set us up for success. The English language is now spoken by the educated in nearly every city on earth. Mass communication now enables us to instantly disseminate our message anywhere. And ours is now a universal urban culture with a youth generation that speaks the same cultural language globally. God has set His kingdom up, not for failure, but for success! If there's anything to learn from the story of Jonah, it's got to be: Let's go!

A WHALE OF A MOBILIZATION—4

Now the Lord spoke to Paul in the night by a vision, "Do not be afraid, but speak, and do not keep silent; for I am with you, and no one will attack you to hurt you; for I have many people in this city." Acts 18:9, 10.

"But there's no way I can move to Tokyo or New York or São Paulo—I'm stuck here at home." Aren't we all? So here are two simple strategies to mobilize yourself for God's cities.

Strategy 1. Begin with the city closest to you. It's hardly as exotic as Rio, but it's a city close to home. If God's heart broke for Nineveh and Jerusalem, He has a heart for your city, too. As today's text today reminds us, God has many of His people inside our cities. How many is many? Enough for Jesus to have given His life, of course. And that means we can no longer sit comfortably, obliviously by on the outskirts of a suburb and pretend that's all there is. We can rejoice that the GI generation conquered "inner space" and the boomers "outer space" and GenXers "cyberspace"—but it's time to move to the top of our agenda, the final frontier to be conquered for God: "urban space." Let's be honest. We've done well, nationally and globally, in the villages and in the country, and not too badly in the suburbs. But our record in the cities is abysmal. They are yet unconquered for Christ and His kingdom. That's why a new generation is desperately needed to seize this last frontier for Him! New pioneers, new missionaries of the third millennium. No need to cross the sea or even the country. Begin in the city nearest to you.

What can we do? For some, to be faithful to the God of Jonah's calling will mean transferring membership from a beloved home church to a needy inner-city church. For others, it will be the radical vision of planting a brand-new church in one of those urban centers. For still others, it will be the organization of teams of volunteers to begin inner-city street ministries (praying door to door, starting neighborhood story hours for children). Our university congregation has embarked on all three of these efforts. The point? We can talk about the great needs of the world's great cities, but if we aren't doing anything to make a difference with the city God has planted us closest to, what good is it? So why not call up a friend, another member of your congregation, your pastor, and invite somebody—anybody—to join you in seeking the "my people" God has in that city of yours?

A WHALE OF A MOBILIZATION—5

Now finish the work, so that your eager willingness to do it may be matched by your completion of it, according to your means. For if the willingness is there, the gift is acceptable according to what one has, not according to what he does not have. 2 Cor. 8:11, 12, NIV.

A second strategy for assisting God in reaching the cities of earth may be easily overlooked. It's the strategy for when you can't go. It's essential even when you *can* go.

Strategy 2. Give for the cities around you. The practical reality is that everyone can't transfer their lives to a city. Family obligations, career choices, professional responsibilities, educational pursuits, financial reasons—there are obviously legitimate and manifold reasons we can't all become missionaries to an inner city or an urban center. But the fact remains that all of us can give—we can all make a financial investment in God's mission for the cities of earth. In fact, as we noted a few days ago, the success of our mission in our home churches is directly proportionate to our investment in the global mission of the kingdom. The phrase was "reflex influence." Remember when your doctor took that silver mallet and "whacked" your knee to see if your leg would reflexively jerk (which it did, making you feel rather foolish and out of control)? The doctor's action produced a corresponding reaction on your part. Giving to the wider mission of the kingdom works the same way. Investing in city missions far away from us actually has a reflex influence on the success of our mission in our own community. "Externally focused churches" (as one team of writers puts it)—churches that focus on the wider needs of the world around them—experience reflexive growth and vitality. It's certainly counterintuitive, since saving your resources for your home church would seem the prudent response. But in God's kingdom it's the reverse—if you want to save yourself, you must lose yourself.

So what would happen if you began to designate some of your offerings for inner-city missions? Can't join a street ministry? Help fund one. Can't volunteer for a soup kitchen? Why not help support one financially? Can't go on television yourself? There are a dozen worthy radio and TV ministries seeking to reach earth's cities in this generation. "Urban space" is our last frontier, and you can help fund its conquest for God. "Let your heart be tender and your vision clear; see mankind as God sees, serve Him far and near. Let your heart be broken by a brother's pain; share your rich resources, give and give again" (*The Seventh-day Adventist Hymnal*, no. 575).

THE LAST STORY

For I was hungry and you gave me something to eat, I was thirsty and you gave me something to drink, I was a stranger and you invited me in, I needed clothes and you clothed me, I was sick and you looked after me, I was in prison and you came to visit me. Matt. 25:35, 36, NIV.

When a man is on death row, you listen very closely and carefully to the last story he tells, don't you? Jesus' parable of the sheep and the goats is the final one recorded in the Gospels before His execution. Why would Matthew save this one to tell at the very end?

Once I was studying the Bible with a woman who raised goats, and when we came to this parable, she took great offense. Why would God save the sheep but condemn the goats? Actually, when Jesus told this story all His agrarian listeners knew that the sheep of Palestine were light in color, while the goats were dark. A shepherd's task in separating the sheep from the goats (the goats were voracious and ravaging eaters and were thus kept apart) was made simple because of the contrast in their hues. Jesus chooses that visual distinction to heighten the contrast between two very different communities of people at the end of time. When He returns, He will separate the nations of earth, like a shepherd separates the sheep and the goats. To the righteous (the sheep) He will offer His eternal kingdom. And to the wicked (the goats) He will render eternal judgment. But both groups in the parable are surprised at the King's unexpected verdict. In our text today the King explains His decision, linking both fates to the way the saved and the lost responded or didn't respond to the physical needs of the poor, the needy, the disenfranchised, and alienated. "'Truly I tell you, whatever you did [or did not do] for one of the least of these brothers and sisters of mine, you did [or did not do] for me'" (Matt. 25:40, TNIV). We all know the story.

But when I read the punch line in *The Desire of Ages,* I was astounded: "Thus Christ on the Mount of Olives pictured to His disciples the scene of the great judgment day. And He represented *its decision as turning upon one point.* When the nations are gathered before Him, there will be but two classes, and their eternal destiny will be determined by *what they have done or have neglected to do for Him in the person of the poor and the suffering*" (p. 637; italics supplied). The final judgment for all rendered on the basis of how we treated the poor? Could it be that Mother Teresa wasn't the only one given the divine mission to serve the poor?

245 REASONS FOR THIS MISSION

Whoever oppresses the poor shows contempt for their Maker,
but whoever is kind to the needy honors God. Prov. 14:31, TNIV.

Are the poor really on God's radar screen for the chosen? Viv Grigg, a New Zealander, felt so compelled by Jesus' solidarity with the poor that he moved from the mountain majesty of his South Pacific homeland into the decaying heart of one of Manila's cardboard-and-tin slum cities. One day beneath the corrugated tin roof of his slum house, Viv sat with a friend and copied by hand onto small white cards every verse in the Bible he could find dealing with the poor. For the next four years he carried them with him, as day and night he meditated upon God's unabashed, uncompromising solidarity with the poor. In the English Scriptures Viv Grigg identified 245 references to the poor, the needy, and poverty. Here are just a handful:

"I rescued the poor who cried for help, and the fatherless who had none to assist him. The man who was dying blessed me; I made the widow's heart sing" (Job 29:12, 13, NIV).

"Have I not wept for those in trouble? Has not my soul grieved for the poor?" (Job 30:25, NIV).

"There will always be poor people in the land. Therefore I command you to be openhanded toward your brothers and toward the poor and needy in your land" (Deut. 15:11, NIV).

"When you give to the poor, it is like lending to the Lord, and the Lord will pay you back" (Prov. 19:17, TEV).

"Religion that God our Father accepts as pure and faultless is this: to look after orphans and widows in their distress. . . . Has not God chosen those who are poor in the eyes of the world to be rich in faith and to inherit the kingdom he promised those who love him?" (James 1:27-2:5, NIV).

Though just a sample of the 245 biblical references to the poor and needy, it is pointedly clear that the Scriptures champion God's unrelenting solidarity with the oppressed, the hungry, the poor, the naked. Surely it is just as clear that when God mobilizes the chosen for His end-time mission, at the top of His list must be the poor. Do you know someone at the top of God's list?

THE CHAMPION

As they were walking along the road, a man said to him, "I will follow you wherever you go." Jesus replied, "Foxes have holes and birds of the air have nests, but the Son of Man has no place to lay his head." Luke 9:57, 58, NIV.

Everybody loves a champion. For years the most famous resident of our little Berrien Springs village was a man the world crowned "The Champion" again and again. In his retirement years Muhammad Ali lived with his small family at the end of one of our lanes. I once visited his training ring in an old reconditioned barn. Lining the overhead rafters were magazine covers from the world over that celebrated this man's athletic prowess. Crippled by Parkinson's now, Ali still flashes a twinkle in his eye and has a warm heart for people.

But the real Champion emerges from a careful reading of the Gospels. Luke in particular intentionally portrays Jesus as the great Champion of the poor. I once tracked the intimations of Jesus' solidarity with the poor and needy in Luke's Gospel. It is astounding. Do it for yourself—you, too, will find the evidence for His advocacy unmistakable.

Viv Grigg, whom we met yesterday, has written a book chronicling his life and mission in that Manila slum. In *Companion to the Poor* he made this provocative observation: "Where can Jesus be found and known today? To find him, we must go where he is. Did he not say, 'Where I am, there shall my servant be also?' Such a search invariably leads us into the heart of poverty. For Jesus always goes to the point of deepest need. Where there is suffering, he will be there binding wounds. His compassion eternally drives him to human need. Where there is injustice, he is there. His justice demands it. He does not dwell on the edge of issues. He is involved, always doing battle with the fiercest of the forces of evil and powers of darkness. That night, in a squatter settlement . . . my heart found rest. There could be no turning back from God's call. I must preach the gospel to the poor" (p. 22).

Is that mission any different for you and for me? Doesn't the very lordship of Jesus mean that the church that champions God's "present truth" to a final generation must also champion Christ's healing presence among the poor, the disenfranchised, the marginalized, the suffering of inner cities near and far? How can the chosen possibly choose to concentrate only on proclamation, when the poor are so near to us and are so dear to God?

REPAIRERS OF THE BREACH—1

Is not this the kind of fasting I have chosen: to loose the chains of injustice and untie the cords of the yoke, to set the oppressed free and break every yoke? Is it not to share your food with the hungry and to provide the poor wanderer with shelter—when you see the naked, to clothe him, and not to turn away from your own flesh and blood? Isa. 58:6, 7, NIV.

It's a bit startling to realize that Isaiah 58 was written to a people not unlike you and me. They were big on the seventh-day Sabbath. They proclaimed the Day of Atonement's cleansing of the sanctuary, and they were the champions of orthodoxy. But they had forgotten and utterly neglected the other side of orthodoxy's coin—orthopraxy. Orthodoxy: [Greek: *orthos*—right, and *doxa*—opinion] "right thinking" or "right believing." Orthopraxy: [Greek: *orthos*—right, *praxis*—acts] "right practicing" or "right behaving." God doesn't fault them for their right beliefs, but He has a heartful to say to them about their lack of right behavior—particularly, as today's text carefully notes, when it comes to their treatment of the poor and suffering.

So how is the orthodoxy/orthopraxy balance with the chosen today? Does God still have issues with people who champion the truth but nothing more? Go online sometime and Google "poverty" or "food insecurity" (the government nomenclature for hunger). Can you believe the numbers? In a nation that boasts such affluence, the tragic divide between the haves and the have-nots is frightful at best and downright obscene at worst. But do the chosen care? Don't ask, "Does God care?" Isaiah 58 is His passionate rejoinder. In fact, the very categories of human need outlined in today's text were co-opted by Jesus in His last story on earth. Food, shelter, clothing—the bare essentials for survival and what one in eight Americans struggles to hang on to are checklisted in both Isaiah 58 and Jesus' sheep and goats parable.

What's the big deal? Thinking back to the parable a few days ago and the startling fact that the final judgment will be based on our response [or lack of it] to the poor and suffering, it becomes evident nothing cuts more quickly or deeply to the core of human selfishness or unselfishness than what we do for those in need. Is there a more visible barometer of my heart than my response to the needs of the poor around me? No wonder Jesus told the rich young ruler to sell everything he had and give it to the poor. He had orthodoxy down pat—but he failed the final exam on orthopraxy. He thought he was chosen, but his choice showed otherwise.

REPAIRERS OF THE BREACH—2

There will always be poor people in the land. Therefore I command you to be openhanded toward those of your people who are poor and needy in your land. Deut. 15:11, TNIV.

I knocked on their basement apartment door. I'd heard that the young couple, members of our congregation and students at the university, were experiencing some financial difficulties. And while such stories are hardly unique in a community of young penniless scholars in training, I decided I had better check this one out. It was not long before Christmas. The young husband invited me in. Sitting there in that nearly bare apartment, the three of us fell into conversation. At some point in our visit, I asked how things were going financially for them. After a momentary glance at each other, the young man stood up and walked to their refrigerator and opened it. He pointed to a half-empty tub of margarine and a jar of corn kernels. "This is what we've been living on lately." They were subsisting on popcorn. How did Jesus put it? "For the poor you have with you always" (John 12:8).

It is a reminder that while the inner cities of the world's great urban centers are thronged with the penniless and the impoverished, God's mobilization of the chosen to minister to the poor is not at the expense of the poor among us. In fact, in a chapter entitled "God's Care for the Poor" Ellen White observes: "There is nothing, after their recognition of the claims of God, that more distinguishes the laws given by Moses than the liberal, tender, and hospitable spirit enjoined toward the poor. Although God had promised greatly to bless His people, it was not His design that poverty should be wholly unknown among them. He declared that the poor should never cease out of the land. There would ever be those among His people who would call into exercise their sympathy, tenderness, and benevolence. Then, as now, persons were subject to misfortune, sickness, and loss of property; yet so long as they followed the instruction given by God, there were no beggars among them, neither any who suffered for food" (*Patriarchs and Prophets*, pp. 530, 531).

"The poor you have with you always." Given that reality, could it be that *the poor are our golden opportunity to exercise the golden rule?* If the tables were turned and your fortunes reversed, how would you want that poor man, that poor woman, that poor child, to treat you? If they had all your money and all your time, how would you want them to treat you in your need?

REPAIRERS OF THE BREACH—3

Woe to him who builds his palace by unrighteousness, his upper rooms by injustice, making his countrymen work for nothing, not paying them for their labor. Jer. 22:13, NIV.

We once convened a Solidarity With the Poor task force to give guidance to our congregation's mission to the inner city. I was surprised at how earnestly these community activists emphasized that we need to take very seriously God's call to social justice in Isaiah 58. Unless the poor can be given skills and tools, they will remain in economic and social bondage, an oppression not unlike a war.

One wintery Sabbath afternoon I was going door to door in Benton Harbor, Michigan, with one of our students, having prayer with those who wished. (This city is the second-most-impoverished city per capita in America.) We came to what looked like a business establishment. The Cadillac parked in front wore a bumper sticker: "Jesus is Lord." This should be a friendly visit. So we stomped the snow off our shoes and stepped into what was a beauty salon. "Who owns the car with 'Jesus is Lord' on it?" I called out. The place went silent. "Because we're from Andrews University, and we're out praying with people. We knew there'd be friends in here!" With that everybody started talking and smiling. One of the men made a comment I will not forget. We somehow got to talking about Iraq, and he told me he had fought there. "In fact," he went on, "I live in Vietnam."

"You do?"

He nodded. And then, his hand pointing out the door, he clarified, "I live in Vietnam here in Benton Harbor." Surprised at his candor, I got his point. Even the occupants of an inner city consider it a war zone.

Isaiah 58 is a divine mobilization of the chosen straight into the war zone of human poverty and injustice. I belong to a community of faith that loves to champion God's great S's—salvation, Sabbath, state of the dead, Second Coming, sanctuary, etc. But Isaiah 58 is clear—without social justice and social action (verses 6 and 7), all the other S's in the world cannot alone fulfill God's mission. For that reason God can begin the chapter calling for social justice and social action and end up with a soliloquy on Sabbath observance, as if to say, "You'll get My day right, only when you get My way right." A point made a century ago as well: "To relieve the afflicted, to comfort the sorrowing, is a labor of love that does honor to God's holy day" (*Welfare Ministry*, p. 77). Why, even the Sabbath is divinely strategic for loving the poor.

REPAIRERS OF THE BREACH—4

Keep the Sabbath day holy. Don't pursue your own interests on that day, but enjoy the Sabbath and speak of it with delight as the Lord's holy day. Honor the Sabbath in every-thing you do on that day, and don't follow your own desires or talk idly. Then the Lord will be your delight. I will give you great honor and satisfy you with the inheritance I promised to your ancestor Jacob. I, the Lord, have spoken! Isa. 58:13, 14, NLT.

The Hebrew greeting is a beautiful one: *Shabbat shalom*—"the peace of the Sabbath be with you." What more appropriate greeting and solution for a time-impoverished postmodern community of faith like ours! It is no accident that after His impassioned appeal for His people to minister to the physical and finan-cial needs of the poor, God concludes with His own *Shabbat shalom* appeal. It is al-most as if He were seeking to remind us that genuine *Shabbat shalom* brings not only divine peace to those who (how did He put it?) "call the Sabbath a delight and the Lord's holy day honorable" (Isa. 58:13, NIV), but it is the day to bring His peace to those of earth's children who need it most.

At the end of our frenetic weeks, do we have little money and no time left for the poor? Jesus declares, "It is right to do good on the Sabbath" (Matt. 12:12, NLT), which interpreted means, *Sabbath afternoons are a gift from God through you to the poor, the suffering, the lonely, and the needy.* Do you need to be with your family? Then on a Sabbath afternoon take your family with you to be with those in need. Do you want to be with your friends? Then take your friends with you to help the poor on a Sabbath afternoon. Do you want to enjoy the Sabbath rest? Then take the rest of Jesus to someone in need on a Sabbath afternoon.

I'm sure you can put together a checklist of *Shabbat shalom* Sabbath afternoon activities longer than this one: outreach to inner-city poor; "Sunshine Bands" to hospitals and foster-care homes; nursing home visitation (singing, reading, praying groups); invite the lonely and disenfranchised family home for Sabbath dinner; adopt a student for *any* dinner; start a "Sabbath Meals on Wheels" ministry for shut-ins; write letters and cards to the lonely (ask your pastor for names); create and maintain a personal Web site for the lonely; shovel a senior citizen's driveway (find creative alternatives in Florida!), etc. For us time-impoverished third millennials who really truly desire to embrace Jesus' solidarity with the poor, isn't the Sabbath the perfect gift?

REPAIRERS OF THE BREACH—5

Your ancient ruins shall be rebuilt; you shall raise up the foundations of many generations; you shall be called the repairer of the breach, the restorer of streets to dwell in. Isa. 58:12, ESV.

One of the glories of England's countryside is its meandering matrix of ancient stone walls. But from the towering stone edifices of Hadrian's second-century wall in northern England to the painstakingly crafted rock walls that wind and wend across the rolling hills of Cornwall, the sad reality of these walls was that they could be breached. And breached they eventually were.

In Isaiah 58 God cries out for a new generation of chosen to become "repairers of the breach," rebuilders of the gaping ruins of an ancient foundation. What breach? The very next words He speaks after our text today are His impassioned appeal to honor the Sabbath. All these millennia later it is more than clear that the protective wall of the divine law has been breached through the fourth commandment: "Remember the Sabbath day to keep it holy" (Ex. 20:8).

The enemy of God calculated that one strategically placed strike could bring the entire wall down. Glen Walker in *Prophecy Made Easy* describes the night of May 16, 1943, when a squadron of Royal Air Force bombers was dispatched on a mission to destroy the Möhne Dam in the Ruhr Valley of Germany. Roaring up the valley just 60 feet above the ground, the bombers carried a specially crafted "dam buster," designed to create a small hole in the towering dam that would eventually explode under the enormous water pressure behind it. And so the bomb struck, the wall was breached, and the dam blew open, sweeping houses and people to their destruction. In the same way the enemy has breached God's law, destroying its protective defense by striking at its very heart in the Sabbath commandment, bringing down the entire wall. Just look at human society today.

No wonder God still cries out for new repairers of the breach, for a generation of the chosen, willing to be mobilized anywhere for the sake of restoring the destroyed foundations of truth. "The breach made in the law at the time the Sabbath was changed by man is to be repaired. God's remnant people, standing before the world as reformers, are to show that the law of God is the foundation of all enduring reform and that the Sabbath of the fourth commandment is to stand as a memorial of creation, a constant reminder of the power of God" (*Prophets and Kings,* p. 678). The divine call and mission are unmistakable. Shall we be the repairers of the breach He is calling for?

O CALCUTTA!

For you know the grace of our Lord Jesus Christ, that though He was rich, yet for your sakes He became poor, that you through His poverty might become rich. 2 Cor. 8:9.

Author and poet T. S. Eliot wrote, "The last temptation is the greatest treason: to do the right deed for the wrong reason." But what would be the *right* reason?

Imagine an amalgamation of soggy cardboard and plastic bags propped up beside a filthy, putrid Calcutta slum gutter. You peer into its stinking interior, and there huddled in a fetal position is the wasted bony form of a man whose hollow eyes and sallow face stare back at you. Crawling into that hovel, holding your breath from the stench, you scoop up this emaciated dreg of humanity and carry him to a waiting black-and-yellow taxi that races you both to the airport. You strap this gangrened stranger beside you on the 747, and 20 hours and half a world away later, you land. Arriving back at your own home, still bearing the foul, wasted form of the man in your arms, you hurry inside, bathe him, clean him, robe him, feed him, and put him to bed—this skeletal stranger. In the morning, when his bewildered eyes finally register the reality of the opulence that now surrounds him, you do a most unthinkable thing. You hand him the keys to your house, your SUV, your boat, your pantry, and file folder with account numbers for your checking, savings, credit cards, and stock portfolio.

Then with hardly a word, you shake his hand, hug his bony shoulders, take off your clothes and pick up the putrid, sticky loincloth you removed from him the night before, and wrap yourself in his decaying rags. With a final nod, you walk out of your home clutching only the return portion of the stranger's round-trip ticket. And boarding another 747, you fly a universe away. When you land in Calcutta, you must walk—you have no money for a taxi. Finally, hours and hours later you straggle into the very slum in which you found him days ago. By the retching smell you recognize the still-rotten cardboard lean-to. Bending to the rancid ground, you crawl into that dank, dismal hole. And curling into a fetal position, you live out the rest of your days in that awful misery of abandoned filth. And the stranger? He now possesses everything of yours—for you gave it to him. And you possess everything of his—he gave it to you. Your riches are forever his, and his poverty is now yours forever and ever.

Why should we serve the poor and needy? Because it is what Jesus did for us.

STAR RISING OVER ISLAM—1

After these things I saw another angel coming down from heaven, having great authority, and the earth was illuminated with his glory. Rev. 18:1.

When the Islamic nation of Malaysia sent its first astronaut into space in 2007, a major quandary was how a faithful Muslim on the international space station was to pray five times a day when each day in space is only 90 minutes long. And so engineers designed a unique computer program, "Muslims in Space," where through spherical trigonometry space-bound Muslims can calculate both when to pray and what direction in space to face in order to pray toward Mecca. The program links all of this with standard Greenwich time, so astronauts can pray at both the correct time on earth and the correct time they perceive on the space station. Just a lot of silly busywork? One could wish we were as carefully focused on praying to God!

Today's text declares that just before Jesus returns, the entire planet will be bathed in a mighty global revival of divine glory. Will that include the 1.4 billion Muslims on earth today? Why would we think otherwise? Consider these statistics regarding contemporary Islam. Like Judaism and Christianity, Islam is classified as an Abrahamic monotheistic religion. Its nearly 1.5 billion adherents make Islam the second-largest religion in the world. It is the second-largest religion in the U.K. and Europe, and it soon will become so in the U.S. as well. The majority of Muslims are not Arabs; only 20 percent of Muslims originate from Middle East countries. In fact, the largest Muslim nation on earth is Indonesia. Muslims today are a majority in 45 African and Asian countries. And a United Nations demographic report forecasts that Muslims will represent at least half of the global birthrate after the year 2055.

And who was Muhammad? He was born into the polytheistic Quraish tribe in Mecca around A.D. 570. Soon orphaned and raised by an uncle, at age 25 Muhammad married a wealthy widow. Fifteen years later, in a cave, he received a vision from the angel Gabriel, visions that continued for 12 years. In obedience to the angel, Muhammad began to teach that there was only one true God, Allah. His message of monotheism met strong resistance. But in 630 he and his forces retook Mecca, making it the center for Islamic worship that it is today. Twenty years after his death his visions were transcribed and codified into the Qur'an. Could it be that into the darkness of paganism God ignited the faint light of truth? After all, He had done it before.

STAR RISING OVER ISLAM—2

And the Angel of the Lord said to her: "Behold, you are with child, and you shall bear a son. You shall call his name Ishmael, because the Lord has heard your affliction." Gen. 16:11.

Tucked away in a familiar story are three surprises you may never have seen be-fore. Once upon a time there was a man with a very beautiful wife. They were homeless but happy. Well, not quite homeless—though their home in this fertile but forsaken stretch of Canaanite land was hardly like the affluent one they'd left behind in Iraq. And, not quite happy—because the couple was childless. And so the wife concocted a plan. Her husband would marry her Egyptian servant, and the baby born would become their heir. He did, and it worked like a charm. Until jeal-ousy won, and the angry wife drove out the servant girl with an attitude.

But the story of Hagar the Egyptian handmaid was just beginning, though you wouldn't think so, given her tears beside a wilderness spring. But suddenly the first of three surprises occured when "the Angel of the Lord found her" (Gen. 16:7). Note that this is the first appearance of the Divine Angel ("I AM") in all of Scripture. And He appeared to an *Egyptian* maid. And if that were not enough, He quickly an-nounced that she would bear a son and she was to name him Ishmael, meaning "God hears," because God indeed had heard the young mother's prayer. Surprise number two—this is the first time in recorded sacred history that God chose to name a baby. And the first baby God named was *Ishmael*, the father of the *Arabs*. And when the Angel had finished His instructions, Hagar responded with reverent joy. "Then she called the name of the Lord who spoke to her, You-Are-the-God-Who-Sees; for she said, 'Have I also here seen Him who sees me?'" (Gen. 16:13). Surprise number three—this is the first time any human in the Bible story testified to seeing God. And she was an Egyptian maid. Three great firsts in Holy Scripture, and they all have to do the Egyptian mother of Ishmael, the father of the Arabs.

Is it all a coincidence? Or did God intentionally plant the seeds of divine des-tiny in the story of the birth of Ishmael and the Arab people? Could it be, then, that in the dark hour of Middle East history, when polytheism raged through the nomadic tribes, the God of Abraham, who longed to rekindle His light and faith among the children of Ishmael, raised up the earthen voice of Muhammad to call His wayward children back to the Creator God? And if the children of Ishmael are that important to God, should they not be the same to us, too?

STAR RISING OVER ISLAM—3

Then Midianite traders passed by; so the brothers pulled Joseph up and lifted him out of the pit, and sold him to the Ishmaelites for twenty shekels of silver. And they took Joseph to Egypt. Gen. 37:28.

Is Islam in Bible prophecy? Martin Luther believed so. So did Isaac Newton, John Wesley, Joseph Mede, Uriah Smith, and J. N. Andrews—to name a few others. For it is the bedrock of the historicist interpretation of Revelation 9 that sees the forces of Islam as divinely guided judgments against the apostate church and nations of the Dark Ages. Consider how strategic the children of Ishmael have been in the divine master plan.

Today's text captures that heartbreaking moment when Joseph's jealous brothers hauled him out of the pit and opted to sell him as a slave, rather than kill him. And who were the traders who came loping by in their caravan? The Ishmaelites—whom God used to transport Joseph to Egypt and a future that would result in the salvation of His people. How did Joseph put it to his brothers when, as governor, he revealed himself to them? "God sent me ahead of you to preserve for you a remnant on earth and to save your lives by a great deliverance" (Gen. 45:7, NIV). Unbeknown to all, the Ishmaelites were divine agents in preserving a remnant.

Story number two concerns the beloved Wise Men of the Christmas gospel. Who were they? We can agree that they were divinely appointed agents to draw the attention of the faith community to the coming Messiah. Scholars concur the Magi were children of the East. Is it coincidental that God has used the descendants of Ishmael to assist Him in preserving truth?

Story number three is beyond the covers of the Bible. In 1529, just as Emperor Charles V was marching on the princes of Germany (who that year embraced the name "Protestant") to crush their spiritual rebellion against Rome's ecclesiastical hegemony, suddenly the Ottoman Turks advanced to the very gates of Vienna, and the emperor was forced to abandon his effort to destroy the fledgling Reformation. A coincidence . . . or a divine intervention just long enough for the Reformation to burst into flames beyond extinguishing once the Turks had retreated?

Could it be that the children of Abraham through his son Ishmael have ever held a special place in God's heart and a unique role in earth's history? Could they even now be providing a critical window once again? Surely the mission of the chosen must embrace the Muslims, too.

STAR RISING OVER ISLAM—4

It has always been my ambition to preach the gospel where Christ was not known, so that I would not be building on someone else's foundation. Rather, as it is written: "Those who were not told about him will see, and those who have not heard will understand."
Rom. 15:20, 21, NIV.

So what shall we do, how shall we respond? First, we can reject the belittling, berating language adopted by some in the West. The epithet "Islamofascists" demeans an entire people and religion on account of a radical minority. How would we like it if someone coined the words "Christofascists" and "Adventistofascists"? Every religion has its fanatical minority. But to call a religion satanic because of extremists is hardly a manifestation of the Christian golden rule.

Second, there is one community of faith on earth that is positioned to bridge God's final appeal to all three monotheistic religions. It is perfectly positioned to reach Christendom, for this community of faith is the heart of Christianity recovered in all the Bible truths. It is perfectly positioned to reach the Jewish world, for, as we noted in August, this community of faith is essentially Judaism with the Messiah. And this same community of faith is perfectly positioned to reach Islam—for with Muslims it embraces the one God of Abraham and His teachings in the sacred Book; with them it champions the body temple of Allah, where neither pork nor alcohol shall reside; with them refusing to bow down to idols; with them serving the poor of earth in works of mercy; with them passionately praying morning and noon and night to God; and with them acknowledging the mighty final judgment of God after which Jesus of Nazareth will return. Seventh-day Adventists have been raised up by God for such a time as this, as a vital bridge to all three monotheistic communities. And now more than ever it is clear that the divine mission includes our Muslim neighbors, colleagues, and communities around us.

Third, let us begin to pray for the vast regions of Islam that one day will be lightened with Revelation 18:1's final burst of divine glory. Some of us reading these words right now will answer our own prayers, becoming cross-cultural bridge builders for God in a Muslim community somewhere on earth. Others of us will provide financial support for organizations seeking to skillfully, sensitively communicate "the everlasting gospel." Paul's ambition in today's text is bold and clear—it's OK to be passionate about mobilizing God's truth to all!

HOME ALONE?

Remember now your Creator in the days of your youth, before the difficult days come, and the years draw near when you say, "I have no pleasure in them." Eccl. 12:1.

Did you know that 75 percent of all Christians in America today accepted Christ *before age 14*? I didn't either. Three out of every four men and women who bear the name of Christ chose Him to be their Savior sometime between birth and 13 years of age. Do you know what that means? It means: (1) that the most fertile, receptive target group for *all spiritual endeavor* is before a child turns 14; (2) that the most successful evangelistic rate on earth is among the literal children of earth; and (3) that the most significant investment the church can make is to pour its resources and personnel into the lives of its youngest. Could that be why both the kingdom of light and the kingdom of darkness are investing so heavily in our children?

In his book *Transforming Children Into Spiritual Champions: Why Children Should Be Your Church's #1 Priority*, George Barna, the Christian demographer, compiles an intriguing statistical profile of American young. Here's a sampling: of the 31 million children in the 5-to-12 age bracket, more than four out of five use a computer regularly in school; kids between ages 2 and 7 average nearly 25 hours per week of mass media, with the number jumping to 48 hours a week for ages 8 to 13. Forty-four percent of all preteens admit they have no role model; when naming the three most important people in the world to them, only one out of three names a mother or father; even so, nine out of 10 of them say they get along well with their parents; and one third of 8- to 12-year-olds say they want to spend more time with their mother.

But setting aside his pages of statistics, consider Barna's most stunning conclusion: "We discovered that the probability of someone embracing Jesus as his or her Savior was 32 percent for those between the ages of 5 and 12; 4 percent for those in the 13-to-18 age range; and 6 percent for those 19 or older. *In other words, if people do not embrace Jesus Christ as their Savior before they reach their teenage years, the chance of their doing so at all is slim*" (p. 34; italics supplied).

Barna isn't Solomon. But they both confirm the same reality. For God and faith, the very best days, the halcyon days of childhood innocence are heaven's prime time for securing a lasting, lifelong relationship with God and our beloved Creator. We may roam the world for Christ, but all the while our greatest and most successful mission waits for us at home.

THE GREAT APPOINTMENT

Son of man, I have made you a watchman for the house of Israel;
so hear the word I speak and give them warning from me. Eze. 33:7, NIV.

Abraham Lincoln once quipped that people who boast about their ancestors are like a field of potatoes—the best part is underground. Could that be true of us who are the inheritors of the Millerite movement's passionate fervor for the return of Christ? A glance at the calendar reminds us that 168 years ago this very moment, men, women, and children up and down the Eastern seaboard of the still-youthful United States were gathered in parlors and kitchens, in fields and barns and tabernacles—clustered together with those they loved in solemn but joyful expectation that sometime between this moment and midnight Jesus would come. What if you and I believed that right now? Can you imagine the comingling of electric hope and restless uncertainty that would grip our hearts while we watched the clock and waited?

Our text today was the fiery-hot injunction that the middle-aged Baptist farmer and Bible student William Miller could not shake. For 13 long years in his Low Hampton, New York, farmhouse he had crunched the numbers of prophecy backward and forward to assure the logic and integrity of his study. And every time his calculations circled back to the same conclusion—Christ would return by the middle 1840s. Shouldn't he sound the warning? But how could he, a country farmer? "When I was about my business," he said, "it was continually ringing in my ears, 'Go and tell the world of their danger.' . . . I felt that if the wicked could be effectually warned, multitudes of them would repent; and that if they were not warned, their blood might be required at my hand" (*The Great Controversy,* p. 330). The internal struggle was so intense that finally in August 1831 Miller promised God that if he received an invitation to share his dramatic conclusion from prophecy, he would accept. Within minutes a knock at the door brought that invitation. Miller stumbled into a nearby maple grove to pray. The man who emerged went on to lead one of the greatest spiritual revivals in American history, with tens of thousands of people eagerly awaiting the return of Jesus on October 22, 1844.

But they were wrong. Or were they? Could it be that as their spiritual children, we have been called to embrace the same fervency, the same mission, the same passion for the same Jesus? Could it be their disappointment is our appointment to finish what they began?

THE RECRUITS — 1

Your people will offer themselves willingly on the day you lead your forces on the holy mountains. From the womb of the morning, like dew, your youth will come to you.
Ps. 110:3, NRSV.

Stephen Ambrose, the biographer of General Dwight D. Eisenhower, described how Eisenhower intentionally chose young, inexperienced, but highly trained troops for the assault on Normandy (D-Day) in World War II. He knew that experienced soldiers are terrified soldiers, cognizant from experience of what a bullet can do. On the other hand, younger troops, full of youthful bluster, are much more willing to march into withering fire. Ambrose observed that there is something to be said for inexperience.

In one stirring line Psalm 110 describes the army recruited by the Messiah for His divine mission. And as today's text reveals, the messianic recruits are young: "On the day you [the Messiah] lead your forces [armies] on the holy mountains . . . like dew, your youth will come to you." What a thrilling prospect! Living as we are on the eve and edge of eternity, the words of this ancient prophecy are a prediction that in the Messiah's last offensive on earth, like the morning dew the young will flock to Him. I love that promise! Having the privilege of watching young adults up close on a university campus—thousands of them over the years—I humbly wish to attest to the wisdom of a Messiah who would heavily recruit among the young. Their refreshing blend of idealism with the savvy realism of this generation, the combination of their value clarification with a strong desire to commit to something worth dying for creates a potential army of raw and yet refined recruits who are ready for mobilization.

No wonder a century ago these words were written: "With such an army of workers as our youth, rightly trained, might furnish, how soon the message of a crucified, risen, and soon-coming Savior might be carried to the whole world! How soon might the end come—the end of suffering and sorrow and sin!" (*Education*, p. 271).

You see, it's true. Wise generals have learned that when you're in a war, young, inexperienced but highly trained recruits are the ones you choose to move to the front lines, if you wish to accelerate your mission and complete it successfully. General Eisenhower was on to something. So is the Messiah. And so must the chosen be—now more than ever—the young!

THE RECRUITS—2

Don't let anyone look down on you because you are young, but set an example for the believers in speech, in life, in love, in faith and in purity. 1 Tim. 4:12, NIV.

Several years ago a young man working at a Boston investment firm applied for a senior leadership position at a Chicago bank. The Chicago bank wrote the Boston company, asking for a recommendation, and the Boston firm happily complied. In fact, they couldn't say enough about the young professional: his father, they wrote, was a Cabot (a storied name in Boston's history); his mother was a Lowell; and further back was a happy blend of Saltonstalls, Peabodys, and others of Boston's first families. Several days later the Chicago bank sent a note back to Boston saying the information supplied was altogether inadequate. The note read: "We are not contemplating using the young man for breeding purposes. Just for work."

God did not raise up this generation to rest on the laurels of our pioneers, admirable though their commitment to Christ was. God instead is raising up a new youthful generation with names from all over the earth. Not for breeding purposes—but for the work of the Messiah. It is the greatest mission ever entrusted to a single generation! Remember yesterday's quotation, "With such an army of workers as our youth . . ."? At the beginning of that same chapter, "The Lifework," appear these words: "Success in any line demands a definite aim. [Those] who would achieve true success in life must keep steadily in view the aim worthy of [their] endeavor. *Such an aim is set before the youth of today.* The heaven-appointed purpose of giving the gospel to the world in this generation is *the noblest that can appeal to any human being.* It opens a field of effort to everyone whose heart Christ has touched" (*Education*, p. 262; italics supplied).

Are you young? And has Christ touched your heart? Then, my young friend, this promise and this passion are yours! The Messiah of heaven is eager to recruit you into His end-time army.

You are on this planet because He chose you to exist. Whatever is focusing your future and your career, remember your King has first claim on your life—to recruit you to His side, to train you for His mission, and then to mobilize you to the place on earth where He needs you. There is no higher calling than His, no greater mission than this. So are you willing to enlist . . . right now?

THE RECRUITS—3

These are the ones who follow the Lamb wherever He goes. These were redeemed from among men, being firstfruits to God and to the Lamb. Rev. 14:4.

What you've just read is a description of the Messiah's last army on earth. Isn't it remarkable that gathered from across the face of the earth, this final generation of recruits is boldly identified as a people "who follow the Lamb wherever He goes"? Are they only the young? Of course not. But as we noted two days ago, Psalm 110 goes out of its way to identify the recruits that flock to the Messiah's army: "Arrayed in holy splendor, your young . . . will come to you like dew from the morning's womb" (Ps. 110:3, TNIV). One author describes the influx of these young recruits "as copious as the dew." Derek Kidner's commentary portrays them as "a splendid army silently and suddenly mobilized." They are the young of the chosen!

And where do they go? They follow the Messiah Lamb wherever He goes. And where does He go? "Many feel that it would be a great privilege to visit the scenes of Christ's life on earth, to walk where He trod, to look upon the lake beside which He loved to teach, and the hills and valleys on which His eyes so often rested. But we need not go to Nazareth, to Capernaum, or to Bethany, in order to walk in the steps of Jesus. We shall find His footprints *beside the sickbed, in the hovels of poverty, in the crowded alleys of the great city, and in every place where there are human hearts in need of consolation.* In doing as Jesus did when on earth, we shall walk in His steps" (*The Desire of Ages,* p. 640; italics supplied). God give us such a generation today!

In a Düsseldorf art gallery a young German university student stood transfixed before the oiled canvass of Domenico Feti's *Ecce Homo* ("Behold the Man"). In silence he stared into that portrayal of Jesus with His crown of thorns. But what won his heart to Christ were the words inscribed at the bottom of the painting: "All this I did for thee—what doest thou for me?" He left the gallery, returned to his campus and formed his friends into the "Order of the Grain of Mustard Seed"—a band of young that eventually would become the most expansive missionary movement in the history of the church, the Moravians. The young man? Count Nicholas von Zinzendorf. He and his followers adopted the Latin motto: *Vicit agnus noster, eum sequamur*—"Our Lamb has conquered, him let us follow." For the mark of a great movement is the ability to follow. And they "follow the Lamb wherever He goes." I, too, want to follow—don't you?

THE RECRUITS—4

May our sons flourish in their youth like well-nurtured plants. May our daughters be like graceful pillars, carved to beautify a palace. Ps. 144:12, NLT.

So how can we mobilize this generation of young within the community of the chosen? Here are seven simple ways to make a spiritual difference in the life of the young.

1. Ask God to make you a mentor to them. In his book *Lost and Found: The Younger Unchurched and the Churches That Reach Them* Ed Stetzer reminds us: "Too many young adults today have no one to turn to when it comes to the tough questions of life (faith, marriage, life, and work) and also the practical questions of life (changing my oil, preparing my taxes, making my budget work, building a resume). . . . Churches that connect generations can be wonderful bodies of believers who respect each other in every facet of congregational life" (pp. 134, 135). I've been surprised at the number of university students who have told me, "Invite us into your homes. We want to be around older adults whose counsel we can trust." Be a mentor.

2. Go deep with them. We mistakenly assume the young aren't interested in serious thought and truth—they just want to play. Not so. They're not interested in "ankle-deep." They want to think, and they want to think deeply. So open up your home on a Friday evening to them and share an old-fashioned Bible study. Invite them to join your Sabbath school class.

3. Model your values to them. We're foolish to think that we must dress like them, talk like them, behave like them in order to influence them. It's the other way around. They want you to be "an old fuddy-duddy" who articulates strong conviction and models it. Compromising our values or standards in an effort to win the young backfires. They'll eventually discern our hypocrisy and reject it. In one major survey, only 31 percent of unchurched young adults said yes to this statement: "If music at church sounded similar to my favorite type of music, I would be more likely to attend" (Stetzer, p. 38). That is, seven out of 10 said we don't have to mimic their music in order to attract their interest. Stand up for your values and win their hearts.

4. Draw them into a community of a small group. A sense of community is huge for the young. Invite them along with a couple of their friends and yours into a small group. Sociological profiles reveal this generation wants to belong and *then* believe. Belong-believe-become is the sequence that can win their hearts to Jesus *and* His mission for them.

310

THE RECRUITS—5

For You are my hope, O Lord God; You are my trust from my youth. By You I have been upheld from birth; You are He who took me out of my mother's womb. My praise shall be continually of You. Ps. 71:5, 6.

How can we recruit the young for the Messiah's mobilization? Our list continues.

5. Do ministry *with* them in the church. It's been that way from the very beginning, hasn't it? When we were just kids, our favorite pastime was trailing behind Daddy or Mommy and with wide eyes (and very retentive memories) watching them polish those shoes or bake that cake or repair that engine. And we nearly burst with joy when our parents actually invited us to turn that screw or stir that bowl or polish that bumper. That's how we've all learned along the way. And it's that way with ministry, too. Invite the young to join you as you lead children's Sabbath school. Enlist them as very junior "leaders" in your Pathfinder club. Have them assist the deacons with the offering, the greeters at the doors, or the PA crew in the booth. Educators the world over will tell you that the best teaching is modeled.

6. Do service *with* them in the community. According to Ed Stetzer, 66 percent of churched young adults and 47 percent of unchurched young adults "rated the opportunity to meet the needs of others (locally and globally) as extremely important in their lives" (p. 111). That is, they are big on plunging into making a difference beyond the walls of the church. Ministry to the poor and disenfranchised? Give the young adults you know the chance to join you in initiating some new community services. The effective key, remember, is to do it together. We've been amazed at how eager young adults are to join us in our inner-city mission nearby.

7. Volunteer to minister to them before they're teenagers. As we noted a few days ago, George Barna has discovered that the most fruitful window in which to lead a person to Jesus is between the ages of 5 and 12. So don't wait to minister to young adults until they're young adults. Win their hearts early; shape their minds while they're children. Mobilize their eager willingness to serve the Master when they're young.

"Remember now your Creator in the days of your youth" (Eccl. 12:1). But let's switch the two words. "Remember now your *youth* in the days of your *Creator*." All heaven is on standby to mobilize the young. So remember—because God needs them, He especially needs *you*.

WILL WE SPEAK CHINESE IN HEAVEN?

After this I looked and there before me was a great multitude that no one could count, from every nation, tribe, people and language, standing before the throne and in front of the Lamb. They were wearing white robes and were holding palm branches in their hands. Rev. 7:9, NIV.

One out of every five of earth's inhabitants lives in China—1.3 billion human beings speak Chinese. (And it seemed we bumped into half of them in the Shanghai traffic!) Look, if God decides to save China, you can count on us speaking Chinese in heaven, because there are more Chinese on earth than anybody else. But, some wonder, will God save China? Can He?

When the elderly John is shown a scene from heaven to come, did you notice how many today's text says will be there? "I looked, and behold, a great multitude which no one could number" (Rev. 7:9). The Greek word for "to number" or "to count" is *arithmesai*, from whence comes our word "arithmetic." John exclaims, "I saw so many people in heaven that nobody could do the arithmetic on them!" So how many is that? Well, it'd have to be more than the biggest number John comes up with in the Apocalypse, wouldn't it? As Dan Smith notes in his book *Lord, I Have a Question*, that number appears two chapters later, where John describes an army of 200 million horsemen (Rev. 9:16). But here John says the number is so great, it's beyond computation. The point? When God does *salvation* arithmetic, you can't begin to count His numbers!

Could that be our problem? Years ago J. B. Phillips wrote a book titled *Your God Is Too Small*. Is He too small to handle big numbers? Jonah thought so. Remember how God reminded the upset prophet that "Nineveh has more than a hundred and twenty thousand people who cannot tell their right hand from their left" (Jonah 4:11, NIV)? Who can't tell the difference between right and left? Why, a 2-year-old, of course! So if Nineveh had 120,000 little children, plus teenagers, plus adults, and seniors, that would make their population between 600,000 and 2 million. "I couldn't destroy that many!" God exclaimed. And so He saved them instead. With a God like that, is it any wonder John couldn't count the number of the redeemed in heaven?

THE GOD OF THE ELEVENTH HOUR

But he answered one of them, "Friend, I am not being unfair to you. Didn't you agree to work for a denarius? . . . Don't I have the right to do what I want with my own money? Or are you envious because I am generous?" Matt. 20:13-15, NIV.

Once upon a time there was a farmer who needed day laborers to help him harvest his sprawling vineyards. So early in the morning he jumped into his rusty pickup truck and drove into town to the corner where all the migrants who need work show up. "You guys want some work? Jump in. I'll pay you the going rate for 12 hours." The farmer drove his battered truck, now filled with migrants, back to the vineyards, where they worked hard. Three hours later the farmer realized he had to have more help if this crop was going to be harvested by sundown. So back down the road in a cloud of dust he raced. And soon another pickup load of migrants joined the crew. Another three hours, and the farmer could tell he was still behind. So for more help back he drove to town, and another pickup load showed up in the vineyards. Finally, one hour before dark the farmer mutters, "I've got to have more help—or we'll never get this done!" And when he hurried back to town he saw still more migrants standing on the corner wishing they had work. "Jump in, fellas! I need help, and I'll pay you what's fair!" That evening when the 12 hours of harvesting were through, the farmer instructed his accountant to begin with the last-hired and pay the workers. With astonished eyes and gaping mouths the eleventh-hour migrants watched as the accountant counted out a full day's wages for them! With glee the migrants who'd been there from sunup did the arithmetic and concluded they were due a bonanza payday. But when they stepped up to the cash box, they were paid the identical amount as all the others. The place erupted in angry voices. Jesus put the words of today's text in the mouth of the farmer, and it's his punch line that catches us: "Are you envious because I am generous?" (Matt. 20:15, NIV).

Could that be our problem, too? Are we envious because God is so generous? How else can you describe this God who declares, "Come to Me in the last hour of life, and I'll give you the same gift I gave to the people who walked with Me all their lives"? No wonder when God does *salvation* arithmetic, you can't even count the numbers. No wonder heaven will be so full. That's why when God mobilizes the chosen He mobilizes their hearts to be as generous as His, so that there is *no human being on earth* that they would not gladly receive into His kingdom.

THE DIVINE AUCTIONEER

Then he said to Jesus, "Lord, remember me when You come into Your kingdom." And Jesus said to him, "Assuredly, I say to you . . . you will be with Me in Paradise." Luke 23:42, 43.

Those who frequent auctions tell me that you'd better be serious when you sit down for that noisy sale. Scratch your head or even raise your little finger and the eagle-eyed auctioneer may spot your movement and declare the goods "Sold!" to you on the spot. Is God that way, too?

I had a parishioner once, a friendly woman who would call every now and then to see how we were doing. On Sabbaths she and her family would greet me. But after a while her calls began coming late at night. And then her words became more garbled. A few Sabbaths later she came through line with the smell of mouthwash heavy on her breath. The next week I drove out to their home. She was out in her garden, and we visited for a bit. Then I asked, "How long have you been struggling with alcohol?" Her gaze dropped, and she nodded her head. We talked of Alcoholics Anonymous and God's power to free her and His merciful forgiveness, and after prayer I left. The midnight calls tapered off. But I wondered how it was. One Sunday afternoon her husband called with word that she was in the hospital intensive-care unit—alcoholic liver failure. It didn't look good; the children were flying in. Could I come? I hurried up to her room. Weak and tired, she couldn't talk much. The three of us prayed. Not long after, she died.

The family requested a private graveside service. One of the children came up to me: "We think you ought to know how Mother died." After she had slipped into a coma, there was a moment in the evening when she came to. Seeing the children about her, she whispered, "Would you sing me the songs of Jesus?" And so with tears they did. Mother smiled faintly as she listened. A short time later she lapsed back into unconsciousness and died. But in her dying request to hear once more the songs of Jesus, the family found great comfort.

And so did I as I drove home from her grave. I could picture Him, the Divine Auctioneer, bent low—breathlessly watching for even the slightest sign that in her eleventh hour His daughter wanted His salvation. And when she had raised, as it were, her little finger toward heaven, He cried out with a joy we shall never quite understand, "Sold to my child in the hospital bed!" Just like the thief on the cross. Is it any wonder Paradise will be so full? And is it any wonder our mission is so urgent? In this eleventh hour we must reach them for Him.

THE PRAYER OF JABEZ

And Jabez called on the God of Israel saying, "Oh, that You would bless me indeed, and enlarge my territory, that Your hand would be with me, and that You would keep me from evil, that I may not cause pain!" So God granted him what he requested. 1 Chron. 4:10.

Look—if all this number crunching is true, and God really is very *big* on saving sinners—then doesn't it follow that the children of God like you and me are to be big on saving them, too? Isn't that what the mobilization of the chosen is all about?

Bruce Wilkinson, who wrote the megabestseller *The Prayer of Jabez*, wrote a sequel, *Beyond Jabez*. In referring to John's vision of heaven being filled with so many saved sinners that no one could possibly count them, Wilkinson makes this stirring appeal: "God has shown us how our story ends—with countless people from every nation on earth crying out joyfully to God [Rev. 7:9, 10]. What part of that throng will be there because of you? What part of God's dream is linked to your destiny?" (p. 108). The truth is—you have a destiny, and God has a dream. And the great object of life is to align our destinies with His dream. Whatever your career choice, whatever your occupation and mine—our destiny remains unchanged. Wilkinson goes on: "Just think what a difference you could make in many, many lives if you were to pray passionately and faithfully for enlarged territory from God, for God. Imagine the miraculous divine partnership that will grow out of your plea, *Let me accomplish more for you.* With His infinite ability and your willing availability, He can literally do anything" (*ibid.*). Do you believe that? Do you believe God believes that . . . that if the chosen were willing and available, He could literally turn the world upside down in a single generation?

But you say, "Oh, that's just a best-selling author filling a page with words." Consider then this solitary line from *The Desire of Ages*: "There is no limit to the usefulness of one who, by putting self aside, makes room for the working of the Holy Spirit upon his heart, and lives a life wholly consecrated to God" (pp. 250, 251). Do you believe that? Enough to act on it?

Then let us end this month with a simple two-question quiz—yes or no. 1. By the grace of God, do you want to be there in heaven's innumerable throng? 2. By the grace of God, do you want to help Him add people to that throng one day? How could we say no to either? Then by the grace of Calvary's God, let us roll up our sleeves and go for Him!

HOLY, HOLELY, WHOLLY—1

For the Lord has chosen Jacob for Himself, Israel for His special treasure. For I know that the Lord is great, and our Lord is above all gods. Ps. 135:4, 5.

I'll never forget that afternoon as long as I live. The countdown clock was ticking toward the first Sabbath of a new school year. But on Thursday as I sat at my study desk, commentaries and books piled high, the sermon just wasn't coming. Everywhere I turned, I kept running headlong into a subject that I had no heart to plunge into. In fact, it was the one subject my pastoral colleagues and I across the land have studiously avoided. But try as I might, I couldn't. Late that evening I pushed away from a blank sheet of paper and headed to the office to sign some letters. Before returning home, I stepped into the dark sanctuary, I prayed that God would somehow move me past the mental logjam and give me a sense of what He wanted me to preach on opening Sabbath. But the next morning my calendar was packed—a devotional at our church school, then opening convocation at the university—when my secretary called to say a woman was at the office, saying she wasn't going to eat until she talked with me. (Now, there's a new dieting twist!) But there was no way I could sit down with her until that afternoon.

She was one of our prayer warriors, and she was there waiting. "I have to talk to you. When I was praying last night, I felt impressed to go to my shelf and pull down a book. And then after further praying, the Lord impressed me to tell you that this is what you should preach on this Sabbath." By now electricity was running up and down my spine. "Let me see that book!" She handed me *The Great Controversy,* open to these words: "We are now living in the great day of atonement. . . . Solemn are the scenes connected with the closing work of the atonement. Momentous are the interests involved therein. The judgment is now passing in the sanctuary above. For many years this work has been in progress. Soon—none know how soon—it will pass to the cases of the living" (pp. 489, 490). When I returned home, my own copy was opened to that same page. I've never had a more dramatic answer to a prayer over what to preach.

But then, what if it were true—that "the hour of his judgment is come" (Rev. 14:7, KJV)? That there really is a sanctuary in heaven where "the court [is] seated, and the books [are] opened" right now (Dan. 7:10)? Would it make a difference in the way you and I lived with Jesus, for Jesus today? But then again, why wouldn't it?

HOLY, HOLELY, WHOLLY—2

And you shall be holy to Me, for I the Lord am holy, and have separated you from the peoples, that you should be Mine. Lev. 20:26.

Could it be that the best way to come to terms with that troublesome four-letter word, "holy," is to learn to misspell it? After all, there is no way we can eliminate the word from the vocabulary of Holy Scripture (there it is again). But why should we? Did you know that it is the only attribute of God that is given trifold expression in the Bible? Nowhere in the Bible do we read, "Love, love, love—God is love," or "Just, just, just—God is just." The only divine characteristic that is magnified with a three-fold expression is "Holy, holy, holy is the Lord of hosts; the whole earth is full of His glory!" and "Holy, holy, holy, Lord God Almighty, Who was and is and is to come!" (Isa. 6:3; Rev. 4:8). Old Testament, New Testament—the holiness of God is exalted before the universe. To the exclusion of His love and His justice? Hardly! Divine holiness is like white light that when refracted by a prism shimmers in all the majestic colors of a rainbow. Even so His holiness is the transcendent summation of all that is glorious and good about our God, refracted out into the love and mercy and righteousness and justice that is He. No wonder both threefold expressions come from the lips of created beings who with unbridled joy and reverent awe bow down to worship the Creator God of the universe. "Holy" is He indeed!

But what is so astounding is that God takes that very attribute of His and calls for it (commands it, really) to be a manifest reality in His chosen ones. Not only in our Old Testament text today. But also in the heart of the New Testament: "But just as he who called you is holy, so be holy in all you do; for it is written: 'Be holy, because I am holy'" (1 Peter 1:15, 16, NIV).

So what would happen if we learned to misspell the word "holy" in order to get it right? That's right—w-h-o-l-l-y for "holy." Isn't that how we've taught our children God made the Sabbath holy, taking seven pennies, spreading them out on a table and sliding the seventh penny (day) to the side to show the Sabbath as "wholly" God's? Didn't we illustrate God's tithe the same way, lining up 10 pennies on a table and then sliding the tenth penny to the side to show the tithe as "wholly" God's? Holy Sabbath, holy tithe, holy people—God puts His finger on them and separates them. "They are mine—wholly mine—holy and mine." And what could be better than to discover that we belong wholly to our loving God—that we are wholly His?

HOLY, HOLELY, WHOLLY—3

Since we have these promises, beloved, let us cleanse ourselves from every defilement of body and of spirit, making holiness perfect in the fear of God. 2 Cor. 7:1, NRSV.

What do being holy (being "wholly God's") and an end-time judgment have to do with each other? In the Hebrew it's called *Yom Kippur*, or "the Day of Atonement." The Jews still celebrate it today, that Leviticus 16 day when the entire community of Israel gathered at the doors of the sanctuary for a solemn liturgical annual ritual that portrayed God's final strategic eradication of sin. It was a mini-judgment day, a symbolic cleansing of the sanctuary and a spiritual cleansing of the chosen ones, expunging from the sanctuary (and from their hearts) the record of their sins. It was a deeply solemn day, since it was the only day of the year that the high priest would enter the very Shekinah glory of God's presence in the small tabernacle cubicle of the Most Holy Place, sprinkling the blood of the sacrifice upon the mercy seat of the golden ark. "On this day atonement will be made for you, to cleanse you. Then, before the Lord, you will be clean from all your sins" (Lev. 16:30, NIV)—a day of "at-one-ment" between God and His chosen ones, cleansing them to be "wholly His," made holy by His relentless grace.

An apocalyptic cleansing of heaven's sanctuary (Heb. 8:1, 2; 9:23, 24) was predicted by Daniel 8:14 and Revelation 14:7 to be the final chapter in heaven's response to Lucifer's earth rebellion before the second coming of Jesus. Since October 22, 1844, the urgent message, "The hour of his judgment has come," has been repeated generation after generation. "Prepare to meet your God, O Israel!" (Amos 4:12, NIV) It's cleansing time. Then why hasn't the divine pre-Advent judgment ended? What is taking God so long to wrap up our rebellion on earth? It is precisely those questions that have kept both pastors and people from relishing any return to a public conversation about heaven's final *Yom Kippur*. To suggest we are simply not ready for Christ to return is to invite the criticism that such thinking is misguided at best and legalistic at worst.

But what if it were the truth? What if all of heaven were poised, ready in a heartbeat to interpose a divine outpouring of spiritual grace and power upon a languishing people? What if the chosen became so passionate about a "wholly yours" devotion to Christ and renunciation of Lucifer that "perfecting holiness ["wholliness"] in the fear of God" (2 Cor. 7:1) were what we sought for most of all in Jesus? Is it legalism to deeply want what God has earnestly promised?

HOLY, HOLELY, WHOLLY—4

How much more, then, will the blood of Christ, who through the eternal Spirit offered himself unblemished to God, cleanse our consciences from acts that lead to death, so that we may serve the living God! Heb. 9:14, NIV.

I was amazed to learn that there is a mountain hidden in the first five books of the Bible—a mountain with two slopes and a towering peak. Scholars call these "hidden" literary mountains "chiasms"—unique devices whereby Bible writers were able to hide thematic mountains of matching parallel thought inside the Hebrew and Greek texts. Writers developed chiasms to draw the discerning reader's attention to the mountain's pinnacle, the apex truth or focus of the passage or book, or, in the case of the Pentateuch, the summit of all five books. For the first five books of the Bible, all written by Moses, are a chiasm. Picture a triangle, and on the left slope at the bottom is Genesis. On the opposite side of the triangle on the bottom is Deuteronomy. Both books share amazing literary parallels. Following Genesis up the left slope of the chiasm comes Exodus, and up the right slope comes its parallel, Numbers (the book before Deuteronomy). And occupying the pinnacle of the chiasm is the remaining book, Leviticus.

But William Shea and Richard Davidson discovered that Leviticus itself is a chiasm with chapter 1 on the left slope and chapter 27 on the right slope, etc. And climbing up the slopes, what is the peak to Leviticus (and by extension, the Pentateuch), the summit chapter? Leviticus 16—the chapter on the Day of Atonement and the cleansing of the sanctuary!

But there's more. Shea and Davidson observe that the key word going up the left slope of the Leviticus chiasm is "blood," used more than 60 times in chapters 1 through 16. And the key word down the right slope is "holy," used more than 60 times from chapter 16 to the end. And at the pinnacle the Day of Atonement takes those twin themes, divine sacrifice ("blood") and human holiness ("holy"), and unites them. Mark it carefully: *God's call for* our *holiness is premised upon God's gift of* His *salvation.* Up one side of the mountain God declares through the sacrifices, "I gave my life *wholly for you.*" Down the other side of the mountain He calls out, "Now live your life *wholly for Me.*" So don't let anybody try to tell you that the cleansing of the sanctuary and an end-time pre-Advent judgment are about grace-less legalism. The two sides of one mountain teach us otherwise. No wonder the chosen thank God for a mountain called Calvary!

THE CHOSEN STORIES—1

*These are all warning markers—DANGER!—in our history books, written down so
that we don't repeat their mistakes. Our positions in the story are parallel—they at the beginning, we at the end—and we are just as capable of messing it up as they were.*
1 Cor. 10:11, Message.

Once upon a time there was a generation of chosen on their way to the
Promised Land. And as our text today provocatively observes, their story was
preserved as a morality play for another generation, also chosen and also on their
way to the Promised Land.

It was one of those glorious, cloudless desert mornings—cloudless, that is, except for the rumbling black mass of billows streaked with lightning atop the summit of this desert mountain. For days now their leader had been gone. Who knew
the fate he had suffered on top? And where was this God that had abandoned them
here in this wilderness? Finally a very large delegation of those disgruntled liberated slaves accosted the second in command and demanded that he, as surrogate
leader, make them a new god. And because he wasn't one to stand up against the
crowd, he complied. "Give me your earrings, the jewelry the Egyptians heaped on
you in the mighty exodus, and I'll sculpt for you a new god."

And sure enough, hours later a shiny golden calf stood in the midst of the camp.
"This is your god, O Israel, that brought you out of the land of Egypt!" (Ex. 32:4).
It's party time for the chosen! And party they did from sunup to sundown, a de-
bauchery so perverted that the story uses the same Hebrew word in Genesis that
describes sexual intercourse. Embracing the debased worship cult of fallen Egypt
they had left behind, the chosen lapsed into a frenzied orgy so loud and raucous that
Moses and his aide-de-camp, Joshua, could hear it from the distant Sinai slope. It
was not a pretty scene when the two of them, cloistered in the very presence of the
living God for 40 days and nights, came striding back into camp. In an instant a
painful hush fell over the mob. With a cry of despair Moses hurled the tablets fresh
with the divine handwriting, shattering them before the cowering crowd.

How quickly our redeemed hearts can return to bondage! One day we are
wholly His. But let our communion with Christ lapse for a spell, and how sad that
we can pull a U-turn in that "path of holiness." No wonder that for us on the borders of the Promised Land, "wholliness" to God is hardly the byproduct of fanati-
cism, but rather the fruit of our walk with Jesus, who has become for us "our
righteousness, holiness and redemption" (1 Cor. 1:30, NIV).

THE CHOSEN STORIES—2

So Moses went back to the Lord and said, "Oh, what a great sin these people have committed! They have made themselves gods of gold. But now, please forgive their sin— but if not, then blot me out of the book you have written." Ex. 32:31, 32, NIV.

A. J. Jacobs, the agnostic editor at large for *Esquire* magazine, set out one day to discover what it meant to "live biblically." So for 12 months he lived by the literal word of the Hebrew Scriptures—no shaving, following the Ten Commandments, no wearing of clothes of mixed fibers, love your neighbor, etc. When the year had passed, he wrote the book *The Year of Living Biblically.* Not a bad idea at all for the chosen, wouldn't you say? Once upon a time there was a people who were the chosen. And they suffered through a terrible moral melt-down. But out of that crisis they were taught two critical lessons, two vital teach-ings in order for the chosen today to learn how to live biblically.

Moses was heartbroken. These were his people—he their surrogate spiritual fa-ther. The camp was in shambles. Those who had survived the terrible plague were broken and repentant. What's a God to do? Moses begged for divine forgiveness on behalf of the chosen. If not, as our text today records, "then blot me out of the book you have written."

The magnitude of such a self-sacrificing love—the love of a leader for his way-ward people—is unparalleled in Scripture save for Paul and Jesus. But the pre-in-carnate Christ, to whom Moses was pleading, knew that for the chosen this was a moment of critical learning.

Lesson 1—a revival of morality leads to a revival of modesty. The orig-inal language of the story makes it clear that in their frenzy the children of Israel had disrobed. And when they became unclothed, they became uncontrolled, be-cause modesty is a protective wall for sexuality. So for whose eyes do we dress today? The pictures that are archived on Facebook and other social network sites can come back to haunt us, as graduate school applicants have discovered too late. But it is no longer just the young in need of modesty. For whose eyes are *we* dress-ing? Jesus was frank: "Whoever looks at a woman to lust for her has already com-mitted adultery with her in his heart" (Matt. 5:28). If you're dressing for his eyes, you may be dabbling with his fall. Men or women—it cuts both ways. That's why the strength of the chosen comes through the gaze of their hearts: "Let us fix our eyes on Jesus" (Heb. 12:2, NIV). So keep your eyes on Him!

THE CHOSEN STORIES—3

*But those who obey God's word truly show how completely they love him.
That is how we know we are living in him. Those who say they live in God
should live their lives as Jesus did. 1 John 2:5, 6, NLT.*

Lesson 2—a revival of spirituality leads to a revival of simplicity. Help me out, please. Having lived on a university campus all these years, I've listened to the honest but frank challenges the young bring to the community of the chosen. "Explain to me, please, why it is that if you move a cluster of five diamonds six inches, the forbidden cluster becomes acceptable." And they point from their earlobe down a few inches to where a broach is pinned on a dress. Or: "Please explain to me how you can condemn $5 ear studs and at the same time drive a $50,000 car or an $80,000 motor home." Fair enough. The truth is, modest simplicity cuts both ways, doesn't it? Isn't it a bit incongruous to imagine a God in the universe who could consistently call us to abandon external ornamentation but not have a word to say about houses that are vastly above our economic station or vastly beyond our personal need?

So what if we all chose to live by the same simplicity? It is more than coincidental that at two crucial junctures in the history of the chosen, the community of faith chose the same response. The runaway Jacob is returning home with a sprawling family and accumulated flocks. God meets him on the borders of the Promised Land and calls him to come to worship at Bethel, the site of the long-ago ladder to heaven. Jacob summons his family to relay God's appeal, and in response they bury their ornaments beneath an oak tree (Gen. 35:1-4). Amazingly, the children of Israel make the identical response at the foot of Mount Sinai after their moral meltdown. "So the sons of Israel stripped themselves of their ornaments, from Mount Horeb onward" (Ex. 33:6, NASB). Scholars believe that this second revival resulted in a lasting abandonment of *ornamental* jewelry by the community of faith (proscribed crowns and signet rings remained). What's up? When the God who initiated both spiritual revivals came in person to live among us—this God who could rightfully wear every gem and crown in the universe—He incarnated the value of divine simplicity. At His death they gambled for the only robe He possessed—no house, no coins, nothing but a life of modest simplicity. Deep spirituality, radical simplicity—therein lies Jesus' example for you and me today. "Follow me wholly." With gratitude!

THE CHOSEN STORIES — 4

The rabble with them began to crave other food, and again the Israelites started wailing and said, "If only we had meat to eat! . . . But now we have lost our appetite; we never see anything but this manna!" Num. 11:4-6, NIV.

This story is accompanied with a small-print warning, since the subject touches arguably the most sensitive nerve within the community of the chosen: "Let us stop passing judgment on one another" (Rom. 14:13, NIV). For nothing stirs up a judgmental spirit more aggressively than *diet*. Which is why skinny people can get to judging heavy people, and vegetarians can get to judging carnivores, and no-dessert vegetarians can get to judging dessert vegetarians, and no-dessert-and-no-in-between-meals vegetarians can get to judging dessert-and-in-between-meals vegetarians, and vegans can judge us all! "Judge not" is Jesus' command.

They were a continual thorn in the flesh for the children of Israel, that "mixed multitude" or "riffraff" (as one commentator puts it). Their bodies were with the chosen, but they had left their hearts in Egypt, like Mrs. Lot with Sodom. And today they howl for a change in diet. "Now the mixed multitude who were among them yielded to intense craving" (Num. 11:4). The Hebrew for "intense craving" is *ta avah avah*, a double craving. And what could be a more telling description of our culture than "double-craving appetite-driven"? In fact, can you name an ad or commercial that does *not* appeal to human appetite—be it appetite for food, possessions, beauty, acceptance, or power? Ours is a "double-craving appetite-driven" world and a generation of addicts. For isn't addiction simply appetite granted ultimate authority, whether for food or alcohol or chocolate or sex or tobacco or cocaine or caffeine? On their way to the Promised Land the chosen fall victim to their own appetites and are left behind, sandy burial mounds this side of Canaan. "So he called the name of that place Kibroth Hattaavah ["the graves of lust or craving"], because there they buried the people who had yielded to craving" (verse 34).

Thank God for appetite—it's His gift. But it is no accident the Creator placed the head above the stomach, elevating reason above appetite, and no coincidence that Satan reverses the order, elevating appetite over reason (as with Adam and Eve), hunger over self-control (as with Esau and Israel). He attempted the same with Daniel and his friends, and with Jesus. But the chosen know that "holy" means an appetite "wholly" obedient to the Creator's diet and will.

THE CHOSEN STORIES—5

They all ate the same spiritual food and drank the same spiritual drink; for they drank from the spiritual rock that accompanied them, and that rock was Christ. 1 Cor. 10:3, 4, NIV.

"Heaven Can Weight." It was a clever headline the Detroit *News* chose for a column on religion and health. "Heaven can weight"—but how much? "Heaven can wait"—but how long? The question for the chosen is: Are my diet and my health a moral issue? Consider for a moment these two New Testament pronouncements:

1. Our diet concerns God's call to *holiness,* for "I am God's temple." Paul is passionate: "Do you not know that your body is a temple of the Holy Spirit, who is in you, whom you have received from God? You are not your own; you were bought at a price. Therefore honor God with your body" (1 Cor. 6:19, 20, NIV). Our physical bodies—these temple palaces in which the Almighty chooses to dwell—were purchased at an infinite price. The last drop of Christ's blood was the crimson currency that bought us back from sin and death. Why wouldn't how I treat my body be a moral issue? "And so, dear brothers and sisters, I plead with you to give your bodies to God. Let them be a living and holy sacrifice—the kind he will accept. When you think of what he has done for you, is this too much to ask?" (Rom. 12:1, NLT).

2. Our diet concerns God's call to *readiness,* for "I am God's witness." That explains the diet of "locusts [carob pods] and honey" God prescribed for John the Baptist. It isn't about being weirdly different—it's all about optimal physical conditioning and maximum mental acuity to enable and empower the chosen's end-time radical witness for Christ. Just like John, we are "to make ready a people prepared for the Lord" (Luke 1:17). "In preparing the way for Christ's first advent, he was a representative of those who are to prepare a people for our Lord's second coming. . . . All who would perfect holiness in the fear of God must learn the lessons of temperance and self-control. . . . For this reason temperance [diet/health] finds its place in the work of preparation for Christ's second coming" (*The Desire of Ages,* p. 101). It really is a moral issue, isn't it?

Jesus' 40 days and nights of fasting prayer are evidence enough that for a mission with stakes as high as ours we cannot afford to allow our appetites to dictate our lives and distract our focus. As every marathon runner knows, if you're in it for the long haul, how you train will determine how you finish. And when heaven is the finish line, how you train *is* a moral issue.

THE CHOSEN STORIES—6

He humbled you, causing you to hunger and then feeding you with manna, which neither you nor your ancestors had known, to teach you that people do not live on bread alone but on every word that comes from the mouth of the Lord. Deut. 8:3, TNIV.

Did you catch that? There are times God lets you and me hunger in order to reveal to us the ferocious power of our own appetite. I struggle with mine. I had flown in for a camp meeting weekend, rented a car, and was trying to find the campsite. All the while I was very hungry, but every exit was bereft of a place to eat. And the longer I drove, the hungrier I grew and the more upset I became, until finally I was loudly complaining to anybody who would listen (which fortunately was only God). In that instant the thought of Jesus enduring 40 days and nights without a morsel flashed in my mind. And I was embarrassed, humbled by the power of my own appetite. What was it Jesus had declared to Satan? "Man and woman shall not live by appetite alone, but by every word that proceeds from the mouth of God."

Reason must supersede appetite. Faith must rise above food. Our lives must be dictated through our minds, not our bellies: "For, as I have often told you before and now say again even with tears, many live as enemies of the cross of Christ. Their destiny is destruction, their god is their stomach, and their glory is in their shame. Their mind is on earthly things" (Phil. 3:18, 19, NIV). Clearly God's call to holiness—to be "wholly His"—is a claim upon our appetites as well. Yes, but alcohol consumption is much worse than plain old food, isn't it? "The word of God places the sin of gluttony in the same catalogue with drunkenness" (*Counsels on Health*, p. 71). What hope is there then for those of us whose appetites so easily can usurp the driver's seat?

The Desire of Ages describes Jesus' grueling wilderness temptation: "By passing over the ground which man must travel, our Lord has prepared the way for us to overcome. It is not His will that we should be placed at a disadvantage in the conflict with Satan. He would not have us intimidated and discouraged by the assaults of the serpent. 'Be of good cheer,' He says; 'I have overcome the world.' John 16:33. Let [the one] who is struggling against the power of appetite look to the Savior. . . . See Him in His agony upon the cross, as He exclaimed, 'I thirst.' He has endured all that it is possible for us to bear. *His victory is ours*" (pp. 122, 123; italics supplied). Then shall we not go out in *His* power and live *His* victory today?

THE CHOSEN STORIES—7

And when they had come to a place called Golgotha, that is to say,
Place of a Skull, they gave Him sour wine mingled with gall to drink.
But when He had tasted it, He would not drink. Matt. 27:33, 34.

May I be blunt? A case for social drinking—the consumption of alcohol on social occasions—cannot be made biblically. The only safe stance, endorsed by the Word of God Himself, is abstinence. The swift death of the two preacher's kids, Nadab and Abihu (when inebriated, they stumbled into the sacred Shekinah presence of God) was a morality play that Israel would long remember. And it is no coincidence that immediately after recounting their tragic deaths, Moses recorded the somber warning of God: "Do not drink wine or intoxicating drink, you, nor your sons with you, when you go into the tabernacle of meeting, lest you die. It shall be a statute forever throughout your generations, that you may distinguish between holy and unholy, and between unclean and clean" (Lev. 10:9, 10).

"But I don't drink that much—just a sip now and then with a meal and some friends. I know my limits." What if the world ran on that logic? What if pilots imbibed in the same philosophy? What if your surgeon rushed to your emergency with "just a sip"? In matters of life and death, nobody challenges the danger of alcoholic consumption. So when is it in life, then, that it's OK to risk benumbing the brain and shutting down the conscience? On a Saturday night?

And what about those who don't know they have a genetic predisposition to alcoholism and cannot risk even a single drink? Is "everybody's doing it" a sane reason? Nobody needs this page filled with the numbing statistics of alcohol consumption's skyrocketing societal, national price tag in mortality, crime, rape, property destruction, illness, and absenteeism. Shall we socially imbibe what nationally destroys? If social drinking met with God's approbation, then why was Daniel and his three friends' abstinence from wine elevated to a prime-time model of appetite "whollyness" to God? Why would God through Solomon forbid even the sipping of wine? Suggesting God meant that we simply shouldn't do it in excess is as logical as concluding His warning against a prostitute means we just shouldn't sleep with her too much! One sip or one night is too much. Even for Jesus, who refused to imbibe a drop of wine for a painkiller. Apparently, keeping your mind open to God 24/7 is the only safe, wise choice for God and us.

THE CHOSEN STORIES — 8

While Israel was staying in Shittim, the men began to indulge in sexual immorality with Moabite women, who invited them to the sacrifices to their gods. The people ate and bowed down before these gods. Num. 25:1, 2, NIV.

Once upon a time there was a movement called "the chosen." They were on the very borders of Canaan. It would not be long until they would be crossing over. And the enemy knew it, even more than they did. And so, in desperation, he reached into his dark, demonic quiver and pulled from it the deadliest arrow of all. Just a single shaft of poison three letters long: S-E-X. And great was his slaughter of the chosen on the borders of the Promised Land.

The sordid narrative of Numbers 25 is hardly a bedtime story! Beguiled by the seducers of Moab (an intentional plant by fallen prophet Balaam as a dagger thrust into the underbelly of the faithful), the children of Israel are bewitched into sexual fornication and rank immorality. Only Hollywood could do it this well. The divine reaction is swift and strong. Unless the cancer is immediately excised, the entire community will be lost. At the end of that bitter and bloody day 24,000 of the chosen perished. Why the divine passion? Because sex has ever been the Creator's gift for ultimate human intimacy. That's why from the beginning the Hebrew word He used for sexual intercourse was "knowing." For only when a man and woman know each other mentally, emotionally, socially, and spiritually are they prepared to know each other physically or sexually. We've been wired for genuine intimacy that is full-orbed and deeply relational. So when Israel consorted with the fallen women of Moab sexually for a fake intimacy, the immediate residual effect was on their consciences, to the stunning place they suddenly abandoned their God to worship the false gods of their temptresses.

It is because unbridled sex eats away the human conscience through fake intimacy that Satan has found it his trump card for our generation. Thus his hypnotic appeal to sexual arousal is everywhere. Billboards, newspaper photographs, magazine covers, television commercials, Internet pop-ups, movie trailers, musical hits, popular fashions, everyday conversations—his reach is nearly universal. "But thanks be to God, who gives us the victory through our Lord Jesus Christ" (1 Cor. 15:57). They crucified Him naked so that our own sexual fallenness might be redeemed and His own genuine intimacy might be restored with us. Ask Him.

THE CHOSEN STORIES—9

To him who is able to keep you from falling and to present you before his glorious presence without fault and with great joy—to the only God our Savior be glory, majesty, power and authority, through Jesus Christ our Lord, before all ages, now and forevermore!"
Jude 24, 25, NIV.

The National Coalition for the Protection of Children reports that 25 percent of all Internet search engine requests are related to pornography. There are 1.3 million pornographic Web sites, visited by 30 million people *every day*, making it a $3 billion-a-year industry. The average age of first Internet exposure to porn—11! Largest consumer of Internet porn: 12- to 17-year-olds. Someone has done a number on us! So here's a fourfold strategy to spiritually survive and grow in the midst of Satan's blitzkrieg assault against the Creator's gift of sex. The devil is desperate. But God is divine—and therein lies our potent secret to sexual victory.

Life and sex strategy 1. Exercise your soul. The psalmist exclaimed, "My soul thirsts for God" (Ps. 42:2). Sexual drive is often described as an insatiable thirst. To the extent that the school board at the King Middle School in Portland, Maine, voted 7-2 to provide a full range of birth-control contraceptives for students as young as 11! Laura Sessions Stepp, in her book *Unhooked: How Young Women Pursue Sex, Delay Love, and Lose at Both*, chronicles the regrets of girls who were casual about sex. I know—I've listened to their heartache. Want to rise above your sexual drive? Then deepen your thirst for God. Jesus told the woman at the well, "Those who drink the water I give them will never thirst" (John 4:14, TNIV). Reread the March readings in this book. Your daily time alone with Christ is the only effective thirst replacement that can bring your sexual drive under His daily control.

Life and sex strategy 2. Exercise your body. If you're struggling with sexual addiction, begin physical exercise, preferably daily. Transference shifts your energies previously focused on sexual stimulation to physical workout. "Flee from sexual immorality. . . . He who sins sexually sins against his own body. Do you not know that your body is a temple of the Holy Spirit, who is in you, whom you have received from God? You are not your own; you were bought at a price" (1 Cor. 6:18-20, NIV). The same Jesus who cleansed the Temple long ago can purify not only your heart, but your body. Work out with Him.

THE CHOSEN STORIES—10

Resist the devil and he will flee from you. James 4:7.

Life and sex strategy 3. Exercise your mind. Remember—that was the difference between Joseph and David. Joseph fled—David fed. The difference was in their mental response to sexual temptation. "Flee also youthful lusts" (2 Tim. 2:22). Exercise your NO (1 Cor. 10:13).

Does our sexual orientation determine our mental and spiritual response? Actually, the biblical prescription for sexual expression levels the playing field for all of us, heterosexual or homosexual. Sidestepping the "nature versus nurture" debate over sexual orientation (foreign to biblical thought), the Bible offers a simple divine principle for all human sexual interaction—*outside of a marriage between a man and a woman, there is to be no interpersonal sexual expression.* Whether heterosexual or homosexual, all children of God outside of marriage between a man and a woman are to live a life of celibacy, sexual abstinence. Richard Hays from Duke University writes: "Despite the smooth illusions perpetrated by mass culture in the United States, sexual gratification is not a sacred right, and celibacy is not a fate worse than death. . . . Surely it is a matter of some interest for Christian ethics that both Jesus and Paul lived without sexual relationships. . . . Within a church, we should work diligently to recover the dignity and value of a single life" (*The Moral Vision of the New Testament*, p. 401). But without the option of homosexual "marriage," where does that leave homosexual Christians (who have shared their stories with me)? Hays goes on: "It leaves them precisely in the same situation as the heterosexual who would like to marry but cannot find an appropriate partner (and there are many such): summoned to a difficult, costly obedience, while 'groaning' for the 'redemption of our bodies' (Rom. 8:23)" (p. 402). Outside of marriage, the divine playing field is even, and the child of God and the children of the chosen will be given the moral purity and divine power to live a life without sex. The same Jesus who lived that same life will bring the same power to you.

Life and sex strategy 4. Exercise your heart. Pastor Bernie Anderson, in his book *Breaking the Silence*, tells that what broke the power of pornography in his life was when he told a pastor friend about his struggle. We need one another (Heb. 10:24, 25). Join a small group of spiritual friends with whom you are safe to share your struggles. When we share our common bond in Christ, He bestows an uncommon power for our collective victory.

329

THE CHOSEN STORIES — 11

There is therefore now no condemnation for those who are in Christ Jesus. Rom. 8:1, NRSV.

All this talk about sex can make us all feel guilty, can't it? So how would you like to become a virgin again, a "spiritual virgin" with a brand-new beginning?

Remember her? They had caught the young woman in the act, in bed with a man who wasn't her husband. Throwing the disheveled sexual sinner at Jesus' sandals one early morning in the Temple courtyard, the clerics loudly demand to know what He recommends as her punishment. Should she be stoned, as commanded by the Law of Moses? The sunup crowd is breathless—what sentence would the Teacher pronounce?

But Jesus doesn't answer. Instead He quietly kneels to the dusty Temple floor and begins to trace with His finger in the dust. Tradition says that what Jesus etched there were the secret sins of the church elders who accused the young woman. What a portrait of God! Twice He is painted in Scripture writing with His finger—once when He carved His eternal law upon two granite tablets, and once when He wrote the sins of the leaders in the dust of the floor. On stone so that time could not efface the truth of his Decalogue. But in the dust so that a single puff of breeze might erase the record of their private sins. Foe or friend alike, He will not embarrass you.

When He's through writing, Jesus rises to His feet with the quiet command, "All right—let the one without sin cast the first stone" (see John 8:7). And the Gospel story reads that beginning with the eldest and ending with the youngest, the clerics slipped away without a word. Raising her chin to meet His eyes, Jesus gazes into that trembling face and asks, "Where are your accusers? Does no one condemn you?" She shakes her tear-streaked face. The incarnate God speaks. "Neither do I condemn you. Go now and leave your life of sin" (verse 11, NIV). Can you believe it? No condemnation for that fallen sinner from the only sinless One who could have cast the first stone that day. Our text today must be true!

And if it is, then "no condemnation" must mean "new creation" (see 2 Cor. 5:17). And a "new creation" can only mean a "new spiritual virginity." For how did the sexually fallen king David pray? "Purify me with hyssop, and I shall be clean; wash me, and I shall be whiter than snow" (Ps. 51:7, NASB). Only a virgin could be that clean! And only a Savior could offer that gift—a Calvary cleansing so deep and so strong that even the chosen can become pure again.

SIGNED, SEALED, DELIVERED— I'M YOURS—1

He said to him, "Walk through the streets of Jerusalem and put a mark on the foreheads of all who weep and sigh because of the detestable sins being committed in their city." Eze. 9:4, NLT.

One morning when we were in Beijing with our friend Doug Martin, he surprised each of us with a gift —a small black-lacquer box containing an official Chinese stamp. On the stamp, he told us (and I'm taking his word for it), are Chinese characters that "spell" our names. It is customary in the Orient to notarize documents with your personal stamp pressed into the red ink pad in the lacquer box and then stamped onto the paper. The affixed Chinese characters authenticate your identity and validate your ownership.

In both the Old and New Testament God reveals that He, too, has an authenticating, validating stamp or seal that He presses into the foreheads of the chosen, those earth children who have chosen Him. In our text today in Ezekiel 9, the stamp is called a "mark"—literally the Hebrew letter *tav*, the last letter of the alphabet that in Ezekiel's time was written like an X. "Put an X on the foreheads of my faithful people" was the divine command. In Revelation 7, rather than a stamp it is called a seal: "Then I saw another angel ascending from the east, having the seal of the living God" (Rev 7:2). It, too, is affixed upon the foreheads of "the servants of our God" (verse 3). And it is clear from both passages that this divine sealing or stamping occurs at the closing of earth's history. For the angel that gives the command in Ezekiel is clothed in linen, the very attire of the high priest on the Day of Atonement (Lev. 16:4). And the angel issuing the command in Revelation does so in the immediate context of Christ's tumultuous second coming (Rev. 6:15-17). Clearly this sealing comes at the close of God's cleansing judgment. But who should be surprised? In earth's final chapter, when the very authority of God will be mocked and His law rejected by the vast majority, why wouldn't He be passionately eager to identify for the universe His chosen ones still loyal to Him?

Does that mean that until then we have no security, no assurance of God's salvation? Hardly! It is no different than what took place that midnight in Egypt. A divine visitant was dispatched in judgment—but every household, every family, every soul that was "under the blood" on the doorposts was secure. Even so God's end-time sealing stamps an entire generation of people who choose to live under the blood of the Lamb. That's your choice. Isn't it?

SIGNED, SEALED, DELIVERED— I'M YOURS—2

Then I saw another angel ascending from the east, having the seal of the living God. And he cried with a loud voice to the four angels to whom it was granted to harm the earth and the sea, saying, "Do not harm the earth, the sea, or the trees till we have sealed the servants of our God on their foreheads." Rev. 7:2, 3.

One Christmas Karen gave me a shiny metal seal. You've probably seen one. With it I can take a brand-new book (or an old one from my library) and, firmly squeezing the clamping seal onto the first page of the book, have in raised imprint the words "Library of Dwight K. Nelson" encircling the monogram DKN. It's a nifty device, and I love using it.

God has a seal, too, with His name in the center: "Then I looked, and behold, a Lamb standing on Mount Zion, and with Him one hundred and forty-four thousand, having His Father's name written on their foreheads" (Rev. 14:1). Why have a seal? Consider these five functions:

1. Proof of Ownership. Once my seal goes in a book, everybody who picks it up immediately learns this book is my property. Since I'm the only one who has a seal with my personal name in it, there can be no dispute. So it is with God and His sealed chosen. "'They shall be Mine,' says the Lord of hosts, 'on the day that I make them My jewels'" (Mal. 3:17).

2. Proof of Authenticity. Have you ever gone to a notary public? Credentialed by the state to validate signatures and documents, when a notary public affixes his or her seal upon a document it is legal proof that the signature is authentic. You need that seal should anyone challenge your claim. So it is with God and the chosen He seals. For that reason the seal symbolically goes in the forehead—because it is in the mind and intellect of His friends that the truth about God's character is authenticated. "The people of God are sealed in their foreheads—it is not any seal or mark that can be seen, but *a settling into the truth, both intellectually and spiritually,* so they cannot be moved" (*Last Day Events,* pp. 219, 220; italics supplied).

3. Proof of Approval. *Good Housekeeping* magazine has earned a national reputation for selecting the best products and merchandise available to American consumers. "The Good Housekeeping Seal of Approval" is a valued mark of distinction. AAA and AARP have their seals of approval, too. With His seal on the chosen God declares to the universe, "See him? See her? I approve!" And who else's approval could be more coveted than that?

SIGNED, SEALED, DELIVERED — I'M YOURS — 3

And you also were included in Christ when you heard the word of truth, the gospel of your salvation. Having believed, you were marked in him with a seal, the promised Holy Spirit. Eph. 1:13, NIV.

Why does God use a "seal"? First, it's a proof of His ownership of His chosen ones. Second, it's proof of the authenticity of their purchase at Calvary. And third, God's seal is His own "Good Heavenkeeping Seal of Approval"—"I approve of them." But there's more to a seal:

4. Proof of Irreversibility. King Darius was duped into signing and sealing a law of the Medes and Persians that doomed his friend Daniel to the lions' den. When he realized the deception, the king tried every legal maneuver he could think of, but to no avail. His seal had made the law irreversible. When our president signs an executive order or an act of Congress and affixes the presidential seal to it, that order or that law is declared binding and essentially irreversible. Even so, when God seals His chosen ones, it is as if He locks them in forever and ever: "Let those who do right continue to do right; and let those who are holy continue to be holy" (Rev. 22:11, TNIV). Once you're sealed, you're locked in to God's glorious eternity!

5. Proof of Likeness. Have you seen these little wax seal kits at a fancy card shop? You can actually stamp your "love letter" with an attractive wax seal that retains your initials for the recipient. Ancient kings used cylindrical seals to roll their likenesses onto the soft wax, so that all who would later see the seal would recognize the likeness of the king. So it is for the King of the universe when He affixes His seal to the foreheads of His loyal people and faithful friends—the very likeness of His character is recognized in their lives. As *The Desire of Ages* puts it: "Christ is sitting for His portrait in every disciple" (p. 827). God's end-time friends become the impressionable wax upon which God seals His moral image and places it permanently on display before the universe. The seal is the finished picture.

And who is the active Agent shaping Jesus' likeness into your character day after day? Today's text is clear—He is the Holy Spirit. His mission? Our sanctification—which in both Hebrew and Greek means our "holy-izing," the lifelong journey in which God seals more and more of *His* character into the impressionable wax of *our* characters until we are "wholly" like Him. They say, "Like Father, like child." Turns out they're right. For that's what "holy" means.

NOT I, BUT CHRIST—1

I am crucified with Christ: nevertheless I live; yet not I, but Christ liveth in me: and the life which I now live in the flesh I live by the faith of the Son of God, who loved me, and gave himself for me. Gal. 2:20, KJV.

I've never particularly relished being the youngest face in the crowd. When you have a baby face, it feels as if you never grow up. You're always "the boy." That's how it was for "John Boy." Not the one from *The Waltons*, but the one with the boyish face, the youngest of Jesus' disciples. Go to Rome and gaze at the Christian art of antiquity and not surprisingly, whether in granite or on canvas, the face of John is portrayed youthful, beardless, with the long hair of a woman—masculine, but still a boy. No wonder he worked so hard at scrambling to the top! Hubris (ego)? In spades. Because we usually hide (or reveal) our inadequacies by our excesses (e.g., Napoleon, the neighborhood "shorty" who grew up to become the global bully).

Remember that sunlit moment when Jesus stopped by the beached fishing skiff of those net-mending brothers? "Come follow me and I'll make you fishers of people." Jumping to their feet, they did just that—James and John. But in a few short days it was surely clear to the Master that in those Zebedee boys He had a handful! "To them he gave the name Boanerges, which means Sons of Thunder" (Mark 3:17, NIV). "I think I'll call you boys 'The Hothead Brothers'!" And they lived up to every nuance of their nickname. Once, you remember, they asked permission to nuke an entire Samaritan village with divine fire. Another time they singlehandedly shut down a one-man independent ministry that detracted from their honor. And remember the time they dragged Mom along to hopefully lock in the top two positions in Jesus' eventual kingdom, igniting an internecine war among all 12 disciples?

Take a look at this catalog of John Boy's character flaws: "John did not naturally possess the loveliness of character that his later experience revealed. By nature he had serious defects. He was not only [1] proud, [2] self-assertive, and [3] ambitious for honor, but [4] impetuous, and [5] resentful under injury. . . . [6] Evil temper, [7] the desire for revenge, [8] the spirit of criticism, were all in the beloved disciple" (*The Acts of the Apostles*, p. 540). Sound familiar? Yet what is so utterly amazing is that this John Boy (with all his psychological and character defects) not only ends up in Jesus' inner circle, but becomes Christ's dearest friend on earth. Amazing, transforming grace!

NOT I, BUT CHRIST—2

Come to me, all you who are weary and burdened, and I will give you rest.
Take my yoke upon you and learn from me, for I am gentle and humble in heart,
and you will find rest for your souls. Matt. 11:28, 29, NIV.

Does Jesus play favorites? Contrary to our first impressions, His having an inner circle—Peter, James, and John—had nothing to do with Teacher's pet. The decisive way in which He nixed James and John's request for the top two positions in the kingdom is evidence enough. But "the depth of their attachment to Him" (*The Desire of Ages,* p. 548) didn't escape the notice of the Master. For you see, the heart of Christ is drawn to the hearts that are drawn to Him. He draws all. But not all will be drawn. And therein lies the difference between John Boy and Judas.

On the eve of Jesus' death it is John and Judas who press nearest to Him at the Last Supper table. But only one of them followed Jesus into the garden. Only one of them refused to run when the rest fled at Jesus' arrest. Only John Boy made his way to the inner courtyard of the kangaroo trial. Only he followed Jesus through the torturous long night and early morning. Only John, of all the disciples, followed his Master to the summit of Calvary. And with only John there beside His mother, Jesus in His supreme anguish looked down and bequeathed His mother to the one disciple who would not forsake Him even in death—John Boy.

Something happened in the heart of this Son of Thunder, some mysterious transformation over the three and a half years the young disciple followed the Master. *Can we not conclude that a daily, prolonged exposure to the Savior transforms the heart of a disciple?* So that what you were, you no longer need to be. For by beholding, you and I can become changed. John did just that: "Day by day, in contrast with his own violent spirit, [1] he beheld the tenderness and forbearance of Jesus, and [2] heard His lessons of humility and patience. [3] He opened his heart to the divine influence, and [4] became not only a hearer but a doer of the Saviour's words. [5] Self was hid in Christ. [6] He learned to wear the yoke of Christ and [7] to bear His burden" (*The Desire of Ages,* pp. 295, 296). How lasting was his sevenfold spiritual quest? Near the end of his life when John wrote his Gospel, five times he humbly, anonymously described himself as "the disciple Jesus *kept on loving*" (Greek). No more thunder. John had removed himself from the picture. His story has only one Hero. "Not I, but Christ" became the song of his life.

HUMILITY'S BEST FRIEND — 1

For those who exalt themselves will be humbled,
and those who humble themselves will be exalted. Matt. 23:12, TNIV.

Let's face it: There are some things in life that are hard to swallow, such as eggshells in your potato salad, slimy okra—and pride. Swallowing pride—it's enough to make you gag, isn't it? Eating humble pie—it's not our favorite culinary pastime, is it? And yet could it be that eating humble pie is a spiritual skill God calls the chosen to develop?

It is one of the greatest rags-to-riches-and-back-to-rags-again stories in all of history! Born a slave, adopted a prince, but turned a fugitive killer. The whole world loves the story of the "Prince of Egypt." From bobbing in a pitch-coated papyrus basket atop the mighty Nile River to an exalted seat at Pharaoh's table as the adopted grandson of the most powerful monarch on earth, it was Horatio Alger's rags-to-riches at its finest for young Moses. Sitting at the feet of the world's brightest intellects, trained as an officer in the world's mightiest army, schooled in governance by the world's most brilliant jurists, the young man's star was in ascendancy. But to the eternal credit of his biological mother, Jochabed, Moses never forsook his Hebrew heritage or his people's God. Deep within himself he knew he was the one to deliver them. "Angels instructed Moses . . . that Jehovah had chosen him to break the bondage of His people" (*Patriarchs and Prophets*, p. 245).

But the young man's modus operandi was utterly foreign to the divine strategy. "'For My thoughts are not your thoughts, nor are your ways My ways,' says the Lord" (Isa. 55:8). And Moses' calculation that murdering an Egyptian taskmaster would be the dramatic catalyst to launch his overthrow of Egypt nearly cost him his life.

"Then . . . Moses fled" (Acts 7:29), a colossal failure with a death warrant on his head. Failure. Who among us doesn't know that twisted knot in the gut, that alkaline taste on the tongue? Failure in life, failure in love. Failure in business, failure in career. Failure in marriage, failure in school. Failure in private, failure in public. The dreaded letter grade F, when we tried so hard to win but lost, when we dreamed so much of succeeding but failed. George Bernard Shaw intoned, "My reputation grows with every failure." And were it not for the story of Moses, it would be the same for us, too. But in his story we learn the counterintuitive truth that for Moses it was *a successful failure*, the very kind of failure the God of Moses can lead us to also.

THANKSGIVING ON THE "TWEEN" DECK

When you have eaten and are full, then you shall bless the Lord your God for the good land which He has given you. Deut. 8:10.

Nathaniel Philbrick's award-winning book *Mayflower* blends the dispassion of an historian with the dramatic flair of a storyteller and is the most detailed and gripping Pilgrim chronicle I have ever read.

After their torturous voyage across the gale-whipped Atlantic on the "tween" deck (the space between the topside deck above and the cargo hold below), the *Mayflower's* 102 passengers, half of them Puritan, the other half adventurers and crew, landed on Cape Cod in frigid November weather. (The "small ice age" of North America still gripped the continent.) Philbrick's account of their ill-prepared splashing ashore the mainland in wet and frozen clothing on December 23, the next two harrowing weeks to construct their first building (a 20-foot square common house), the deadly onslaught of a winter made even more bitter with so many falling ill or dying that only six of the decimated colony were strong enough to care for the sick, the late-night and unmarked burials to hide from any native spies the dwindling of the Pilgrim band—you cannot help reading this narrative with an almost sacred awe. By spring 52 of the 102 *Mayflower* passengers were dead. "We think of the Pilgrims as resilient adventurers upheld by unwavering religious faith, but they were also human beings in the midst of what was, and continues to be, one of the most difficult emotional challenges a person can face: immigration and exile" (p. 76).

Nearly four centuries later, here we are, ourselves on a voyage this Thanksgiving, occupying the "tween" deck between the past and the future, exiles in a foreign land, "strangers and pilgrims on the earth" (Heb. 11:13). And what shall be our spirit? Do we have the same dogged determination to be faithful to the vision that launched our movement? No matter the contrary odds, the devastating price, these were a people not unlike the heroes of Hebrews 11, who "having seen [the promises] from afar off were assured of them." They did not turn back. And neither must we. "Let us fix our eyes on Jesus, the author and perfecter of our faith" (Heb. 12:2, NIV). For in Christ the Promised Land is assured. The Pilgrims lived with that sense of "the chosen." So must we. It may not be long now to the "crossing over."

HUMILITY'S BEST FRIEND—2

Now Moses was a very humble man, more humble than anyone else on the face of the earth.
Num. 12:3, NIV.

Forty years in Egypt were soon swallowed up by the 40 long, hot years of the Midian wilderness. Moses has enrolled in the school of failure: "Man would have dispensed with that long period of toil and obscurity, deeming it a great loss of time. But Infinite Wisdom called him who was to become the leader of his people to spend forty years in the humble work of a shepherd. . . . No advantage that human training or culture could bestow, could be a substitute for this experience. . . . Shut in by the bulwarks of the mountains, Moses was alone with God. . . . [He] seemed to stand in His presence and to be overshadowed by His power. Here *his pride and self-sufficiency were swept away.* In the stern simplicity of his wilderness life, the results of the ease and luxury of Egypt disappeared. *Moses became patient, reverent, and humble,* 'very meek, above all the men which were upon the face of the earth' (Num. 12:3), yet strong in faith in the mighty God of Jacob" (*Patriarchs and Prophets,* pp. 247-251; italics supplied).

Failure is humility's best friend, isn't it? Apparently God allows us to fail with the counterintuitive hope that we might through Him *successfully* fail. For what is there that stuns our ego and wounds our pride more quickly and deeply than failure, be it public or private? And are we ever more teachable than when we have failed? Are we ever more "humble-able" than in the grip of failure? Some years ago someone handed me a book and said, "You need this." It was Andrew Murray's classic, *Humility.* It has so blessed me I've brooded my way through it three times: "Accept with gratitude everything that God allows from within or without, from friend or enemy, in nature or in grace, to remind you of your need of humbling, and to help you do it. Reckon humility to indeed be the mother-virtue, your very first duty before God, the one perpetual safeguard of the soul, and set your heart upon it as the source of all blessing" (p. 88).

After all, didn't Jesus embrace all that humbled Him? A towel for our feet, a cross for our souls, "He humbled Himself and became obedient to the point of death" (Phil. 2:8). And what is His invitation to us? "Learn from me, for I am gentle and humble in heart" (Matt. 11:29, NIV). Then shall we not ask Him to help us to come to the place where we can embrace that which humbles us, whatever it might be? For how else shall we become like Jesus?

A TALE OF TWO SAULS—1

And he had a choice and handsome son whose name was Saul. There was not a more handsome person than he among the children of Israel. From his shoulders upward he was taller than any of the people. 1 Sam. 9:2.

Don't you wish we chose presidents the same way today, by casting lots? Think of all the acrimony and money we could save. Put the names in a hat—draw the state, draw the town, draw the family, draw the person. "Ladies and gentlemen, the president of the United States!" That's how the first king of Israel was "elected." Tall, dark, and handsome from the tribe of Benjamin—how could you go wrong? But they did, terribly.

In his book *Good to Great* Jim Collins documents the most successful leaders he calls Level 5 leaders: "Level 5 leaders are a study in duality: modest and willful, shy and fearless. . . . Those who worked with or wrote about the good-to-great leaders continually used words like *quiet, humble, modest, reserved, shy, gracious, mild-mannered, understated, did not believe his own clippings;* and so forth" (pp. 22-27). The most successful leaders are noted for their humility. Would to God that King Saul had remained one of them, but sadly his tale unravels with almost breathtaking speed. Chosen because he was *little* in his own eyes, he was rejected because he became *all* that was in his own eyes. His is a tragic tale of humility and its demise.

Given that ignominious record, one could wonder why a mother would ever again name her baby boy Saul. But in the Roman city of Tarsus, a Hebrew mother and her Pharisee husband chose that very name for their newborn son, nicknaming him "Paul" for their Greco-Roman culture. Like father, like son, Saul was sent off to boarding school in Jerusalem to eventually become a Pharisee scholar of sacred law, a brilliant one at that. And he hated to lose—as he did that day in the synagogue in Jerusalem when he was outwitted and outscriptured by another young man, a Greek Jew-turned-disciple of the dead Jesus of Nazareth. The stoning of Stephen, the conversion of Saul—the rest is the fiery history of that intrepid champion of Christ.

A tale of two Sauls—one who began in humility and ended in suicidal pride, the other who began with proud self-confidence and ended in Christlike humility. The critical difference? How they both responded to adversity. One was driven inward by it, the other was driven upward. And in that little-known chapter of Paul's great pain lies humility's greatest secret of all.

A TALE OF TWO SAULS—2

But he said to me, "My grace is sufficient for you, for my power is made perfect in weakness." Therefore I will boast all the more gladly about my weaknesses, so that Christ's power may rest on me. 2 Cor. 12:9, NIV.

There is an obscure chapter in the second Saul's life that seldom is reviewed, and yet which holds perhaps the greatest secret of all to humility. The newly converted Paul disappeared for several years. Piecing together the New Testament record, we conclude he eventually returned to his hometown of Tarsus. While there Paul was granted some spectacular visions by God. That divine entrustment precipitated one of the great crises and principles of humility.

"I know a man in Christ who fourteen years ago was caught up to the third heaven. Whether it was in the body or out of the body I do not know—God knows" (2 Cor. 12:2, NIV). Paul uses the same literary device as John did by intentionally, humbly, cloaking himself in the third person. But from his description it is clear that through visions Paul was granted personal access to Paradise where he heard and saw "inexpressible things." Because of that singular divine privilege, God placed in His friend's hands a new crucible to drink: "To keep me from becoming conceited because of these surpassingly great revelations, there was given me a thorn in my flesh, a messenger of Satan, to torment me" (verse 7, NIV). The Greek word for "thorn" is not the one used for Christ's crown of thorns, but rather describes a wooden sliver jammed into the flesh, like a splinter beneath your nail. Because Paul describes it as "in my flesh," scholars have gathered a series of clues throughout Paul's Epistles (from the Galatians offering him their own eyes, to his use of an amanuensis or scribe, to his statement "See how I write with big letters" at the end of a letter) to suggest that it was Paul's eyesight that was afflicted. Was it the physical consequence of his Damascus road encounter with Jesus? We don't know. But clearly it was a constant reminder of his limitations and physical inadequacy, making him dependent on others for his ministry functions and causing him inconvenience, embarrassment, and painful discomfort. No wonder Paul describes its source as a demonic angel ("messenger of Satan") to "torment me" (Greek: "strike with a fist"). Why such pain? "To keep me from becoming conceited," i.e., to keep me humble. It makes you wonder. Could it be that suffering *sometimes* is a divinely permitted antidote to our pride? And could we like Paul come to where we glory in it?

A TALE OF TWO SAULS—3

That is why, for Christ's sake, I delight in weaknesses, in insults, in hardships, in persecutions, in difficulties. For when I am weak, then I am strong. 2 Cor. 12:10, NIV.

Have you ever begged and pleaded with God to remove something from your heart, from your body, from your life—and He didn't? Then you know the passionate depth behind Paul's admission that on three separate occasions "I pleaded with the Lord to take it away from me" (2 Cor. 12:8, NIV).

Obviously not quick "Now I lay me down to sleep" prayers before jumping into bed, these three prayer events were wrestling-to-the-mat pleadings for Jesus to take it away.

Given my own battles, I find comfort in knowing that Paul struggled with the same weakness: "The life of the apostle Paul was a constant conflict with self. . . . His will and his desires every day conflicted with duty and the will of God. Instead of following inclination, he did God's will, however crucifying to his nature" (*The Ministry of Healing,* pp. 452, 453). And because this greatest Christian of all time battled self, God allowed in Paul's life—even as He does in ours—that which Paul very much wished were not in his life. This is humility's hard path of suffering. For it is one thing to embrace failure when you were the cause of your own failure—embrace it and learn from it. But it is quite another to embrace the suffering we endure as intentionally *allowed* by God to lead us deeper into the godlike quality of humility. I cannot walk into your hospital room and declare to you that you are suffering because God has chosen to make you more humble. That would be ludicrous and possibly very mistaken. Suffering is caused, not by God, but by the "messenger of Satan" (Jesus said, "An enemy has done this"). But I can walk into my own room of suffering and whisper to myself that perhaps that which I am suffering has possibly been allowed by God for the sake of drawing me more deeply into His love and humility. Paul nowhere describes someone else's suffering as a divine lesson. But without equivocation he here declares that through divine revelation he has learned that what he is suffering is intended by God to keep him from becoming exalted in his own eyes.

Suffering is the hard pathway to humility. How else shall we explain Paul's bursting into song when after the third prayer event Jesus came to him with a no and a promise: "My grace is sufficient for you." Amazing, amazing grace that can transform the one who suffers into one who glories in the very suffering that glorifies the Savior and humbles himself! Shall we not follow?

THE JOHN THE BAPTIST GENERATION — 1

And he will go on before the Lord, in the spirit and power of Elijah, to turn the hearts of the fathers to their children and the disobedient to the wisdom of the righteous—to make ready a people prepared for the Lord. Luke 1:17, NIV.

Why all this talk about holiness and humility? Because God is calling the children of the chosen to be "wholly" His and humbly His in the midst of a generation that unabashedly is not. He is calling for a new John the Baptist generation of men, women, young adults, and children to live boldly, radically for Christ in this "hour of the judgment" (Rev. 14:7). Blaise Pascal, the French mathematician and Christian philosopher, wrote words I have scribbled on the Luke 1 page of my Bibles: *"When everyone is moving toward depravity, no one seems to be moving; but if someone stops, he shows up the others who are rushing on, by acting as a fixed point."*

The nature of crowds is such (try it the next time you're on a crowded subway platform) that when everybody is sweeping the same direction, you can hardly tell you're moving. But let one person suddenly stop, and in that instant the crowd knows very well the direction it is headed. John the Baptist was raised up before the Messiah's first coming to be that "fixed point"—to refuse to flow with the crowds, but rather to call them to stop and get ready. Before the Messiah comes the second time, there will be a generation of His friends who, just like John, will refuse to flow along mindlessly with the crowd, but will stand firm and unmoving, thus becoming God's new "fixed point" for the world to see. Why? "To make ready a people prepared for the Lord." Even as you read these words, the court of heaven is in session. What may appear to be business as usual here on earth only masks the somber reality that we are now living in the most urgent hour in human history. Jesus is coming soon!

"The destiny of earth's teeming multitudes is about to be decided. Our own future well-being and also the salvation of other souls depend upon the course which we now pursue. . . . We need to humble ourselves before the Lord, with fasting and prayer, and to meditate much upon His word, especially upon the scenes of the judgment. We should now seek a deep and living experience in the things of God. We have not a moment to lose" (*The Great Controversy*, p. 601).

It is high time for the John the Baptist generation to take their stand as "fixed points" for Christ. He is calling for you. Can you hear Him? Will you answer? Stand up. Stand up for Jesus!

THE JOHN THE BAPTIST GENERATION—2

Behold, I send My messenger before Your face, who will prepare Your way before You. The voice of one crying in the wilderness: "Prepare the way of the Lord; make His paths straight."
Mark 1:2, 3.

What does it mean to be countercultural? Henry David Thoreau wrote: "If a man does not keep pace with his companions, perhaps it is because he hears a different drummer. Let him step to the music which he hears, however measured or far away." It is that faraway music that the John the Baptist generation steps to today, a measured strain that is radically countercultural. Just like Elijah, who thundered atop Mount Carmel, "How long will you falter between two opinions? If the Lord is God, follow Him; but if Baal, follow him" (1 Kings 18:21). Choose your God! Because as Jesus said, it is impossible to serve two competing cultures—you'll either love one and hate the other, or hate one and love the other (see Matt. 6:24). Which is why the Apocalypse ends with an urgent countercultural appeal: "Babylon is fallen—come out of her!" (see Rev. 18:4).

But you protest, "I'm not in that doomed kingdom or that fallen culture." Perhaps not. But I wonder if that doomed kingdom and culture are in us. I saw a newspaper cartoon of two parents standing in the driveway. Mother is patting shell-shocked Father on the back, while she clutches a newspaper with the headline "Fall Lineup." Junior walks away from the garbage can, where he has just tossed out their television. Mother consoles Father: "Well, you did tell him to take out the *trash*." Has TV made its insidious inroads into the hearts and homes of the chosen? There is no more potent purveyor of this world's fallen culture than the television. Of course the mechanical medium isn't fallen! We have television cameras in our sanctuary. It's what the medium purveys that is fallen. Have the chosen become marinated in the fallen culture of a lost world . . . through noncritical indulgence of TV's daily, nightly fare? Social commentator Neil Postman wrote a biting exposé of American television, *Amusing Ourselves to Death*. His premise: television has essentially dumbed down every major activity into entertainment, and thus corrupted our society to its core—the news, politics, sports, even church and religion, have all become entertainment because the crowds and culture demand it.

The more pressing question is Are the chosen amusing themselves to death too? Living on the eve of Christ's return, how much of what we watch is holy, "wholly" like Jesus?

THE JOHN THE BAPTIST GENERATION—3

In those days John the Baptist came preaching in the wilderness of Judea, and saying,
"Repent, for the kingdom of heaven is at hand!" Matt. 3:1, 2.

Marinated! It means to be soaked in a liquid so long that eventually every pore is saturated with that brine—so that like Harvard beets, when someone takes a bite the salty vinegar is all they can taste. Television, movies, video games, Internet, music, dress, entertainment, diet—the Western lifestyle that boasts 1,000 enticing expressions has marinated an entire generation with the brine of a sick and fallen culture.

Then shall we make a bonfire of the 2.5 televisions per Adventist household and call it a day? For some that will be the only successful remedy for withdrawing from the marinating culture of this fallen world. "If your right eye causes you to sin, pluck it out" (Matt. 5:29). Jesus could be embarrassingly radical at times. But better to be saved minus that television than be lost with it. I have friends who have made that countercultural decision and much to their joy discovered that there is life beyond television. (It's called reading, family time, worship, etc.)

Want to know what John the Baptist did with his television? "To him the solitude of the desert was a welcome escape from society in which suspicion, unbelief, and impurity had become well-nigh all-pervading [welcome to the third millennium]. He distrusted his own power to withstand temptation, and *shrank from constant contact with sin* [what television offers—constant contact with sin until it no longer is offensive to you], lest he should lose the sense of its exceeding sinfulness. . . . *In solitude, by meditation and prayer,* he sought to gird up his soul for the lifework before him. Although in the wilderness, he was not exempt from temptation. *So far as possible, he closed every avenue* by which Satan could enter, yet he was still assailed by the tempter. But his spiritual perceptions were clear; he had developed strength and decision of character, and through the aid of the Holy Spirit he was able to detect Satan's approaches, and to resist his power" (*The Desire of Ages,* pp. 101, 102; italics supplied).

The Off switch is how you close almost every avenue to Satan. Meditation and prayer are how you find the wisdom and courage to keep them closed. And John's message of Calvary, "Behold the Lamb of God," is how the marinating brine is cleansed from your soul. Then when you do sit down before a TV or computer, you say: "Jesus, please watch this with me."

THE JOHN THE BAPTIST GENERATION—4

He went into all the country around the Jordan, preaching a baptism of repentance for the forgiveness of sins. Luke 3:3, NIV.

We were in Europe trying to find Neuschwanstein, that fairy book castle in Austria our daughter, Krissi, had long wanted to see. We stopped in Innsbruck to grab lunch, then drove on, discovering a glorious four-lane highway through spectacular mountain country. But it felt like we were heading south. We finally pulled off at a small house on the slope and in our "pidgin" English asked the family how to find the castle. Looking at our map and then up at us, they shook their heads, "No, no—this Italy, this Italy!" Long ago we'd taken a wrong turn onto a wrong highway going in the wrong direction in the wrong country. How embarrassing! But that's precisely what John the Baptist's call to "Repent!" means. Turn your life around! You're headed in the wrong direction. And he preached it to the saved, of all people.

Christ turns to Laodicea, the last church on earth, and pleads: "Be earnest, and repent" (Rev. 3:19, NIV). So what shall the chosen repent of? Some of us are shamed by a laundry list of dirty clothes and sins. Others can't think of a thing, so they contrive some "minor" infraction. "The nearer we come to Jesus, and the more clearly we discern the purity of His character, the more clearly shall we see the exceeding sinfulness of sin, and the less shall we feel like exalting ourselves. There will be a continual reaching out of the soul after God, a continual, earnest, heartbreaking confession of sin and humbling of the heart before Him. *At every advance step in our Christian experience our repentance will deepen*" (*The Acts of the Apostles*, p. 561; italics supplied).

If repentance for the chosen is to deepen as we go, then shouldn't we pray David's prayer, "Search me, O God, . . . and see if there be any wicked way in me" (Ps. 139:23, 24, KJV)? And shouldn't we then ask to "behold the Lamb of God who takes away" the sins He reveals? After all, aren't all our sins against *Him* in the end? One day I was mad at Karen and lobbed at her words that were cruel and cutting. And I'd have been very satisfied if she'd simply fired back at me a broadside of her own. But she didn't. Instead she burst into tears. And in that instant—when I saw those tears—I knew the depth of the pain my sin had inflicted on her. And it broke my heart to realize I had broken her heart. Even so, don't you suppose that if we kneel at the foot of the cross long enough each day, the heart we broke will break our hearts, too?

THE ISSACHAR FACTOR—1

Of Issachar, those who had understanding of the times, to know what Israel ought to do, two hundred chiefs, and all their kindred under their command. 1 Chron. 12:32, NRSV.

As we count down to the hope of "crossing over"—an entire generation of the chosen watching, working, and waiting for the return of Jesus—don't you wish we could predict the future as well as this little device predicts the weather? It's a cheerful little ribbon of yarn woven in all the colors of the rainbow. The instructions that come with it are simple: 1. Hang outside the window. 2. Check each morning. 3. If it's wet, it's raining. 4. If it's stiff, it's freezing. 5. If it's white, it's snowing. 6. If it's moving, it's windy. 7. If it's faded, it's sunny. And, 8, if it's gone, it's ripped off. What an ingenious device! Works every time.

Don't you wish forecasting the future were that simple? Once upon a time there was an ancient tribe who had the uncanny ability to do just that. David had just vanquished his enemies. King Saul was dead. In today's text the tribes of Israel were aligning themselves with their new young monarch. And in the middle of their listing came the small tribe of Issachar with a unique identification marker: *They understood the times and knew what Israel ought to do.*

What if that were the identification marker of the chosen today? Didn't Jesus all but command us to embrace this "Issachar factor"? In Luke 12:54-56 and Matthew 16:1-3, He exclaimed: "Look at you! You can read the *signs in the skies*—'red sky at night, sailor's delight; red sky in the morning, sailors, take warning' [He really did refer to that pithy meteorological proverb]—but you can't discern *the signs of the times!*" That is, why don't you become like the little tribe of Issachar and understand the times to know what the chosen ought to be doing? For example, what should the chosen understand about the endemic fear that throttles our society? We're afraid of everything: pandemics, terrorism, economic collapse, ecological meltdown, migrants, our neighbors—we fear even fear itself. But didn't Jesus predict a global pandemic of fear just before He returns? "People will faint from fear and foreboding of what is coming upon the world" (Luke 21:26, NRSV). Should the chosen be afraid? Hardly! People who are afraid wring their hands and hang their heads. But not My followers, Jesus declared! The pandemic of fear must be met by the posture of hope: "Now when these things begin to take place, stand up and raise your heads, because your redemption is drawing near" (verse 28, NRSV).

THE ISSACHAR FACTOR—2

As long as it is day, we must do the work of him who sent me.
Night is coming, when no one can work. John 9:4, NIV.

For a generation getting ready to cross over, should the hedgehog or the fox be our mascot? Isaiah Berlin, the English philosopher, once said that there are two kinds of thinkers in the world—hedgehogs (who embrace one big idea and stick to it) and foxes (who dart from idea to idea). Then along came Joshua Cooper Ramo, author of *The Age of the Unthinkable*, which reported on the research of political scientist and psychologist Philip Tetlock, who decided to test the hedgehog and fox difference in making predictions. After interviewing hundreds of experts in economics, politics, and international relations, Tetlock and his team discovered that when it came to prediction accuracy the fox thinkers outscored the hedgehog thinkers. The difference was in the fox thinkers' "wide-ranging curiosity." Was that the secret to Issachar, too—a wide-ranging curiosity of the trends of the times that informed their strategic response?

In Matthew 24 (called "the little Apocalypse" because of its focus on end-time events), Jesus thinks more like a fox than a hedgehog when He describes a wide-ranging list of seven global trends that will peak together just before He returns. Utilizing the Issachar factor today means that we must keep a watchful eye on all seven of these trends: (1) religious deception; (2) military conflicts; (3) political upheaval; (4) natural disasters; (5) legal breakdown; (6) social collapse; and, (7) spiritual revival. If you haven't already, why not start a file for each of these predicted trends—collect news clippings, Internet reports, press releases, economic predictions, social indicators, etc. Like Issachar, we must understand the times to know what we must do.

Some think what we must do is convince God to accelerate all seven trends right now, so that society will collapse, the world will plunge into chaos, and the end will have to come. How wrong they are! "The work which the church has failed to do in a time of peace and prosperity she will have to do in a terrible crisis under most discouraging, forbidding circumstances" (*Testimonies for the Church,* vol. 5, p. 463). Which is why Jesus' appeal in our text today is so urgent. "Work, for the night is coming" sings that old gospel hymn. But notice Jesus' very good news: "*We* must do the work," that is, together with Him. It's a CO-mission. Parents can get their work done much faster without their little children's help. But it's the "we" part that binds their hearts *together*—you and Jesus.

THE ISSACHAR FACTOR—3

But when he, the Spirit of truth, comes, he will guide you into all truth. He will not speak on his own; he will speak only what he hears, and he will tell you what is yet to come.
John 16:13, NIV.

Would you like the Issachar factor's unusual ability to understand the times and know what ought to be done? Here are seven simple ways the gift of discernment can be yours, too.

1. Pray for discernment. Read again our text for today. Jesus specifically promised that the Holy Spirit "will tell you what is yet to come." Begin asking Him now.

2. Study the Word. There's no point in trying to understand the times without pondering what God has already spoken about these times. Revisit old prophecies, examine new passages, immerse yourself in Holy Scripture. It's the one Book the chosen must master. "The entrance of Your words gives light; it gives understanding to the simple" (Ps. 119:130).

3. Believe the prophets. The tribe of Issachar already had a track record. Long before David, the leaders of Issachar knew the importance of aligning themselves with the divine gift of prophecy: "And [in that day of battle] the princes of Issachar were with Deborah" (Judges 5:15). And she was a prophet. In the day of battle it is the better part of wisdom to align yourself with the prophet. "Believe in the Lord your God, and you shall be established; believe His prophets, and you shall prosper" (2 Chron. 20:20). A century ago one like Deborah wrote: "The present is a time of overwhelming interest to all living. Rulers and statesmen, men who occupy positions of trust and authority, thinking men and women of all classes, have their attention fixed upon the events taking place about us. They are watching the strained, restless relations that exist among the nations. They observe the intensity that is taking possession of every earthly element, and they recognize that something great and decisive is about to take place—that the world is on the verge of a stupendous crisis. Angels are now restraining the winds of strife, that they may not blow until the world shall be warned of its coming doom; but a storm is gathering, ready to burst upon the earth; and when God shall bid His angels loose the winds, there will be such a scene of strife as no pen can picture" (*Education*, pp. 179, 180). The Issachar factor—the divinely enabled ability to discern the times and decide the response—is predicated upon a trust in God's prophets, "which you do well to heed as a light that shines in a dark place, until the day dawns" (2 Peter 1:19).

THE ISSACHAR FACTOR — 4

And He said to them, "It is not for you to know times or seasons which the Father has put in His own authority." Acts 1:7.

Yesterday we discussed three ways the gift of discernment can be yours. Today we'll look at two more.

4. Avoid all date setting. The only One in the universe who has the date of Jesus' return circled in bright red in the calendar on His wall is the Father, Jesus told His disciples. Anybody else who comes riding into town with "new light" for a new date (almost) should not be believed. "Watch therefore, for you do not know what hour your Lord is coming" (Matt. 24:42). But having established that, don't forget that God's endgame is stunningly rapid.

Researcher Chris Martenson warns his Web site readers (www.chrismartenson.com) how quickly events can accelerate. Imagine, he says, that at noon I handcuff you to the highest seat in the bleachers of Fenway Park, stadium home of the Boston Red Sox. Then I place a single drop of water on the pitcher's mound far below—a drop that magically doubles in size every minute. If Fenway were watertight, how long will you have to flee that stadium to survive? For minutes you would see no appreciable increase in water—one drop becomes two, two drops become four, etc. At 12:44 p.m. there would be just five feet of water in the stadium, still leaving 93 percent of the stadium empty. But if you do not extricate yourself within five minutes, your seat in the highest bleacher will be under water at 12:49 p.m.! It is the power of compounding. Albert Bartlett observes, "The greatest shortcoming of the human race is our inability to understand the exponential function." For 44 minutes we think we have all the time in the world—but five minutes later, it's all over! A century ago the same point was made: "Great changes are soon to take place in our world, and the final movements will be rapid ones" (*Testimonies for the Church*, vol. 9, p. 11). The point? While no one knows the date, be forewarned that the "exponential function" means that suddenly all the indicators will simultaneously spike—with blinding speed. Watch!

5. Maintain a healthy caution. As you seek the Spirit's discernment to understand the times, avoid dogmatic prognostications and those who insist on them. The Internet flourishes with "prophetic" scenarios. Keep a healthy tentativeness and flexibility in your conclusions, "for you do not know which [idea] will succeed, whether this or that" (Eccl. 11:6, NIV). Jesus has called you to live and serve with a spirit of trust in your heavenly Father and hope in your soon-coming Savior, mingled with an earnest love for those you'll meet today.

THE ISSACHAR FACTOR—5

Call to me and I will answer you, and will tell you great and hidden things that you have not known. Jer. 33:3, NRSV.

I used to think that the gift of discernment was a spiritual gift reserved only for a select few. But the more I study, the more convinced I am that God wants to bestow this gift on all His friends. Why else would He invite us in our text today to ask Him to give us the ability to discern "great and hidden things" we haven't known before? Why else would Jesus promise that the Holy Spirit "'will guide you into all truth . . . and He will tell you things to come'" (John 16:13)? How? Consider these final two steps to understanding the times and knowing how to respond:

6. Keep your focus on God. Remember—He's the hero in earth's final chapter, not the chosen. "Look to Me, and be saved, all you ends of the earth! For I am God, and there is no other" (Isa. 45:22). All trend analyses and "signs of the times" exposés must have as their shared quest the compelling mission to draw the attention of this generation to the Savior. How?

7. Testify to your hope. My friend Jon Paulien, who has spent his life reflecting on and studying the book of Revelation, has written extensively on the Apocalypse. While he maintains a healthy tentativeness even with his own research and conclusions, one point he reiterates: no matter how the endgame is deciphered in Revelation, Christ makes it clear throughout that book that the "everlasting gospel" must go "to every nation, tribe, tongue, and people" (Rev. 14:6) *before He will return.* You see, the Issachar factor of discerning the times (what will yet come) must lead us to the Issachar factor of determining the response (what must yet be done). And Jesus is unequivocal: "And this gospel of the kingdom will be preached in all the world as a witness to all the nations, and then the end will come" (Matt. 24:14). Think about it: *the surest of all "signs of the times" that Jesus is soon to come is the only sign that is left in the hands of His followers*—telling the world about Jesus. And what could be a more calming antidote for this generation of fear than the simple truth: *He died for me*—I can live without guilt (no more drinking or drugging it away); *He rose for me*—I can live without fear (for what can man do to me that the Son of man cannot undo for me); and *He's coming for me*—I can live with hope (not in a president or an economy, but in the only One who will have the last word).

With good news that great, let the children of Issachar go out today and share the hope!

FOUR SECRETS TO SURVIVING THE COMING ECONOMIC EARTHQUAKE—1

Owe no one anything except to love one another, for he who loves another has fulfilled the law.
Rom. 13:8.

Do you know how much a *million* dollars is? If we tightly stacked $1,000 bills on top of each other, a million dollars would be four inches high. How about a *billion* dollars? You'd need a stack 300 feet tall. And how about a *trillion* dollars? That requires a stack of $1,000 bills 63 *miles* up into the stratosphere! And how much is our government in debt today? The stack to pay it off would stretch past the international space station more than 700 miles into space! And that doesn't include the interest. But if we took all of our indebtedness—public and private, government and personal—some estimates say we collectively owe up to 95 63-mile-high stacks of $1,000 bills. No wonder "debt" is a four-letter word in today's society. Is there any hope for you and me? Yes, there is. For the economic earthquake rumbling beneath us right now, there are four vital survival secrets for the chosen. As you worship, ponder them.

Secret 1. Get out of debt. All the wise financial counselors I know are univocal about this one. What kind of debt? All debt! But start with your credit cards. Perform what Dave Ramsey calls a "plasectomy"—cut up your plastic. "But I pay off my credit card(s) every month." Ramsey estimates we spend 12 to 18 percent more using plastic, even when we pay them off monthly. Why? Because nothing slows down spending like counting out the cash. "But I already owe a huge credit card balance." Then begin paying more than the minimum. Credit card companies want you to be indebted for life. Pay off your cards beginning with the lowest balance, so you can experience success as soon as possible. Reduce your interest rate. Call the company. They'd rather have your business than lose your payments completely. And talk to someone. Break debt's shame chain. You're not alone. Talking is the first step to help.

It was raining, and so I was running on my treadmill, troubled over some circumstances and wondering how it was all going to turn out. Suddenly two blue jays alighted in the wet tree outside my window. I stared at them as I ran. They hopped to another branch, and both turned my way, as if they wanted me to take a good long look. Do they look worried or anxious? And didn't the heavenly Father they trust also make me? Then why should I be worried or anxious? Should I not trust Him? For am I not of more value to Him than two little blue jays?

FOUR SECRETS TO SURVIVING THE COMING ECONOMIC EARTHQUAKE—2

You can be sure that God will take care of everything you need, his generosity exceeding even yours in the glory that pours from Jesus. Phil. 4:19, Message.

Ever wonder why commercials were invented? I once read a book by former advertising executive Jerry Mander. Its title betrays its premise—*Four Arguments for the Elimination of Television.* In it he made a point that has stuck with me over the years. The dominant purpose of advertising is to create in the viewer a state of discontent. Think about it. Do I need advertising to remind me I must eat food and wear clothing to survive? Do you need commercials to remind you to brush your teeth and wash your hands and your dirty clothes? Hardly! Advertising seeks to sell us what we wouldn't have bought had we not seen the ad. It creates "a scarcity of contentment." I just gotta have that iPhone, drive that SUV, wear those name-brand jeans. And so we buy what we don't need. But we are paying far too high a price for the *more* that no longer feels like *much.*

Secret 2. Discover the joy of contentment. (And watch less television would be an auxiliary secret, I suppose.) Don't only *get* out of debt, but also *stay* out of debt. What will keep us from succumbing to Madison Avenue's hypnotic chant (especially during this Christmas season)? "For I have learned to be content whatever the circumstances. I know what it is to be in need, and I know what it is to have plenty. I have learned the secret of being content in any and every situation, whether well fed or hungry, whether living in plenty or in want" (Phil 4:11, 12, NIV). You see, *contentment is a quiet state of mind based upon a simple way of life.* Paul was not a Zen Buddhist. He was a follower of Christ who learned to be happy and contented with whatever he had or didn't have. "My God will meet all your needs according to his glorious riches in Christ Jesus" (verse 19, NIV). It's a promise to supply all our *needs,* not our *wants.* When we reduce our wants, we're contented to trust God with our needs.

"The whole treasury of heaven is open to those He seeks to save. Having collected the riches of the universe, and laid open the resources of infinite power, He gives them all into the hands of Christ, and says, All these are for man. Use these gifts to convince him that there is no love greater than Mine in earth or heaven. His greatest happiness will be found in loving Me" (*The Desire of Ages,* p. 57). Can you think of a dearer Friend to trust and love?

FOUR SECRETS TO SURVIVING THE COMING ECONOMIC EARTHQUAKE—3

"Bring the whole tithe into the storehouse, that there may be food in my house. Test me in this," says the Lord Almighty, "and see if I will not throw open the floodgates of heaven and pour out so much blessing that there will not be room enough to store it." Mal. 3:10, TNIV.

Would you like to be one of Warren Buffett's close friends—this man who started out as a newspaper delivery boy and ended up one of the richest people on earth (estimated net worth, $62 billion)? Can you imagine him handing you his business card one day, with his private phone number and "should you ever need me" scribbled on the back? How could you keep his friendship secret!

Once upon a time there was a God even richer than Warren Buffett. He's been quoted to say, "The silver is Mine, and the gold is Mine" (Haggai 2:8), and apparently He means all of it! "The cattle on a thousand hills are Mine" (Ps. 50:10), and from the reports we've received, even the hills under the cattle are His. "The earth is the Lord's, and everything in it, the world, and all who live in it" (Ps. 24:1, NIV), leading Maltbie Babcock to compose a hymn that sings the truth: "This Is My Father's World." Would you like to be one of this God's close friends? To carry in your heart His inside number, "should you ever need Me"? How could you keep His friendship secret! It is precisely God's ownership of the entire universe that is the truth behind the third secret.

Secret 3. Sign God on as your CEO, CFO, and COO. In the parlance of Warren Buffett's corporate world, God offers to become our chief executive officer, chief financial officer, and chief operating officer—all Three in One. We gladly (who wouldn't!), humbly (you'll partner with *me?*) accept His gracious offer by a single signature—on a tithe envelope. From the beginning, tithe has defined the first 10 percent of our income as exclusively belonging to the God who enabled us to earn the entire 100 percent. It's counterintuitive, especially for those of us struggling for economic survival. But truly, we can't afford *not* to tithe. Moses reminded the chosen: "During the forty years that I led you through the desert, your clothes did not wear out, nor did the sandals on your feet" (Deut. 29:5, NIV). Tires lasting longer, money stretching farther—I can't explain how God fulfills His promise in our text today. All I know from my personal experience is that there is no one greater to have on your side in the midst of this economic meltdown. So give Him your signature today.

FOUR SECRETS TO SURVIVING THE COMING ECONOMIC EARTHQUAKE—4

Give away your life; you'll find life given back, but not merely given back—given back with bonus and blessing. Giving, not getting, is the way. Generosity begets generosity.
Luke 6:38, Message.

I love the story, don't you? There she is, picking up a few sticks in that drought- and famine-ravaged land, preparing a final supper for her son and herself—when a bushy-bearded prophet asks her not only for a glass of water but for a meal, as well. "Do me this favor and your food will never run out." Counterintuitive? Totally. But the widow's faith response still teaches the truth—*if you make God first, He will make it last.* Isn't that what Jesus was trying to tell us when He promised, "Give, and it will be given to you" (Luke 6:38)? How could the widow's giving up the little she had possibly result in more than she could ever have dreamed? You may be wondering the same thing as you stare at that stack of bills on your desk or the pink slip in your hand. *How can God possibly provide what unemployment has taken from me?*

Secret 4. Turn your surviving into thriving! Why don't you find out? Go ahead and give, and see if the God of Elijah and the widow won't turn your sur- viving into thriving, too? The truth is, the happiest people on earth are all givers, whether rich or poor. Research now shows that giving boosts your immune sys- tem, fighting off stress and depression, and increasing your life expectancy in the process. "Give, and it will be given to you." Jesus knew what He was talking about. Give your treasure, give your talents, give your time—give yourself. "For God so loved the world that he gave." You're in great company. "Giving touches a nerve in us that nothing else does. We look a lot like God when we do it. When you give, you defy the fear that you won't have enough. You insult greed, the impulse to ac- quire or possess more than one needs or deserves. If you really believe that God owns it all and that He is your source and provider, giving will be a simple matter. . . . According to Jesus, giving keeps your heart in motion toward God and away from material things. . . . Your heart will follow the direction of your giving" (Ed Gungor, in *Leadership*, Summer 2006, p. 36).

Four-year-old Elizabeth Johnston was learning her memory verse, "God loveth a cheerful giver." But her mother, Madeline, told me that the words got a bit jumbled, for all that week she could hear Beth repeating the verse to her dol- lies: "God is a lovely cheerful giver." How true!

A CHRISTMAS LIST CHECKLIST

But store up for yourselves treasures in heaven, where moth and rust do not destroy, and where thieves do not break in and steal. For where your treasure is, there your heart will be also.
Matt. 6:20, 21, NIV.

Sometimes the chosen can be like the two young brothers who were spending the night at their grandparents' home. At bedtime the boys knelt beside their beds to say their prayers. The youngest one began praying at the top of his lungs: "I PRAY FOR A NEW BICYCLE. I PRAY FOR A NEW NINTENDO. I PRAY FOR A NEW IPOD." His older brother leaned over and nudged him: "Why are you shouting? God isn't deaf!" To which the little brother replied, "No, but Grandma is."

As we count down to this most commercial of all seasons of the year, has God become a kind of doting but benevolent heavenly grandma to us? Reviewing our prayer journey this year, could it be our prayer seasons have ended up becoming Christmas wish list inventories—all year long? "Dear God, blessed be Your name. And thank You for Your goodness. And please be rich toward me, because I need . . . and . . . and . . . In Jesus' name. Amen."

One of the bold lessons of life that few human beings ever learn is that the journey of faith and religion is not so that God might be rich toward us, but rather so that we might learn to be rich toward Him. That was Jesus' stunning punch line to that somber parable of His about a rich farmer who one night crawled into bed and commenced an absolutely delicious soliloquy about how utterly successful he was and how gloriously rich he had become. His midnight conversation with himself is laced with 13 first-person pronouns. And just as he is sighing contentedly off to sleep, the midnight curtains tremble lightly, a chilling breeze sweeps into the room, and on that cold wind a Voice in the dark: "You fool!" The wealthy farmer suffers cardiac arrest and is dead. The End. Jesus' point? "This is how it will be for those who store up things for themselves but are not *rich toward God*" (Luke 12:21, TNIV).

In all of earth's history, can you think of a more critical year to put our gifts for God at the top of our Christmas list? One day soon the little we have will be worth nothing. While he was away, John Wesley's home burned to the ground. When he received the news of that terrible loss, Wesley responded: "The *Lord's* house burned. One less responsibility for me!"

THE JESUS GENERATION: "ARE WE STILL OURSELVES?"

Blessed is the nation whose God is the Lord,
the people He has chosen as His own inheritance. Ps. 33:12.

One night our little girl, Kristin, was carrying on a rather ponderous philosophical conversation with her mother. At age 5 she was still sorting out the "yesterday-today-tomorrow" delineation of time. Then as Karen tucked her into bed, out of the blue Kris asked, "Mommy, now that it's *tonight,* is this *tomorrow?*" Karen replied, "No, Krissie, it's not *tomorrow.*" But looking up from her pillow, she probed further, "Well, is it *yesterday,* then?" Obviously in 5-year-old logic, if tonight is not today and not tomorrow, then it must be yesterday. "No, sweetie, this is *today.*" "Then when does it become *tomorrow?*" To which Karen replied, "When you wake up in the morning, it will be *tomorrow.*" Kristin thought long and hard for a moment, and then with her brow furrowed with perplexity, she asked, "Mommy, are we still ourselves?"

You start out with a philosophical discussion of time and end up with the great ontological debate—are we still ourselves? Well, are we? For nearly 170 years people across this nation and around the earth have proclaimed the soon coming of Christ. "Tomorrow is almost here!" the chosen have cried out. Today has almost become yesterday, and tonight is nearly tomorrow. So before tonight becomes yesterday—it's time to get ready!

We dare not abandon that time-bound hope. After all, the word "imminent" has been woven into the collective conversation of the chosen from the beginning. The dictionary defines it as an event that is impending, hanging over one's head, close at hand in its incidence, coming on shortly. "The end of all things is at hand" (1 Peter 4:7). Like our spiritual progenitors, do we still link "imminent" to Jesus' coming? Are we still ourselves?

Some suggest that as long as Jesus comes, it doesn't really matter if it's soon or not. Tell that to a young couple passionately in love and eagerly tearing off the pages of the calendar until their glorious wedding day. "Soon" makes all the difference in the world! And so it must for the chosen of this generation, too. If we ever let go of tomorrow, we will quickly lose hold of today.

A fast-food restaurant sign reads, "Thank you for coming. Please return soon." It's a third-millennial version of the Apocalypse's last prayer, "Even so, come, Lord Jesus." When that becomes our daily prayer, then we are still ourselves—the Jesus generation.

THE JESUS GENERATION: 144,000 — 1

For we know, brothers and sisters loved by God, that he has chosen you. 1 Thess. 1:4, TNIV.

There has been a simple yes-or-no question I've wrestled over. Perhaps you have too. It's this: Does God have a different standard for the final Jesus generation on earth than He has had for all the previous generations? Is there a "translation" standard (for the chosen who will go to heaven without experiencing death) that is different from a "resurrection" standard (for the chosen who will be resurrected at Jesus' return)? You say, "Who cares? What difference does it make?" Well, if God does have two different standards for His friends, depending on when they lived in salvation's history—and given that we now live in the most unsettled and unpredictable time in earth's history, giving our generation the very real potential of becoming the last generation on earth—then wouldn't you want to know what God's standard is for this potentially final Jesus generation? But of course! So let's explore for the answer.

Enter now the 144,000. "Then I looked, and there before me was the Lamb, standing on Mount Zion, and with him 144,000 who had his name and his Father's name written on their foreheads" (Rev. 14:1, NIV). Ever notice how countercultural these apocalyptic end-time friends of God are? **1.** They have His name on their foreheads at a time when the rest of the world has "the mark of the beast" on theirs (13:16). **2.** They sing "a new song" (14:3) at a time when the rest of the world is marinated in the music of fallen Babylon (18:22). **3.** They refuse to go to bed with the great prostitute when the rest of the earth has slept with this fallen geo-religio-political alliance (18:3). **4.** They "follow the Lamb wherever He goes" (14:4) when the whole world has "followed the beast," that end-time demonic confederacy (13:3). **5.** They have "no lie . . . in their mouths" (14:5, NIV) when deceit and subterfuge are the rule of the age (13:14). **6.** They are "blameless" (14:5, NIV) in the midst of a society morally fallen and spiritually bankrupt (18:4, 5).

Clearly God's 144,000 are the Jesus generation on the eve of His return. But are they held to a higher divine standard than all the chosen who have lived before them? Whatever the answer, it is abundantly clear they are a countercultural people with an unshakable passion for Christ. If that were all—wouldn't you want that portrait for your own?

THE JESUS GENERATION: 144,000—2

This is the account of Noah. Noah was a righteous man, blameless among the people of his time, and he walked with God. Gen. 6:9, NIV.

Are the 144,000 a literal number? The way life is unraveling on earth these days, one wonders sometimes if God even has 144,000 loyal followers and friends left (you and I being exceptions, of course)! But play that violin very long, and soon we'll echo the self-pity of Elijah, who pined to God, "And I alone am left," when in fact God had 7,000 others who had not bowed to that fallen culture and had not become marinated in that pagan world. Clearly 144,000 is a symbolic number, as symbolic as the "male virgin Jew" (Rev. 7:4; 14:4) description of this end-time generation of God's chosen ones. Fact is, God has His faithful all over the earth.

But will they be held to a different standard than God's friends of previous generations? Let's enlarge yesterday's six-point description from Revelation 14 and see if there are precedents for this generation. **1.** Are the 144,000 the only "blameless" ones in history? Look at our text for today. Noah was too. And so were Abraham and Job (Gen. 17:1; Job 1:1). **2.** Are they the first not to lie? No, for Jesus described Nathanael as one "in whom is no deceit" (John 1:47). **3.** Are they the first to follow the Lamb? "Enoch walked with God" (Gen. 5:24). **4.** Are they the first to be pure morally and spiritually? No, for so were Joseph and Daniel and his three companions (Gen. 39:10; Dan. 3:12). **5.** Are they the first to sing a new song? Moses and Israel sang such a song on the far banks of the Red Sea (Ex. 15:1). **6.** Are they the first to be sealed? God-fearing Jews were sealed long ago (Eze. 9:4), and God-fearing Christians have been sealed throughout history (Eph. 1:13). **7.** Are they the first to obey the commandments of God (Rev. 14:12)? No, for Daniel did (Dan. 6:13). **8.** Are they the first to hold fast to the faith of Jesus (Rev. 14:12)? No, for Paul admonished Timothy to do the same (2 Tim. 4:7).

Looking at this list, how would you now answer the question—is the Jesus generation held to a different or higher standard than the rest of God's friends and saints and forgiven sinners down through history? The answer is clear. What God has asked of His friends from the very beginning He still seeks today. The standard is unchanged. "My grace is sufficient for you" (2 Cor. 12:9) remains the divine bedrock upon which God has always built His household of faith. Then are the 144,000 not unique at all? They are indeed, as we will discover tomorrow.

THE JESUS GENERATION: 144,000—3

*At that time Michael, the great prince who protects your people, will arise. There will be a time
of distress such as has not happened from the beginning of nations until then. But at that time
your people—everyone whose name is found written in the book—will be delivered.*
Dan. 12:1, NIV.

There are two unique ways in which the 144,000 will be unparalleled in salvation history. **1. They will be unique in number.** The very size of the number 144,000 reveals that there will be literally thousands upon thousands of earth children who will rise to the standard of God's holiness that He has always held before His friends. Only now, instead of an isolated Enoch or Noah or Joseph or Ruth or Nathaniel or Paul here or there, there will be an entire generation of Enochs and John the Baptists and Marys and Esthers and Daniels ("Dare to be a Daniel, dare to stand alone, Dare to have a purpose firm! Dare to make it known!") in every nation, tribe, culture, and people. By the thousands God will have Jobs who will be so loyal to Him that they will cry out: "Though He slay me, yet will I trust Him" (Job 13:15). How do we know? "And they overcame [the dragon] by the blood of the Lamb and by the word of their testimony, and they did not love their lives to the death" (Rev. 12:11). All over the face of this fallen and crumbling earth there will be a people who have God's name in their foreheads and His character in their hearts.

2. They will be unique in history. For they will be the generation that will live *through* the final gavel of the cosmic judgment. "The hour of his judgment has come" (Rev. 14:7). And when that gavel falls, all hell will break loose. Our text today describes "a time of trouble, such as never was since there was a nation" (NKJV). God reveals this impending crisis, not to frighten us, but to remind us there will be a people on earth who, in the midst of an unprecedented time of trouble, will remain as Daniel did, utterly loyal to the Creator God of heaven. The Jesus Generation. The Chosen. And that is why they will sing a new song "no one can learn . . . except the hundred and forty-four thousand who were redeemed from the earth" (Rev. 14:3). Which is precisely why God is so earnest now "to make ready a people prepared for the Lord" (Luke 1:17). The stakes have never been higher, the times never more urgent—"But be of good cheer, I have overcome the world" (John 16:33)—and His promise never more hopeful!

THE JESUS GENERATION: ONE LINE, ONE LIFE, ONE GENERATION

He must increase, but I must decrease. John 3:30.

And what is the one line that guides the one life of that one generation at the end of time—that crossing-over generation that refuses to imbibe what C. S. Lewis called the "sweet poison of the false infinite," and embraces instead God's call to radical countercultural holiness?

Ponder the last recorded words of that friend of God's before he was arrested by a guilty king, incarcerated in a lonely fortress, and then on a starry, starry night beheaded at the behest of an insanely vengeful queen. For it is through his last words that the John the Baptist generation and the Jesus generation are conjoined in a common bond. "He must increase, but I must decrease," John instructed his dwindling followers. "Christ must increase, but I must decrease."

Could there be a nobler desire for a generation living at the edge of time? As one writer expressed it: "May I take ten looks at Christ, O God, for every look I take at me." May my preoccupation for Jesus be 10 times greater for Him than for me. *The Desire of Ages* describes the paradox: "Looking in faith to the Redeemer, John had risen to the height of self-abnegation [self-renunciation]. . . . The soul of the prophet, emptied of self, was filled with the light of the divine" (pp. 179, 180). The paradoxical height of self-abnegation—no wonder Job himself could exclaim, "Therefore I abhor myself, and repent in dust and ashes" (Job 42:6).

"He must increase, but I must decrease." For that is how the 144,000 choose to live. "They follow the Lamb wherever he goes" (Rev. 14:4, NIV). They live by John's credo, for there is no other way for the brine of self's fallen kingdom to be expunged from their lives and cleansed from their souls. "Christ must increase, but I must decrease." More and more of Him—less and less of me.

Theodore Monod composed a hymn that sings John's prayer: "O the bitter pain and sorrow, that a time could ever be, when I proudly said to Jesus, 'All of self and none of Thee.' . . . Yet He found me; I beheld Him bleeding on th' accursed tree; and my wistful heart said faintly, 'Some of self and some of Thee.' . . . Day by day His tender mercy, healing, helping, full and free, brought me lower, while I whispered, 'Less of self and more of Thee.' . . . Higher than the highest heavens, deeper than the deepest sea, Lord, Thy love at last has conquered, *'None* of self and *all* of Thee' " (*Christ in Song*, no. 218).

THE JESUS GENERATION: R.I.P.

And a great windstorm arose, and the waves beat into the boat, so that it was already filling. But He was in the stern, asleep on a pillow. And they awoke Him and said to Him, "Teacher, do You not care that we are perishing?" Mark 4:37, 38.

I don't sleep very well when the plane I'm traveling in is pitching and rolling through the midnight skies at 35,000 feet. I'd rather be in my own bed. How Jesus could possibly remain asleep through that furious, heaving, water-drenching midnight gale on the lake is nothing short of miraculous. But do you suppose it's the very miracle God longs to store deep in the hearts of the Jesus generation to prepare them for the massive storm that is brewing?

Oswald Chambers in *My Utmost for His Highest* defines trusting faith this way: "Faith is unutterable trust in God, trust which never dreams that He will not stand by us" (Aug. 29). In the fury of that storm Jesus slept peacefully because He never dreamed the Father wouldn't stand by Him. "It was in faith—faith in God's love and care—that Jesus rested" (*The Desire of Ages,* p. 336). Trusting faith.

Like the day Jesus died. "Now it was about the sixth hour, and there was darkness over all the earth until the ninth hour. Then the sun was darkened, and the veil of the temple was torn in two. And when Jesus had cried out with a loud voice, He said, *'Father, "into Your hands I commit My spirit."'* Having said this, He breathed His last" (Luke 23:44-46).

I don't want to sound morbid, but if I am able to choose the last words I breathe before I die, I would like to die with these words of absolute trust on my lips, wouldn't you? As he became the first Christian martyr, Stephen did that: "Lord Jesus, receive my spirit" (Acts 7:59). So did John Huss, the Bohemian pastor and Reformer, whose last words tethered to that fiery stake were: "I do commit my spirit into Thy hands, O Lord Jesus, for Thou hast redeemed me." They were Bernard's last words, and Luther's and Melanchthon's as well.

And those last words will be the *life words* of earth's last generation of the chosen. How else do you suppose they will pass through the most turbulent storm in earth's history? Radical trusting faith: "Father, into Your hands we commit our lives." "The season of distress and anguish before us will require a faith that can endure weariness, delay, and hunger—a faith that will not faint though severely tried. The period of probation [now] is granted to all to prepare for that time" (*The Great Controversy,* p. 621). Let us pray it together: "Lord, increase our faith" (Luke 17:5). And He will.

THE JESUS GENERATION: "TO LONELY PLACES"

But Jesus often withdrew to lonely places and prayed. Luke 5:16, NIV.

Dallas Willard tells of experiments conducted with mice and amphetamine (a drug to induce increased wakefulness). When a mouse is kept alone, it takes 20 times more amphetamine to kill it than when it is in a group. In fact, researchers found that if they placed an amphetamine-free mouse in the midst of a group already on the drug, that poor, drug-free mouse would be dead within 10 minutes! So strong was the erratic group behavior of the drugged mice that the healthy mouse began to imitate their frenzied dysfunction and eventually dropped over dead from simply trying to keep up with them. Willard's point? "Our conformity to social pattern is hardly less remarkable than that of the mice—and just as deadly" (*Spirit of the Disciplines*, p. 161). And therein lies the necessary lesson for the Jesus generation. The hypnotic draw of this culture's social pattern can be broken only by our withdrawal from it just as Jesus did.

"But he would withdraw to desolate places and pray" (Luke 5:16, ESV). Why? "No other life was ever so crowded with labor and responsibility as was that of Jesus; yet how often He was found in prayer! How constant was His communion with God! . . . In a life wholly devoted to the good of others, the Saviour found it necessary to withdraw from the thoroughfares of travel and from the throng that followed Him day after day. He must turn aside from a life of ceaseless activity and contact with human needs, to seek retirement and unbroken communion with His Father. As one with us, a sharer in our needs and weaknesses, He was wholly dependent upon God, and in the secret place of prayer He sought divine strength, that He might go forth braced for duty and trial. . . . Through continual communion He received life from God, that He might impart life to the world. *His experience is to be ours*" (*The Desire of Ages,* pp. 362, 363; italics supplied).

For a generation praying to cross over, it isn't rocket science to suggest that the state of earth's civilization at that final hour will be like amphetamine-drugged mice in spades! It is utterly essential, therefore, that you and I preserve and protect our daily solitude with Jesus, *no matter what.* The enemy of us all knows that if he can woo us into conformity to the social patterns and fallen culture of this society, the absolute frenzy of trying to imitate it and them will destroy us. For the sake of His soul and mission, our Master and Example *often* withdrew to lonely places in order to pray. For the sake of our soul and mission, can we afford to do any less?

THE JESUS GENERATION: "WE ARE DRIVEN"

Immediately the Spirit drove Him into the wilderness. Mark 1:12.

The automotive giant Nissan once touted its shiny creations with the advertising slogan "We are driven!" Of course we are—all of us. Some of us are driven by the need to be loved and accepted. Others of us are driven by the need to be fêted and applauded. Still others are driven by the need to constantly please our significant others, be it a parent, a spouse, an employer, or even the memory of one. But lest we conclude that somehow it is morally wrong to be driven, our text today reminds us that Jesus Himself was driven—not by the emotional quirks that drive us, to be sure, but driven nonetheless by the Spirit Himself. I am ever amazed at this piece of inspired reflection on the life of Jesus: "From hours spent with God [Jesus] came forth morning by morning, to bring the light of heaven to men. *Daily he received a fresh baptism of the Holy Spirit*" (*Christ's Object Lessons,* p. 139; italics supplied). Did you catch that? *Daily* He was infilled with the power of the mighty third person of the Godhead. The Spirit-driven life was the *daily* quest and experience of Jesus. Would that we all were so driven!

By why is this Gift so essential, especially for the chosen? Simple. The Holy Spirit is the divine secret to the Christlike life lived by the 144,000 just before He returns. Note carefully how *The Desire of Ages* describes this cause and effect: "The Holy Spirit is the breath of spiritual life in the soul. *The impartation of the Spirit is the impartation of the life of Christ.* It imbues the receiver with the attributes of Christ" (*The Desire of Ages,* p. 805; italics supplied). In a world where humanity's most popular heroes have a star embedded in the sidewalk along Hollywood Boulevard, God is raising up a new generation driven to emulate a radically different and exponentially greater Hero. How does that old gospel song go? "Be like Jesus, this my song, in the home and in the throng; be like Jesus, all day long! I would be like Jesus." Why, it could be the theme song of the Jesus generation, so simple yet focused that prayer. A Spirit-driven life is the answer, for only when the Spirit drives us can we reach the destination of a Christlike life.

So, trying to find the right Christmas gift this year for the person who has everything? Want to find the perfect gift for yourself? How about the one Present that "brings all other blessings" in its box? (see *The Desire of Ages,* p. 672). What more potent prayer for the Jesus generation to be praying on the edge of eternity! Let's ask for the Gift right now.

THE JESUS GENERATION:
THE LAST TEMPTATION

During the days of Jesus' life on earth, he offered up prayers and petitions with loud cries and tears to the one who could save him from death, and he was heard because of his reverent submission. Heb. 5:7, NIV.

Oscar Wilde quipped, "I can resist anything except temptation!" But then we humans capitulate too easily, too readily, don't we? The searing showdown with the fallen Lucifer that our Lord Himself walked into—remember, the gospel record is clear: Jesus was driven by the Spirit (Mark 1:12) or "led by the Spirit" (Luke 4:1) straight into that explosive desert battle—is evidence enough that the path of temptation is the way of God for even those who are closest to Him. "Lead us not into temptation" notwithstanding, the reality is that all of God's chosen friends are led just like Jesus into the demonic fury of temptation.

And what is temptation? "Temptation is the suggested shortcut to the realization of the highest at which I aim—not towards what I understand as evil, but towards what I understand as good" (Oswald Chambers, *My Utmost for His Highest*, Sept. 17). The devil does not stalk us with the offer to do evil—we would quickly resist. Rather he approaches us with the offer of a shortcut to what surely is good. It was that way with Joseph's sexual temptation from Mrs. Potiphar, offering him the possibility of what was good—his freedom from slavery. It was that way with Jesus' three wilderness barrages from Satan—all three offering what was truly good: deliverance from starvation, protection from danger, conquest of the world. But for Joseph and for Jesus, having been led into temptation, the obedient response was the same—it may be the "good" way, but it is not the God way. "Your will be done on earth as it is in heaven."

And because the divine will will indeed be done on earth in the lives of the final Jesus generation, you and I don't have Wilde's luxury of laughing off our temptations. Rather, like our Master, we too must offer up "prayers and petitions with loud cries and tears" to the only One who can save us (Heb. 5:7, NIV). There is no shortcut for the chosen. But there is this promise: "The soul that is yielded to Christ becomes His own fortress, which He holds in a revolted world, and He intends that no authority shall be known in it but His own. A soul thus kept in possession by the heavenly agencies is impregnable to the assaults of Satan" (*The Desire of Ages*, p. 324).

THE JESUS GENERATION: THE TIPPING POINT

"Let's go across to the outpost of those pagans," Jonathan said to his armor bearer. "Perhaps the Lord will help us, for nothing can hinder the Lord. He can win a battle whether he has many warriors or only a few!" 1 Sam. 14:6, NLT.

In his best-seller *The Tipping Point: How Little Things Can Make a Big Difference* Malcolm Gladwell examines the strategic key to cultural trends. He concludes that massive social change behaves like a viral epidemic (the flu, measles, AIDS). All you need is a single virus with the ability to stick to someone else, and given the right context the right virus can explode in exponential multiplication until an entire populace is infected. To illustrate that process of geometric progression, Gladwell takes a sheet of paper and folds it in half. Is the paper now twice as thick as before? (This is not a trick question.) Yes. Fold it again. Now is it four times as thick? Yes. If you could fold that paper 50 times, how thick would it be? I guessed a few inches; a friend guessed 10 feet. The answer? The thickness would stretch from the earth to the sun. And if you folded it 51 times? From the earth to the sun and back again. Something very small—be it an idea, a person, or even a movement—if given the opportunity to replicate and duplicate itself, can end up infecting or affecting the entire world!

Just two young adults—Jonathan and his armorbearer—but they were all God needed to infect the craven heart of Israel's cowering army. Two young men crawling hand over hand up the rocky face of an enemy-held cliff demonstrated the radical faith and bold courage that Heaven knew would turn the tide and rout the enemy. Who can't help but admire the courage of Jonathan who cried out to his fighting companion, "Come, let's go. . . . Nothing can hinder the Lord from saving, whether by many or by few" (1 Sam. 14:6, NIV).

Good news for the chosen, who like Jonathan will need from God one of those geometric progression finishes at the end of time! How else will an entire generation be reached for Christ in a matter of weeks? "After these things I saw another angel coming down from heaven, having great authority, and the [whole] earth was illuminated with his glory" (Rev. 18:1). If the first Pentecost began with a handful, couldn't the last Pentecost begin the same way? God doesn't need millions in this hour of earth's closing history. All He needs are two of you. And if He can't find two, then one will do—even if it's one boy against a towering giant for God's glory.

THE JESUS GENERATION: "THE UPSIDE-DOWN KINGDOM"

I tell you the truth, unless a kernel of wheat is planted in the soil and dies, it remains alone. But its death will produce many new kernels—a plentiful harvest of new lives.
John 12:24, NLT.

Welcome to Jesus' "upside-down kingdom," as Donald Kraybill described it. It's the only kingdom on earth where in order to win, you must lose; in order to be first, you must be last; in order to be a leader, you must become a servant; in order to be the greatest, you must become the least; in order to live, you must die. Let's be honest—it's not the kind of stuff that will make you a winner on *Survivor* or any other of the ad nauseam reality TV shows. With Jesus, surviving isn't the driving premise for those who follow Him. Sacrificing is.

Take a kernel of wheat or corn, Jesus illustrates. Think of all you can do with corn kernels: with some glue kids can create funny faces for the refrigerator; with a microwave you pop up a bag of Saturday night nutrition; with some string you can decorate a Christmas tree; or with a glass jar you spice up your shelves with some pretty colors. But you don't have to be a horticulturalist to know that none of these is the highest calling of a kernel or seed. Because a seed has one solitary purpose in life. Anything else falls short of its raison d'être. In our text today Jesus declares that the best seed is a buried seed. You can leave the seeds crammed together in a jar [a church] on the shelf forever—but they will never become more than a jarful of seeds. Every farmer knows that you've got to sacrifice the seed in order to save the seed.

So are you, am I . . . are the chosen a buried seed? "All who would bring forth fruit as workers together with Christ must first fall into the ground and die. The life must be cast into the furrow of the world's need. Self-love, self-interest, must perish. But the law of self-sacrifice is the law of self-preservation [the upside-down kingdom]. The seed buried in the ground produces fruit, and in turn this is planted. Thus the harvest is multiplied. The [farmer] preserves his grain by casting it away. So in human life, to give is to live [upside down again]. *The life that will be preserved is the life that is freely given in service to God and man.* Those who for Christ's sake sacrifice their life in this world will keep it unto life eternal" (*Christ's Object Lessons*, pp. 86, 87; italics supplied).

That's why the Christmas story commences in a stable, not a palace. Because self-sacrifice is the rule of the King who came and the life of the chosen who follow.

THE JESUS GENERATION:
"HAST THOU NO SCAR?" — 1

When He had called the people to Himself, with His disciples also, He said to them, "Whoever desires to come after Me, let him deny himself, and take up his cross, and follow Me. For whoever desires to save his life will lose it, but whoever loses his life for My sake and the gospel's will save it." Mark 8:34, 35.

So what is this cross that Jesus said we're supposed to take up? Some men have concluded that their cross is an irritable postmenopausal wife—"God gave me a cross to bear." Some women have decided that their cross is a hopelessly dead and comfortless marriage from which they cannot be legally or ecclesiastically released—"It's my cross to bear for Jesus." But marriages gone sour are hardly the crosses Jesus had in mind. (In fact, if Jesus could have His way, He'd seek to fix that marriage and probably start with the "cross bearer"!) So what is this cross? Financial straits? Professional failure? Terminal disease?

How did Jesus put it? "If any of you would come after Me, you must deny yourself, take up your cross daily, and follow Me." Clearly, you have to choose it—choose to deny yourself, choose to take up your own cross, choose to bear it right behind Jesus (like Simon the Cyrenian). The cross Jesus calls us to isn't something we got stuck with. It's something we choose. Which means it *can* be a loveless marriage, if you choose for the sake of loyalty to Jesus to bear it and to be faithful to your spouse in spite of little reciprocation. It *can* be professional failure, if your choice to be faithful to Jesus places you at odds with the commands or expectations of your job superiors, so that you're fired or harassed in hopes you'll leave that employment. Your cross *can* be racial discrimination that has dogged your path and harassed your soul, if you choose to embrace that "unrightful" if not unlawful discrimination you are suffering, for the sake of Jesus. Your cross *can* be that terminal disease, if you choose to embrace your physical crisis as an opportunity to testify to your unshaken trust in God in the midst of impending pain and death.

But the choice must be yours, and really in the end only yours. Terry Wardle observes: "The Christian life brings enormous blessing. . . . But Jesus never once hid the fact that the Christian life would be demanding and costly" (*The Transforming Path*, p. 139). In our "rights-conscious" society—where people sue at the drop of the hat to make certain they get their just deserts—Bethlehem and Calvary remind us that our just deserts are a cross, just like Jesus'.

THE JESUS GENERATION:
"HAST THOU NO SCAR?" — 2

If you refuse to take up your cross and follow me, you are not worthy of being mine. If you cling to your life, you will lose it; but if you give up your life for me, you will find it.
Matt. 10:38, 39, NLT.

You can read her story on Wikipedia. As a girl she begged God to take away her brown eyes and give her eyes of blue. But no matter how hard she pleaded, their color never changed. Years later Amy Carmichael remarked that had her prayers been answered, she would never have been able to draw close to the sufferers God called her to, who found in her brown eyes a compassionate likeness to their own. For the Irish girl with the brown eyes grew up to become the beloved missionary to India, serving on that mighty subcontinent 55 years without a furlough until her death. Adopting native garb, dying her skin with dark coffee, Amy Carmichael plunged into her incarnational ministry, rescuing young girls forced into prostitution, founding a mission, and raising up an orphanage. But in spite of joy in her Master's service, through her life she suffered from neuralgia, a painful disease that left her in bed for weeks at a time.

Undeterred, she bore her cross in the steps of her Savior. A young woman once wrote her asking what missionary life was like. Carmichael wrote back, "Missionary life is simply a chance to die." And she nearly did, after a tragic fall, which instead left her bedridden most of the last 20 years of her life. But cheerfully she continued to bear her cross with a life motto that has inspired many: "One can give without loving, but one cannot love without giving." She asked that no gravestone be erected for her. And so the children she served placed a birdbath over her grave inscribed with the word, *Amma*, "Mother" in Tamil. Jesus was right: "She who loses her life for My sake will find it."

Amy Carmichael wrote the poem "No Scar," with its provocative, probing question: "Hast thou no scar? No hidden scar on foot, or side, or hand? I hear thee sung as mighty in the land, I hear them hail thy bright ascendant star, hast thou no scar? Hast thou no wound? Yet I was wounded by the archers, spent, leaned Me against a tree to die; and rent by ravening beasts that encompassed Me, I swooned: Hast thou no wound? No wound? no scar? Yet, as the Master shall the servant be, and, pierced are the feet that follow Me; but thine are whole: can he have followed far who has no wound nor scar?" (in Terry Wardle, *The Transforming Path*, p. 143).

"THE TWELVE DAYS OF CHRISTMAS"

For God so loved the world, that he gave his only begotten Son, that whosoever believeth in him should not perish, but have everlasting life. John 3:16, KJV.

Have you ever sung "The Twelve Days of Christmas"? The song is not only interminably long—it is unabashedly materialistic in its obsession with gift-getting. Since 1984 PNC Wealth Management has been calculating the costs of Christmas via these 12 gifts ("a partridge in a pear tree," etc). They've calculated that if you buy each item in the song just once it will cost you $19,507. Make that $128,886 if you buy the gifts the proscribed number of times!

So how much does Christmas really cost? How much was spent that first Christmas nearly 2,000 years ago? Let's see. We have a blue-collar self-employed carpenter and his pregnant fiancé, both of the lower class, whose income no doubt was best rendered "hand to mouth." Because of the Roman tax edict, the couple locked up his carpenter shop (planning to be back in a few days) and journeyed to "O little town of Bethlehem," where all they got was a string of "No Vacancy" signs. So in the damp smelly darkness of a backyard cave stable the woman's Babe was born, His crib a prickly box of cow feed, His visitors a motley band of unsavory shepherds who, in astonishment, bowed before this Baby the herald angels declared to be the Messiah. But angelic pronouncement notwithstanding, the Baby-makes-three little family was still dirt poor. Had it not been for the extravagant gifts of that band of nomadic Arab sages, the family would never have financially survived their flight to Egypt as impoverished migrants. That first Christmas could hardly be described as much more than a bargain basement bust.

Unless, of course, you calculate the costs from the other side of the universe, the astronomical costs of the One who did all the giving that one-star night long ago. "For God so loved the world that he gave . . ." Wooden manger, wooden cross, He gave it all. "The gift of Christ reveals the Father's heart" (*The Desire of Ages,* p. 57). On Christmas He emptied His treasury for us.

The young mother, frazzled and spent from hanging on to her two children and all their Christmas shopping bags, stepped into the crowded elevator. The holiday mania had taken its toll. As the doors closed, she blurted out, "Whoever started this whole Christmas thing should be found, strung up, and shot." From the back of the car a voice responded, "Don't worry; we've already crucified Him." They said the rest of the way down you could have heard a pin drop.

"I WONDER AS I WANDER"

Beyond all question, the mystery of godliness is great: He appeared in a body, was vindicated by the Spirit, was seen by angels, was preached among the nations, was believed on in the world, was taken up in glory. 1 Tim. 3:16, NIV.

I once saw a painting by Julius Gari Melchers entitled simply *The Nativity.* Perhaps it was the way the artist captured the brooding face of the husband-not-father as he leans forward on his squatted knees and pensively stares at the bedded Newborn tucked at his feet in that crude box of hay. Or maybe it was the utter "spentness" of the young birth mother, exhausted, now prone on the cold floor, save for her slumping shoulders propped against the stable wall, her tired eyes at half mast, her weary face expressionless and resting upon the side of her betrothed. It makes you wonder: What is it the husband broods upon? What thoughts are hers, the young mother? In the heavy, still air do they wonder that the "infant lowly" is the "infant holy"?

The ancient words of our Christmas text today are as provocative in the Greek as they are in the English—*mega musterion*—a truly "mega mystery." How else shall we describe the immersing incarnation (literally, "infleshment") of the Infinite into this shadowland we finites still call home? G. K. Chesterton was right: "We walk bewildered in the light, for something is too large for sight, and something much to plain to say." The Seed of God planted in the womb of humanity—why the very mechanics and genetics of such a divine-human anatomical transfer are more than even our third-millennial science can fathom. But in the end the great mystery that Christmas bids us ponder isn't so much that God *could* do it, but rather that God *would* do it. "The work of redemption is called a mystery, and it is indeed the mystery by which everlasting righteousness is brought to all who believe. . . . Christ, at an infinite cost, by a painful process, mysterious to angels as well as to men, assumed humanity. Hiding His divinity, laying aside His glory, He was born a babe in Bethlehem" (*The SDA Bible Commentary,* Ellen G. White Comments, vol. 7, p. 915).

It was the day before Christmas. Busily wrapping packages, the boy's mother asked if he'd please shine her shoes. Soon, with the proud smile of a 7-year-old, he brought her shiny shoes for inspection. She was so pleased, she handed him a quarter. On Christmas morning she felt a strange lump in one shoe. Taking it off, she shook the shoe and out dropped a quarter wrapped in a small piece of paper. On it in a child's scrawl were the words: "I done it for love."

SNAKES IN THE CRADLE

And as Moses lifted up the serpent in the wilderness, even so must the Son of Man be lifted up, that whoever believes in Him should not perish but have eternal life.
John 3:14, 15.

For 40 hot, long, wearying years the chosen have been camping their way in circles through the barren wilderness. And now with the Promised Land nearly in sight, comes word that Moses and God are taking a detour around Edom. "But the people grew impatient on the way; they spoke against God and against Moses, and said, 'Why have you brought us up out of Egypt to die in the desert?' " (Num. 21:4, 5, NIV). In the words of Yogi Berra, it was déjà vu all over again. Will the chosen ever learn to radically trust their divine Leader?

Now it's not that I'm afraid of snakes—I just don't want to be there when they're there. What follows is the stuff of snake-infested nightmares. The camp of Israel suddenly swarmed with "fiery serpents," so described because of the searing pain and rapidly ensuing death the vipers' fangs inflicted on their victims. I cannot imagine the horror of a deadly adder slithering up onto my bed and sliding beneath my covers and along my very exposed leg. I grew up with too many missionary stories of swaying cobras coiled and cocked at the foot of the bed!

Shall we blame God for this toxic serpentine plague? No. Deuteronomy 8:15 makes it clear that the wilderness was already infested with the adders. For 40 years God shielded His children from their poison. But now only days from the Promised Land, God honors their free choice to reject His leadership. And when He quietly removes His protective presence, the heretofore held-at-bay poisonous reptiles come slithering into camp—and the Israelites begin dropping like flies. "In almost every tent were the dying or dead. None were secure. Often the silence of the night was broken by piercing cries that told of fresh victims" (*Patriarchs and Prophets,* p. 429). And the very leader they had cursed just hours earlier they now begged to plead with God on their behalf. So Moses turned his face before God, pleading for the chosen. The divine response? "Mold a bronze serpent, hoist it on a pole, and command the stricken to look. All who look will live."

Raw faith. You either look and live, or refuse to look and die. For the chosen the choice has always been that stark. Magic serpent? No, just the image of a God who would become the very curse that the sins of the chosen have caused, so that they might yet enter the Promised Land.

THE HIPPOCRATIC OATH

And I, if I am lifted up from the earth, will draw all peoples to Myself. John 12:32.

The Hippocratic Oath is a physician's pledge to practice medicine for the sake of preserving life and protecting the patient—"and do no harm." And what is the visual symbol of these practitioners of the healing art? A serpent entwined about a pole.

But because of Jesus' clandestine midnight conversation with Nicodemus, we know that the story of the bronze serpent is much more than a precedent for medicine. With their portable sanctuary God dramatically taught the chosen at every wilderness encampment that through the substitutionary sacrificial lamb, their sins—indeed, the sins of the entire human race—are atoned for and freely pardoned by a gracious and forgiving God. But with the bronze serpent God adds another essential metaphor for His gift of atonement—healing. For the chosen must not only be forgiven their sins—they must also be healed of their sins in order to enter the Promised Land.

How? Well, how are you saved from a rattlesnake bite today? The poison of the rattler is injected into a horse or cow in order to cause the animal to create an antibody to the snake's toxin. Then that antibody is extracted from the blood, frozen and stored for the day you are bitten, and rushed to an emergency room. *You are saved because another was injected with the same poison.* In unmistakable language to Nicodemus, Jesus linked Moses' bronze serpent with His own being lifted up at Calvary, where He would become sin, "who knew no sin" (2 Cor. 5:21), for the sake of the healing of this race of sinners. "And the Lord has laid on Him the iniquity of us all" (Isa. 53:6). He was injected with our sins, so that "by his wounds we are healed" (verse 5, NIV). No wonder we must hurry to His cross morning after morning!

I am concerned that with so distinctive a message and so countercultural a lifestyle, the chosen might be deceived into thinking that our salvation is somehow predicated upon our unique teachings or radical obedience. But the divine Serpent on the pole declares otherwise. "If you will only do your part and bow at the cross of Calvary, you will receive the blessing of God. God loves you. He does not wish to draw you nigh to Him to hurt you, oh, no; but to comfort you, to pour in the oil of rejoicing, to heal the wounds that sin has made, to bind up where Satan has bruised. . . . Will you bow low at the foot of the cross? Jesus will place his arms around you, and comfort you. Will you do this without further delay?" (*Review and Herald*, Mar. 4, 1890).

THE GOSPEL ACCORDING TO A $20 BILL

And who would dare tangle with God by messing with one of God's chosen? Who would dare even to point a finger? The One who died for us—who was raised to life for us!—is in the presence of God at this very moment sticking up for us. Rom. 8:33, 34, Message.

My retired preacher friend Phil Dunham, in his book *Sure Salvation*, tells of a speaker who held up a $20 bill: "Anybody want this?" Hands shot up. The speaker wadded and crumpled the bill. "Still want it?" Hands up again. He dropped the bill to the floor, grinding it with his heel. "Want it now?" Hands in the air. "You see, my friends, no matter what I do to the money, you still want it, because what happens to it doesn't decrease its value. So with us—crumpled, dropped, ground into the dirt by decisions we make, by circumstances in life—we feel worthless. But the truth is, no matter what has happened or what will happen, you will never lose your value in God's eyes. Dirty or clean, crumpled or finely pressed, you are still priceless to Him." Amen!

Throughout the year we've been tracking God's chosen, who have messed up time and time again. And truth be known (and it is), so have we! But what glad year-end news is this simple reminder: we have never lost our value in the eyes of God. We are still priceless to Him. Even when we crash and burn just days from the Promised Land. Just like did Moses and Aaron.

We come now to the last story with a lump in our throats. For whose heart doesn't ache over the bitter sentence that because of these two leaders' very rash, very public denial of God on the borders of Canaan, both of them would have to forfeit crossing over with Israel—both would have to die this side of the Promised Land. Just because they lost their tempers and beat the rock instead of speaking to it? But remember: "That rock was Christ" (1 Cor. 10:4), which was to be smitten only once—at the beginning of their journey—a bold symbol of Jesus' "once for all" smiting upon Calvary (Isa. 53:4). To beat Him again, to publicly thrash Him in a fit of self-righteous rage, not only destroyed the salvation metaphor but also denied the divine Giver—"Must *we* fetch you water out of this rock?" (Num. 20:10, KJV). In Moses and Aaron's meltdown are two somber lessons for the chosen: Those who receive much will be required much (the chosen and their leaders are held to a high standard), and the closer we come to the Promised Land, the closer must be our walk with God (the more radical must be our trust in Him). But never forget—even when you crumple, you're still precious in His sight. And God will have the last word!

THE LAST WORD

He opened the rock, and water gushed out; like a river it flowed in the desert. . . . He brought out his people with rejoicing, his chosen ones with shouts of joy. Ps. 105:41-43, NIV.

Poor Moses. For 40 long bone-wearying years he has been both nursemaid and leader to a congregation of grown-up kids. For 40 years he has begged the Lord to please give the people one more chance—"if not, I pray, blot me out of Your book" in their place (Ex. 32:32). And now on the very borders of the Promised Land the leader loses it, melts down, and in a flash hears the divine sentence—"You will not cross over." In his farewell address Moses tells the children of Israel how he begged God to reverse the verdict, until finally Christ could take no more. When your child weeps, it breaks your heart, too. "Speak no more to Me of this matter" (Deut. 3:26).

One last time Moses stands before his people. With arms outstretched before that sea of faces, his last words are an unforgettable promise for the chosen of every age: "Happy are you, O Israel! Who is like you, a people saved by the Lord, the shield of your help and the sword of your majesty! Your enemies shall submit to you, and you shall tread down their high places" (Deut. 33:29). And then the man of God slowly turns from these who have been his life and all alone now begins the final ascent up his last mountain. There atop Mount Nebo the Lord showed him all the land, then Moses died and He buried him, "but no one knows his grave to this day" (see Deut. 34:1-6)—no one, that is, but God, who never forgets where His friends are buried.

One day on heaven's History Channel I want to watch the divine replay of that heart-stopping moment from Jude 9, when Mercy came calling from the throne room of the universe. Towering over the dusty remains of His faithful and forgiven friend, there He is, the preincarnate Christ, robed in the fiery white light of eternity. He raises His hands. The angels who've accompanied Him and Lucifer with his demons who have futilely resisted him *all* stare wide-eyed—for no one in galactic history has yet witnessed what is about to transpire. A triumphant shout rings out: "Awake, O sleeper, and arise from the dead" (Eph. 5:14, ESV). And "in the twinkling of an eye" (1 Cor. 15:52), before the gasping universe, the dust atop the mountain trembles, and suddenly Moses is—young and forever! And in the ensuing ecstatic pandemonium as Christ and friend embrace, the universe bows in wonder before the shining truth that not even death can keep the chosen out of the Promised Land! Blessed be the God who will ever have the last word.

THE STAR SAPPHIRE

I have seen and I testify that this is God's Chosen One. John 1:34, TNIV.

John the Baptist is right. When in the end all is said and done, the shining truth will be the truth about Jesus—that He alone is the truly chosen one. Yes, God has had His friends throughout the ages of earth's history—loyal men, faithful women, courageous young adults, and even obedient children—who have made the radical, and oftentimes countercultural choice to live and die true to their Creator and faithful to their God. They are the chosen of earth. But the truth that has sustained this innumerable throng over the millennia, the resplendent light that has gleamed upon their pathways in every land in every age has ever been "the light of the knowledge of the glory of God in the face of Jesus Christ" (2 Cor. 4:6). And ". . . were thousands of the most gifted [men and women] to devote their whole time to setting forth Jesus always before us, studying how they might portray his matchless charms, they would never exhaust the subject" (*Review and Herald,* June 3, 1890). For He alone is the chosen one.

Professional gemologist Roy Whetstine was strolling through an amateur rock collectors' exhibit when he stopped by the collection of a rock hound from Idaho. On the card table amid the prized and polished rocks of the collector sat a Tupperware bowl containing a menagerie of rocky duplicates and discards. The masking tape on the front of the bowl read "For Sale—$15 Each." Whetstine reached into the dusty bowl and fingered the rocks. One felt strange. He lifted a potato-shaped gray-violet rock into the air, twisting it before his trained eye. "You want $15 for *this*?"

The collector grabbed the rock and looked at it closely. "No," he finally replied. "You can have this one for $10."

Whetstine pulled out a wrinkled $10 bill and walked away with the world's largest star sapphire—700 more carats than the previous record holder, the Black Star from Queensland, Australia. Estimated value? $1.7 million. Marked down to $10!

All year long we have examined the divine calling of the chosen. But wouldn't it be the greater loss if the chosen made the same mistake—glorying in their plastic bowl of distinctive teachings and countercultural lifestyles, all the while discounting the Star Sapphire of the universe? As the waning year dwindles to its final hours, isn't this the right time for you and me to make a new resolution for the new year? "Everything else is worthless when compared with the infinite value of knowing Christ Jesus my Lord" (Phil. 3:8, NLT).

THE HOMECOMING

Therefore the redeemed of the Lord shall return, and come with singing unto Zion; and everlasting joy shall be upon their head: they shall obtain gladness and joy; and sorrow and mourning shall flee away. Isa. 51:11, KJV.

Delayed (or deferred) gratification is the term psychologists use to describe the mature ability to wait in order to experience that which is desirable. (It would *not* describe choosing to consume that piece of apple pie before dutifully eating the broccoli—unless, of course, one considers broccoli dessert.) Delayed gratification is what the chosen have had to live with throughout the millennia. "These all died in faith, not having received the promises, but having seen them afar off" (Heb. 11:13, KJV). The long and winding road of their pilgrimage never reached heaven—they saw it "afar off"—but died this side of the Promised Land, hope still deferred. And so it may be that you and I, too, shall die this side of heaven, our final gratification delayed for a season, our shared hope still deferred. But on this New Year's Eve let us choose to live in Christ as "prisoners of hope" (Zech. 9:12), chained to His promise of the homecoming.

Henry Gariepy, in *100 Portraits of Christ,* tells of Theodore Roosevelt, the former president of the United States, returning home from Africa after a grand hunting safari. As he boarded the ocean liner at that African port, crowds cheered his walk up the red carpet. He was feted with the finest suite aboard the ship. Stewards waited on him hand and foot during the transoceanic journey home. The former president was the center of the entire ship's attention.

Also on board that vessel was another passenger, this one an elderly missionary who had given his life for God in Africa. His wife dead, his children gone, he was now returning to his homeland alone. Not a soul on that ship noticed him. Upon the ocean liner's arrival at San Francisco, the president was given a hero's welcome—whistles blowing, bells ringing, and the awaiting crowd cheering as Roosevelt descended the gangplank in beaming glory. But nobody came to welcome the returning missionary. Alone, the elderly man found a small hotel for the night. As he knelt beside his bed, his heart broke: "Lord, I'm not complaining. But I don't understand. I gave my life for You in Africa. But it seems that no one cares. I just don't understand."

And then in the darkness it was as if God reached down from heaven and placed His hand upon the old man's shoulder and whispered, "Missionary, you're not home yet."

A WORD AFTER . . .

In his book *Einstein*, a biography of the celebrated genius of the last century, Walter Isaacson describes how the young Albert received a gift from his mother that lasted a lifetime. It was a violin. And with the gift came her maternal insistence (God bless our mothers) that her boy take violin lessons. At first the lad resisted the notion of rote repetition and endless mechanical exercises. But then one day young Einstein was exposed to Mozart's sonatas. And in that encounter "music became both magical and emotional to him." Years later, reflecting on his boyhood discovery of Mozart, Einstein remarked: "I believe that love is a better teacher than a sense of duty, at least for me" (p. 14).

And that is true at least for the chosen as well, is it not? For if we mechanically follow Jesus and obey God out of a sullen sense of duty, then of all men and women and teens we should be the most pitied in this world. But if we shall follow Christ and obey God with joy-filled, worshipful gratitude to Him who "has loved us and given Himself for us" (Eph. 5:2), then for us—for you and for me—love is truly "a better teacher." For love is the best teacher of all.

Then let us begin the new year the way we began the year that is ended, sitting at the feet of our Teacher, memorizing the harmonies of heaven so that His music might yet be played out upon the strings of our lives.

For the chosen, could there be a higher destiny?